Pink 💗 Innocent

1

Kotori Momoyuki

Translated and adapted by
Joshua Weeks

Lettered by
North Market Street Graphics

Ballantine Books ★ New York

Pink Innocent volume 1 is a work of fiction. Names, characters, places, and incidents are the products of the author's imagination or are used fictitiously. Any resemblance to actual events, locales, or persons, living or dead, is entirely coincidental.

A Del Rey Manga/Kodansha Trade Paperback Original

Published in the United States by Del Rey, an imprint of The Random House Publishing Group, a division of Random House, Inc., New York.

Publication rights arranged through Kodansha Ltd.

First published in Japan in 2007 by Kodansha Ltd., Tokyo

ISBN 978-0-345-51468-4

Printed in the United States of America

www.delreymanga.com

9 8 7 6 5 4 3 2 1

Translator/Adapter: Joshua Weeks
Lettering: North Market Street Graphics

CONTENTS

HONORIFICS EXPLAINED

Throughout the Del Rey Manga books, you will find Japanese honorifics left intact in the translations. For those not familiar with how the Japanese use honorifics and, more important, how they differ from American honorifics, we present this brief overview.

Politeness has always been a critical facet of Japanese culture. Ever since the feudal era, when Japan was a highly stratified society, use of honorifics—which can be defined as polite speech that indicates relationship or status—has played an essential role in the Japanese language. When addressing someone in Japanese, an honorific usually takes the form of a suffix attached to one's name (example: "Asuna-san"), is used as a title at the end of one's name, or appears in place of the name itself (example: "Negi-sensei," or simply "Sensei").

Honorifics can be expressions of respect or endearment. In the context of manga and anime, honorifics give insight into the nature of the relationship between characters. Many English translations leave out these important honorifics and therefore distort the feel of the original Japanese. Because Japanese honorifics contain nuances that English honorifics lack, it is our policy at Del Rey not to translate them. Here, instead, is a guide to some of the honorifics you may encounter in Del Rey Manga.

-san: This is the most common honorific and is equivalent to Mr., Miss, Ms., or Mrs. It is the all-purpose honorific and can be used in any situation where politeness is required.

-sama: This is one level higher than "-san" and is used to confer great respect.

-dono: This comes from the word "tono," which means "lord." It is an even higher level than "-sama" and confers utmost respect.

-kun: This suffix is used at the end of boys' names to express familiarity or endearment. It is also sometimes used by men among friends, or when addressing someone younger or of a lower station.

-chan: This is used to express endearment, mostly toward girls. It is also used for little boys, pets, and even among lovers. It gives a sense of childish cuteness.

Bozu: This is an informal way to refer to a boy, similar to the English terms "kid" and "squirt."

Sempai/
Senpai: This title suggests that the addressee is one's senior in a group or organization. It is most often used in a school setting, where underclassmen refer to their upperclassmen as "sempai." It can also be used in the workplace, such as when a newer employee addresses an employee who has seniority in the company.

Kohai: This is the opposite of "sempai" and is used toward underclassmen in school or newcomers in the workplace. It connotes that the addressee is of a lower station.

Sensei: Literally meaning "one who has come before," this title is used for teachers, doctors, or masters of any profession or art.

-[blank]: This is usually forgotten in these lists, but it is perhaps the most significant difference between Japanese and English. The lack of honorific means that the speaker has permission to address the person in a very intimate way. Usually, only family, spouses, or very close friends have this kind of permission. Known as *yobisute*, it can be gratifying when someone who has earned the intimacy starts to call one by one's name without an honorific. But when that intimacy hasn't been earned, it can be very insulting.

Pink Innocent

1

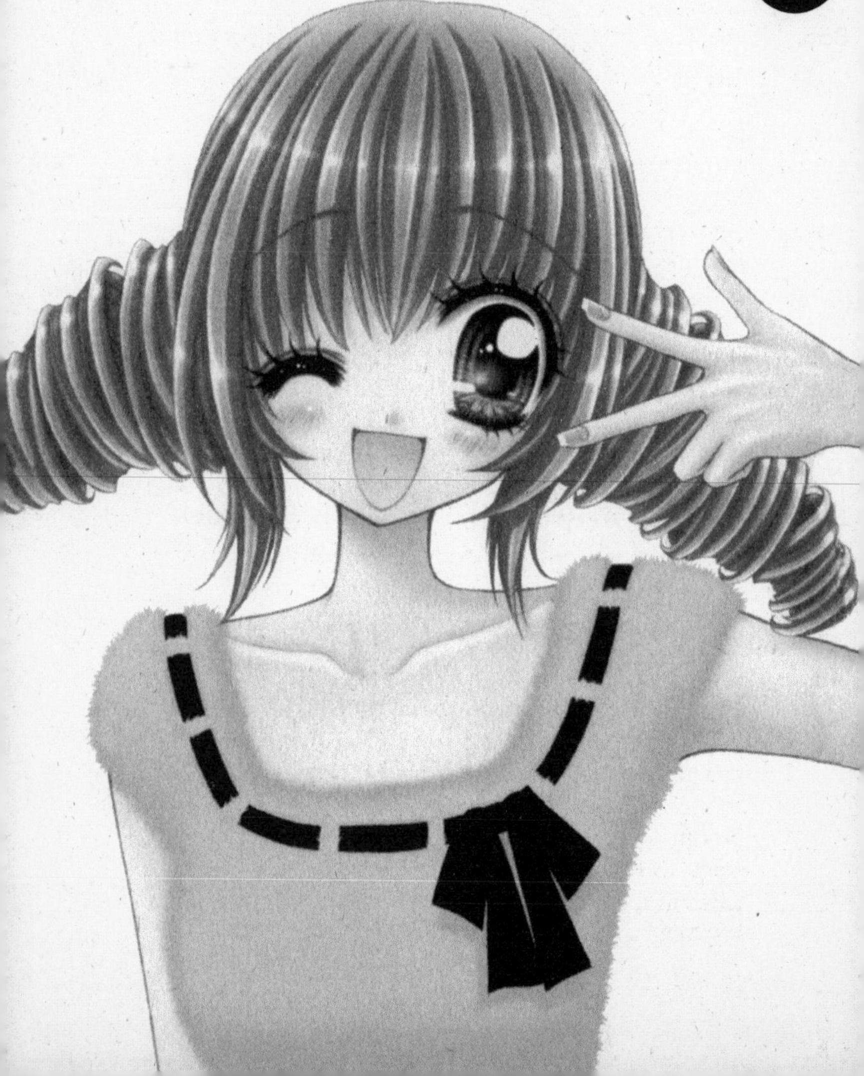

Pink Innocent

Contents

❦

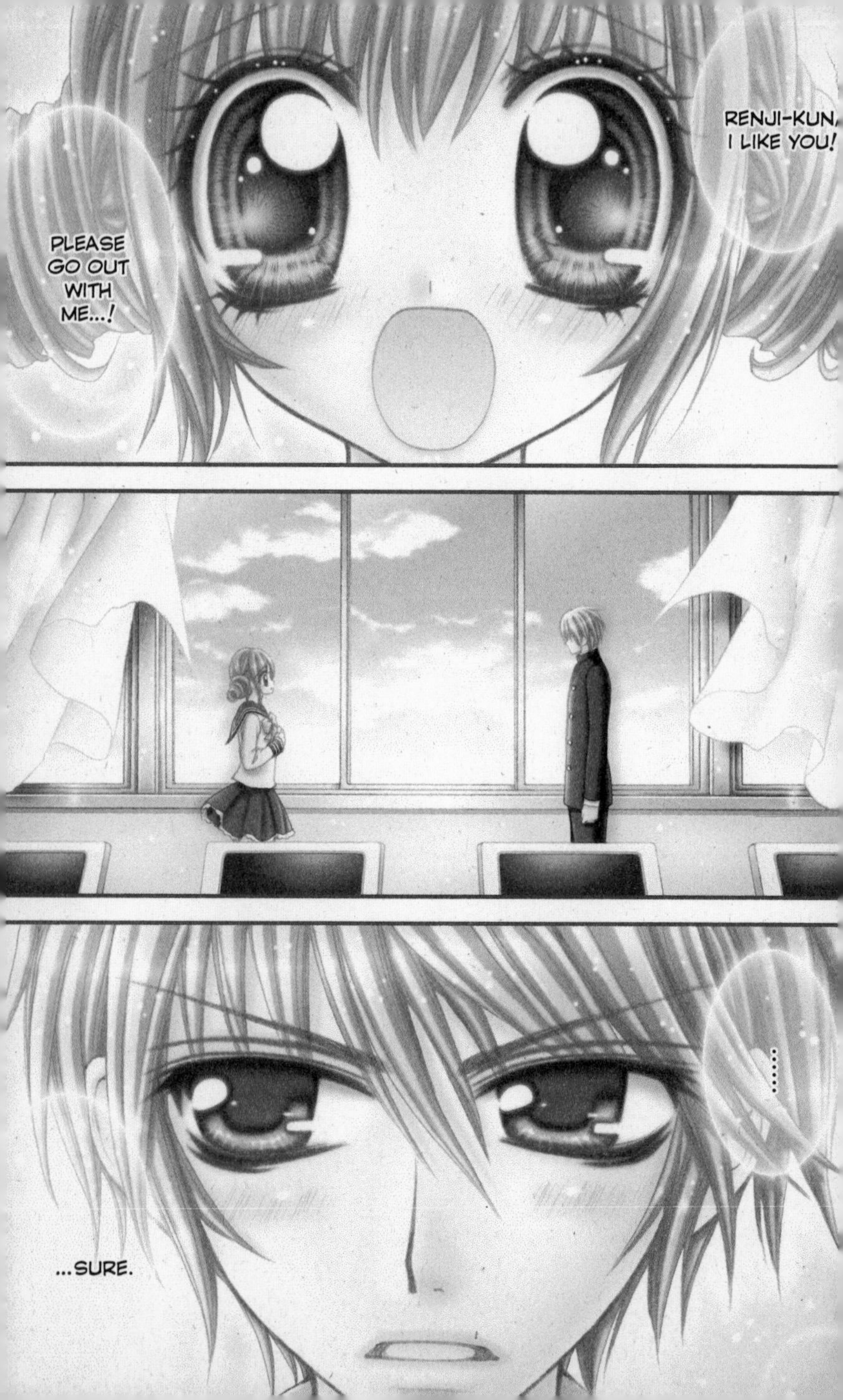
RENJI-KUN, I LIKE YOU!
PLEASE GO OUT WITH ME...!
......
...SURE.

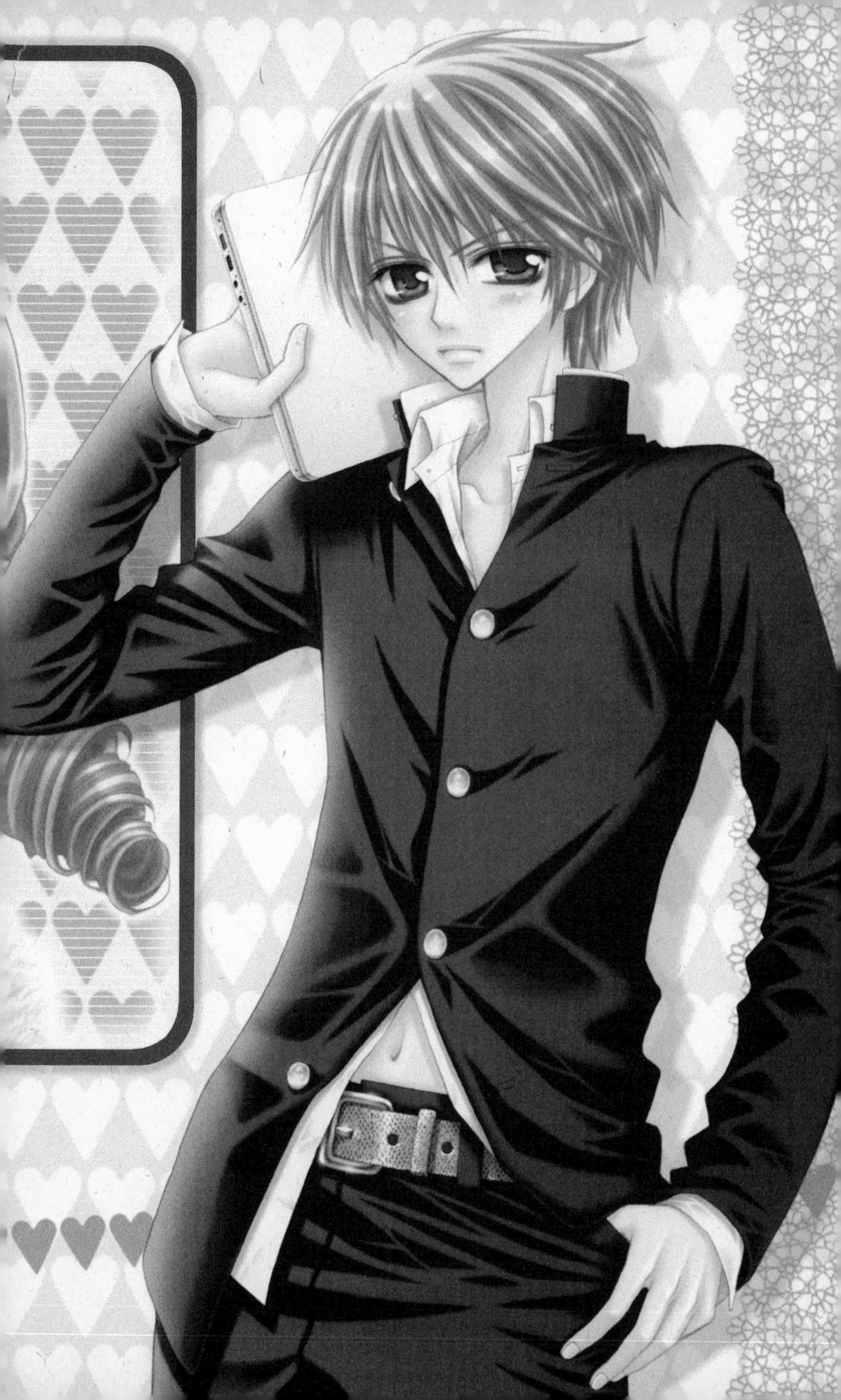

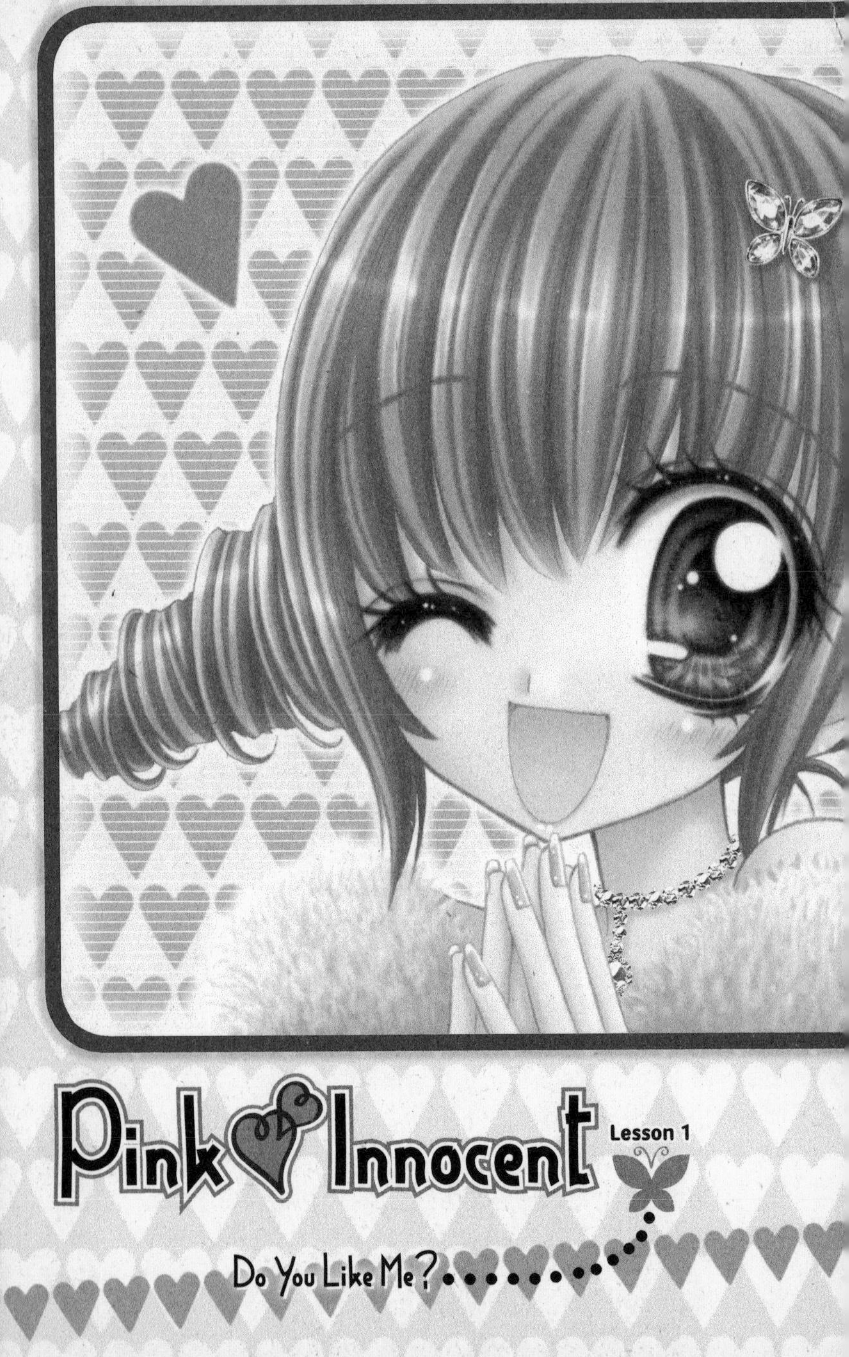

Pink Innocent

Lesson 1

Do You Like Me?

Hello! Kotori Momoyuki here. Thank you very much for reading this first volume of *Pink Innocent*. This is my fourth comic book volume. It's because of all the readers who have supported me that I've been able to have my work serialized and publish these volumes. Thank you all so much! Well then, I hope you enjoy reading through this first volume of *Pink Innocent*!

♥♥♥♥♥♥♥♥♥♥♥♥♥♥♥♥♥♥♥

This series was my first serialized work in four months.... The deadline for the first chapter was so soon that I had to finish the preliminary drawings 1.5 times faster than my last series, *Ōji-sama no Tsukurikata* (*How to Make a Prince*). I surprised myself. I became able to draw even faster and faster for the second and following chapters—although I'm still quite slow! I think my goal is to become twice as fast as I am now. Oh, and my pen work hasn't gotten faster at all....

→I really like this preview collage.♪

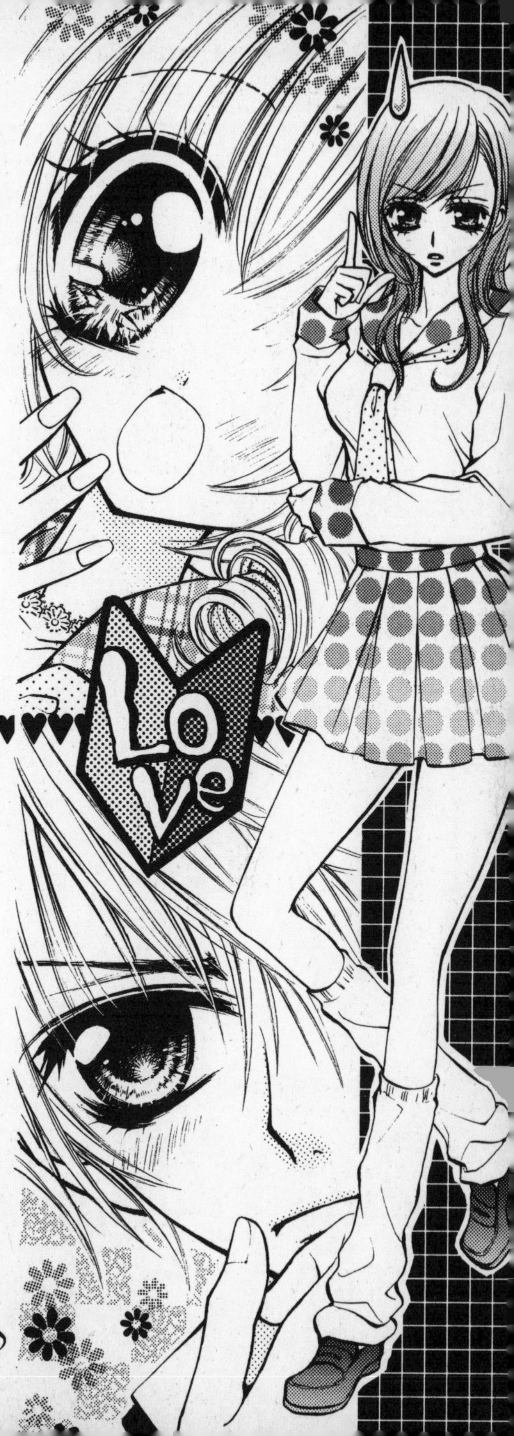
LoVe

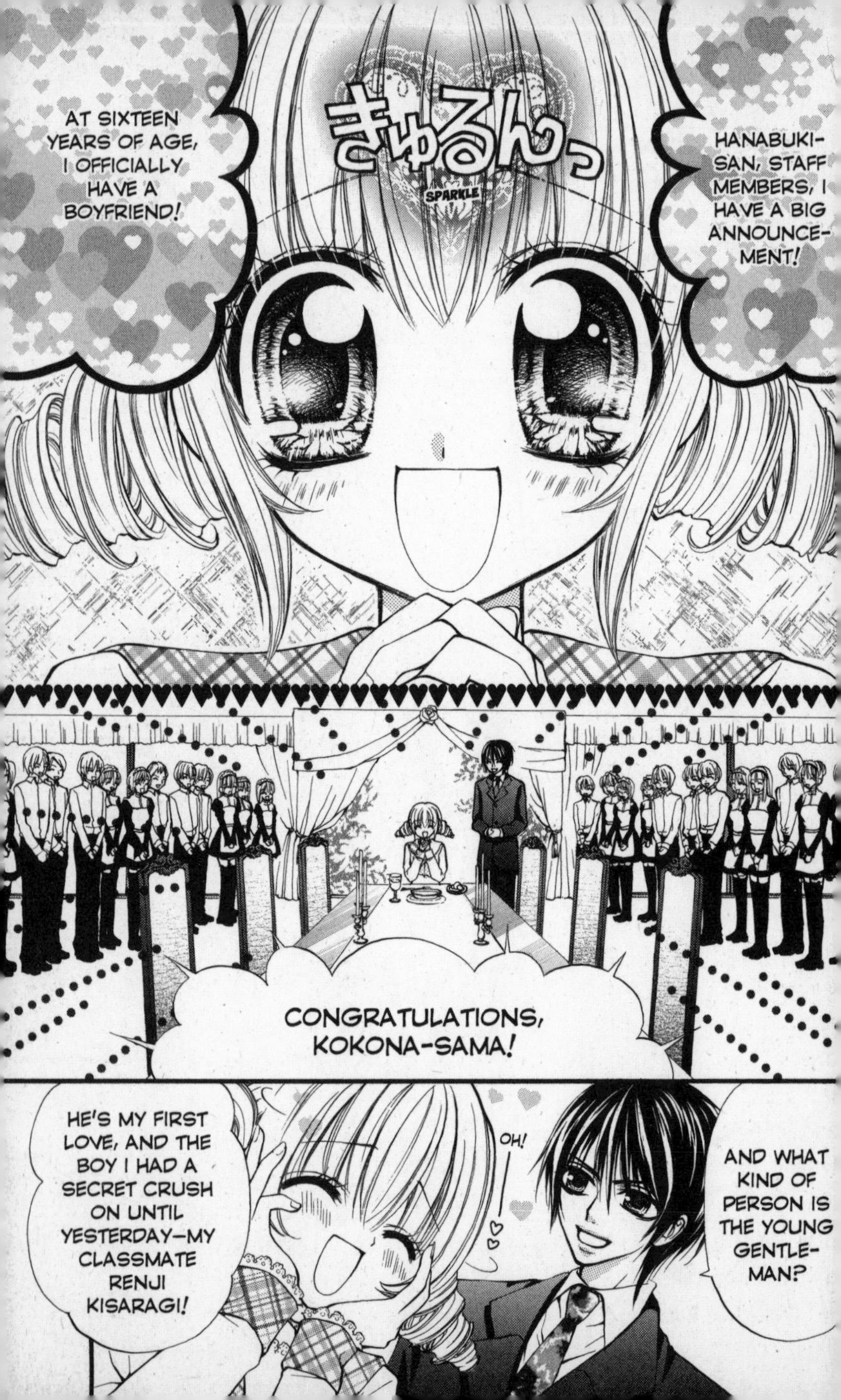
HANABUKI-SAN, STAFF MEMBERS, I HAVE A BIG ANNOUNCEMENT!
きゅるんっ
SPARKLE
AT SIXTEEN YEARS OF AGE, I OFFICIALLY HAVE A BOYFRIEND!
CONGRATULATIONS, KOKONA-SAMA!
AND WHAT KIND OF PERSON IS THE YOUNG GENTLEMAN?
OH!
HE'S MY FIRST LOVE, AND THE BOY I HAD A SECRET CRUSH ON UNTIL YESTERDAY—MY CLASSMATE RENJI KISARAGI!

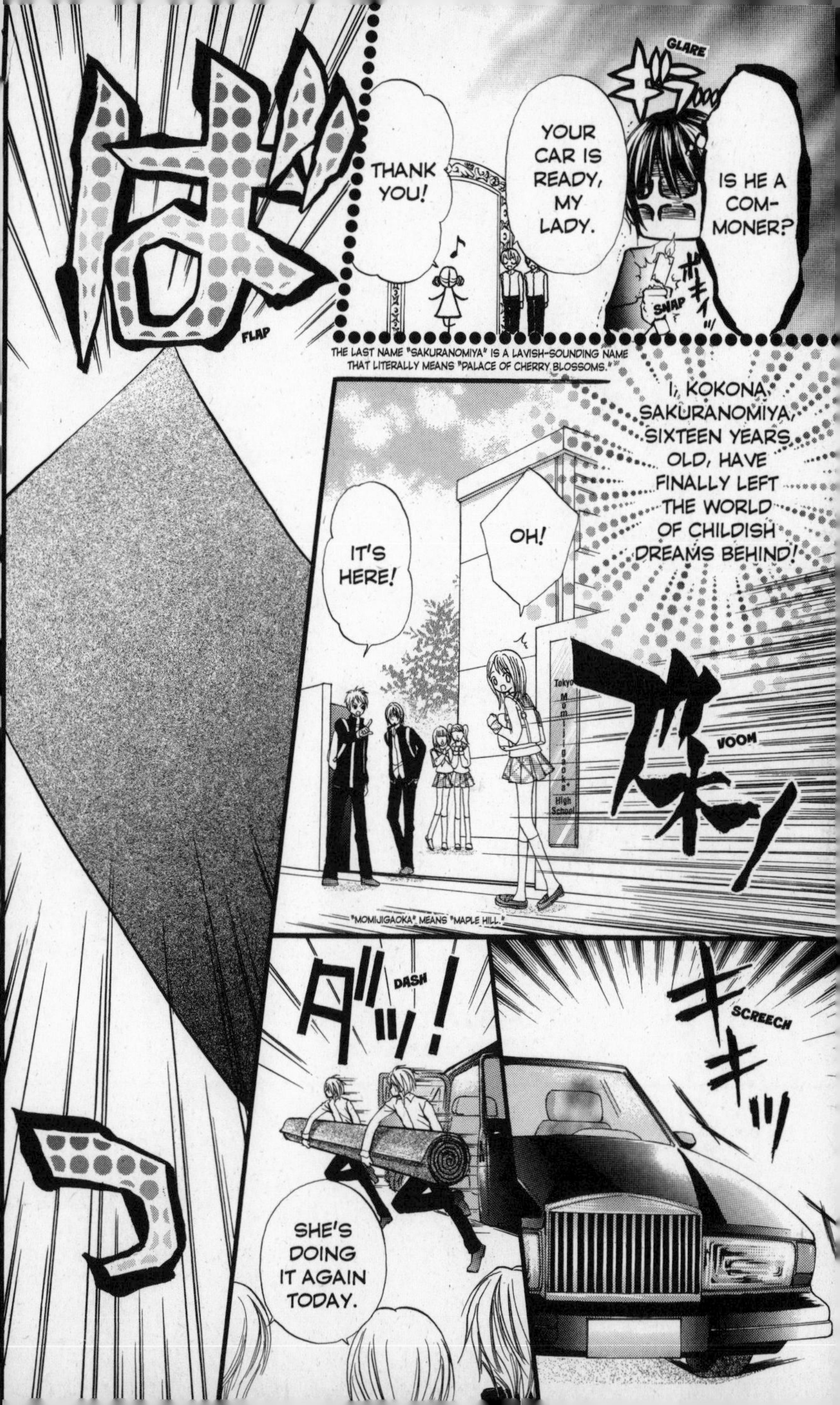
GLARE
IS HE A COMMONER?
SNAP
YOUR CAR IS READY, MY LADY.
THANK YOU!
THE LAST NAME "SAKURANOMIYA" IS A LAVISH-SOUNDING NAME THAT LITERALLY MEANS "PALACE OF CHERRY BLOSSOMS."
I, KOKONA SAKURANOMIYA, SIXTEEN YEARS OLD, HAVE FINALLY LEFT THE WORLD OF CHILDISH DREAMS BEHIND!
OH!
IT'S HERE!
VOOM
Tokyo Momijigaoka High School
"MOMIJIGAOKA" MEANS "MAPLE HILL."
SCREECH
DASH
SHE'S DOING IT AGAIN TODAY.
FLAP

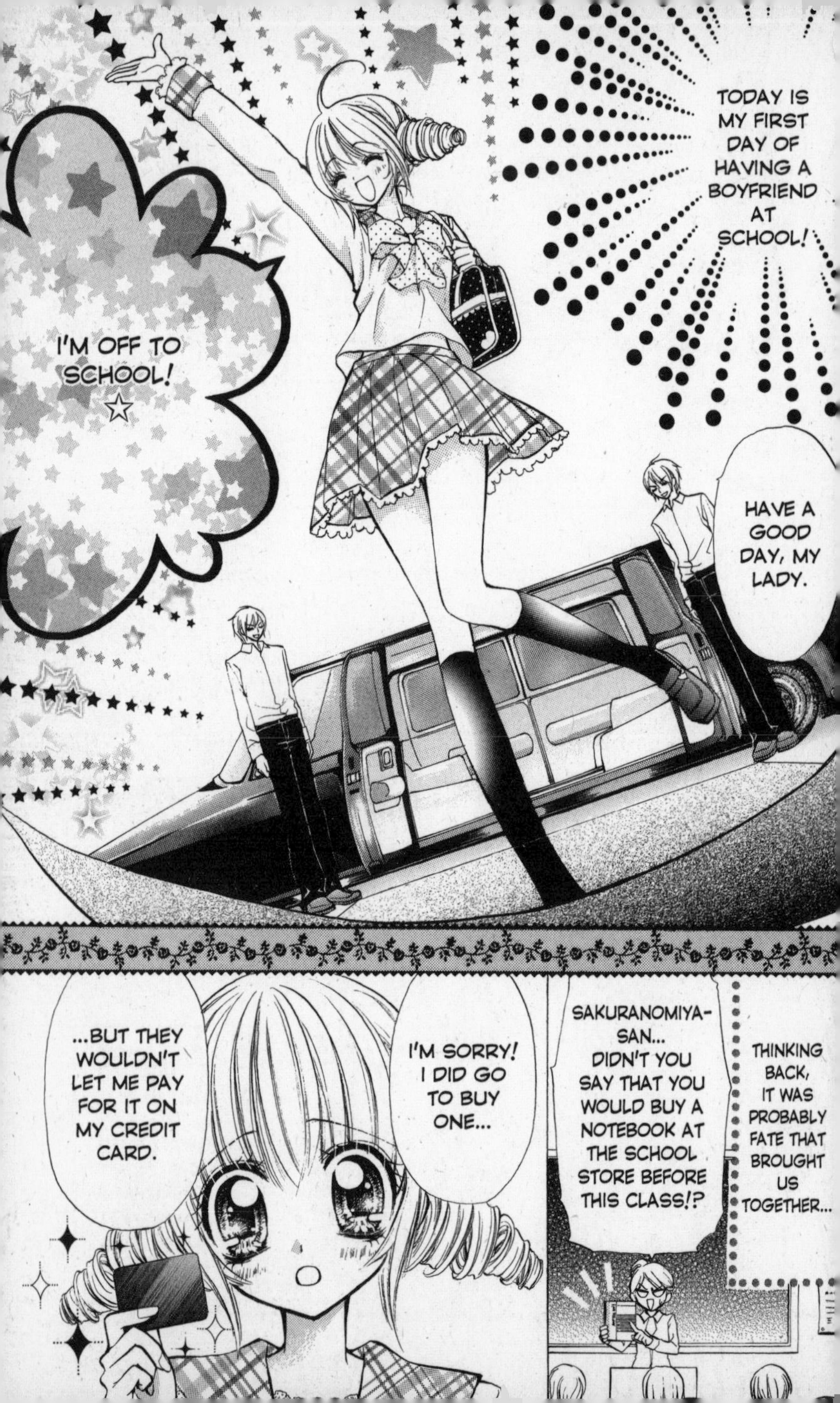
TODAY IS MY FIRST DAY OF HAVING A BOYFRIEND AT SCHOOL!
I'M OFF TO SCHOOL! ☆
HAVE A GOOD DAY, MY LADY.
THINKING BACK, IT WAS PROBABLY FATE THAT BROUGHT US TOGETHER...
SAKURANOMIYA-SAN... DIDN'T YOU SAY THAT YOU WOULD BUY A NOTEBOOK AT THE SCHOOL STORE BEFORE THIS CLASS!?
I'M SORRY! I DID GO TO BUY ONE...
...BUT THEY WOULDN'T LET ME PAY FOR IT ON MY CREDIT CARD.

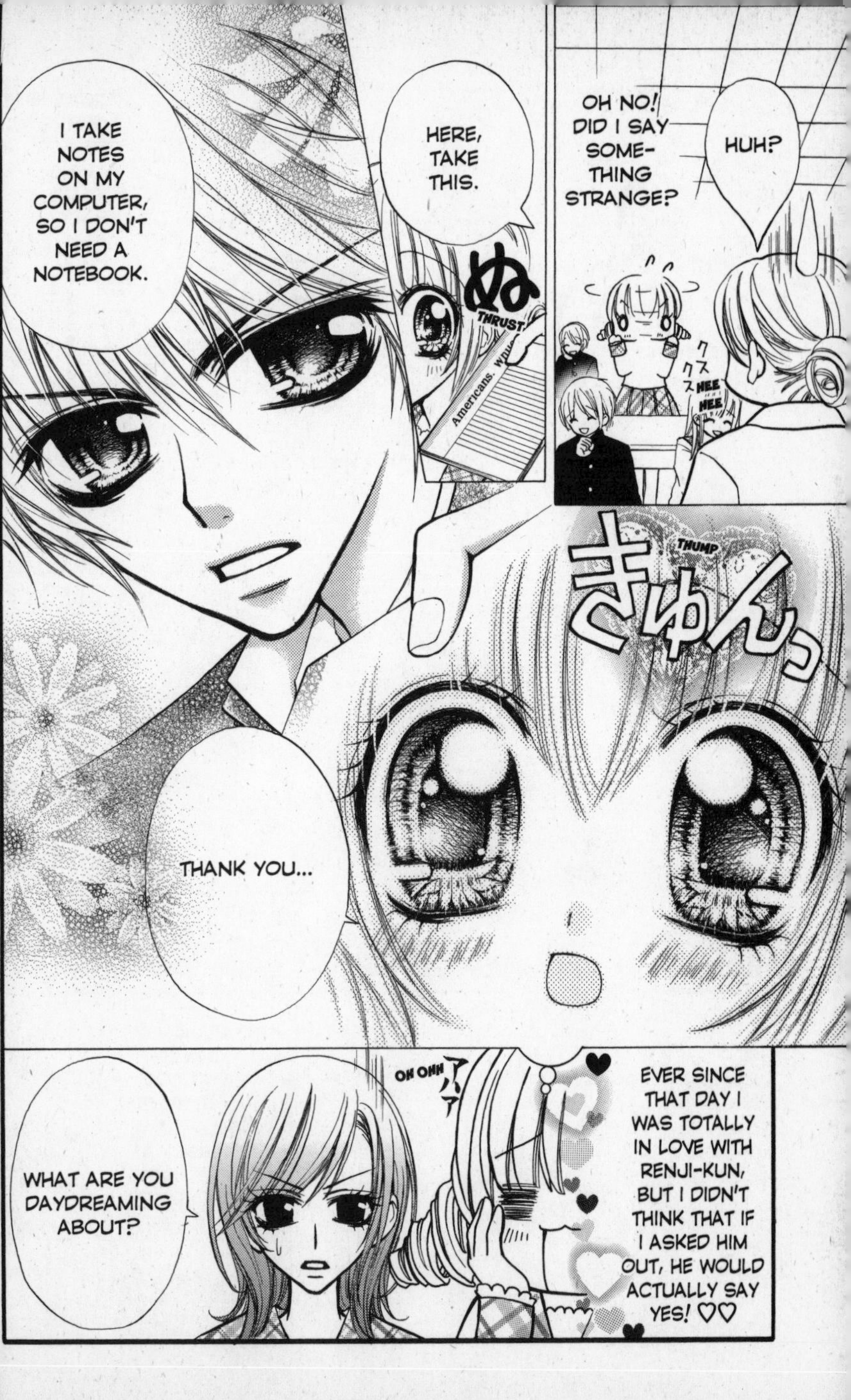
HUH?
OH NO! DID I SAY SOME-THING STRANGE?
クスクス
HEE HEE
HERE, TAKE THIS.
ぬ
THRUST
I TAKE NOTES ON MY COMPUTER, SO I DON'T NEED A NOTEBOOK.
きゅんっ
THUMP
THANK YOU...
EVER SINCE THAT DAY I WAS TOTALLY IN LOVE WITH RENJI-KUN, BUT I DIDN'T THINK THAT IF I ASKED HIM OUT, HE WOULD ACTUALLY SAY YES! ♡♡
アハァ
OH OHH
WHAT ARE YOU DAYDREAMING ABOUT?

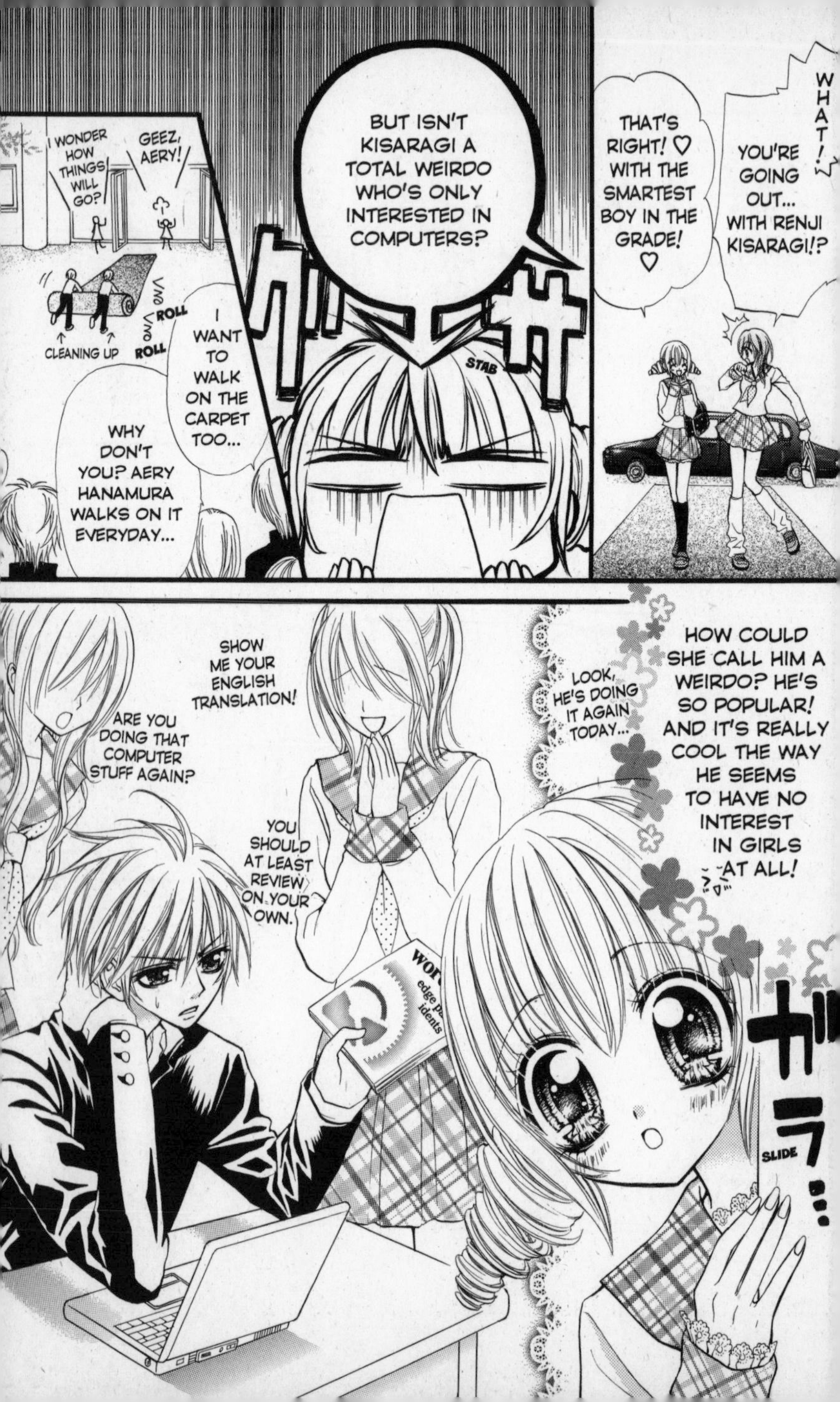
WHAT!
YOU'RE GOING OUT... WITH RENJI KISARAGI!?
THAT'S RIGHT! ♡ WITH THE SMARTEST BOY IN THE GRADE! ♡
BUT ISN'T KISARAGI A TOTAL WEIRDO WHO'S ONLY INTERESTED IN COMPUTERS?
STAB
GEEZ, AERY!
I WONDER HOW THINGS WILL GO?
ROLL
ROLL
CLEANING UP
I WANT TO WALK ON THE CARPET TOO...
WHY DON'T YOU? AERY HANAMURA WALKS ON IT EVERYDAY...
HOW COULD SHE CALL HIM A WEIRDO? HE'S SO POPULAR! AND IT'S REALLY COOL THE WAY HE SEEMS TO HAVE NO INTEREST IN GIRLS AT ALL!
SLIDE
LOOK, HE'S DOING IT AGAIN TODAY...
SHOW ME YOUR ENGLISH TRANSLATION!
ARE YOU DOING THAT COMPUTER STUFF AGAIN?
YOU SHOULD AT LEAST REVIEW ON YOUR OWN.

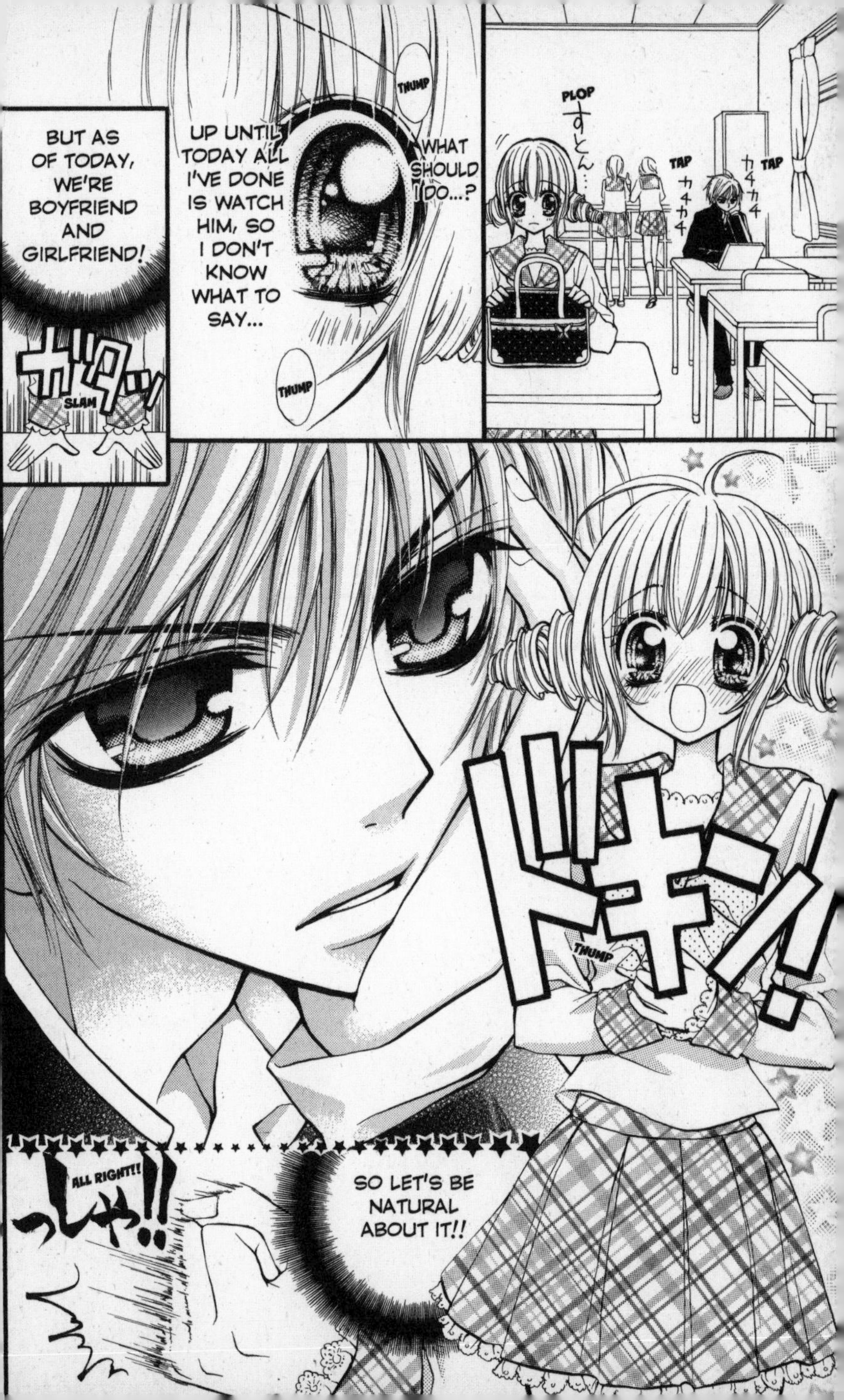
PLOP
すとん…
TAP
カチカチ
TAP
THUMP
UP UNTIL TODAY ALL I'VE DONE IS WATCH HIM, SO I DON'T KNOW WHAT TO SAY...
WHAT SHOULD I DO...?
THUMP
BUT AS OF TODAY, WE'RE BOYFRIEND AND GIRLFRIEND!
ガタッ
SLAM
ドキン!
THUMP
SO LET'S BE NATURAL ABOUT IT!!
ALL RIGHT!!
っしゃ!!

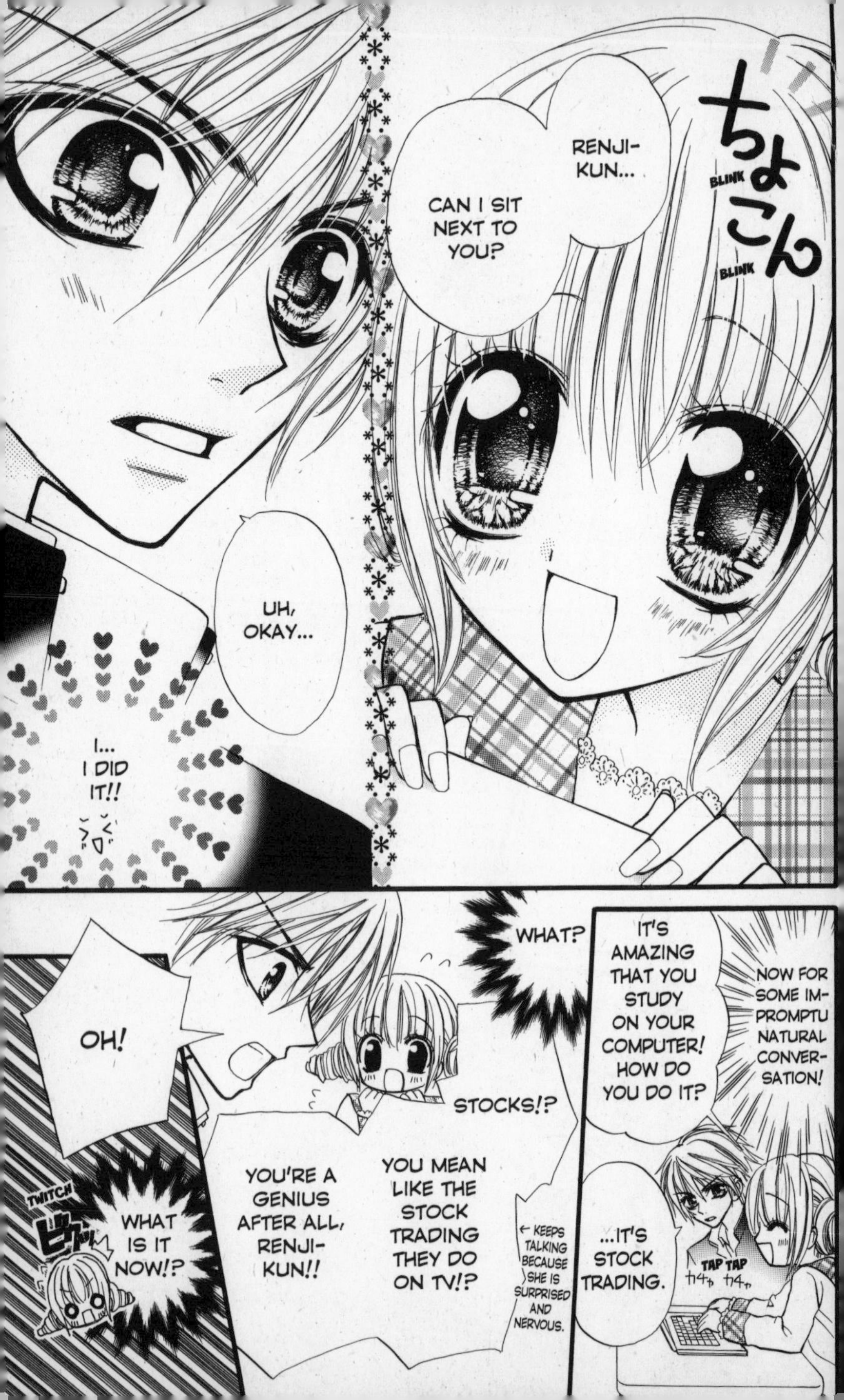
ちょこん
BLINK
BLINK
RENJI-KUN...
CAN I SIT NEXT TO YOU?
UH, OKAY...
I... I DID IT!!
NOW FOR SOME IMPROMPTU NATURAL CONVERSATION!
IT'S AMAZING THAT YOU STUDY ON YOUR COMPUTER! HOW DO YOU DO IT?
...IT'S STOCK TRADING.
TAP TAP
WHAT?
STOCKS!?
YOU MEAN LIKE THE STOCK TRADING THEY DO ON TV!?
← KEEPS TALKING BECAUSE SHE IS SURPRISED AND NERVOUS.
YOU'RE A GENIUS AFTER ALL, RENJI-KUN!!
OH!
TWITCH
WHAT IS IT NOW!?

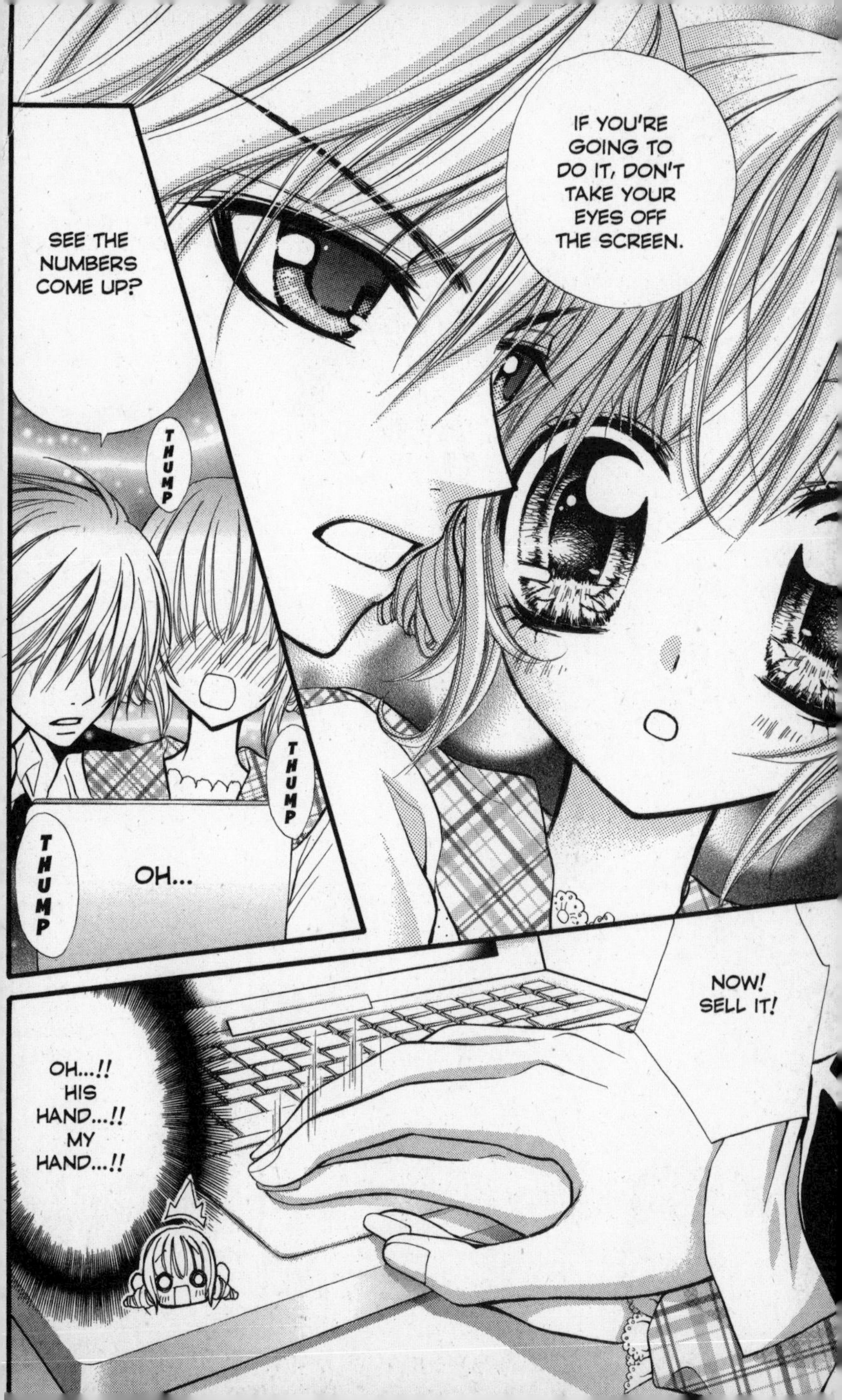
IF YOU'RE GOING TO DO IT, DON'T TAKE YOUR EYES OFF THE SCREEN.
SEE THE NUMBERS COME UP?
THUMP
THUMP
THUMP
OH...
NOW! SELL IT!
OH...!! HIS HAND...!! MY HAND...!!

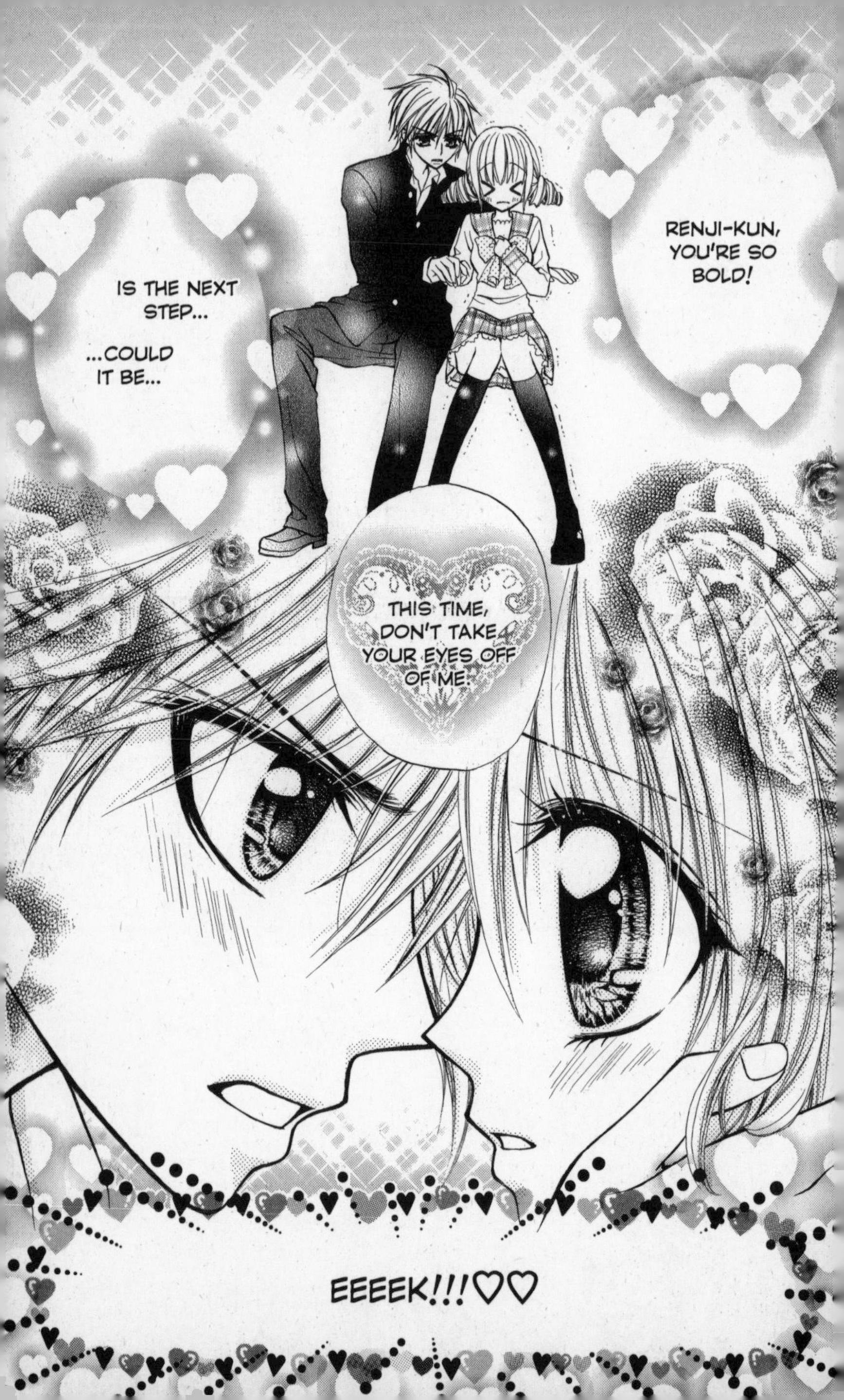
RENJI-KUN, YOU'RE SO BOLD!
IS THE NEXT STEP...
...COULD IT BE...
THIS TIME, DON'T TAKE YOUR EYES OFF OF ME.
EEEEK!!!♡♡

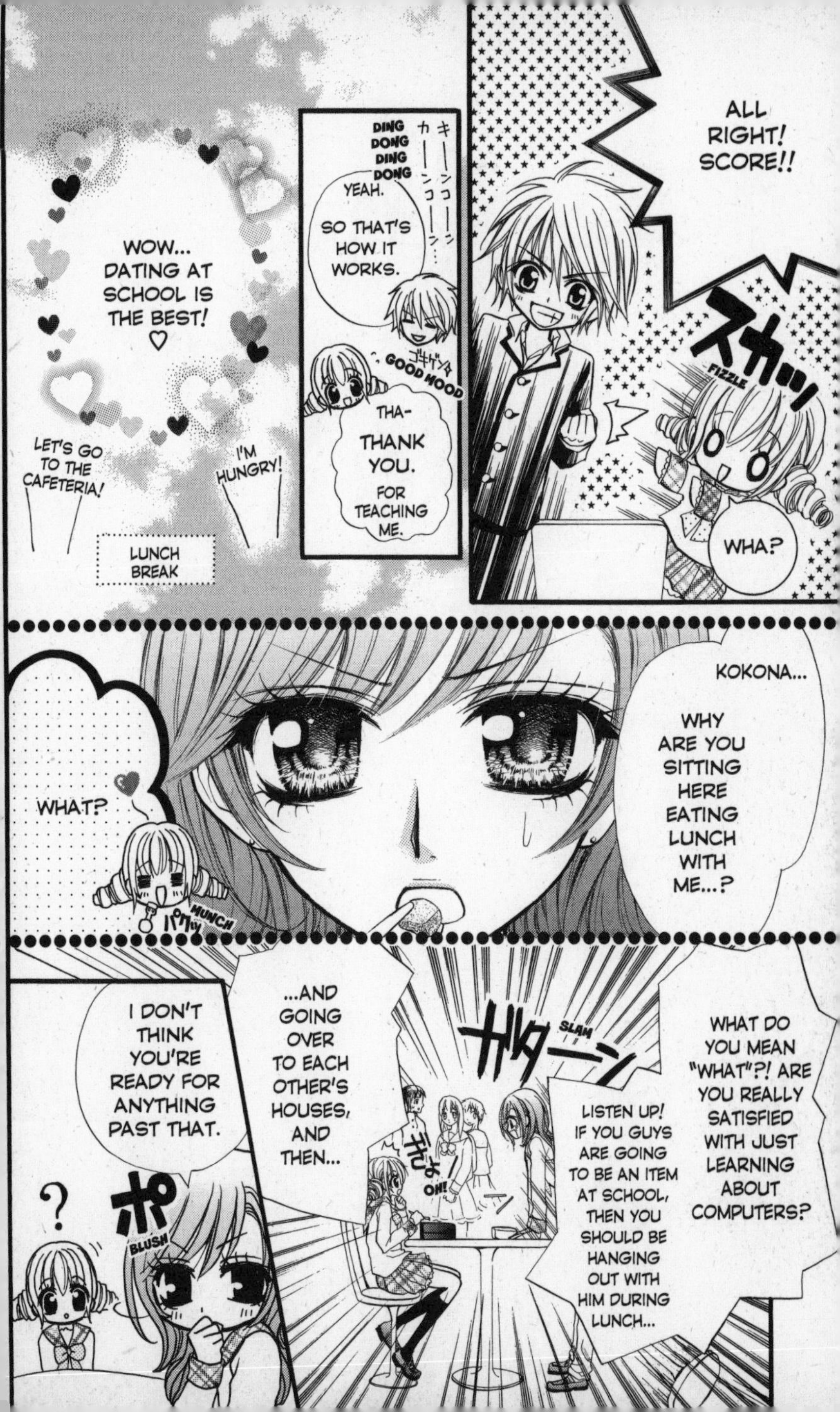
ALL RIGHT! SCORE!!
スカッ
FIZZLE
WHA?
キーンコーン カーンコーン…
DING DONG DING DONG
YEAH.
SO THAT'S HOW IT WORKS.
ゴキゲン♪
GOOD MOOD
THA- THANK YOU. FOR TEACHING ME.
WOW... DATING AT SCHOOL IS THE BEST! ♡
I'M HUNGRY!
LET'S GO TO THE CAFETERIA!
LUNCH BREAK
KOKONA...
WHY ARE YOU SITTING HERE EATING LUNCH WITH ME...?
WHAT?
パクッ
MUNCH
WHAT DO YOU MEAN "WHAT"?! ARE YOU REALLY SATISFIED WITH JUST LEARNING ABOUT COMPUTERS?
LISTEN UP! IF YOU GUYS ARE GOING TO BE AN ITEM AT SCHOOL, THEN YOU SHOULD BE HANGING OUT WITH HIM DURING LUNCH...
ガターン
SLAM
ギョッ
OH!
...AND GOING OVER TO EACH OTHER'S HOUSES, AND THEN...
I DON'T THINK YOU'RE READY FOR ANYTHING PAST THAT.
ポ
BLUSH
?

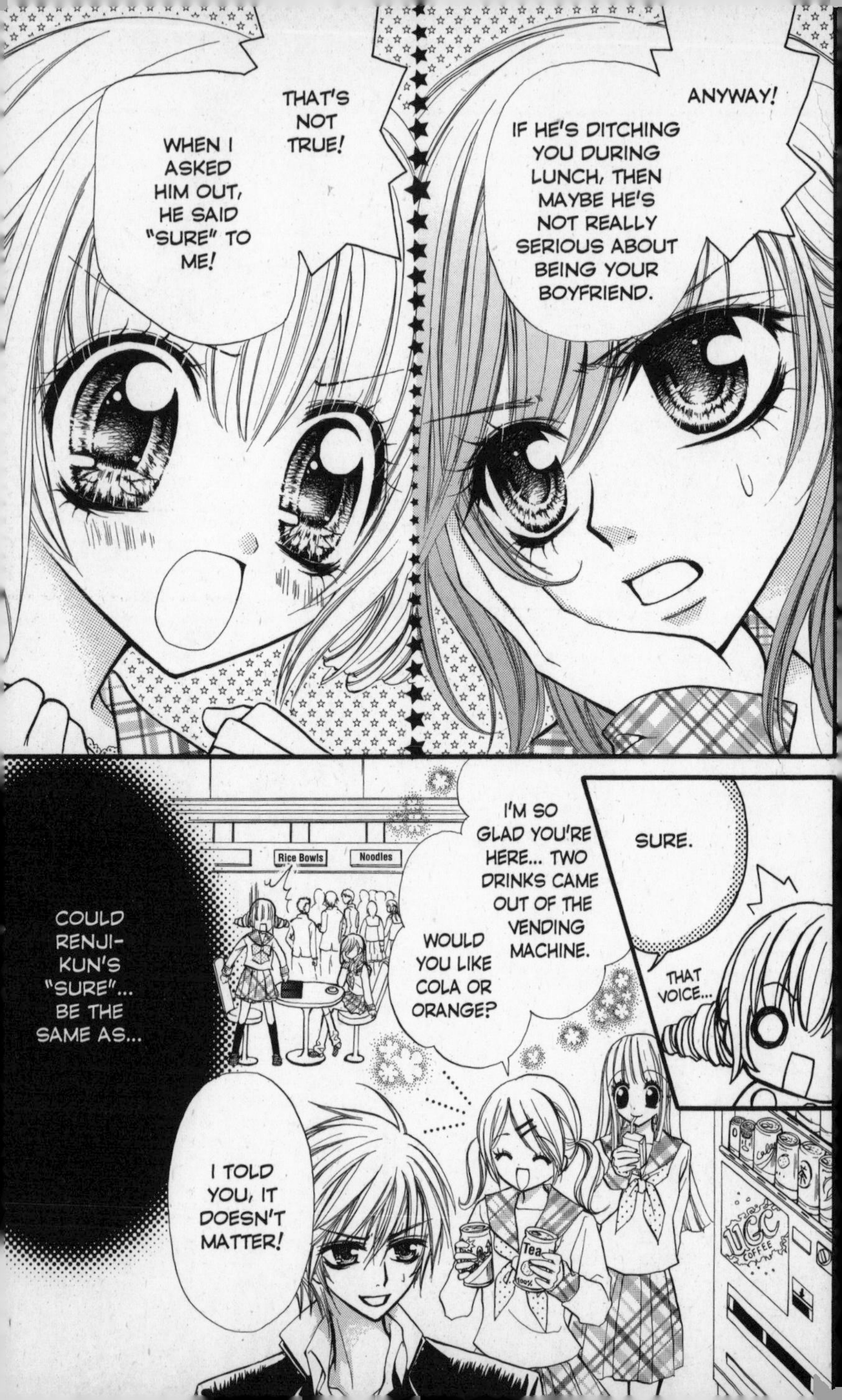
ANYWAY!
IF HE'S DITCHING YOU DURING LUNCH, THEN MAYBE HE'S NOT REALLY SERIOUS ABOUT BEING YOUR BOYFRIEND.
THAT'S NOT TRUE!
WHEN I ASKED HIM OUT, HE SAID "SURE" TO ME!
SURE.
THAT VOICE...
I'M SO GLAD YOU'RE HERE... TWO DRINKS CAME OUT OF THE VENDING MACHINE.
WOULD YOU LIKE COLA OR ORANGE?
Rice Bowls
Noodles
I TOLD YOU, IT DOESN'T MATTER!
COULD RENJI-KUN'S "SURE"... BE THE SAME AS...

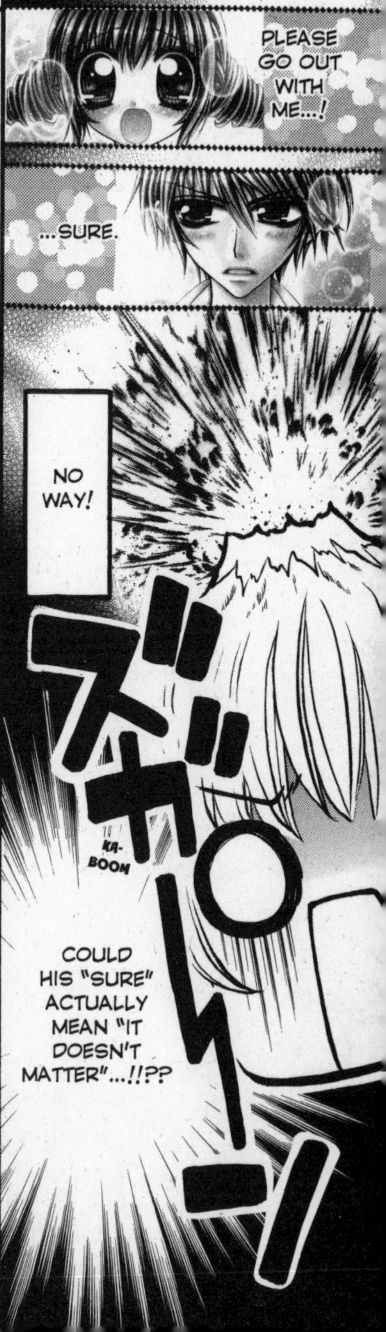
PLEASE GO OUT WITH ME...!
...SURE.
NO WAY!
KA-BOOM
COULD HIS "SURE" ACTUALLY MEAN "IT DOESN'T MATTER"...!!??

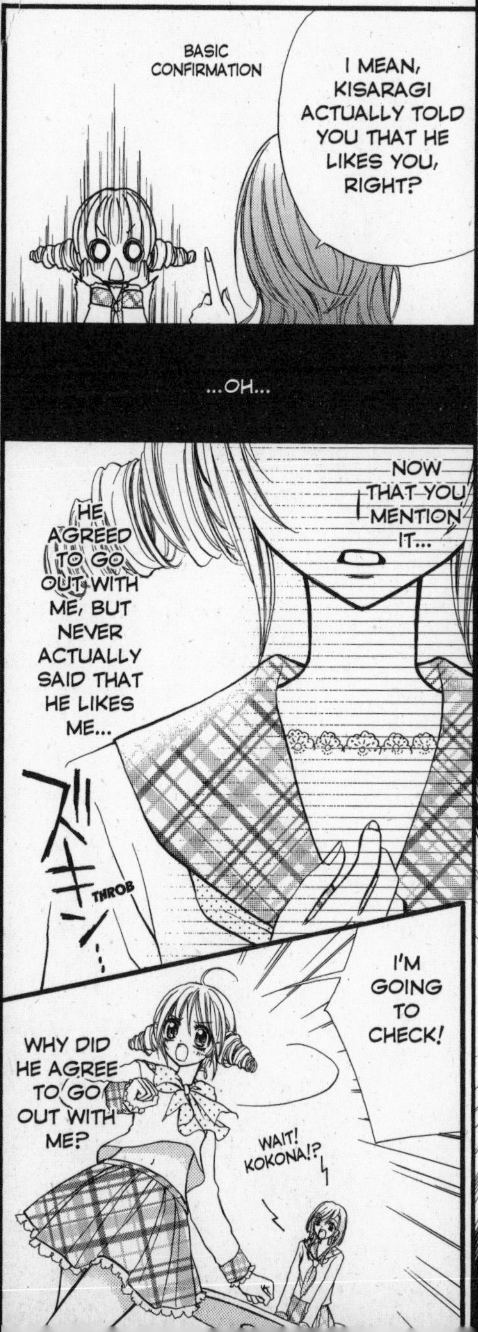
I MEAN, KISARAGI ACTUALLY TOLD YOU THAT HE LIKES YOU, RIGHT?
BASIC CONFIRMATION
...OH...
NOW THAT YOU MENTION IT...
HE AGREED TO GO OUT WITH ME, BUT NEVER ACTUALLY SAID THAT HE LIKES ME...
THROB
I'M GOING TO CHECK!
WHY DID HE AGREE TO GO OUT WITH ME?
WAIT! KOKONA!?

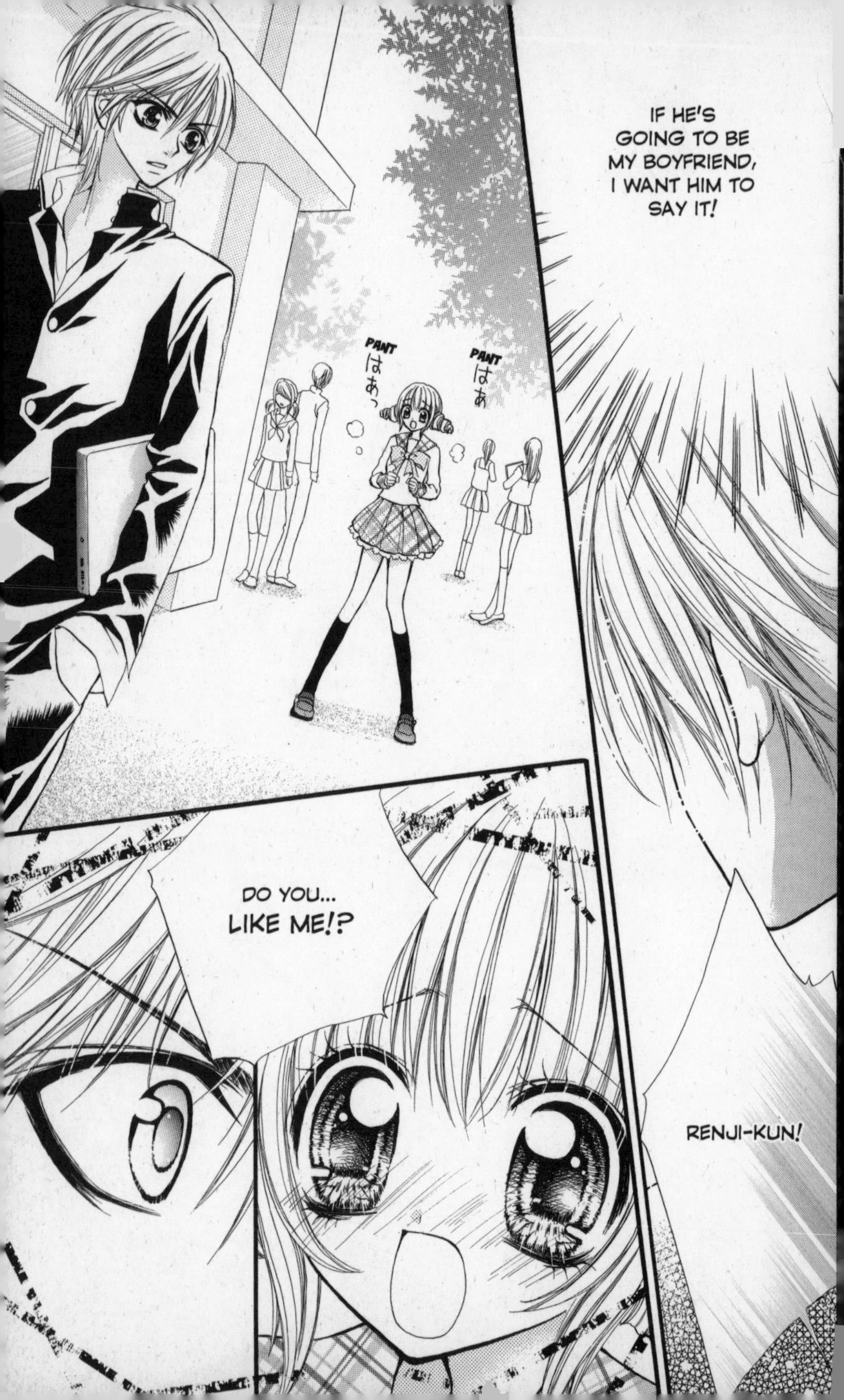
IF HE'S GOING TO BE MY BOYFRIEND, I WANT HIM TO SAY IT!
RENJI-KUN!
PANT はぁ
PANT はあっ
DO YOU... LIKE ME!?

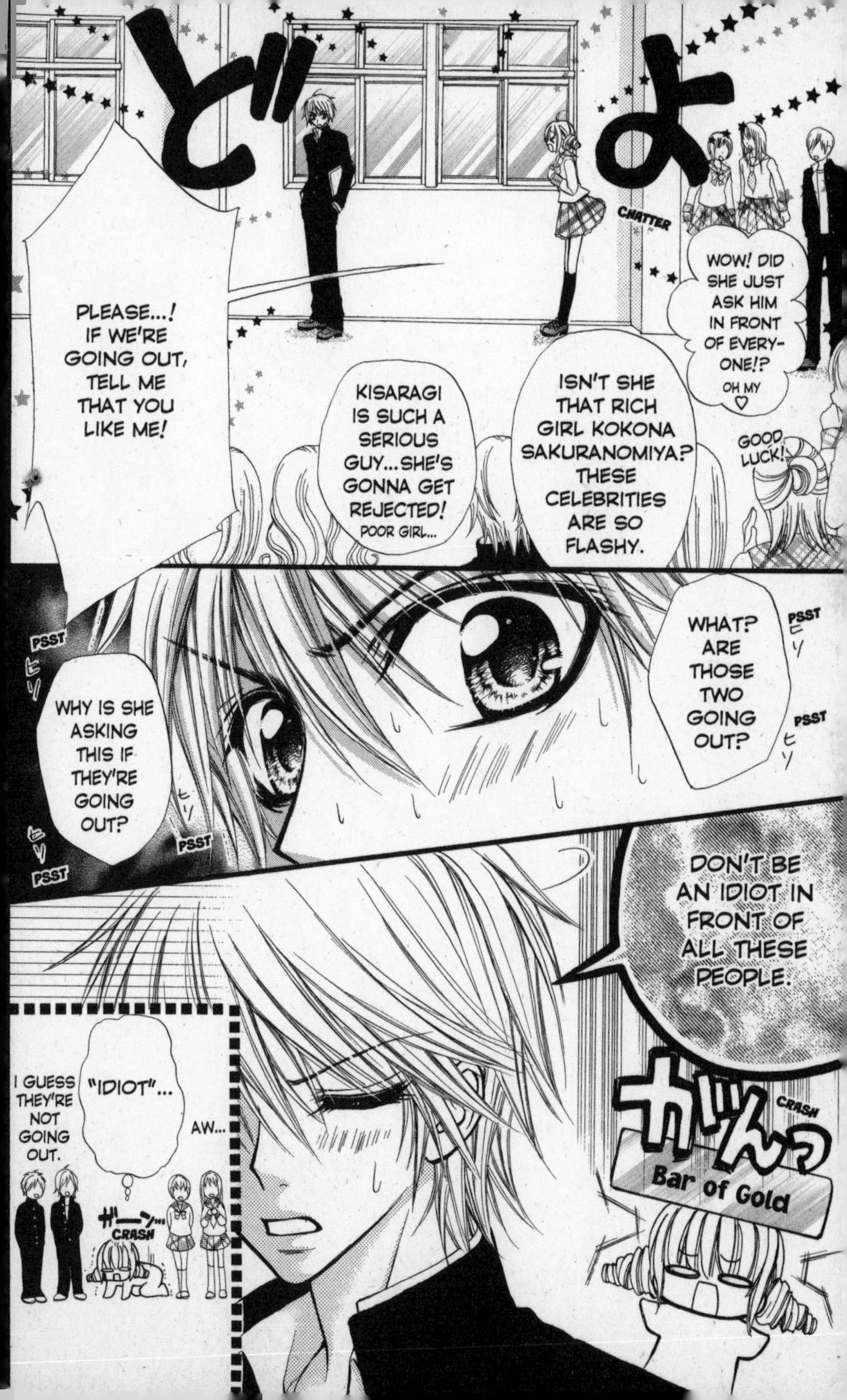
どよ
CHATTER
WOW! DID SHE JUST ASK HIM IN FRONT OF EVERY-ONE!? OH MY ♡
GOOD LUCK!
ISN'T SHE THAT RICH GIRL KOKONA SAKURANOMIYA? THESE CELEBRITIES ARE SO FLASHY.
KISARAGI IS SUCH A SERIOUS GUY...SHE'S GONNA GET REJECTED! POOR GIRL...
PLEASE...! IF WE'RE GOING OUT, TELL ME THAT YOU LIKE ME!
PSST ヒソ
WHAT? ARE THOSE TWO GOING OUT?
PSST ヒソ
WHY IS SHE ASKING THIS IF THEY'RE GOING OUT?
PSST ヒソ
PSST ヒソ
DON'T BE AN IDIOT IN FRONT OF ALL THESE PEOPLE.
がんっ CRASH
Bar of Gold
"IDIOT"...
AW...
I GUESS THEY'RE NOT GOING OUT.
ガーン... CRASH

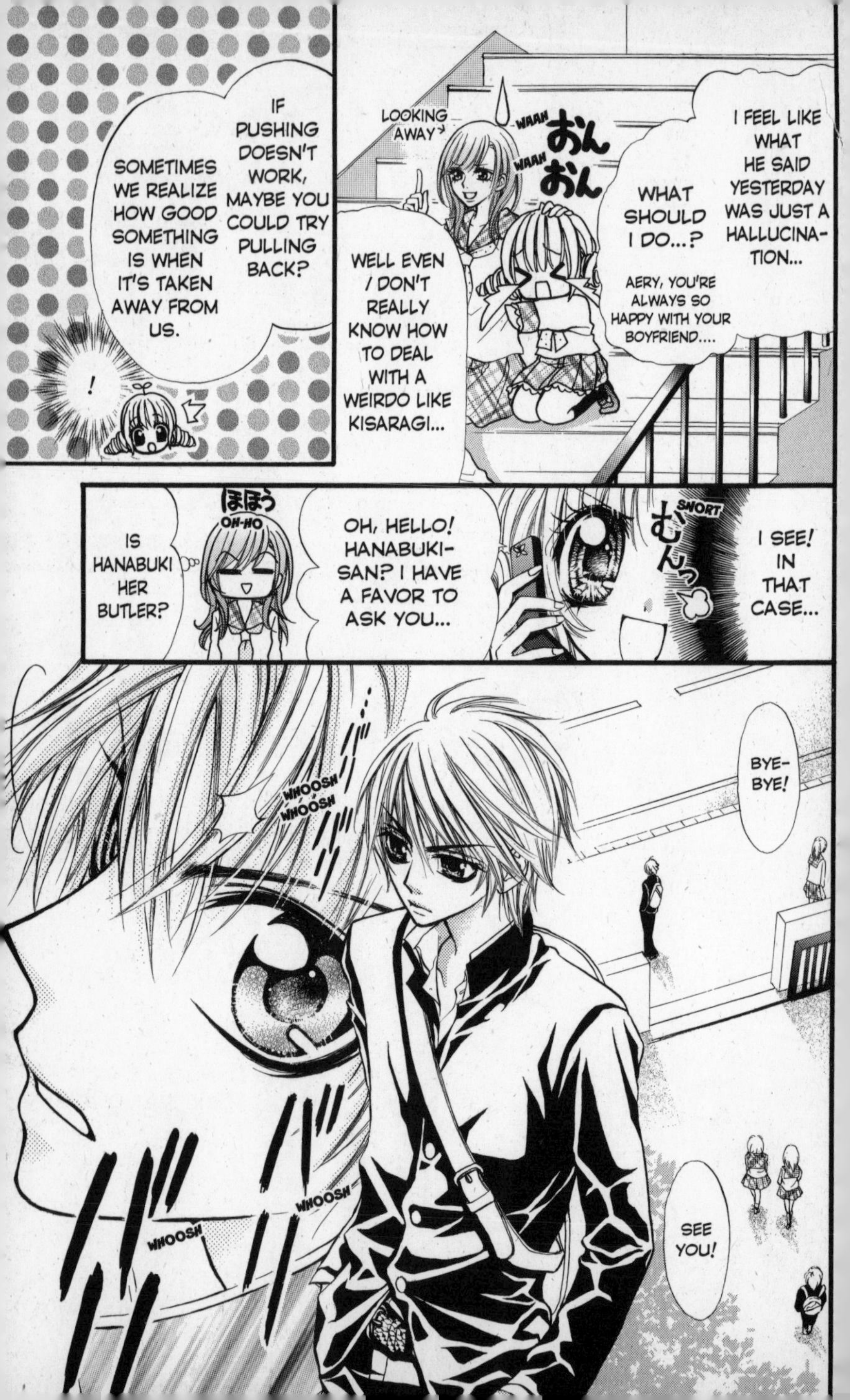
I FEEL LIKE WHAT HE SAID YESTERDAY WAS JUST A HALLUCINATION...
WHAT SHOULD I DO...?
AERY, YOU'RE ALWAYS SO HAPPY WITH YOUR BOYFRIEND....
WAAH おん
WAAH おん
LOOKING AWAY
WELL EVEN I DON'T REALLY KNOW HOW TO DEAL WITH A WEIRDO LIKE KISARAGI...
IF PUSHING DOESN'T WORK, MAYBE YOU COULD TRY PULLING BACK?
SOMETIMES WE REALIZE HOW GOOD SOMETHING IS WHEN IT'S TAKEN AWAY FROM US.
!
I SEE! IN THAT CASE...
SNORT むんっ
OH, HELLO! HANABUKI-SAN? I HAVE A FAVOR TO ASK YOU...
ほほう OH-HO
IS HANABUKI HER BUTLER?
BYE-BYE!
WHOOSH WHOOSH
SEE YOU!
WHOOSH
WHOOSH

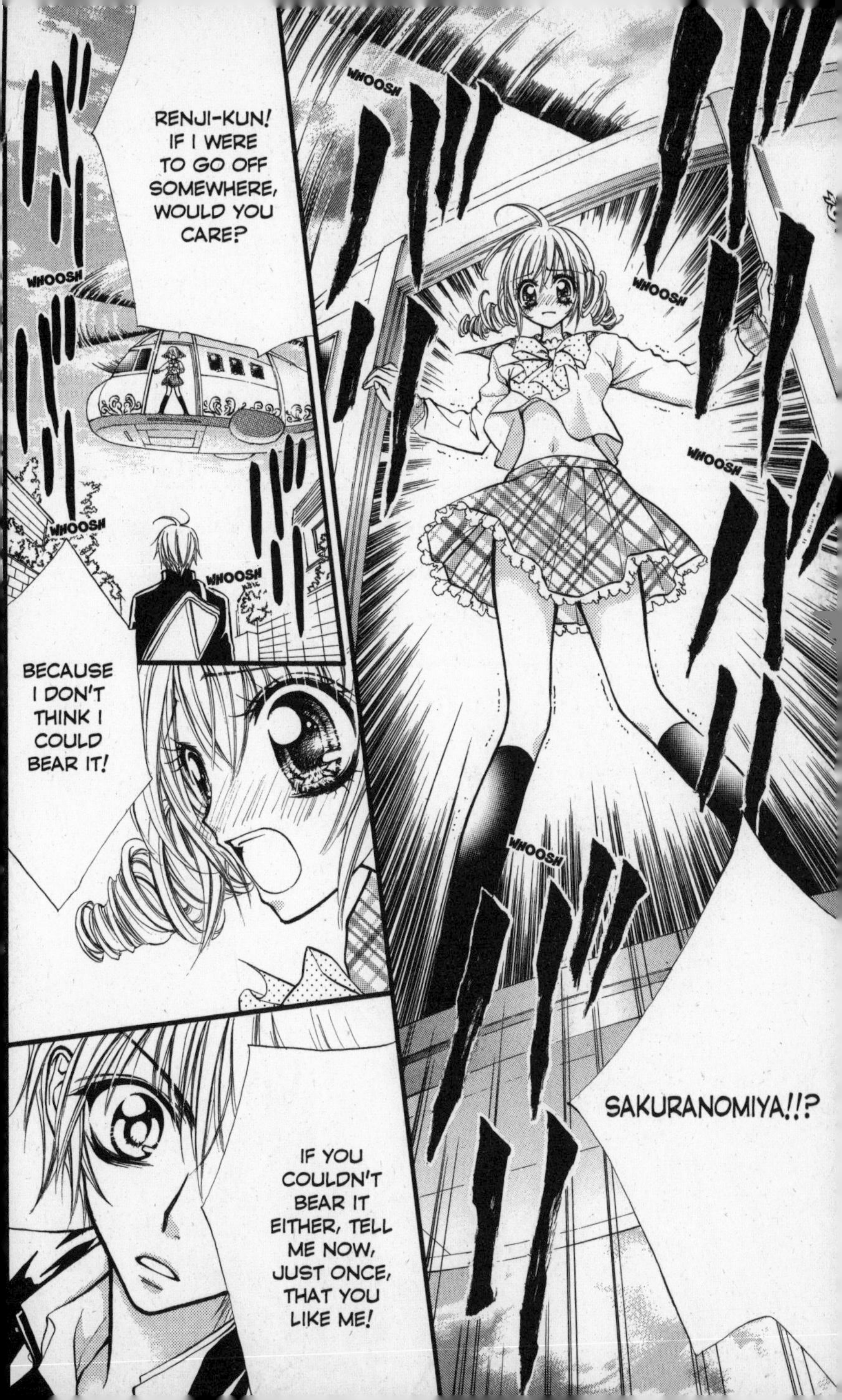
WHOOSH
WHOOSH
WHOOSH
WHOOSH
SAKURANOMIYA!!?
RENJI-KUN! IF I WERE TO GO OFF SOMEWHERE, WOULD YOU CARE?
WHOOSH
WHOOSH
WHOOSH
BECAUSE I DON'T THINK I COULD BEAR IT!
IF YOU COULDN'T BEAR IT EITHER, TELL ME NOW, JUST ONCE, THAT YOU LIKE ME!

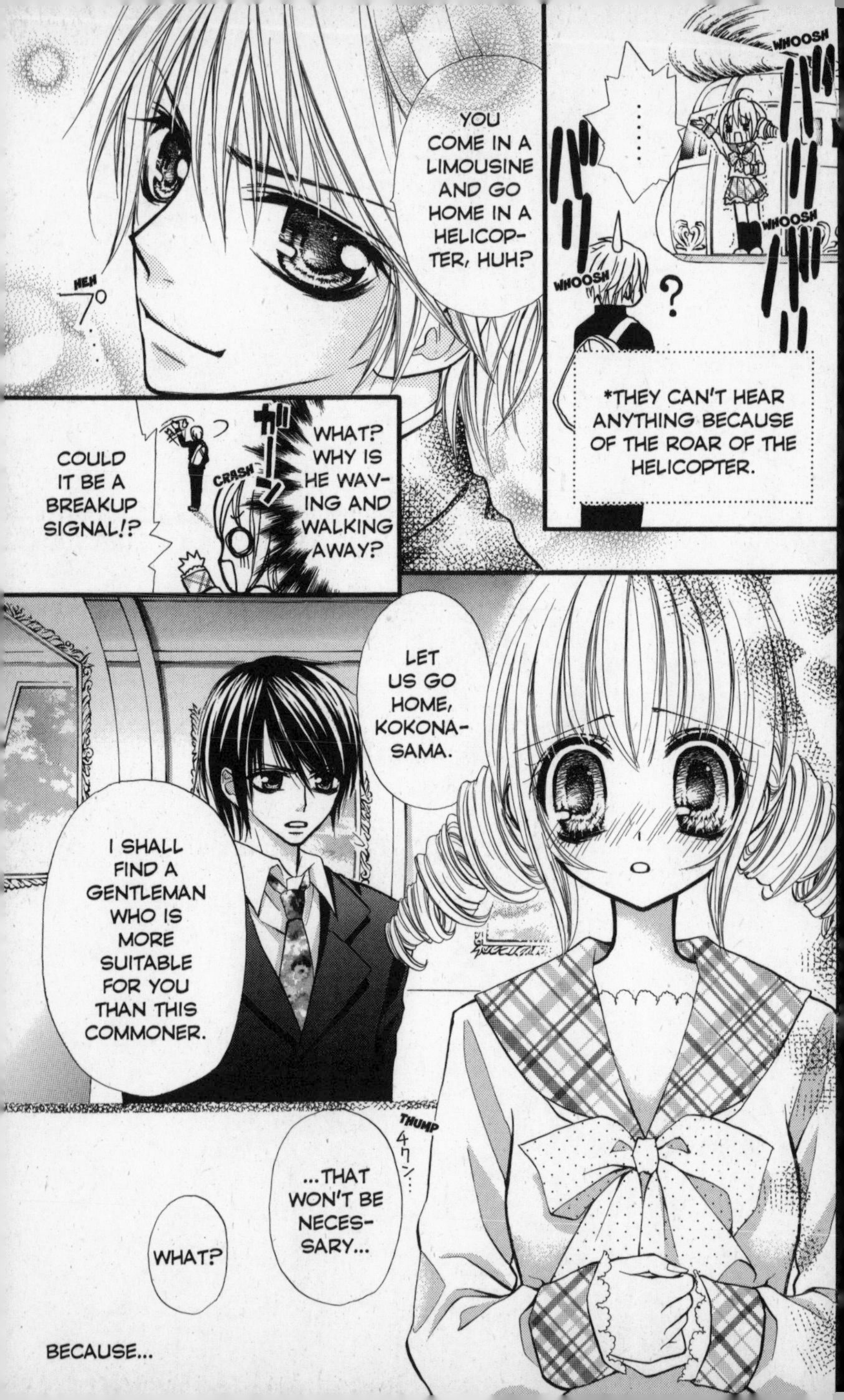
WHOOSH
......
WHOOSH
WHOOSH
?
*THEY CAN'T HEAR ANYTHING BECAUSE OF THE ROAR OF THE HELICOPTER.
YOU COME IN A LIMOUSINE AND GO HOME IN A HELICOPTER, HUH?
HEH
WHAT? WHY IS HE WAVING AND WALKING AWAY?
CRASH
COULD IT BE A BREAKUP SIGNAL!?
LET US GO HOME, KOKONA-SAMA.
I SHALL FIND A GENTLEMAN WHO IS MORE SUITABLE FOR YOU THAN THIS COMMONER.
THUMP
...THAT WON'T BE NECESSARY...
WHAT?
BECAUSE...

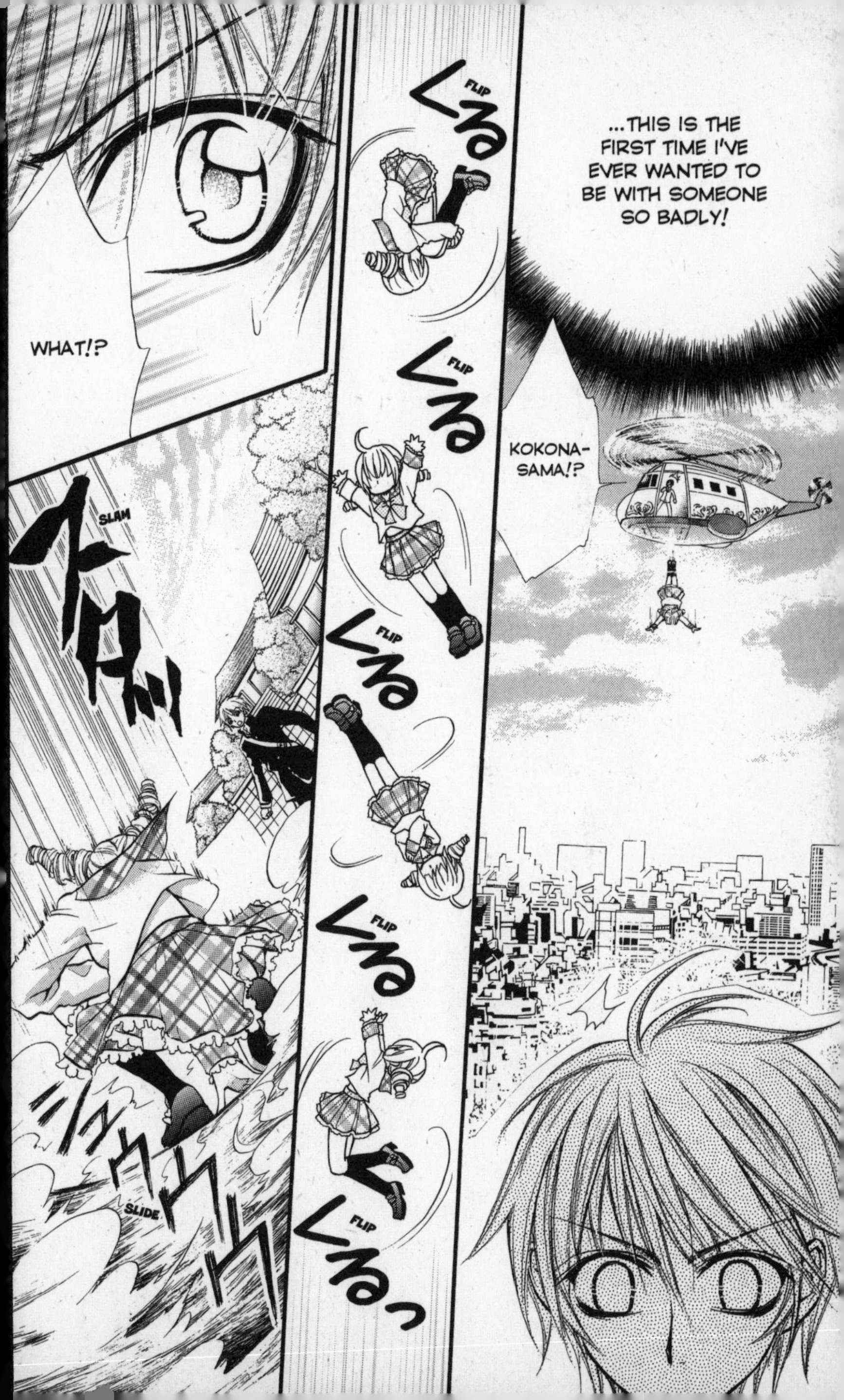
...THIS IS THE FIRST TIME I'VE EVER WANTED TO BE WITH SOMEONE SO BADLY!
KOKONA-SAMA!?
くる FLIP
くる FLIP
くる FLIP
くる FLIP
くるっ FLIP
WHAT!?
SLAM
SLIDE

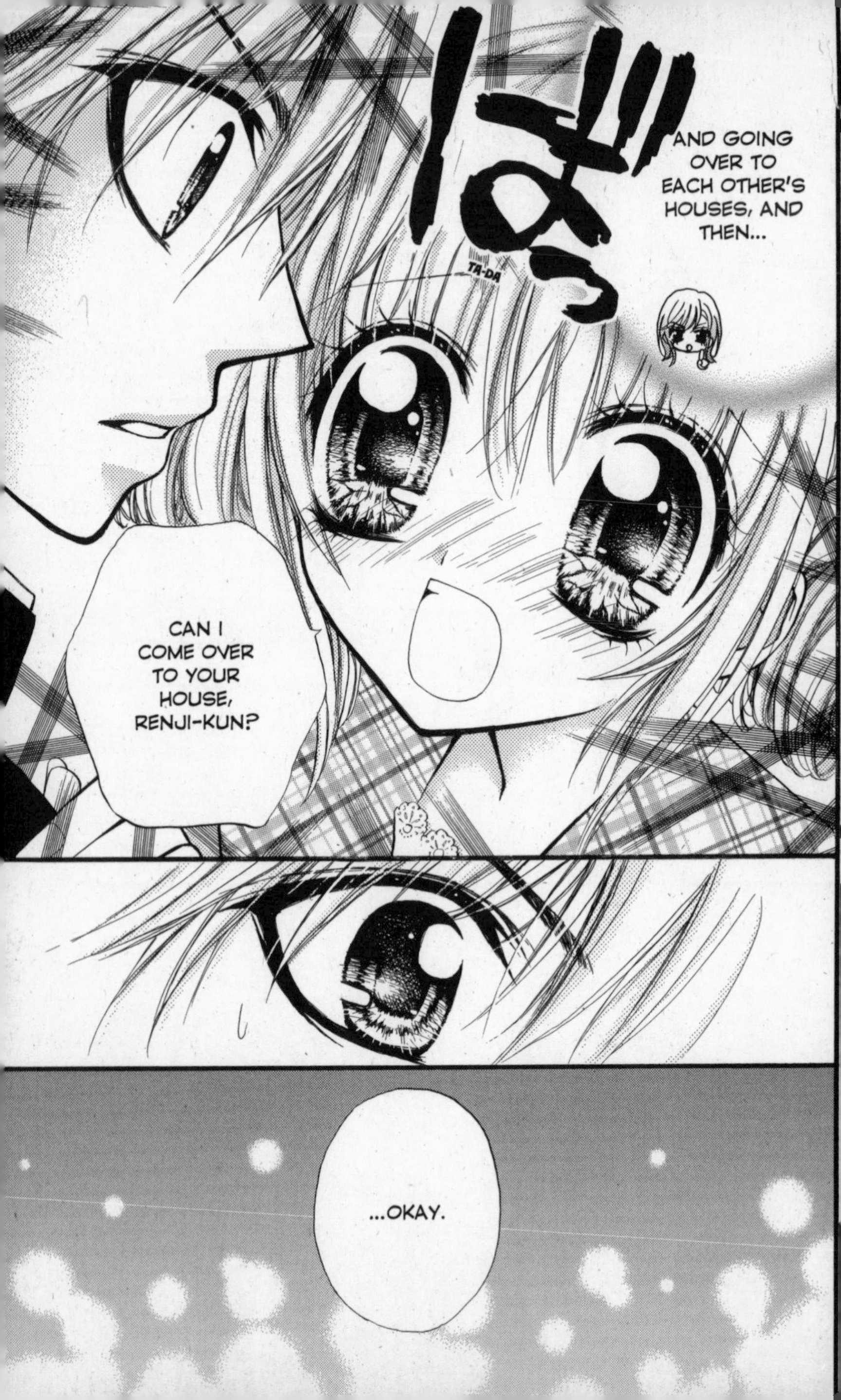
AND GOING OVER TO EACH OTHER'S HOUSES, AND THEN...
ぱっ
TA-DA
CAN I COME OVER TO YOUR HOUSE, RENJI-KUN?
...OKAY.

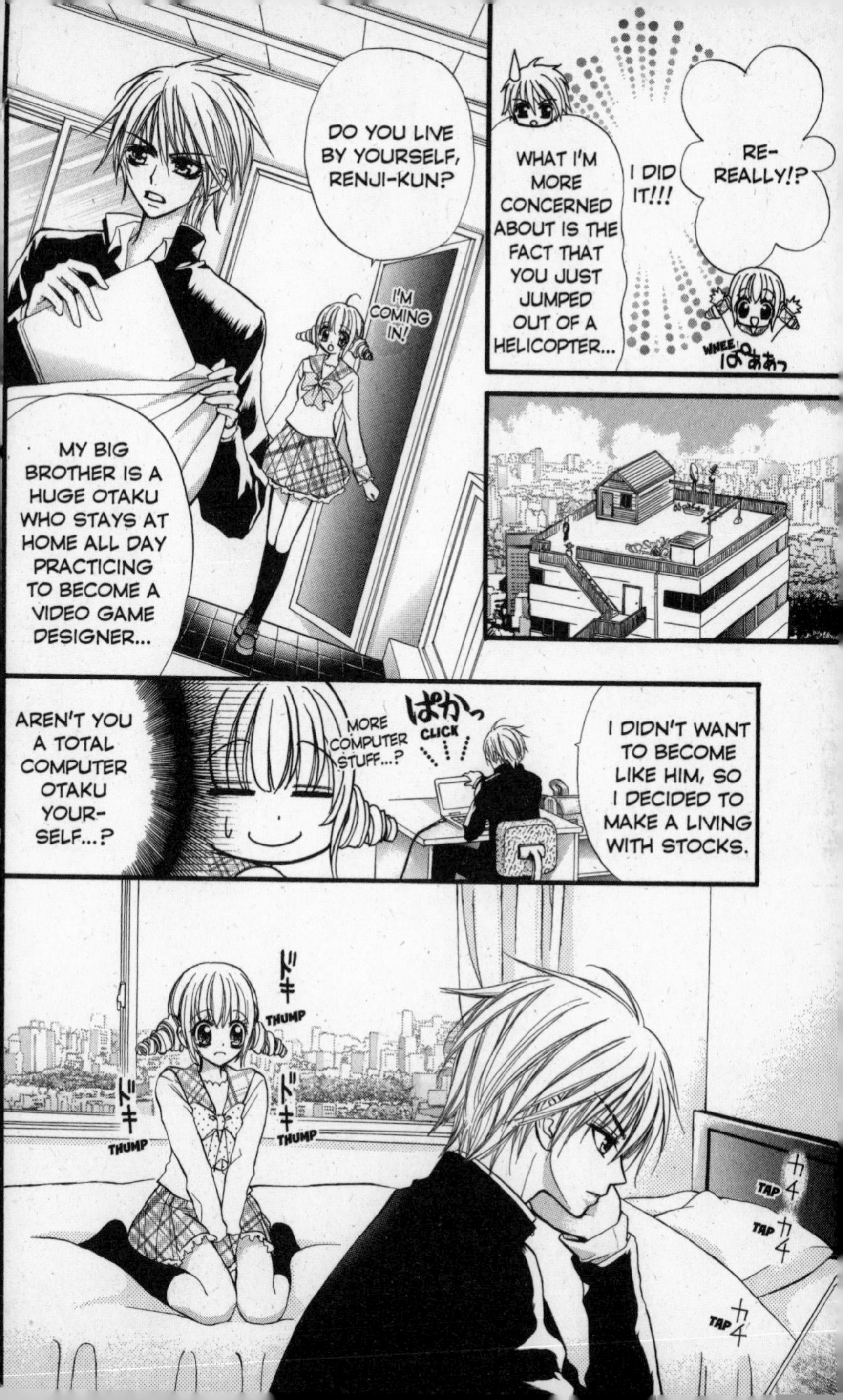
RE-REALLY!?
I DID IT!!!
WHAT I'M MORE CONCERNED ABOUT IS THE FACT THAT YOU JUST JUMPED OUT OF A HELICOPTER...
WHEE ぱあぁっ
DO YOU LIVE BY YOURSELF, RENJI-KUN?
I'M COMING IN!
MY BIG BROTHER IS A HUGE OTAKU WHO STAYS AT HOME ALL DAY PRACTICING TO BECOME A VIDEO GAME DESIGNER...
I DIDN'T WANT TO BECOME LIKE HIM, SO I DECIDED TO MAKE A LIVING WITH STOCKS.
ぱかっ CLICK
MORE COMPUTER STUFF...?
AREN'T YOU A TOTAL COMPUTER OTAKU YOURSELF...?
TAP カタ
TAP カタ
TAP カタ
ドキ THUMP
ドキ THUMP
ドキ THUMP

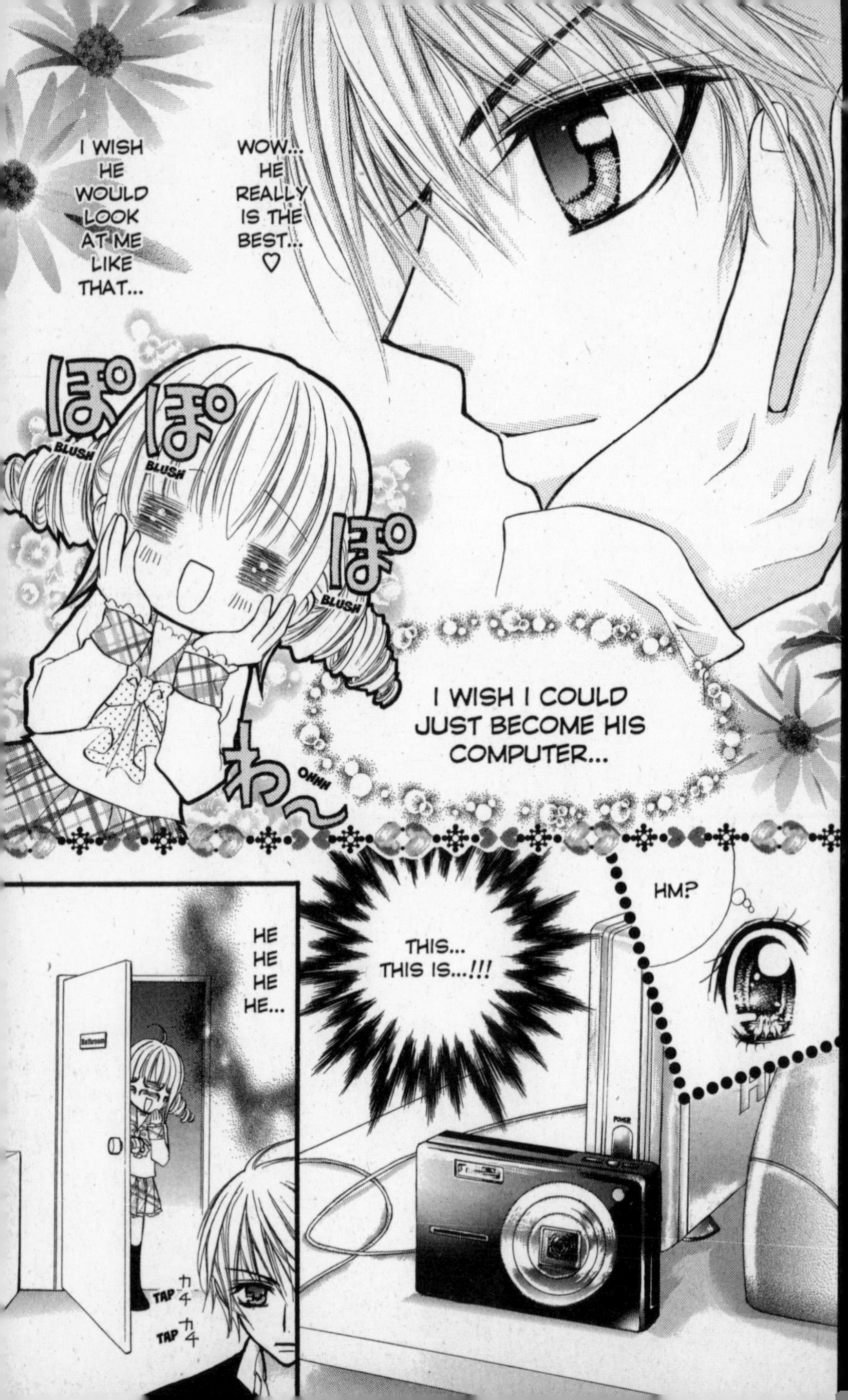
WOW... HE REALLY IS THE BEST... ♡
I WISH HE WOULD LOOK AT ME LIKE THAT...
ぽ BLUSH
ぽ BLUSH
ぽ BLUSH
I WISH I COULD JUST BECOME HIS COMPUTER...
わ～ OHNN
HM?
THIS... THIS IS...!!!
HE HE HE HE...
TAP カチ
TAP カチ

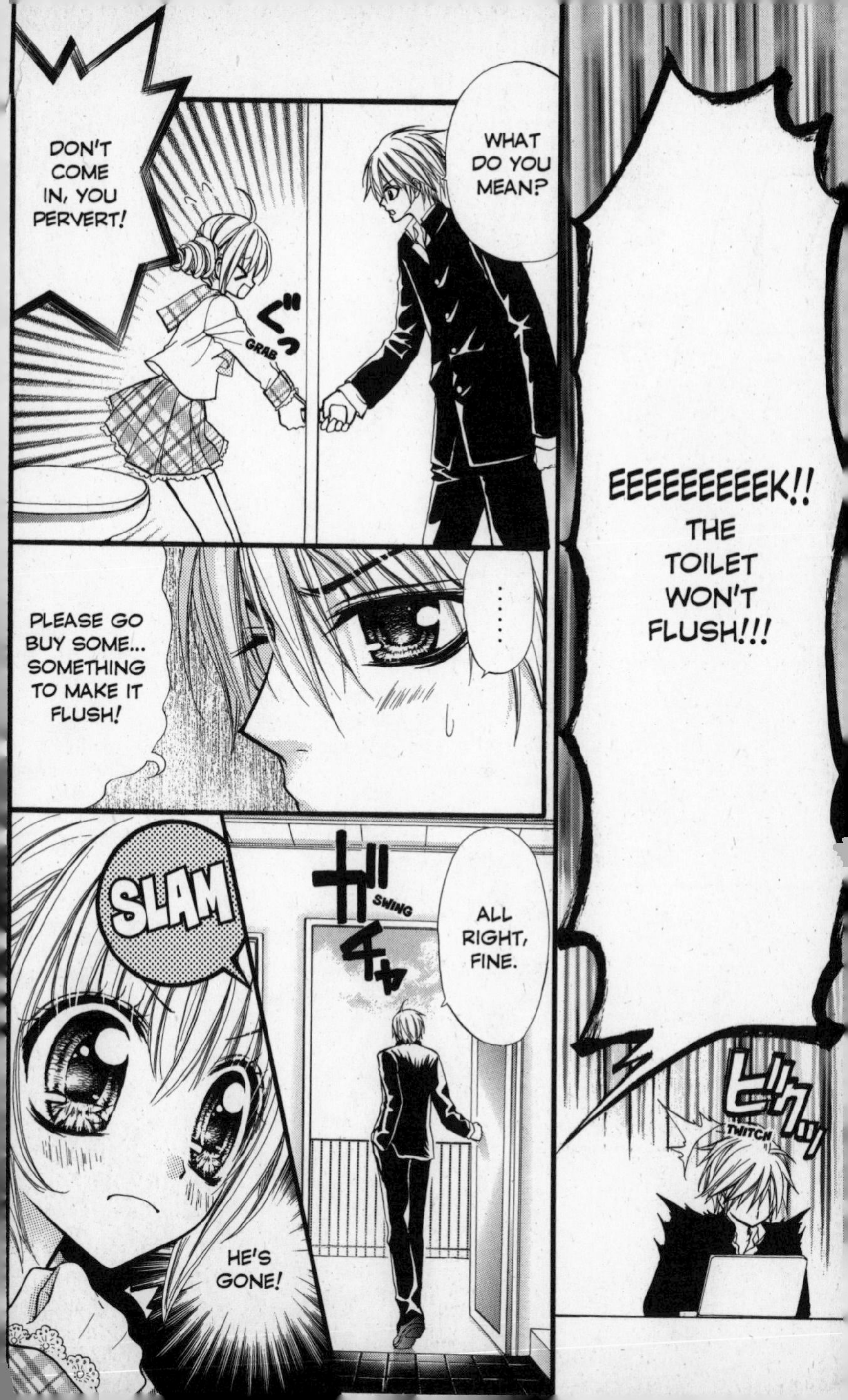

EEEEEEEEEEK!! THE TOILET WON'T FLUSH!!!
TWITCH
WHAT DO YOU MEAN?
DON'T COME IN, YOU PERVERT!
GRAB
......
PLEASE GO BUY SOME... SOMETHING TO MAKE IT FLUSH!
ALL RIGHT, FINE.
SWING
SLAM
HE'S GONE!

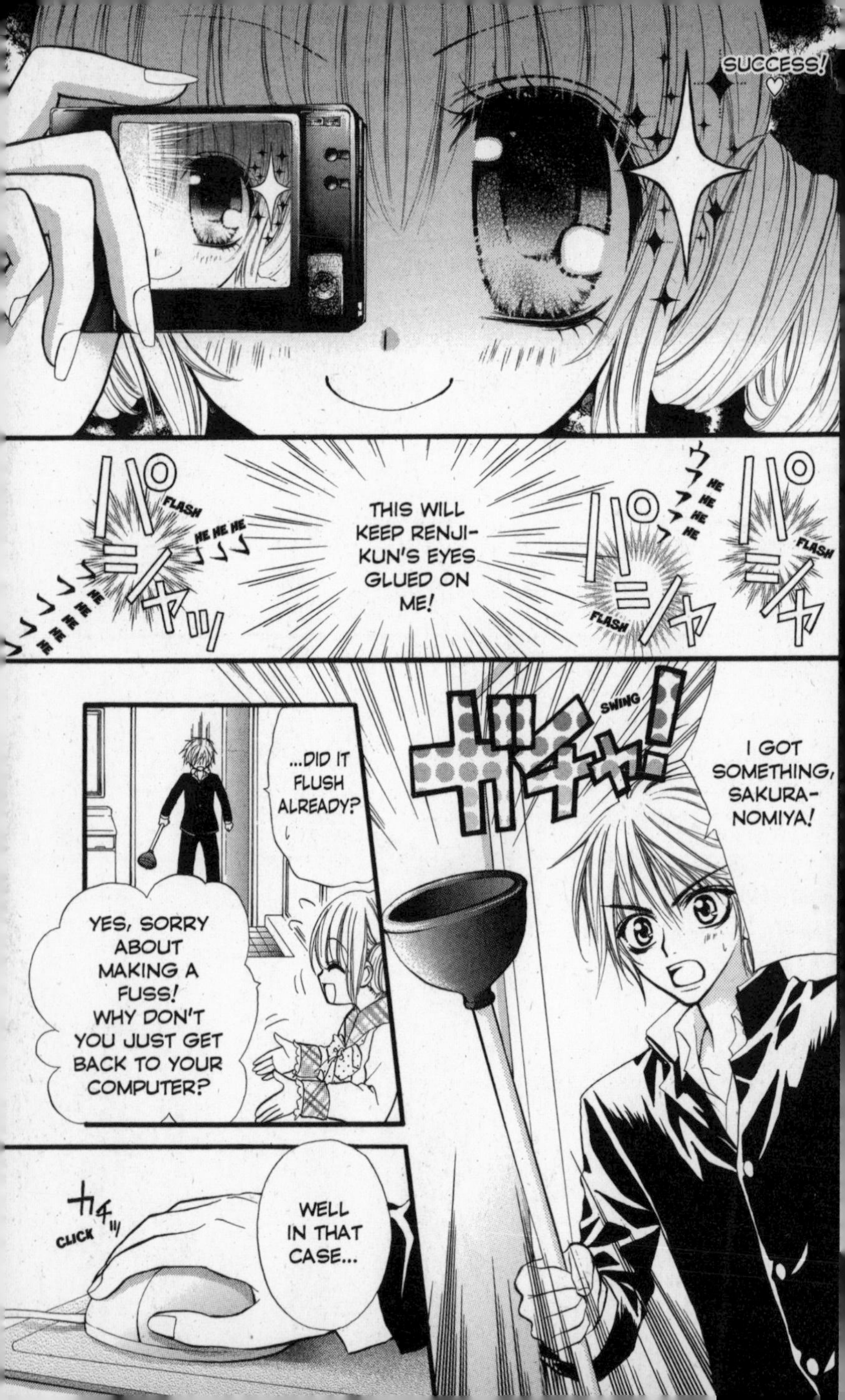
SUCCESS! ♥
パシャ
FLASH
ウフフフ
HE HE HE HE
パシャ
FLASH
THIS WILL KEEP RENJI-KUN'S EYES GLUED ON ME!
パシャッ
FLASH
HE HE HE
HE HE HE HE HE
ガチャ!
SWING
I GOT SOMETHING, SAKURA-NOMIYA!
...DID IT FLUSH ALREADY?
YES, SORRY ABOUT MAKING A FUSS! WHY DON'T YOU JUST GET BACK TO YOUR COMPUTER?
WELL IN THAT CASE...
カチッ
CLICK

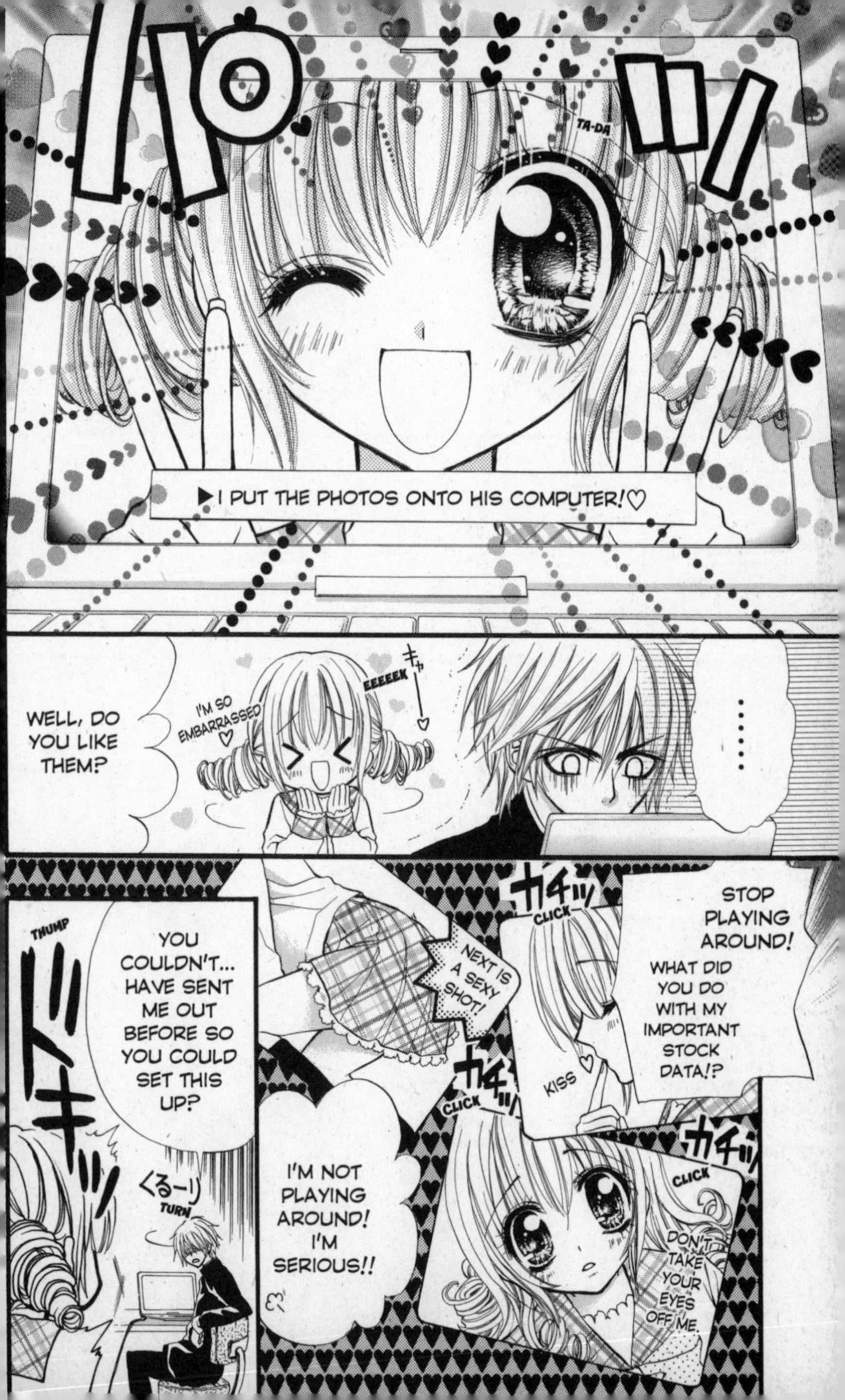
TA-DA
▶I PUT THE PHOTOS ONTO HIS COMPUTER!♡
......
キャー♡
EEEEEK
I'M SO EMBARRASSED ♡
WELL, DO YOU LIKE THEM?
カチッ
CLICK
STOP PLAYING AROUND!
WHAT DID YOU DO WITH MY IMPORTANT STOCK DATA!?
KISS ♡
NEXT IS A SEXY SHOT!
カチッ
CLICK
カチッ
CLICK
DON'T TAKE YOUR EYES OFF ME.
I'M NOT PLAYING AROUND! I'M SERIOUS!!
YOU COULDN'T... HAVE SENT ME OUT BEFORE SO YOU COULD SET THIS UP?
ドキッ
THUMP
くるーり
TURN

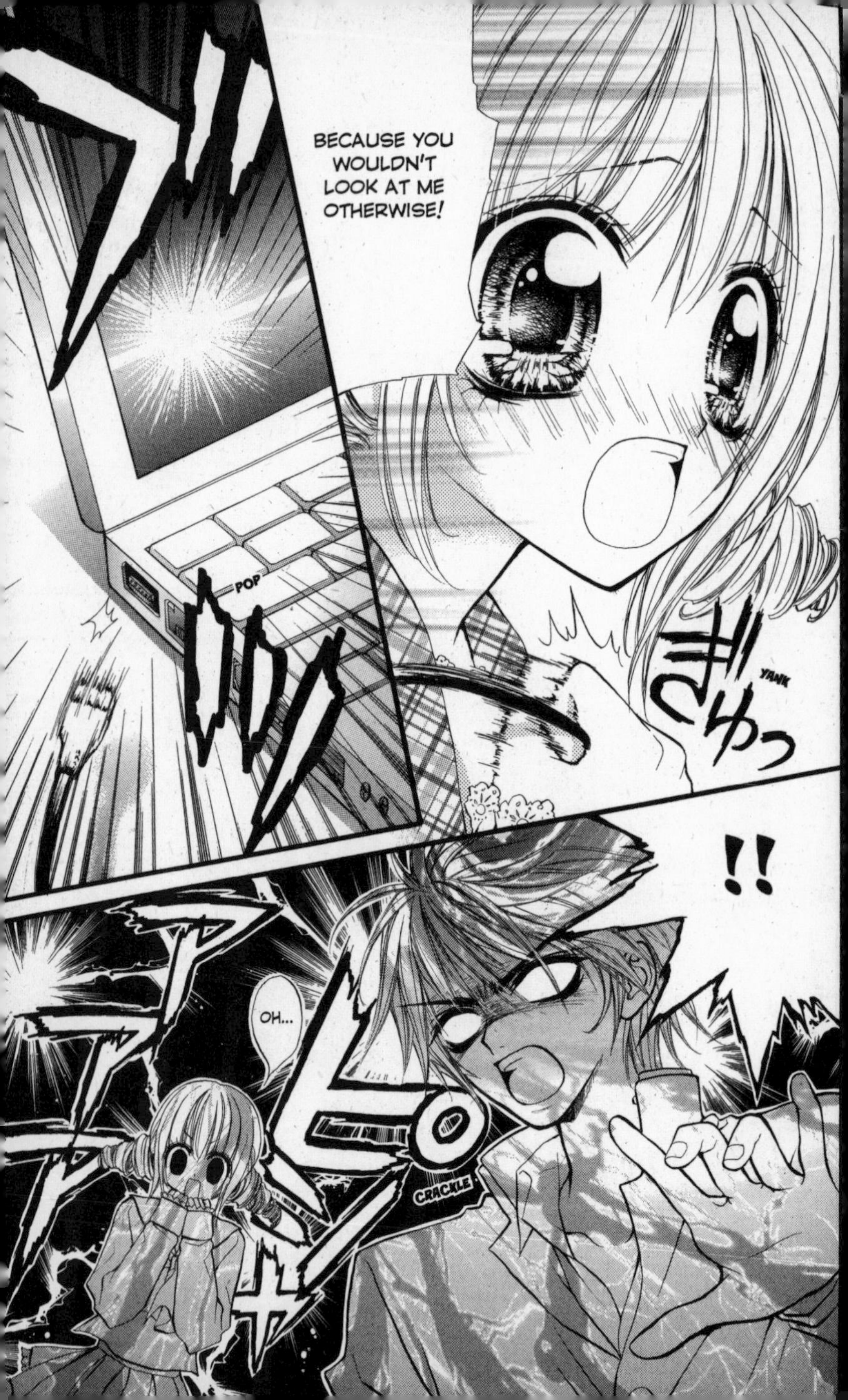
BECAUSE YOU WOULDN'T LOOK AT ME OTHERWISE!
ぎゅっ
YANK
POP
!!
CRACKLE
OH...

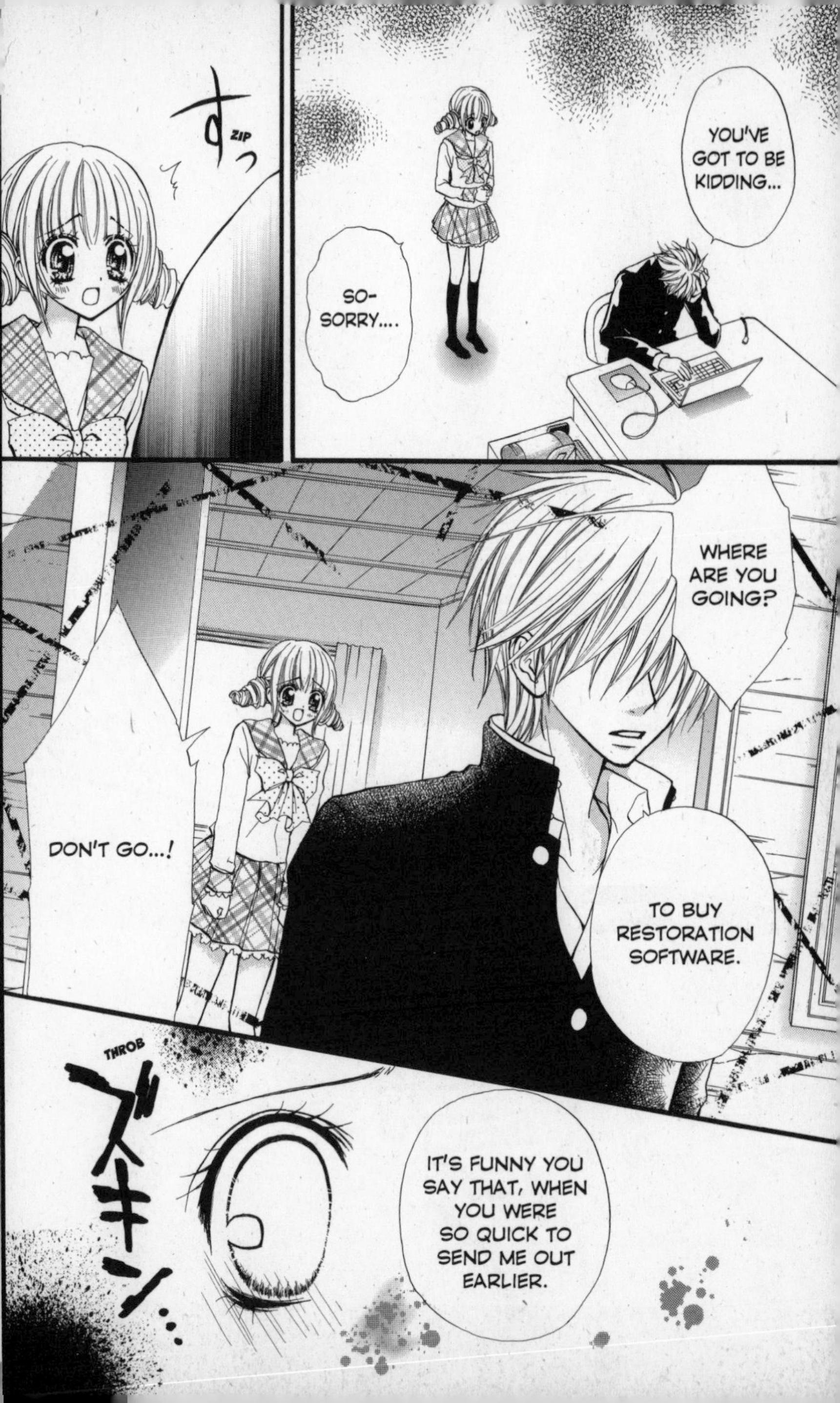
YOU'VE GOT TO BE KIDDING...
SO-SORRY....
すっ
ZIP
WHERE ARE YOU GOING?
TO BUY RESTORATION SOFTWARE.
DON'T GO...!
IT'S FUNNY YOU SAY THAT, WHEN YOU WERE SO QUICK TO SEND ME OUT EARLIER.
ズキン…
THROB

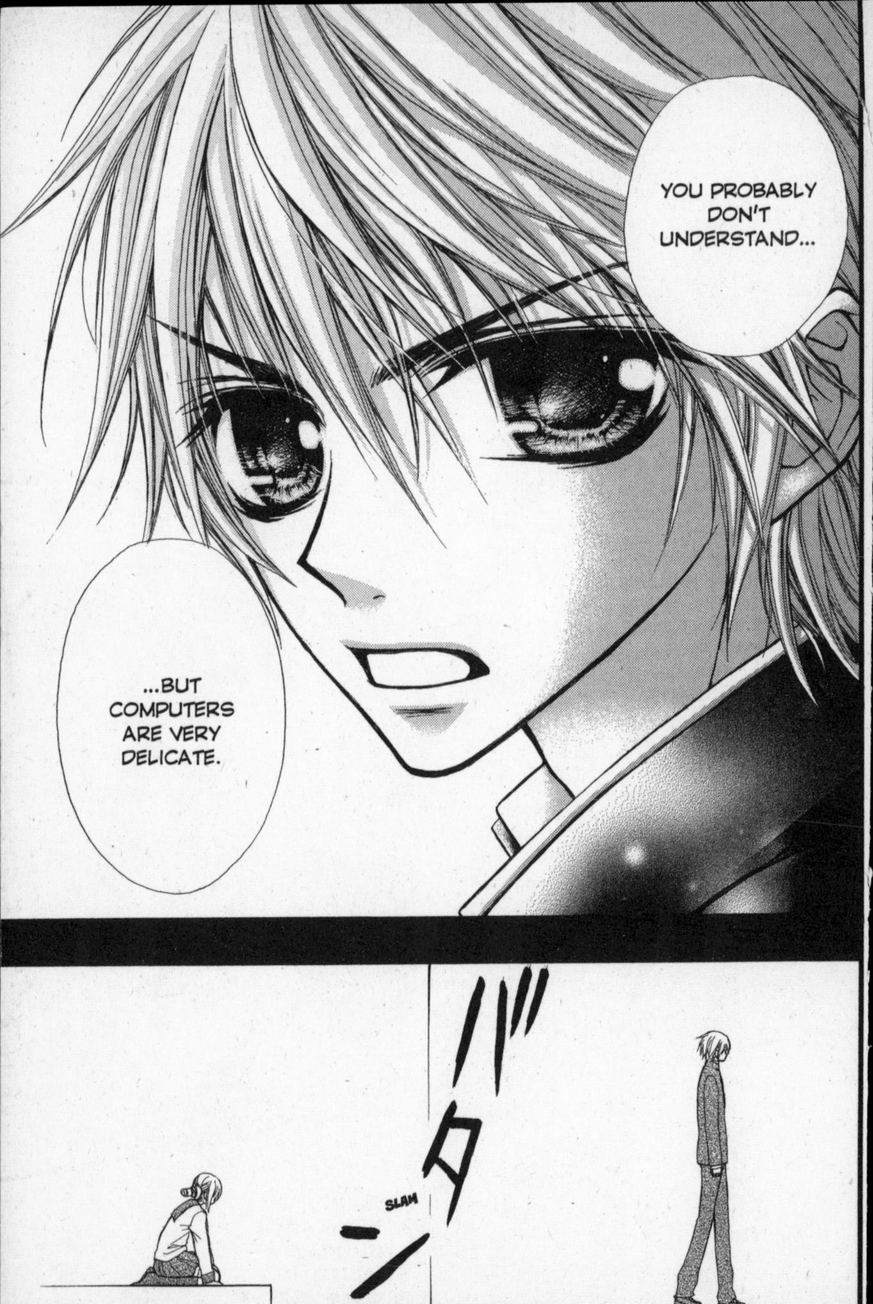
YOU PROBABLY DON'T UNDERSTAND...
...BUT COMPUTERS ARE VERY DELICATE.
バタン
SLAM

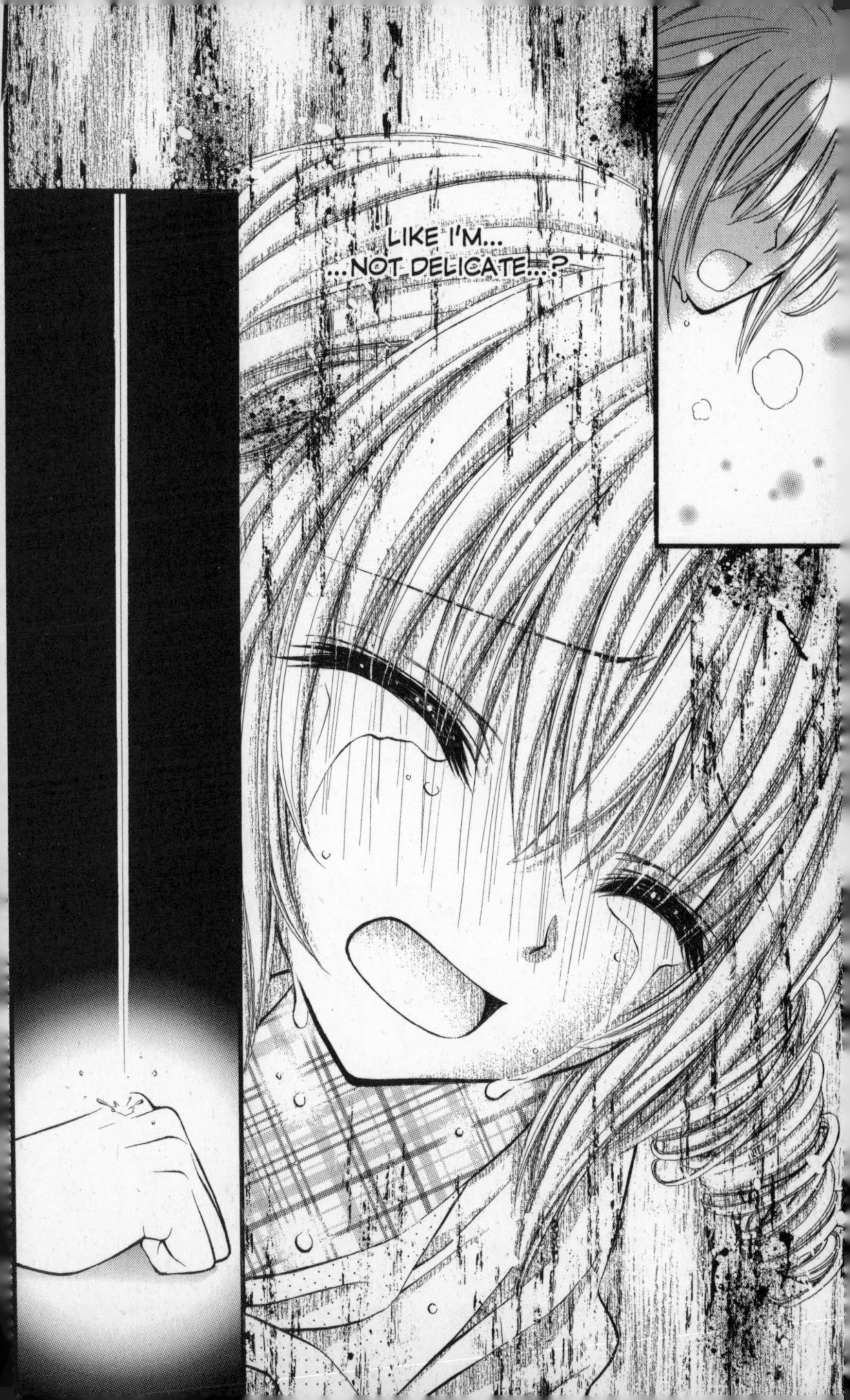
LIKE I'M...
...NOT DELICATE...?

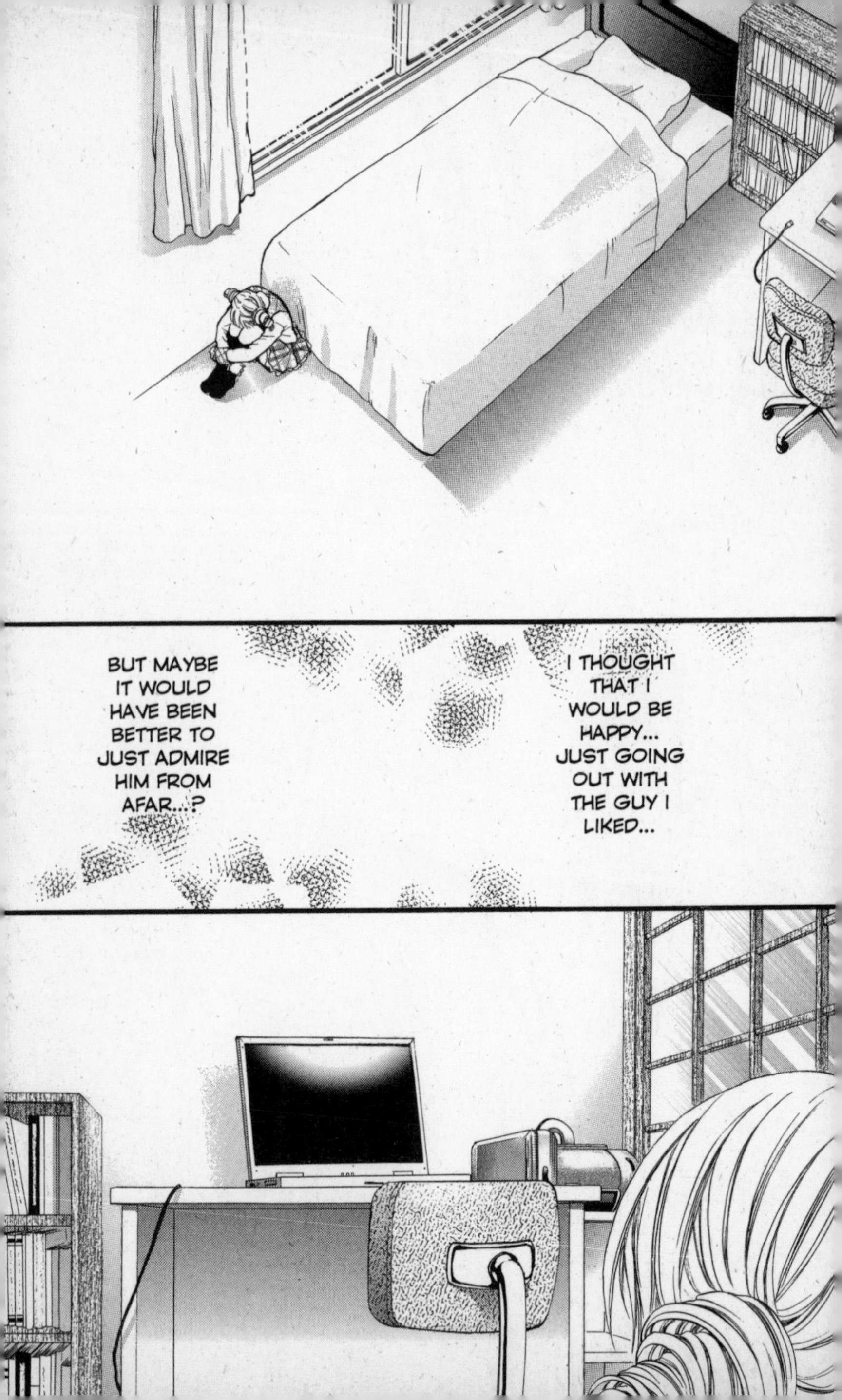
I THOUGHT THAT I WOULD BE HAPPY... JUST GOING OUT WITH THE GUY I LIKED...
BUT MAYBE IT WOULD HAVE BEEN BETTER TO JUST ADMIRE HIM FROM AFAR...?

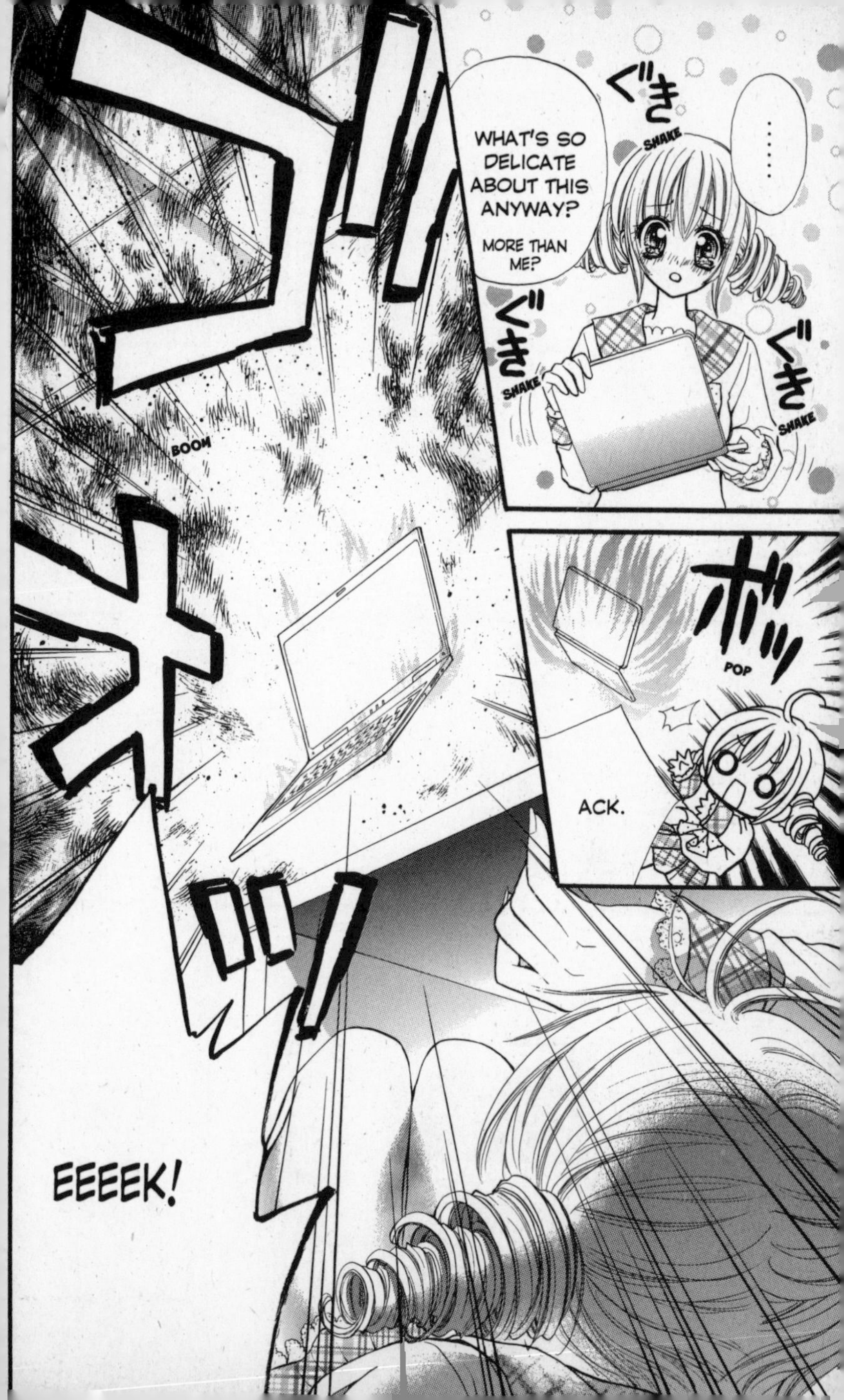

……
WHAT'S SO DELICATE ABOUT THIS ANYWAY?
MORE THAN ME?
ぐき
SHAKE
ぐき
SHAKE
ぐき
SHAKE
ボッ
POP
ACK.
BOOM
EEEEK!

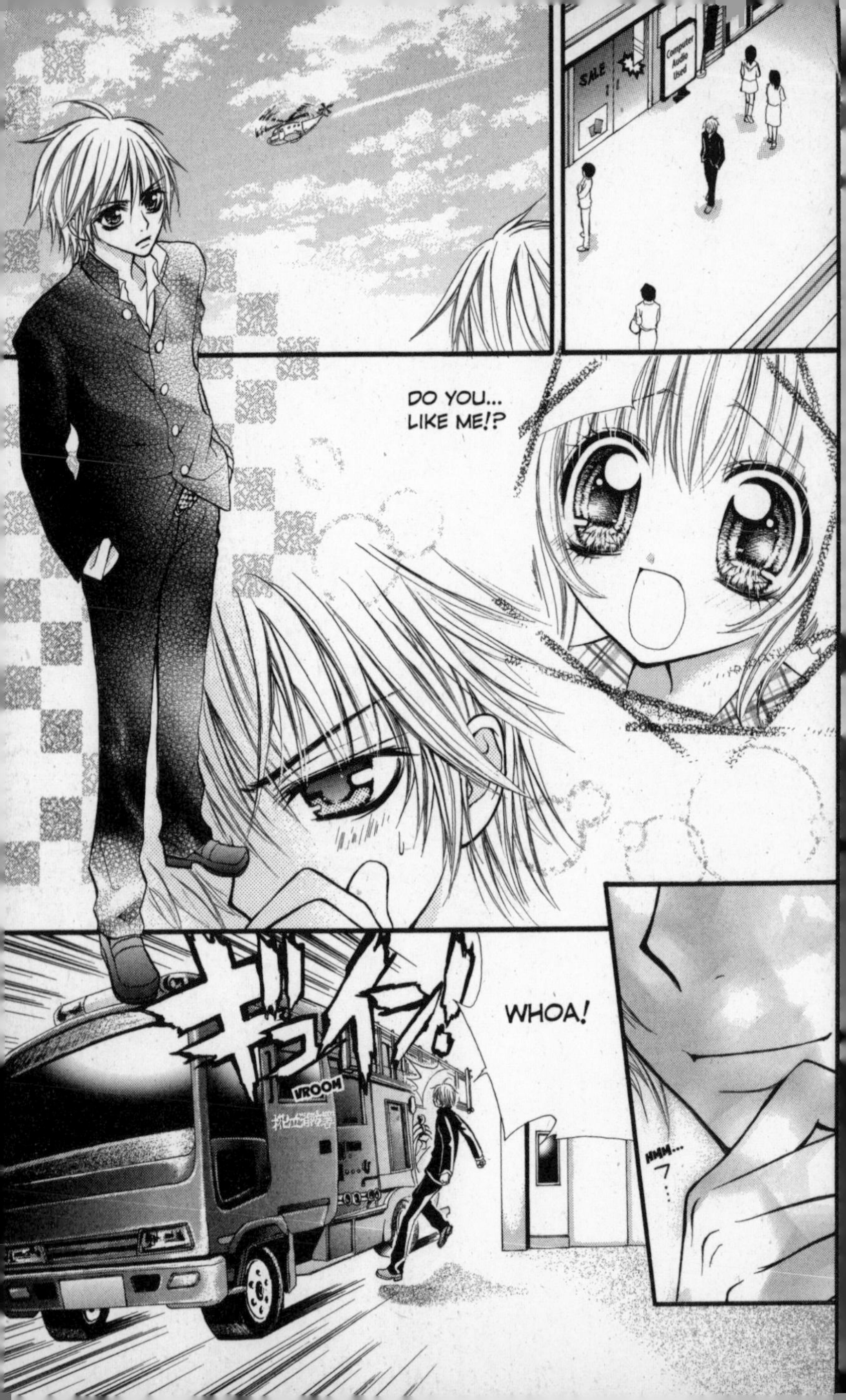
SALE
Computer Audio Used
DO YOU... LIKE ME!?
HMM...
WHOA!
VROOM

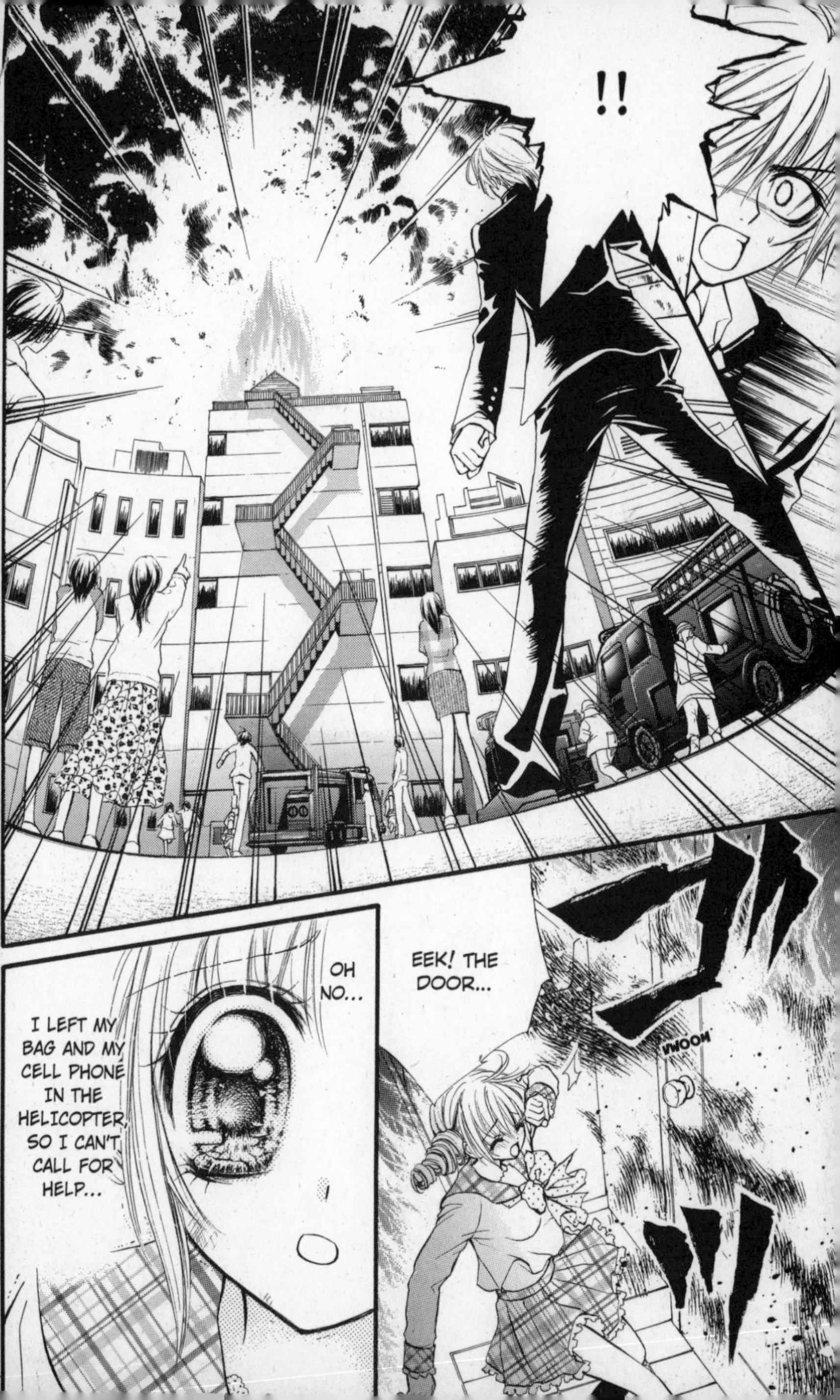
!!
EEK! THE DOOR...
VWOOM
OH NO...
I LEFT MY BAG AND MY CELL PHONE IN THE HELICOPTER, SO I CAN'T CALL FOR HELP...

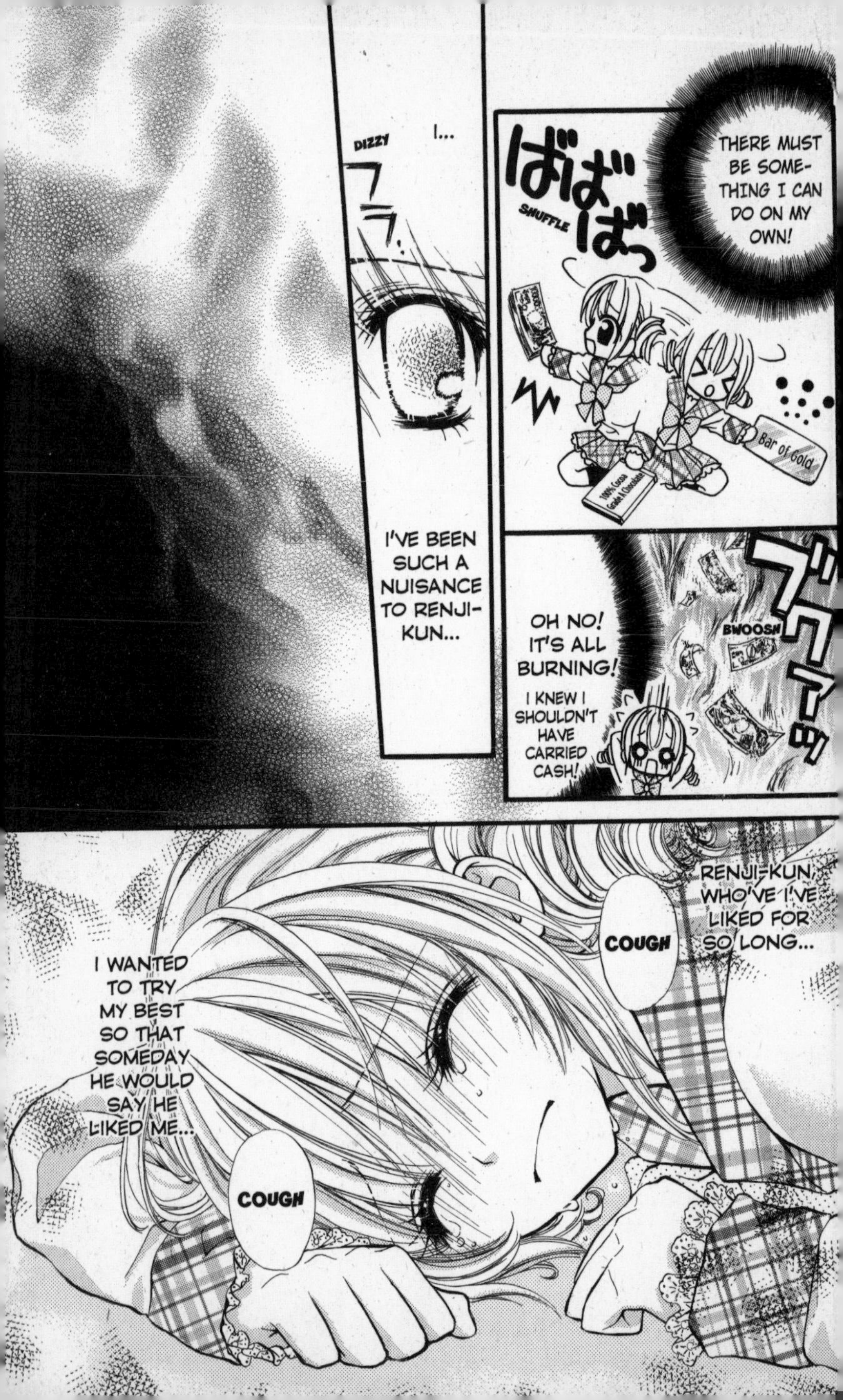
THERE MUST BE SOMETHING I CAN DO ON MY OWN!
ばばばっ
SHUFFLE
Bar of Gold
100% Cocoa Grade A Chocolate
ブワァッ
BWOOSH
OH NO! IT'S ALL BURNING!
I KNEW I SHOULDN'T HAVE CARRIED CASH!
I...
DIZZY
フラ
I'VE BEEN SUCH A NUISANCE TO RENJI-KUN...
RENJI-KUN, WHO'VE I'VE LIKED FOR SO LONG...
COUGH
I WANTED TO TRY MY BEST SO THAT SOMEDAY HE WOULD SAY HE LIKED ME...
COUGH

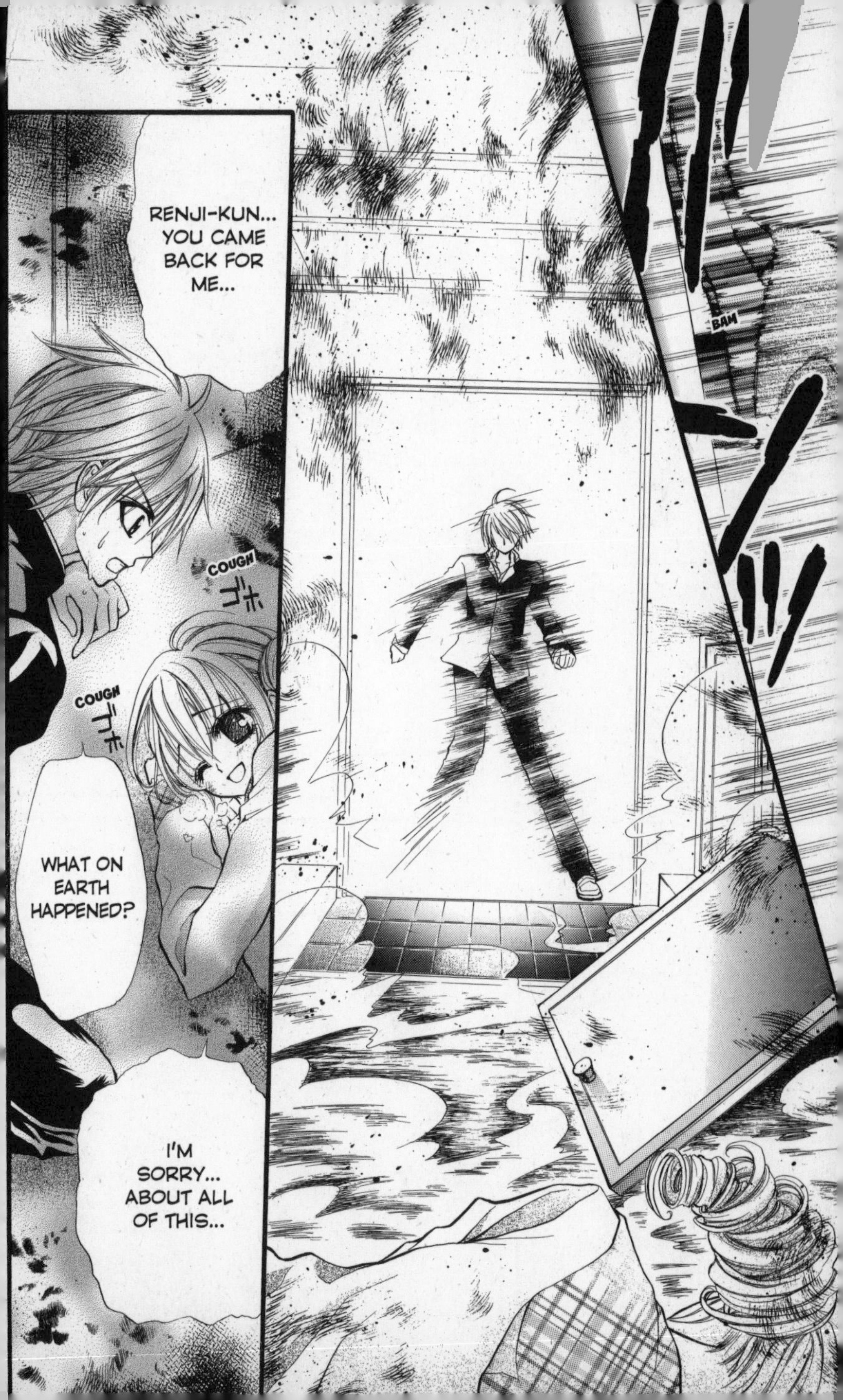
BAM
RENJI-KUN... YOU CAME BACK FOR ME...
COUGH
ゴホ
COUGH
ゴホ
WHAT ON EARTH HAPPENED?
I'M SORRY... ABOUT ALL OF THIS...

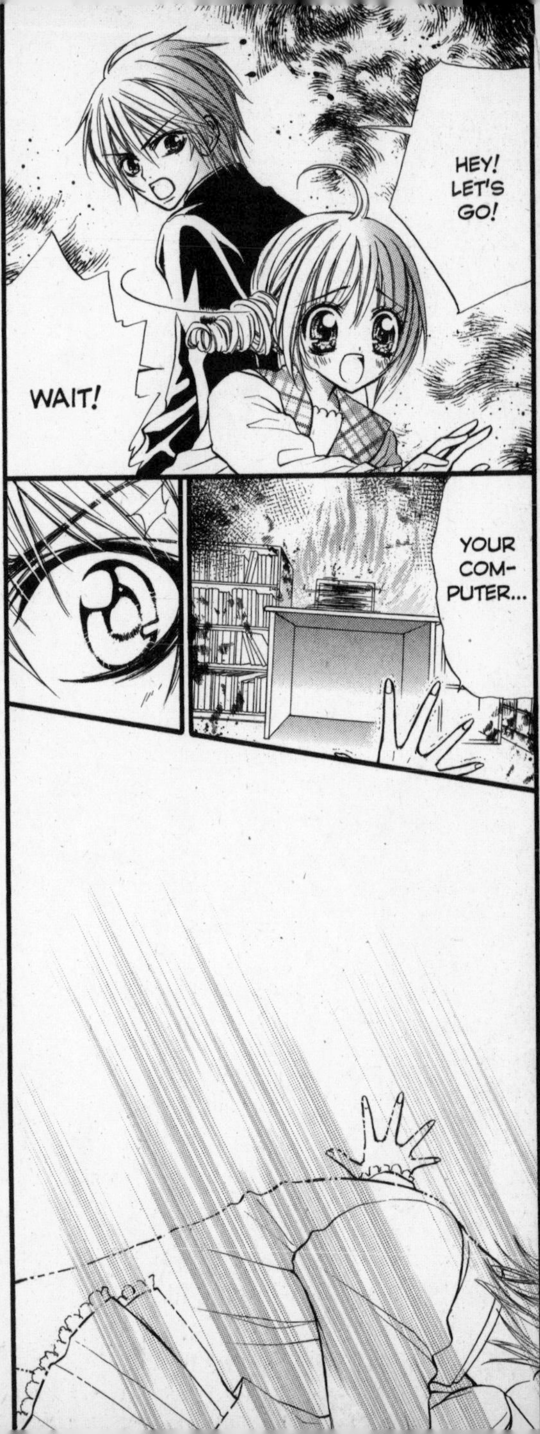
HEY! LET'S GO!
WAIT!
YOUR COM-PUTER...

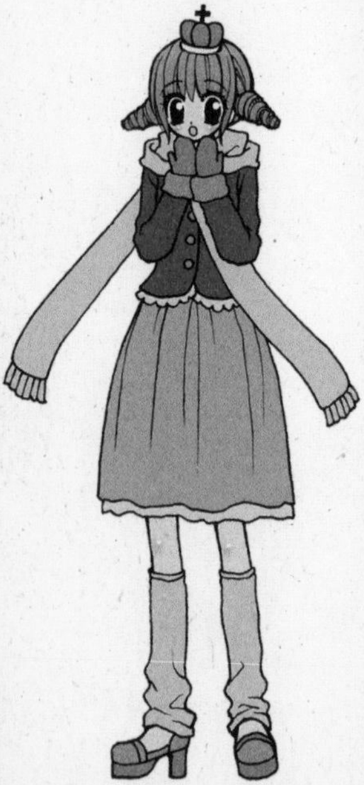

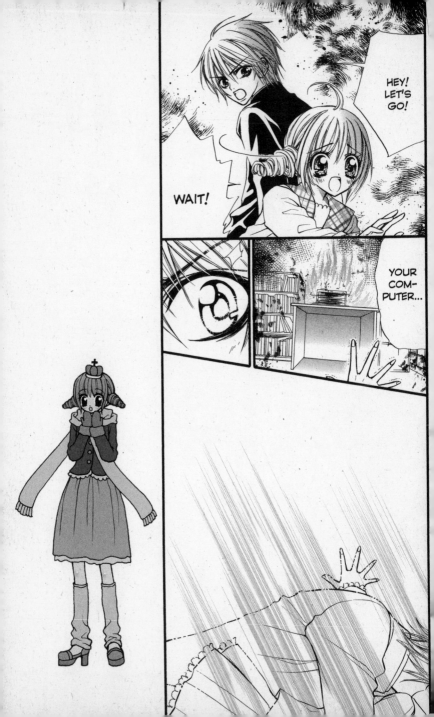

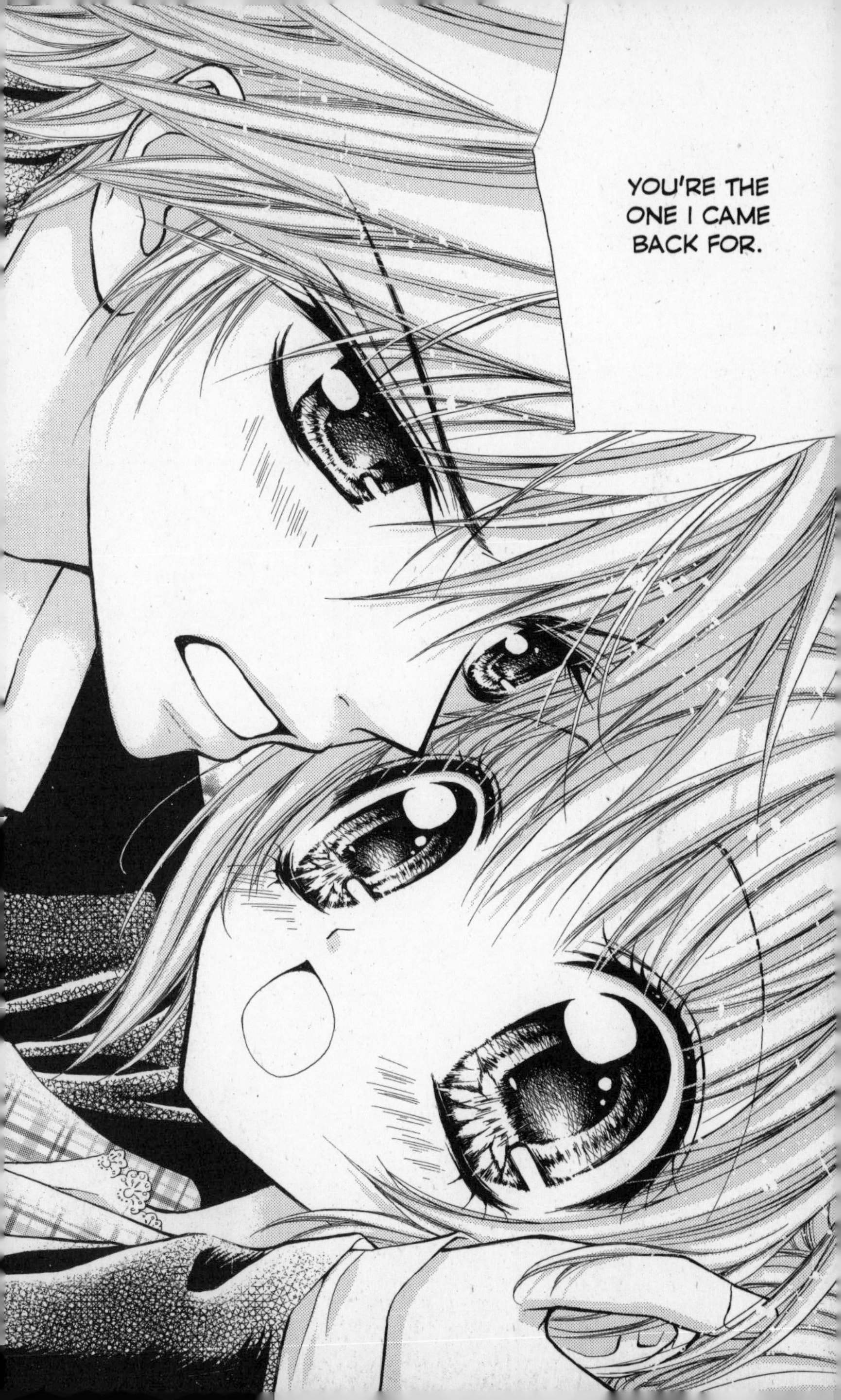
YOU'RE THE ONE I CAME BACK FOR.

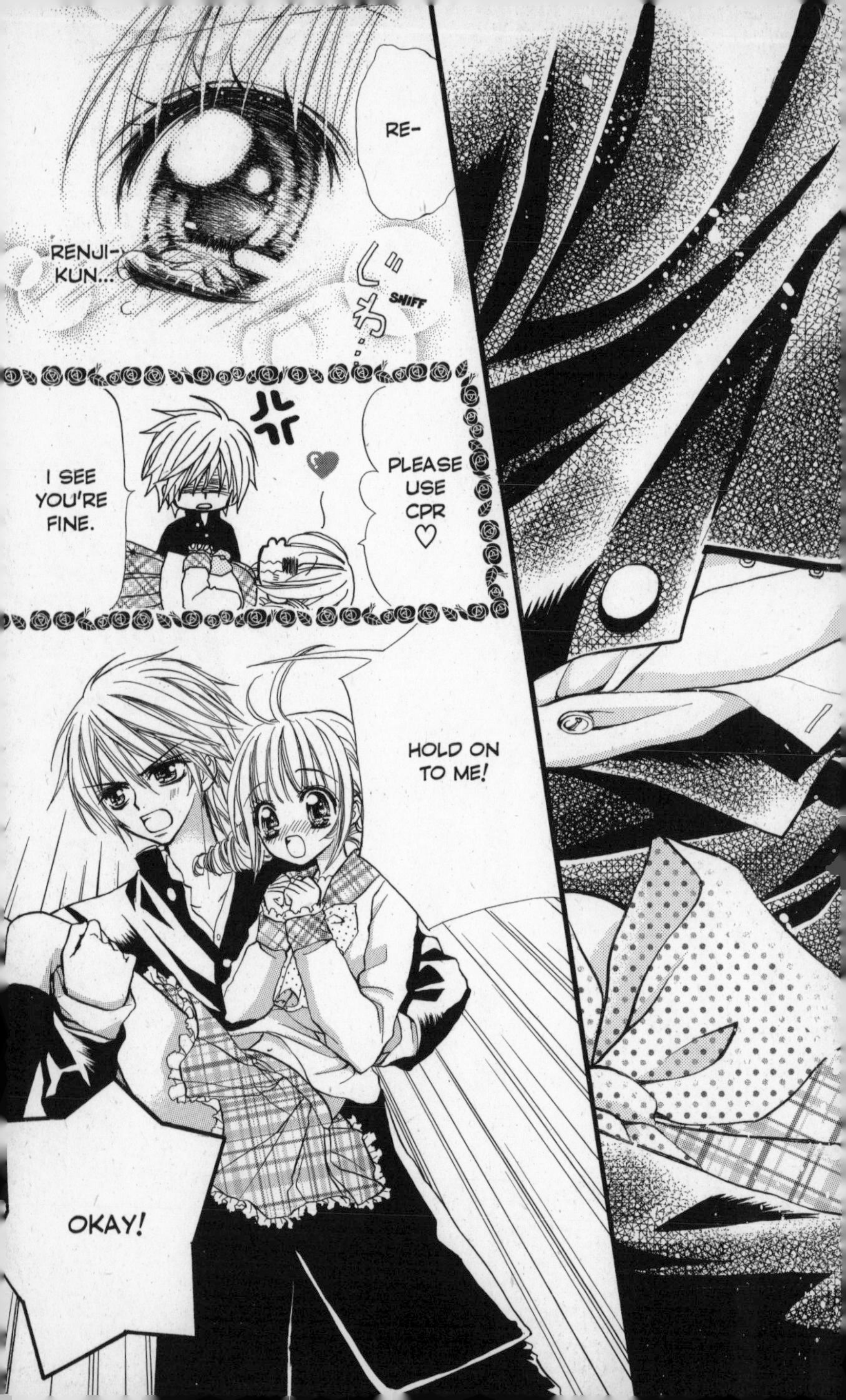
RE-
じわ
SNIFF
RENJI-KUN...
PLEASE USE CPR ♡
I SEE YOU'RE FINE.
HOLD ON TO ME!
OKAY!

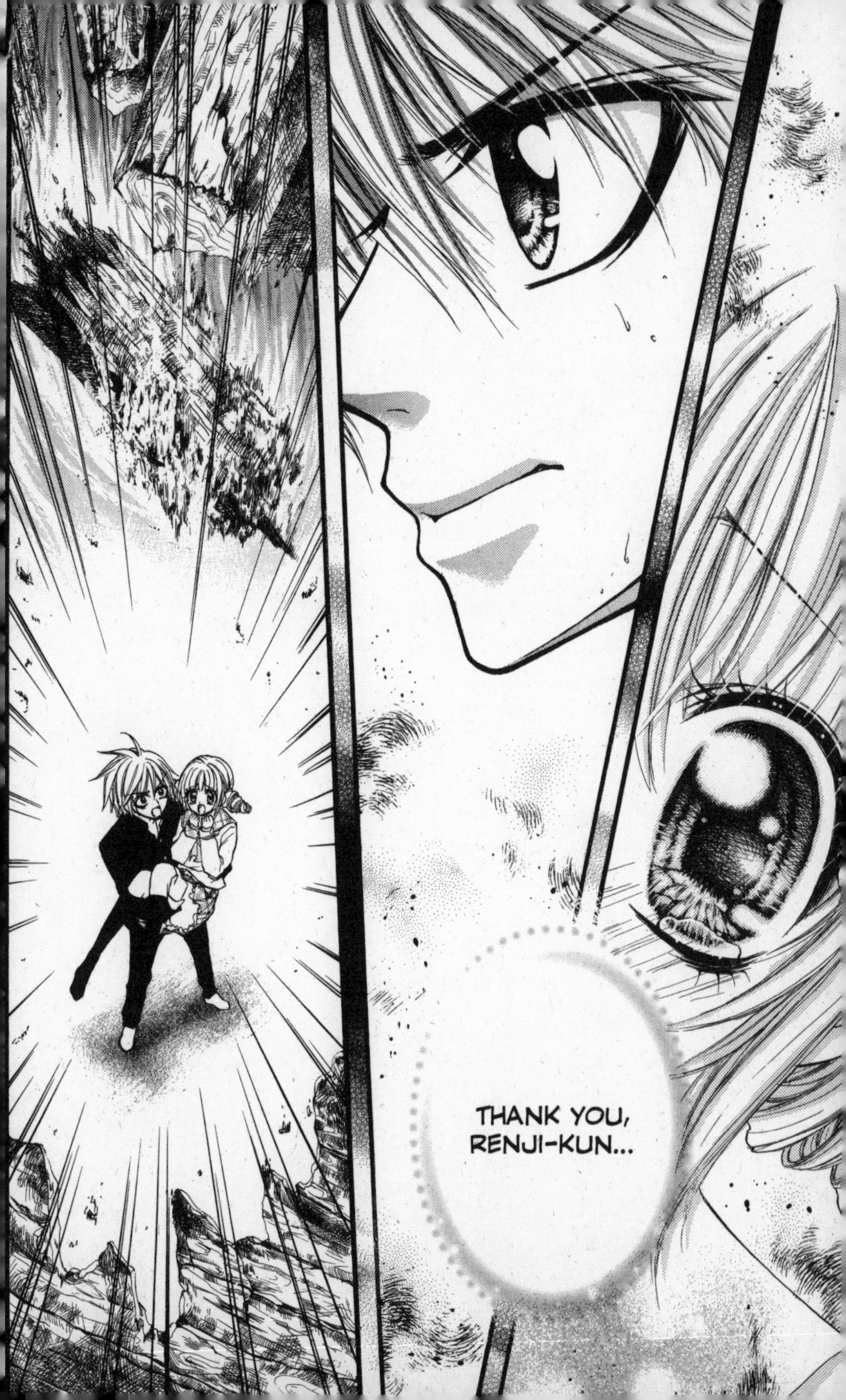
THANK YOU, RENJI-KUN...

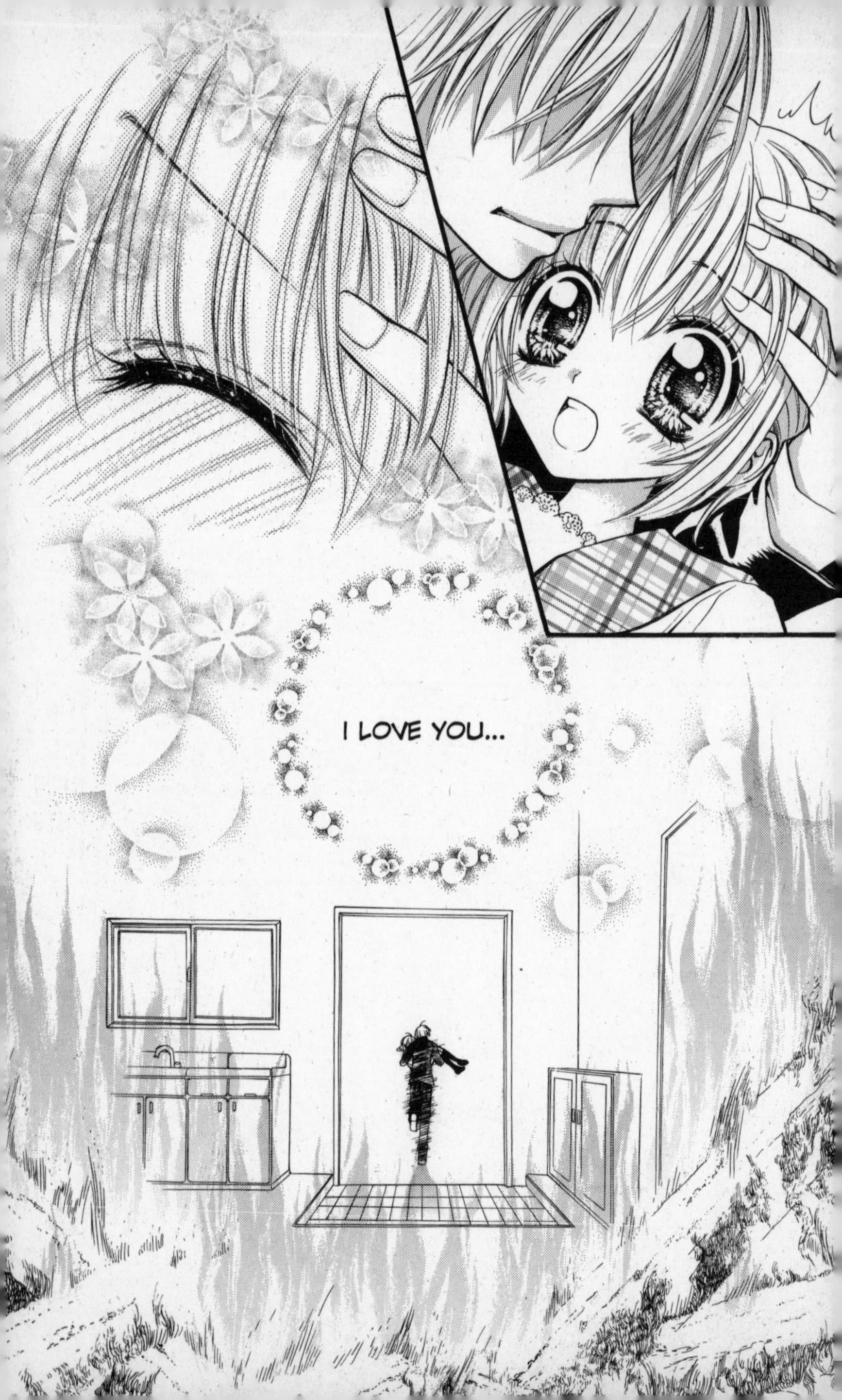
I LOVE YOU...

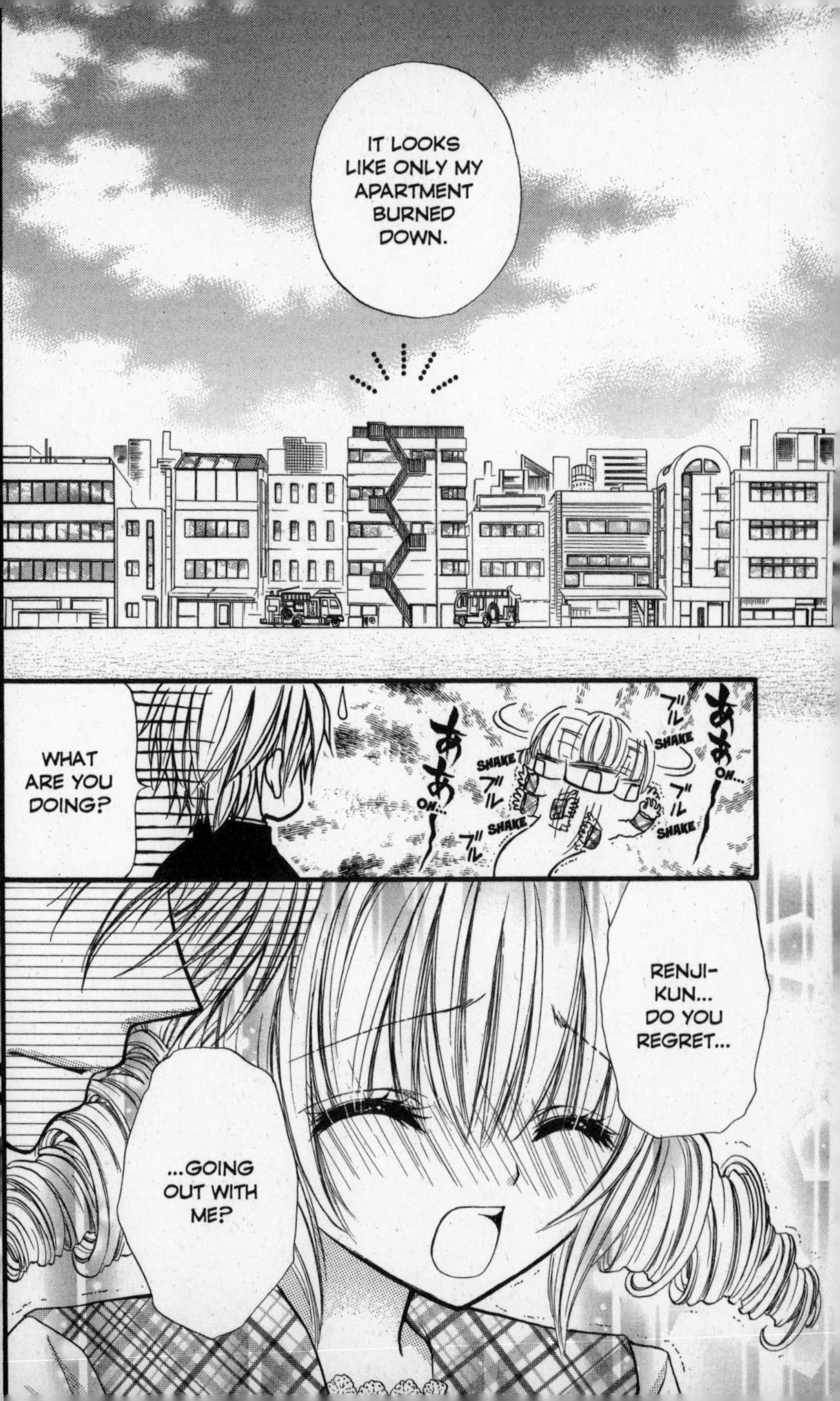
IT LOOKS LIKE ONLY MY APARTMENT BURNED DOWN.
......
ああ～ OH...
ブル SHAKE
ブル SHAKE
ああ～ OH...
ブル SHAKE
ブル SHAKE
WHAT ARE YOU DOING?
RENJI-KUN... DO YOU REGRET...
...GOING OUT WITH ME?

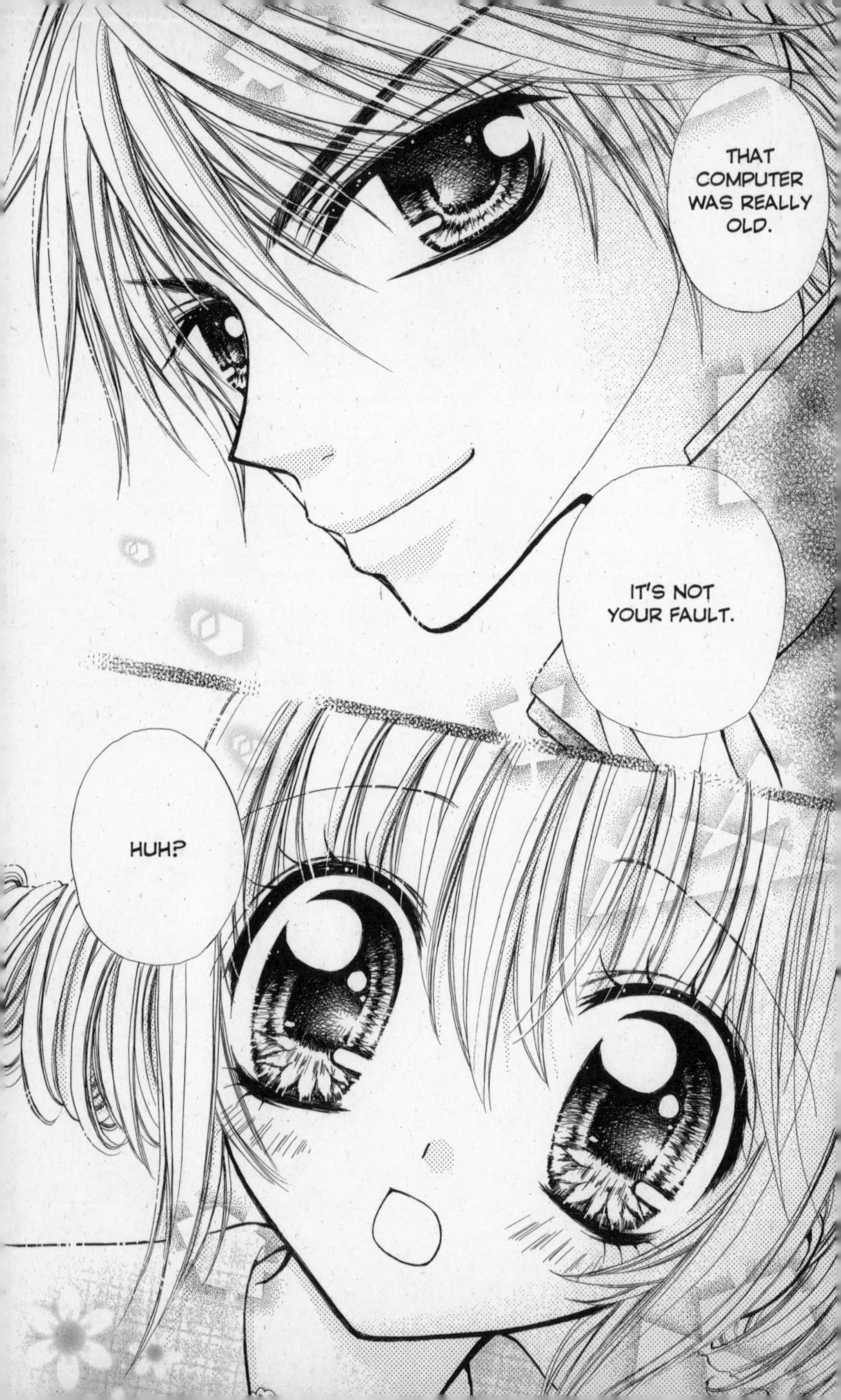
THAT COMPUTER WAS REALLY OLD.
IT'S NOT YOUR FAULT.
HUH?

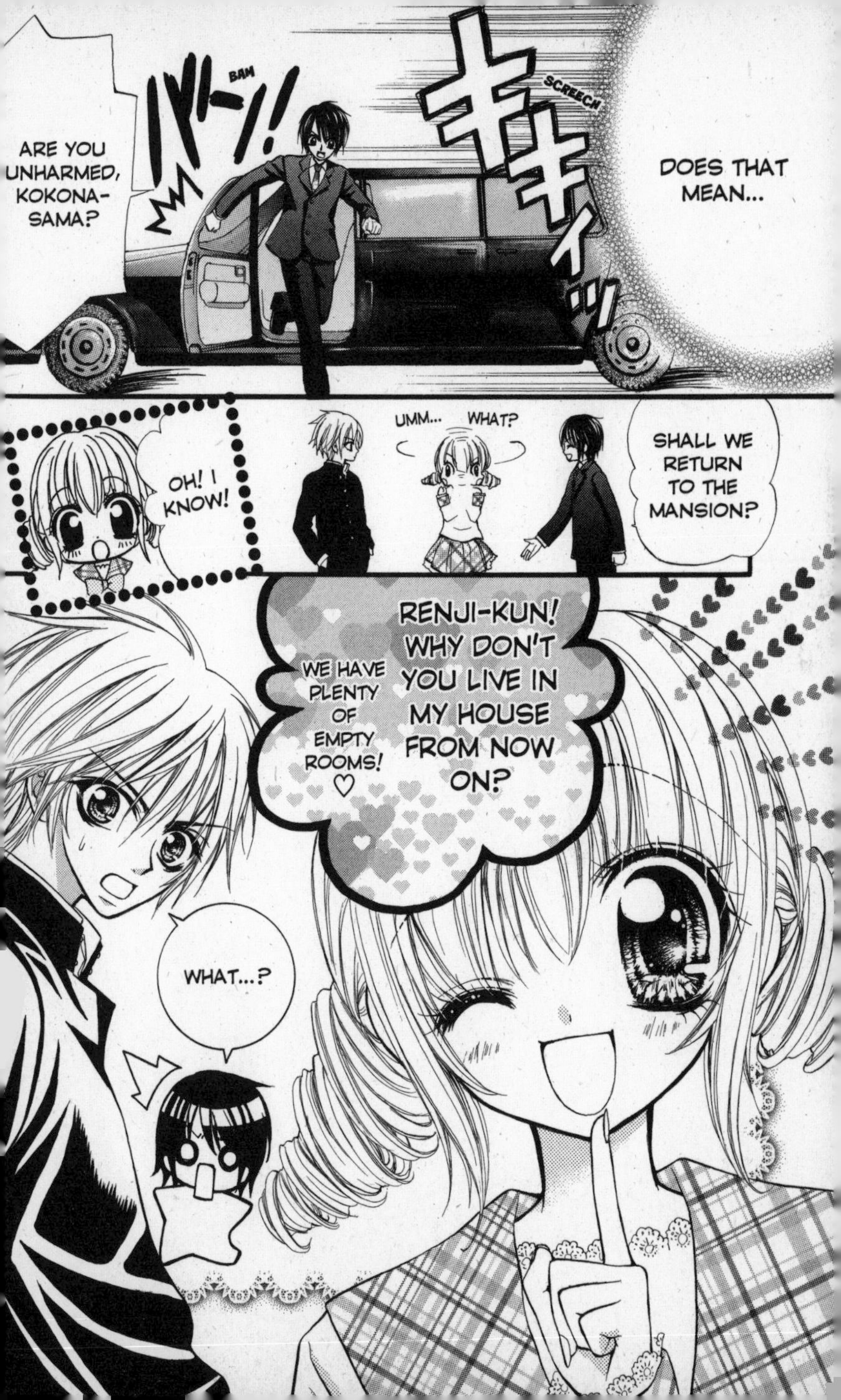
DOES THAT MEAN...
SCREECH
BAM
ARE YOU UNHARMED, KOKONA-SAMA?
SHALL WE RETURN TO THE MANSION?
UMM... WHAT?
OH! I KNOW!
RENJI-KUN! WHY DON'T YOU LIVE IN MY HOUSE FROM NOW ON?
WE HAVE PLENTY OF EMPTY ROOMS! ♡
WHAT...?

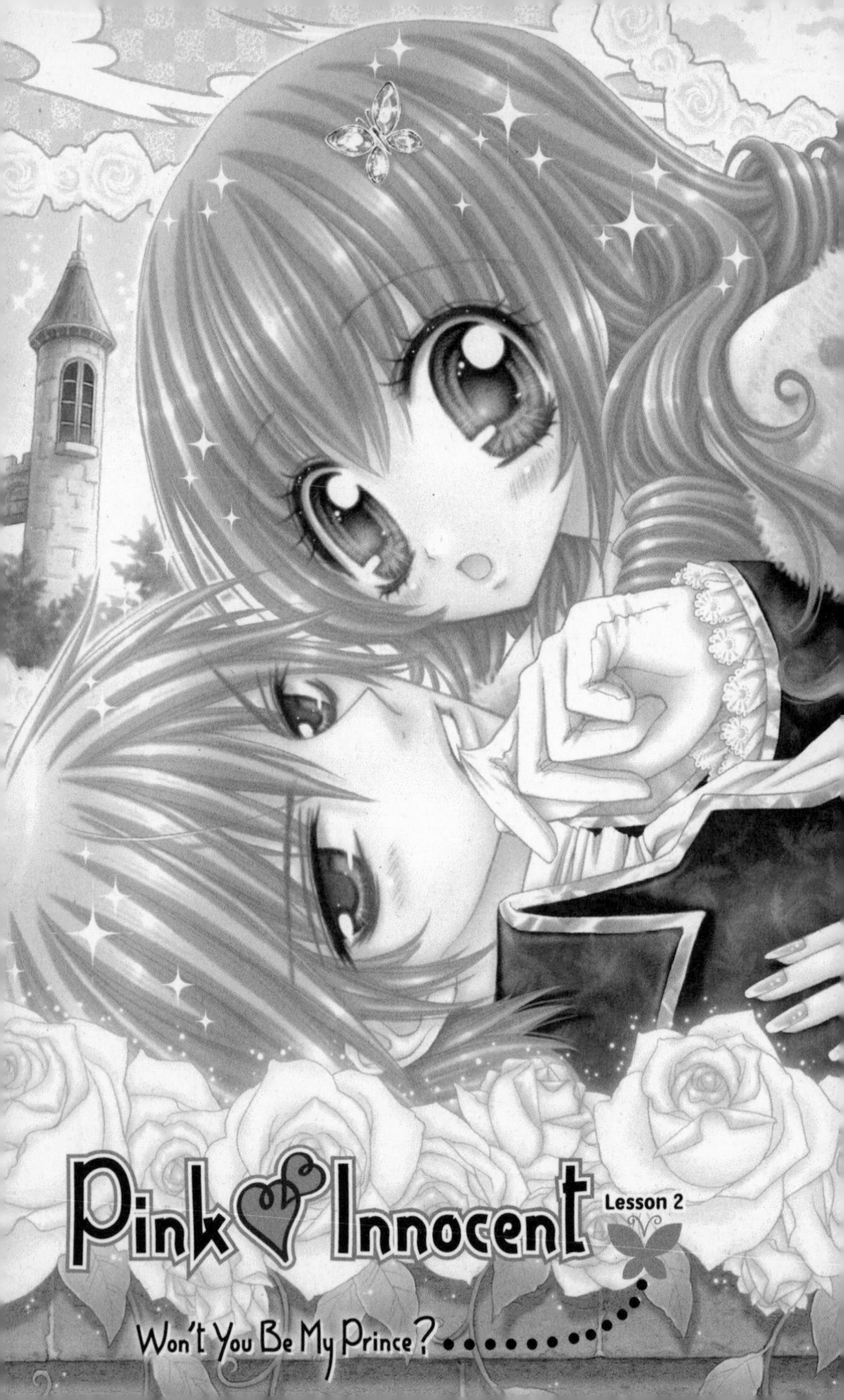
Pink Innocent
Lesson 2
Won't You Be My Prince?

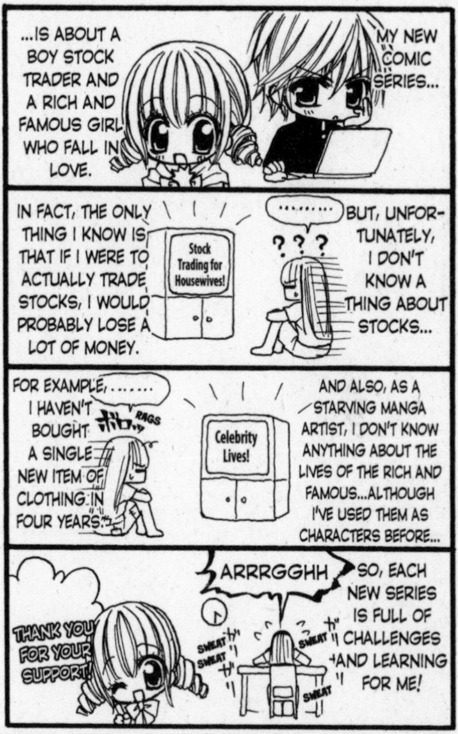
MY NEW COMIC SERIES...
...IS ABOUT A BOY STOCK TRADER AND A RICH AND FAMOUS GIRL WHO FALL IN LOVE.
BUT, UNFORTUNATELY, I DON'T KNOW A THING ABOUT STOCKS...
....
? ? ?
Stock Trading for Housewives!
IN FACT, THE ONLY THING I KNOW IS THAT IF I WERE TO ACTUALLY TRADE STOCKS, I WOULD PROBABLY LOSE A LOT OF MONEY.
AND ALSO, AS A STARVING MANGA ARTIST, I DON'T KNOW ANYTHING ABOUT THE LIVES OF THE RICH AND FAMOUS...ALTHOUGH I'VE USED THEM AS CHARACTERS BEFORE...
Celebrity Lives!
RAGS
FOR EXAMPLE, ...
I HAVEN'T BOUGHT A SINGLE NEW ITEM OF CLOTHING IN FOUR YEARS.
SO, EACH NEW SERIES IS FULL OF CHALLENGES AND LEARNING FOR ME!
ARRRGGHH
SWEAT
SWEAT
SWEAT
SWEAT
THANK YOU FOR YOUR SUPPORT!

This mini four-panel comic printed as a preview in the volume before *Pink* began serialization. Soon I will have gone five years without buying any clothes *sob*....

I cut back on things even more in 2006 than in 2005. I thought that no matter what I would never quit piano, but poverty finally forced me to stop taking classes....But I'm glad that I got my teaching certificate before I quit....Something to make me feel like I accomplished something.... Now that I think about it, I guess I should have lied and said that I quit because I was too busy working on this series....(!!!)

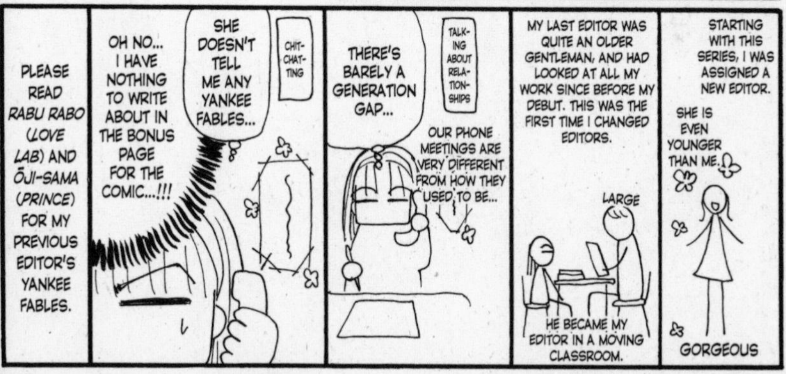
STARTING WITH THIS SERIES, I WAS ASSIGNED A NEW EDITOR.
SHE IS EVEN YOUNGER THAN ME.
GORGEOUS
MY LAST EDITOR WAS QUITE AN OLDER GENTLEMAN, AND HAD LOOKED AT ALL MY WORK SINCE BEFORE MY DEBUT. THIS WAS THE FIRST TIME I CHANGED EDITORS.
LARGE
HE BECAME MY EDITOR IN A MOVING CLASSROOM.
TALKING ABOUT RELATIONSHIPS
THERE'S BARELY A GENERATION GAP...
OUR PHONE MEETINGS ARE VERY DIFFERENT FROM HOW THEY USED TO BE...
CHIT-CHATTING
SHE DOESN'T TELL ME ANY YANKEE FABLES...
OH NO... I HAVE NOTHING TO WRITE ABOUT IN THE BONUS PAGE FOR THE COMIC...!!!
PLEASE READ RABU RABO (LOVE LAB) AND ŌJI-SAMA (PRINCE) FOR MY PREVIOUS EDITOR'S YANKEE FABLES.

Changing editors was really difficult for me at first....If I had come out of my shell a little more it might not have been such a big deal....But the change made me realize my own ability to adapt, which then frightened me....

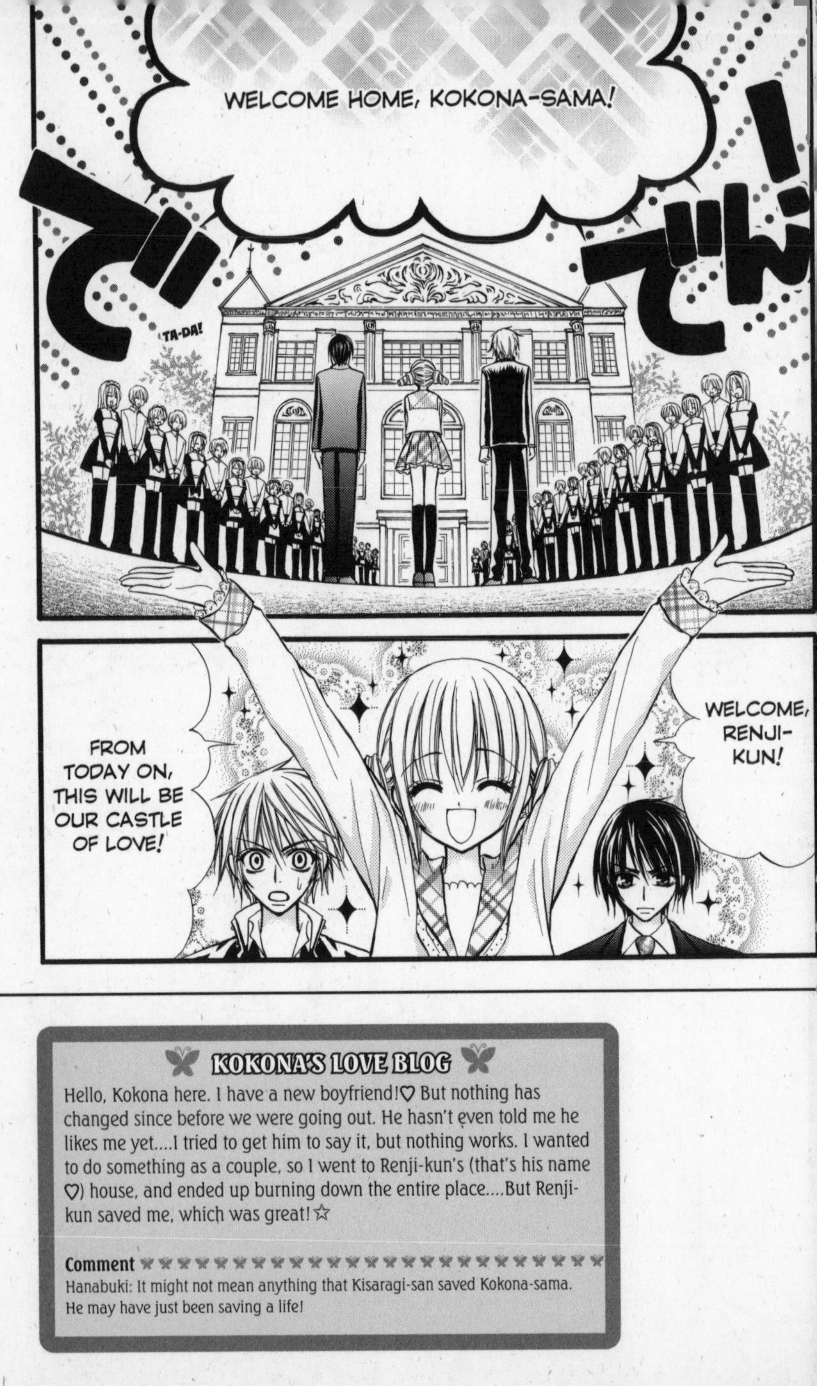
WELCOME HOME, KOKONA-SAMA!
でん!
で
TA-DA!
WELCOME, RENJI-KUN!
FROM TODAY ON, THIS WILL BE OUR CASTLE OF LOVE!

KOKONA'S LOVE BLOG

Hello, Kokona here. I have a new boyfriend!♡ But nothing has changed since before we were going out. He hasn't even told me he likes me yet....I tried to get him to say it, but nothing works. I wanted to do something as a couple, so I went to Renji-kun's (that's his name ♡) house, and ended up burning down the entire place....But Renji-kun saved me, which was great! ☆

Comment

Hanabuki: It might not mean anything that Kisaragi-san saved Kokona-sama. He may have just been saving a life!

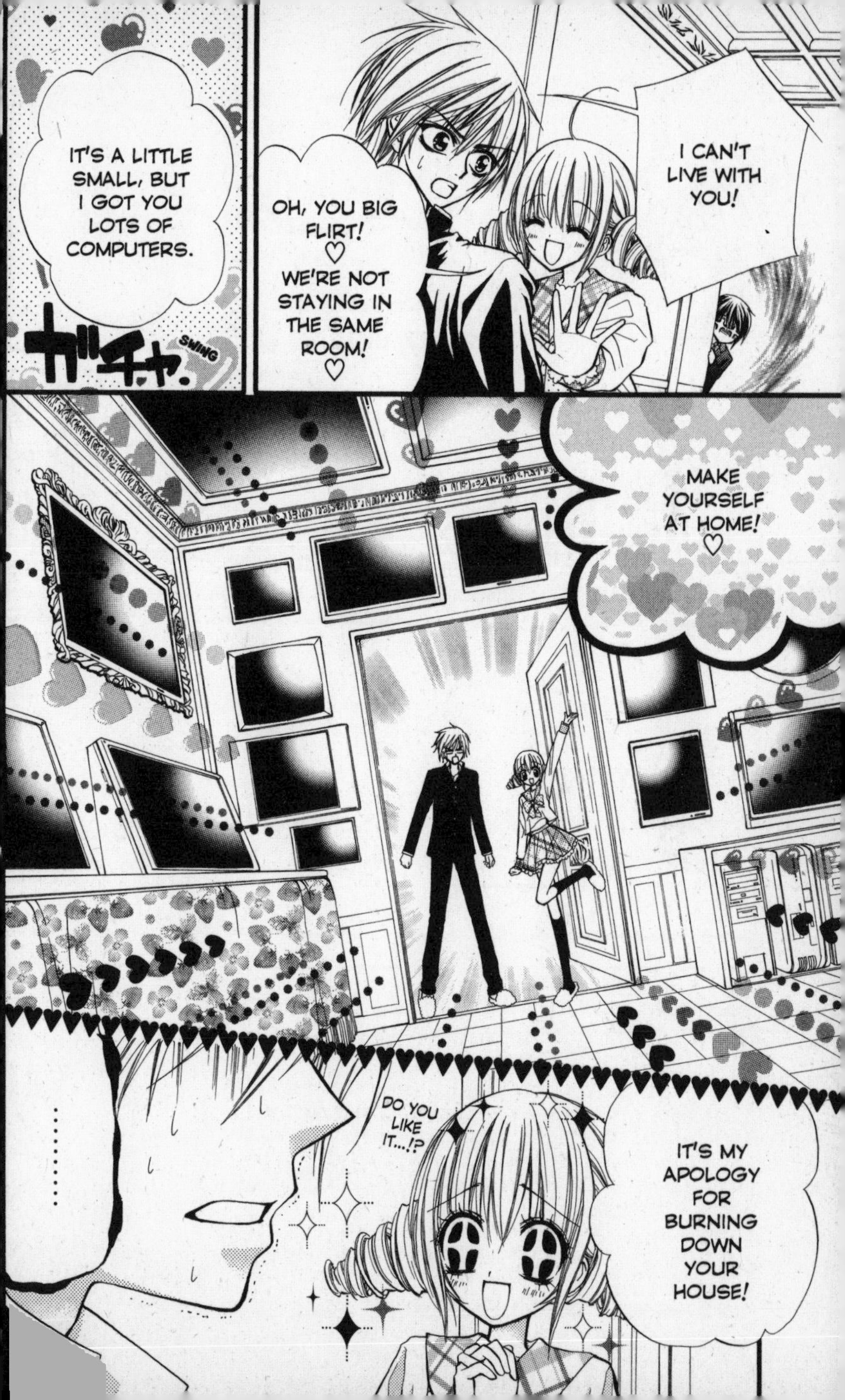
I CAN'T LIVE WITH YOU!
OH, YOU BIG FLIRT! ♡ WE'RE NOT STAYING IN THE SAME ROOM! ♡
IT'S A LITTLE SMALL, BUT I GOT YOU LOTS OF COMPUTERS.
ガチャ
SWING
MAKE YOURSELF AT HOME! ♡
IT'S MY APOLOGY FOR BURNING DOWN YOUR HOUSE!
DO YOU LIKE IT...!?
......

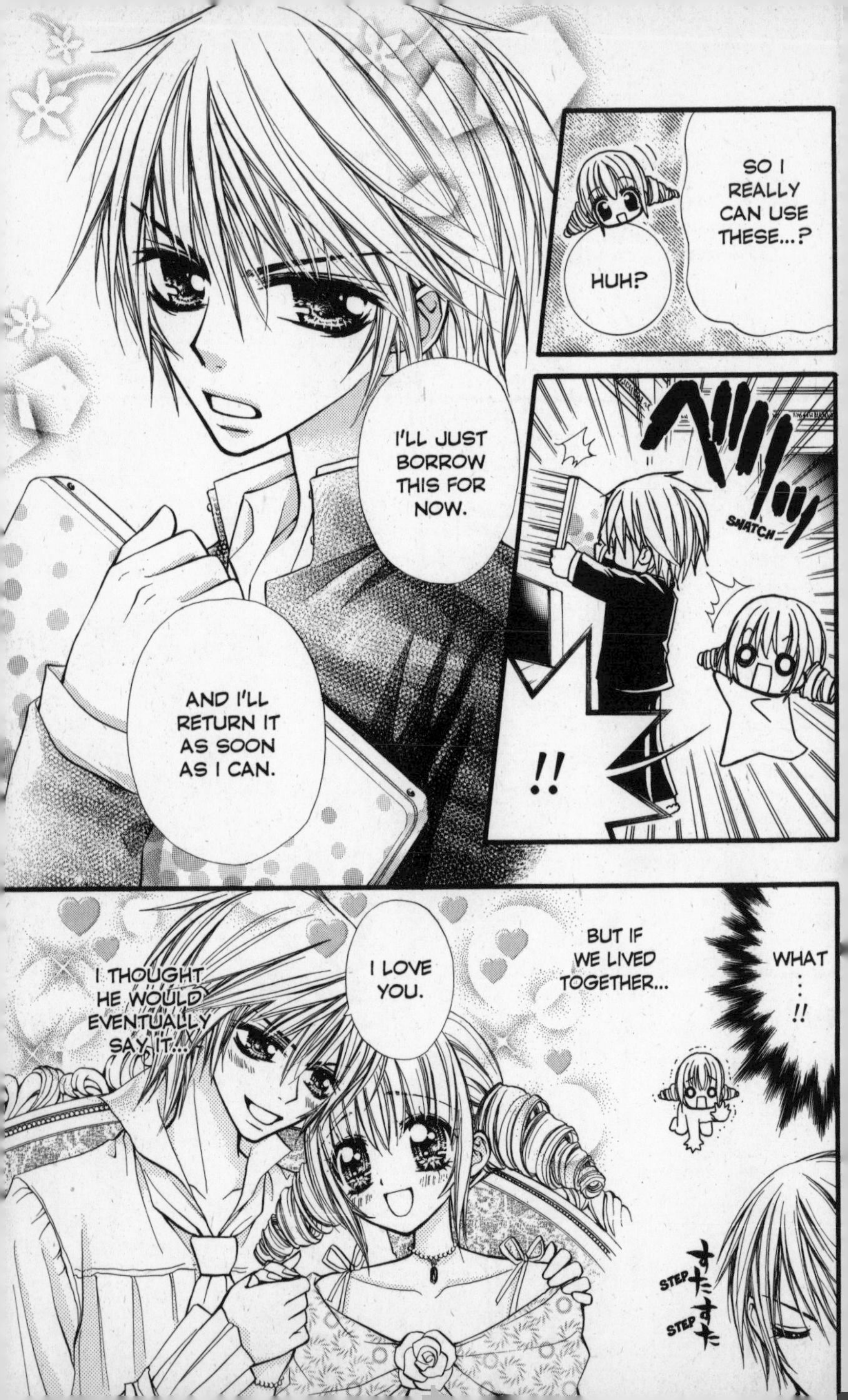
SO I REALLY CAN USE THESE...?
HUH?
SNATCH
!!
I'LL JUST BORROW THIS FOR NOW.
AND I'LL RETURN IT AS SOON AS I CAN.
WHAT...!!
BUT IF WE LIVED TOGETHER...
I LOVE YOU.
I THOUGHT HE WOULD EVENTUALLY SAY IT...
STEP
STEP

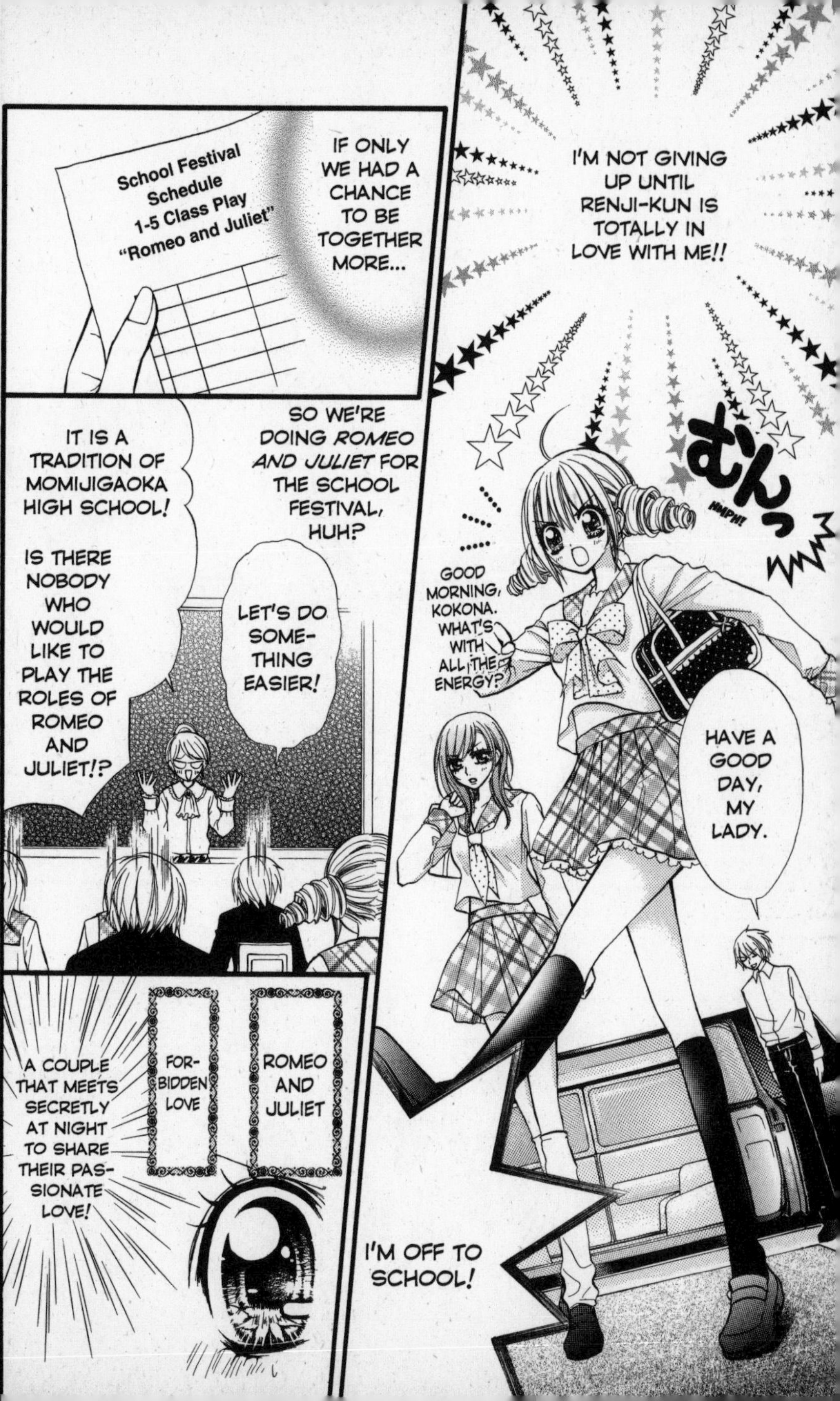
I'M NOT GIVING UP UNTIL RENJI-KUN IS TOTALLY IN LOVE WITH ME!!
むんっ
HMPH!
HAVE A GOOD DAY, MY LADY.
GOOD MORNING, KOKONA. WHAT'S WITH ALL THE ENERGY?
I'M OFF TO SCHOOL!
IF ONLY WE HAD A CHANCE TO BE TOGETHER MORE...
School Festival Schedule 1-5 Class Play "Romeo and Juliet"
SO WE'RE DOING *ROMEO AND JULIET* FOR THE SCHOOL FESTIVAL, HUH?
IT IS A TRADITION OF MOMIJIGAOKA HIGH SCHOOL!
IS THERE NOBODY WHO WOULD LIKE TO PLAY THE ROLES OF ROMEO AND JULIET!?
LET'S DO SOME-THING EASIER!
ROMEO AND JULIET
FOR-BIDDEN LOVE
A COUPLE THAT MEETS SECRETLY AT NIGHT TO SHARE THEIR PAS-SIONATE LOVE!

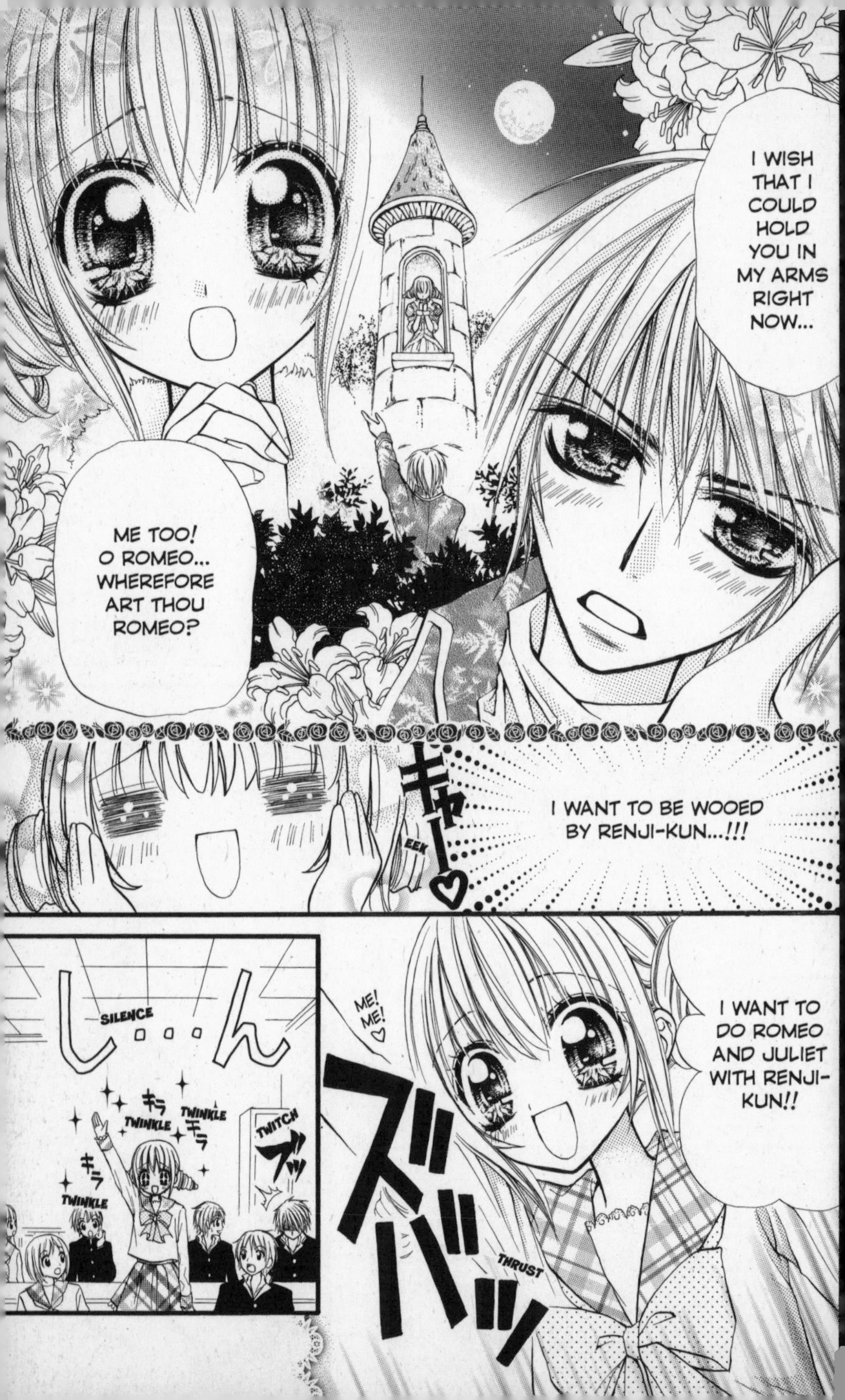
I WISH THAT I COULD HOLD YOU IN MY ARMS RIGHT NOW...
ME TOO! O ROMEO... WHEREFORE ART THOU ROMEO?
I WANT TO BE WOOED BY RENJI-KUN...!!!
キャー
EEK
I WANT TO DO ROMEO AND JULIET WITH RENJI-KUN!!
ME! ME! ♡
ズバッ
THRUST
し...ん
SILENCE
キラ
TWINKLE
キラ
TWINKLE
キラ
TWINKLE
ブッ
TWITCH

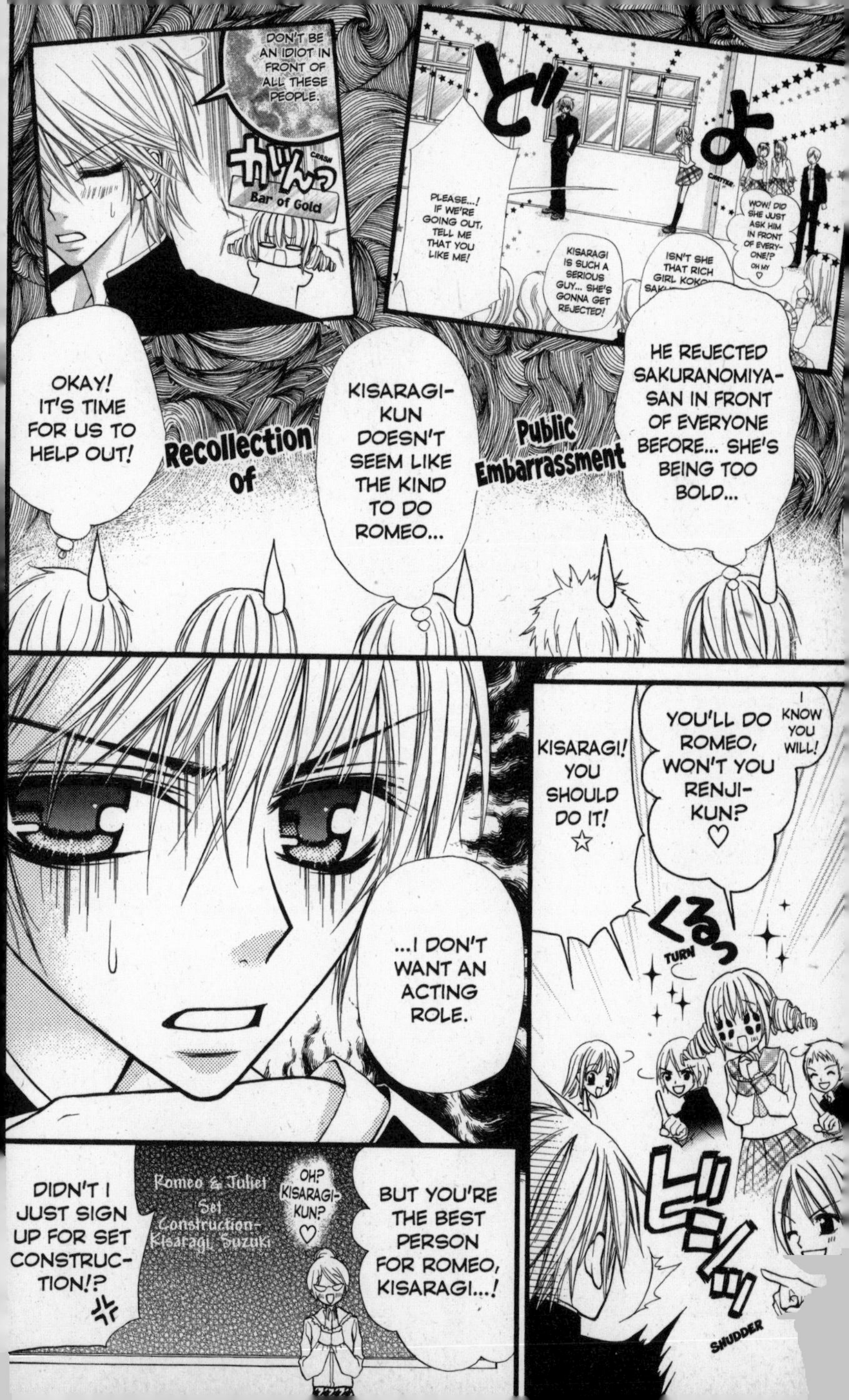

どよ
CHATTER
WOW! DID SHE JUST ASK HIM IN FRONT OF EVERY-ONE!? OH MY ♡
PLEASE...! IF WE'RE GOING OUT, TELL ME THAT YOU LIKE ME!
ISN'T SHE THAT RICH GIRL
KISARAGI IS SUCH A SERIOUS GUY... SHE'S GONNA GET REJECTED!
DON'T BE AN IDIOT IN FRONT OF ALL THESE PEOPLE.
がんっ
CRASH
Bar of Gold
HE REJECTED SAKURANOMIYA-SAN IN FRONT OF EVERYONE BEFORE... SHE'S BEING TOO BOLD...
KISARAGI-KUN DOESN'T SEEM LIKE THE KIND TO DO ROMEO...
Recollection of Public Embarrassment
OKAY! IT'S TIME FOR US TO HELP OUT!
I KNOW YOU WILL!
YOU'LL DO ROMEO, WON'T YOU RENJI-KUN? ♡
KISARAGI! YOU SHOULD DO IT! ☆
くるっ
TURN
SHUDDER
...I DON'T WANT AN ACTING ROLE.
BUT YOU'RE THE BEST PERSON FOR ROMEO, KISARAGI...!
OH? KISARAGI-KUN? ♡
Romeo & Juliet Set Construction- Kisaragi, Suzuki
DIDN'T I JUST SIGN UP FOR SET CONSTRUCTION!?

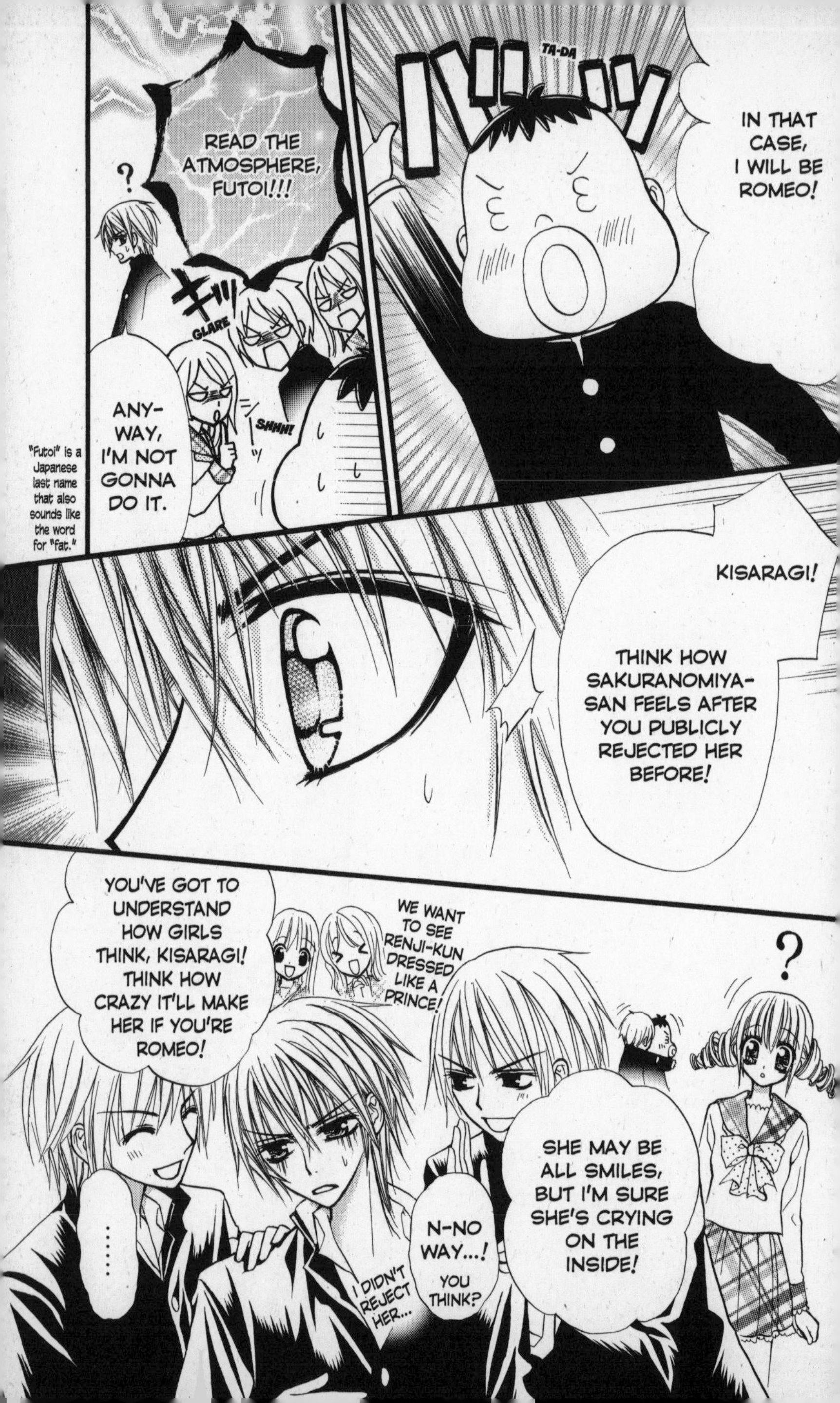
TA-DA
IN THAT CASE, I WILL BE ROMEO!
READ THE ATMOSPHERE, FUTOI!!!
?
GLARE
SHHH!
ANY-WAY, I'M NOT GONNA DO IT.
KISARAGI!
THINK HOW SAKURANOMIYA-SAN FEELS AFTER YOU PUBLICLY REJECTED HER BEFORE!
?
SHE MAY BE ALL SMILES, BUT I'M SURE SHE'S CRYING ON THE INSIDE!
WE WANT TO SEE RENJI-KUN DRESSED LIKE A PRINCE!
N-NO WAY...!
YOU THINK?
I DIDN'T REJECT HER...
YOU'VE GOT TO UNDERSTAND HOW GIRLS THINK, KISARAGI! THINK HOW CRAZY IT'LL MAKE HER IF YOU'RE ROMEO!
......

"Futoi" is a Japanese last name that also sounds like the word for "fat."

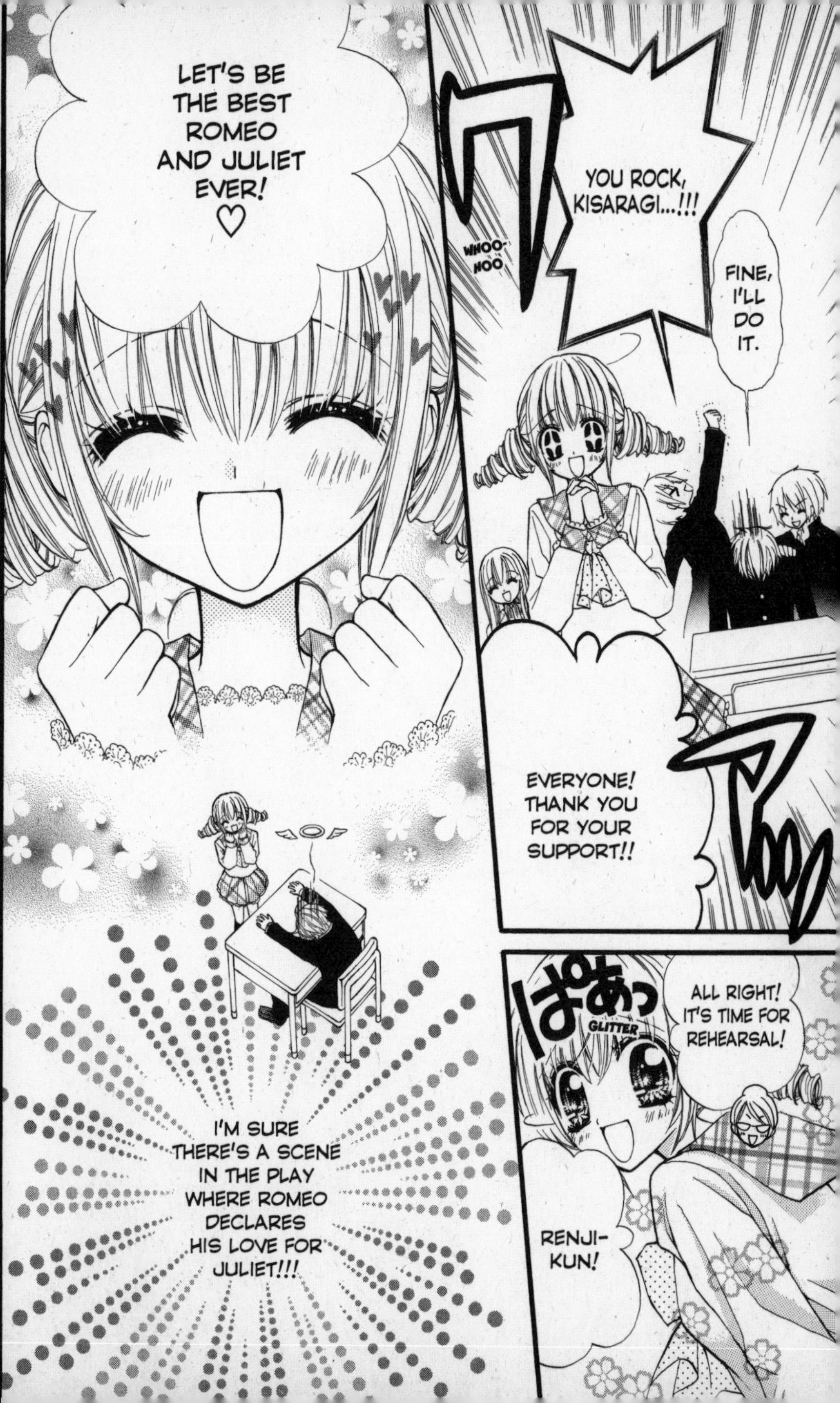
YOU ROCK, KISARAGI...!!!
WHOO-HOO
FINE, I'LL DO IT.
EVERYONE! THANK YOU FOR YOUR SUPPORT!!
ぱあっ
GLITTER
ALL RIGHT! IT'S TIME FOR REHEARSAL!
RENJI-KUN!
LET'S BE THE BEST ROMEO AND JULIET EVER! ♡
I'M SURE THERE'S A SCENE IN THE PLAY WHERE ROMEO DECLARES HIS LOVE FOR JULIET!!!

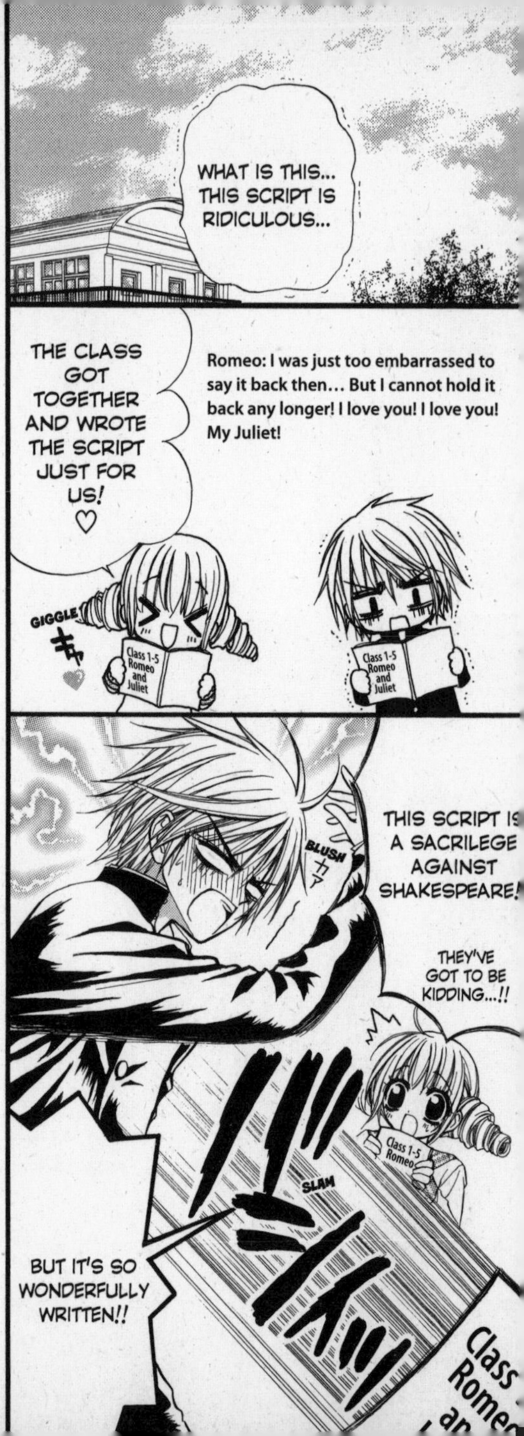
WHAT IS THIS... THIS SCRIPT IS RIDICULOUS...
Romeo: I was just too embarrassed to say it back then... But I cannot hold it back any longer! I love you! I love you! My Juliet!
THE CLASS GOT TOGETHER AND WROTE THE SCRIPT JUST FOR US! ♡
Class 1-5 Romeo and Juliet
GIGGLE
Class 1-5 Romeo and Juliet
THIS SCRIPT IS A SACRILEGE AGAINST SHAKESPEARE!
BLUSH
THEY'VE GOT TO BE KIDDING...!!
Class 1-5 Romeo
SLAM
BUT IT'S SO WONDERFULLY WRITTEN!!

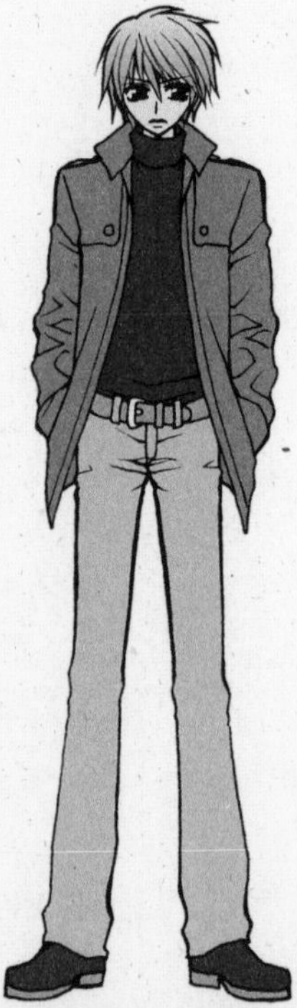

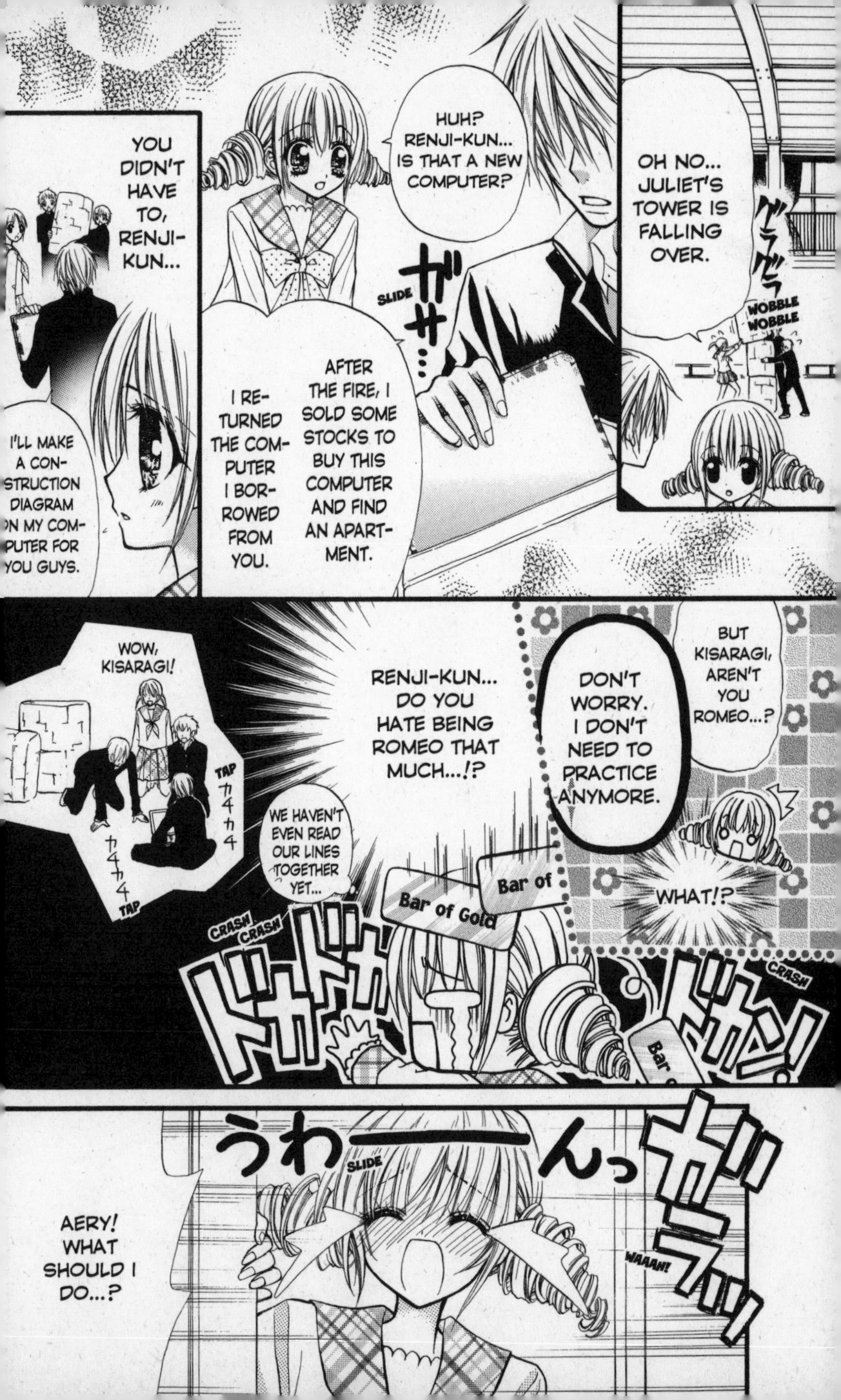

OH NO... JULIET'S TOWER IS FALLING OVER.
グラグラ
WOBBLE WOBBLE
HUH? RENJI-KUN... IS THAT A NEW COMPUTER?
ザザ…
SLIDE
AFTER THE FIRE, I SOLD SOME STOCKS TO BUY THIS COMPUTER AND FIND AN APARTMENT.
I RETURNED THE COMPUTER I BORROWED FROM YOU.
YOU DIDN'T HAVE TO, RENJI-KUN...
I'LL MAKE A CONSTRUCTION DIAGRAM ON MY COMPUTER FOR YOU GUYS.
BUT KISARAGI, AREN'T YOU ROMEO...?
DON'T WORRY. I DON'T NEED TO PRACTICE ANYMORE.
WHAT!?
RENJI-KUN... DO YOU HATE BEING ROMEO THAT MUCH...!?
WE HAVEN'T EVEN READ OUR LINES TOGETHER YET...
Bar of
Bar of Gold
Bar
ドカッ
CRASH
ドカドカ
CRASH CRASH
WOW, KISARAGI!
カタカタ
TAP
カタカタ
TAP
ガラッ
うわーーーんっ
SLIDE
WAAAH!
AERY! WHAT SHOULD I DO...?

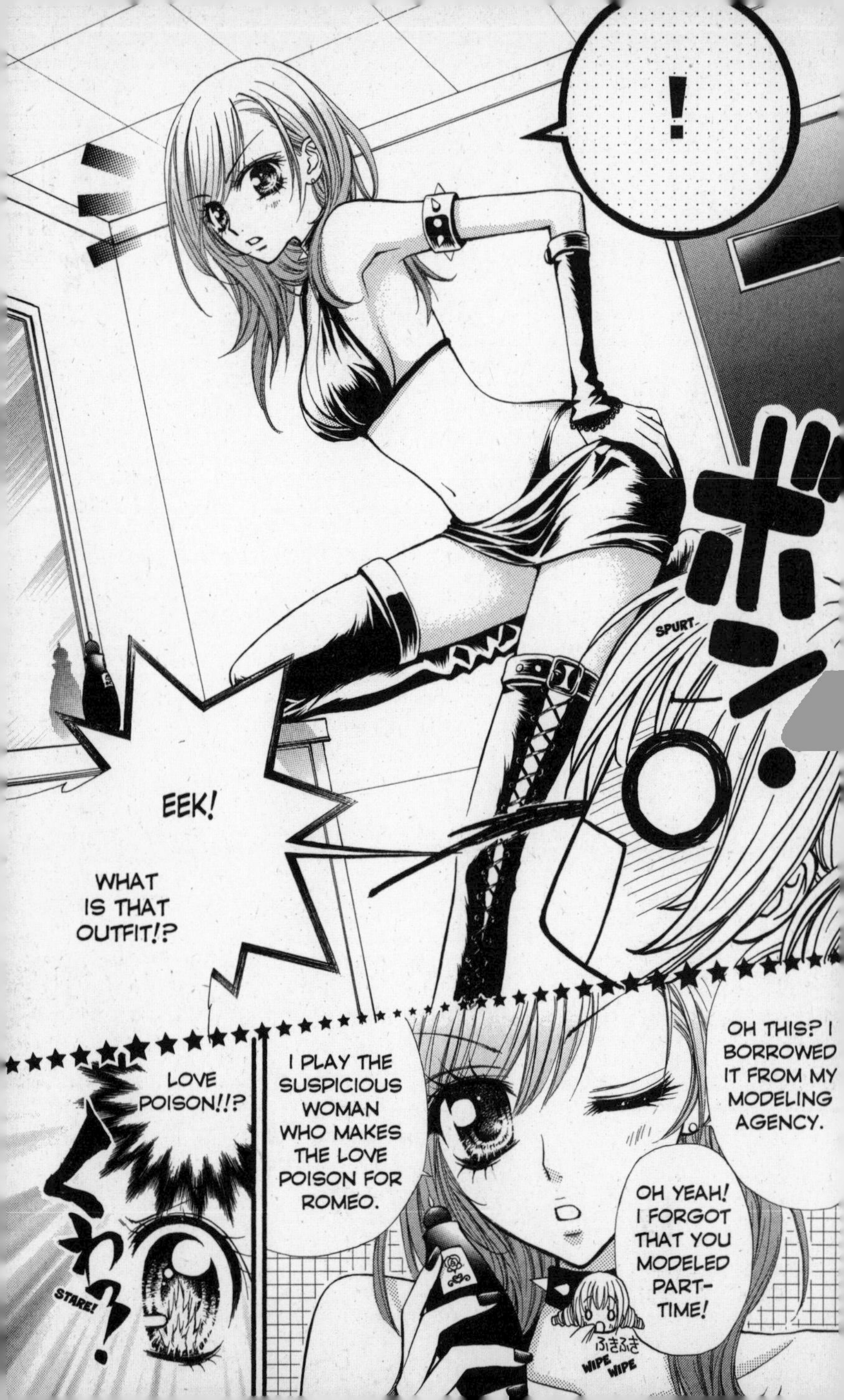
!
ボン!
SPURT
EEK!
WHAT IS THAT OUTFIT!?
OH THIS? I BORROWED IT FROM MY MODELING AGENCY.
OH YEAH! I FORGOT THAT YOU MODELED PART-TIME!
ふきふき
WIPE WIPE
I PLAY THE SUSPICIOUS WOMAN WHO MAKES THE LOVE POISON FOR ROMEO.
LOVE POISON!!?
くわっ!
STARE!

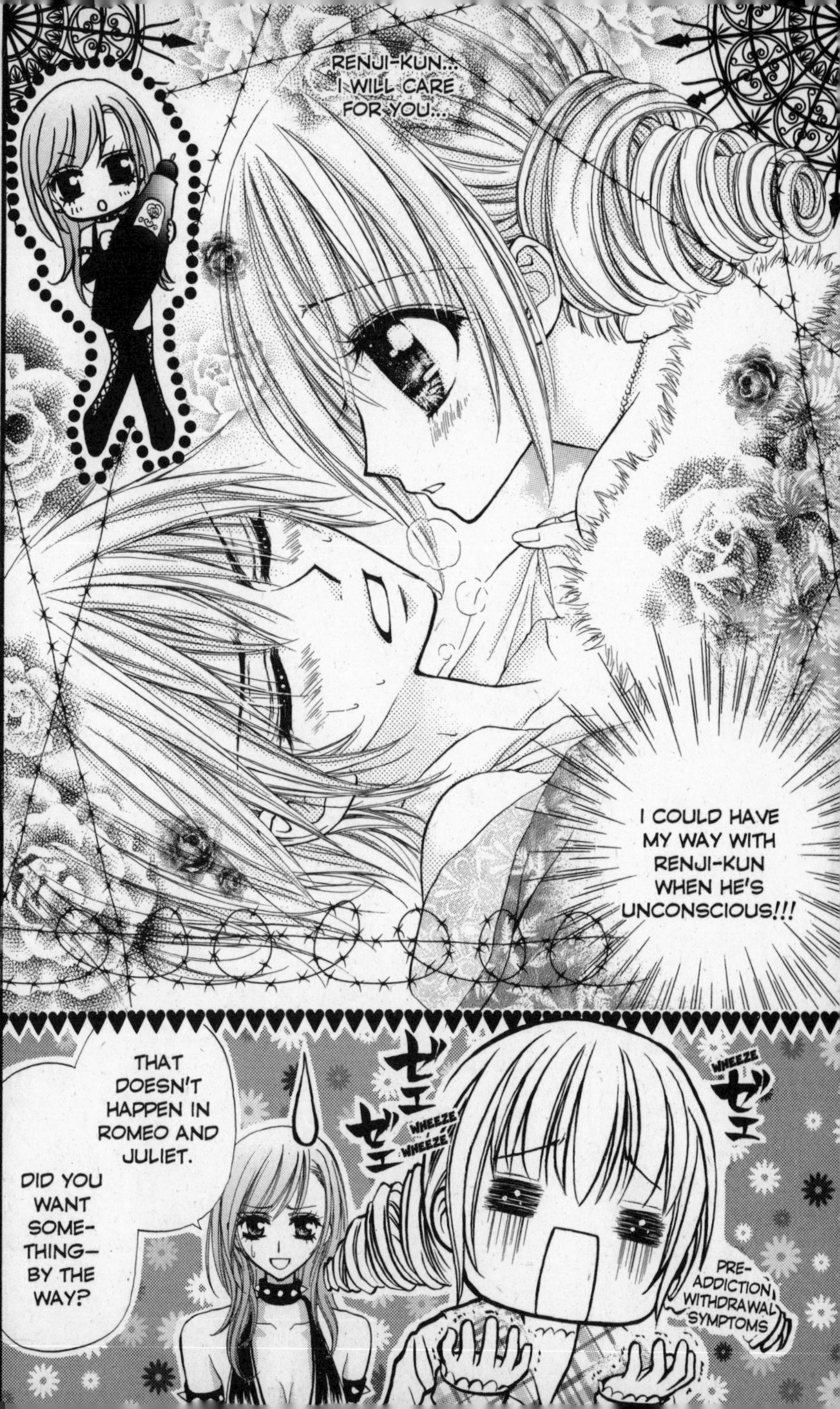
RENJI-KUN... I WILL CARE FOR YOU...
I COULD HAVE MY WAY WITH RENJI-KUN WHEN HE'S UNCONSCIOUS!!!
ゼェ WHEEZE
ゼェ ゼェ WHEEZE WHEEZE
PRE-ADDICTION WITHDRAWAL SYMPTOMS
THAT DOESN'T HAPPEN IN ROMEO AND JULIET.
DID YOU WANT SOME-THING— BY THE WAY?

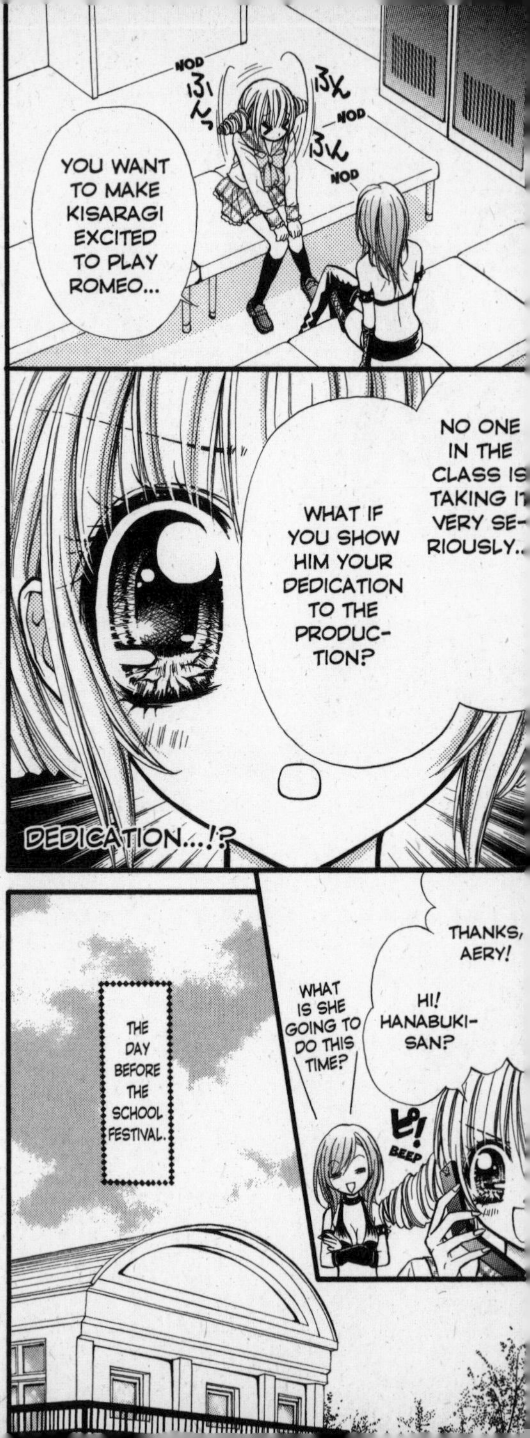
ふん
NOD
ふん
NOD
ふんっ
NOD
YOU WANT TO MAKE KISARAGI EXCITED TO PLAY ROMEO...
NO ONE IN THE CLASS IS TAKING IT VERY SERIOUSLY...
WHAT IF YOU SHOW HIM YOUR DEDICATION TO THE PRODUCTION?
DEDICATION...!?
THANKS, AERY!
HI! HANABUKI-SAN?
WHAT IS SHE GOING TO DO THIS TIME?
ピ!
BEEP
THE DAY BEFORE THE SCHOOL FESTIVAL.

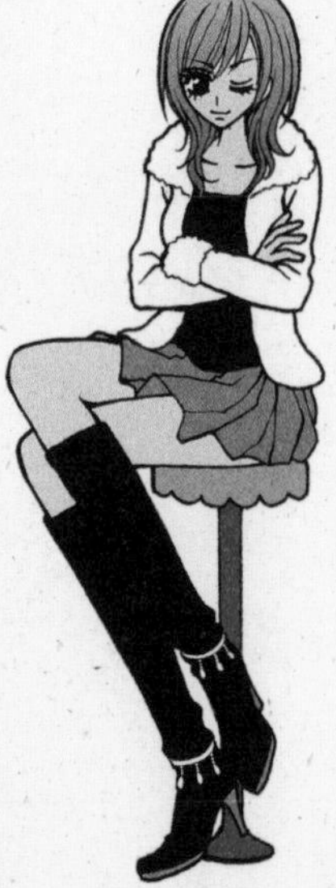

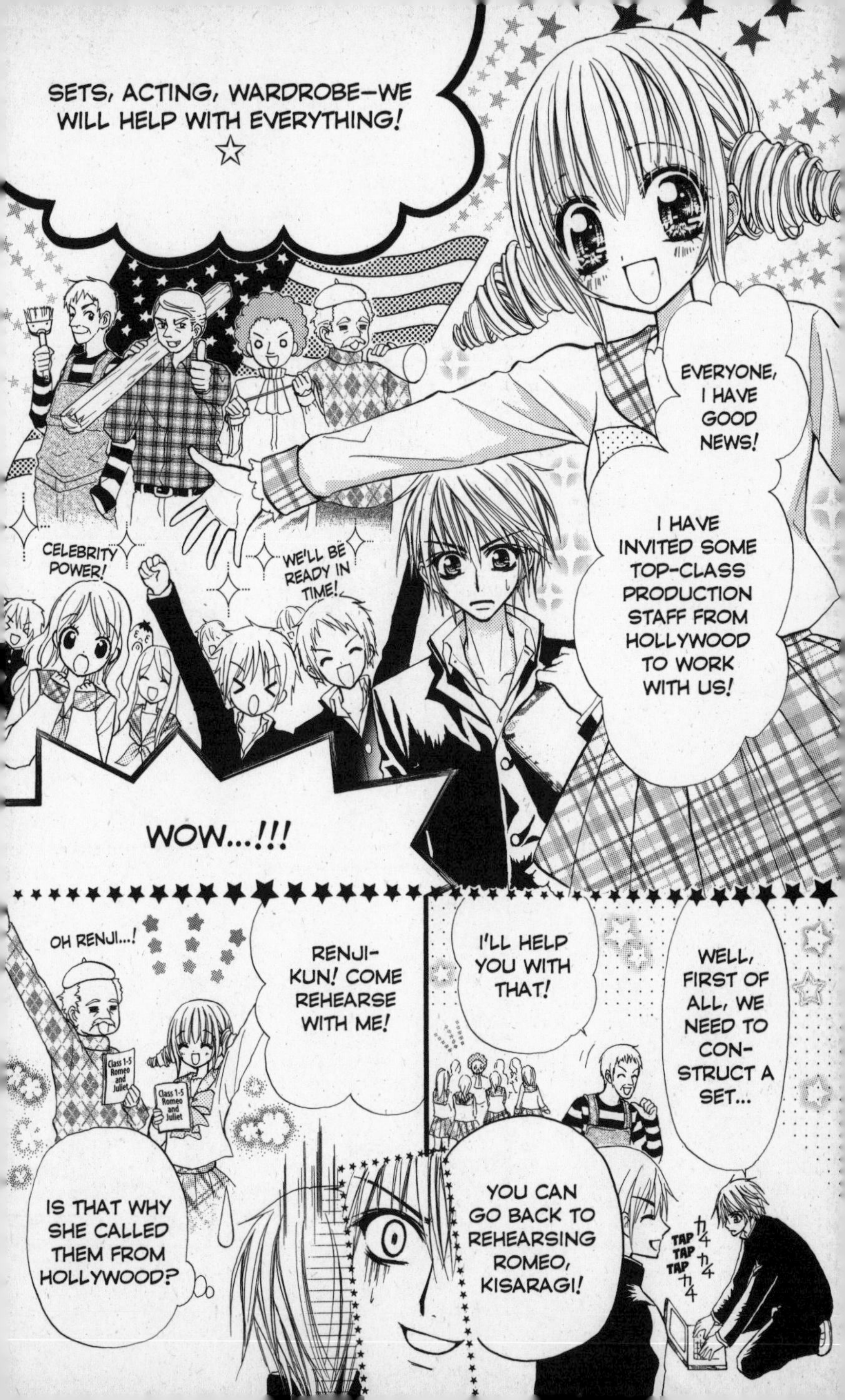
EVERYONE, I HAVE GOOD NEWS!
I HAVE INVITED SOME TOP-CLASS PRODUCTION STAFF FROM HOLLYWOOD TO WORK WITH US!
SETS, ACTING, WARDROBE—WE WILL HELP WITH EVERYTHING! ☆
WE'LL BE READY IN TIME!
CELEBRITY POWER!
WOW...!!!
WELL, FIRST OF ALL, WE NEED TO CON-STRUCT A SET...
I'LL HELP YOU WITH THAT!
YOU CAN GO BACK TO REHEARSING ROMEO, KISARAGI!
TAP TAP TAP
RENJI-KUN! COME REHEARSE WITH ME!
OH RENJI...!
Class 1-5 Romeo and Juliet
Class 1-5 Romeo and Juliet
IS THAT WHY SHE CALLED THEM FROM HOLLYWOOD?

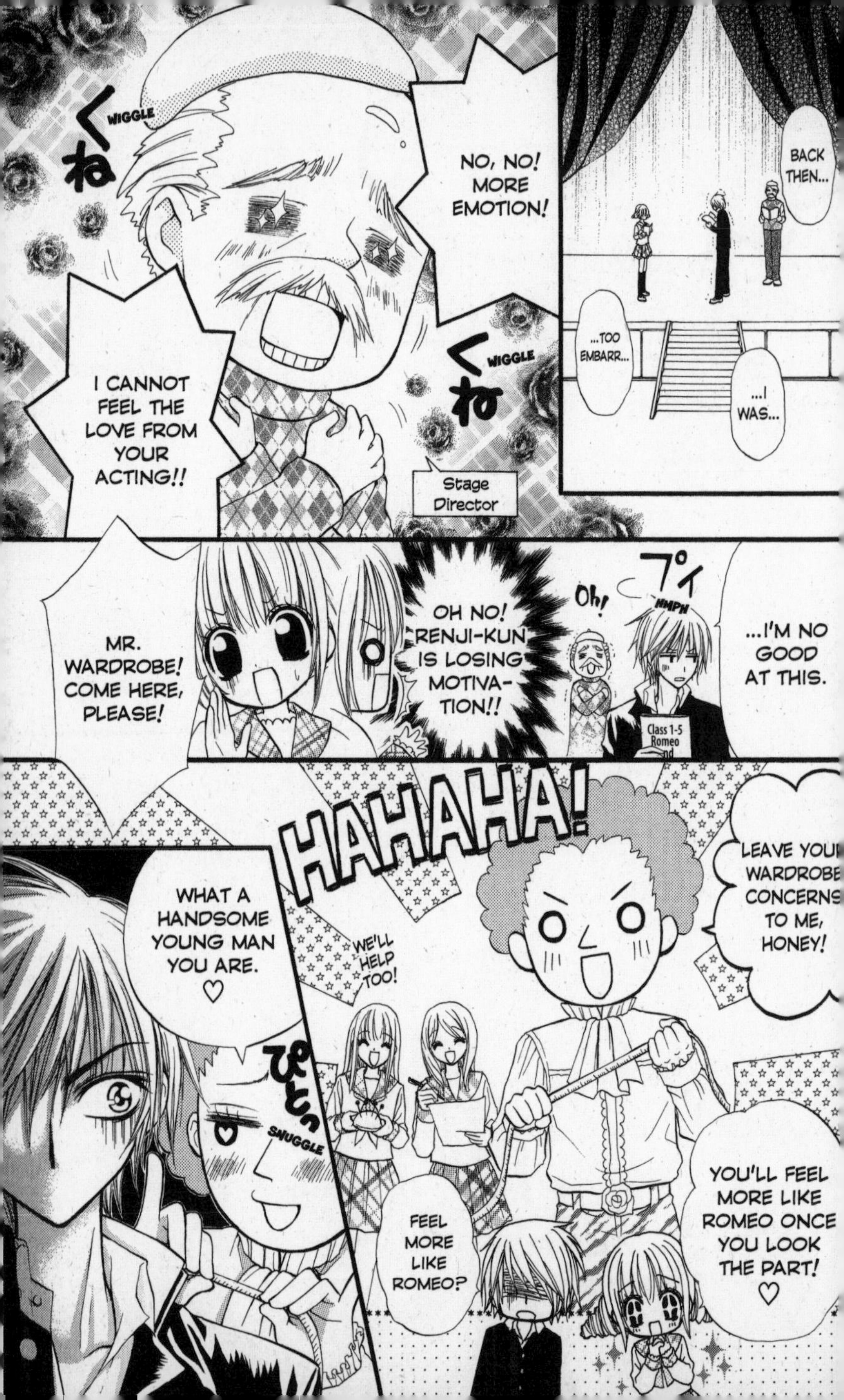
BACK THEN...
...I WAS...
...TOO EMBARR...
NO, NO! MORE EMOTION!
くね WIGGLE
くね WIGGLE
I CANNOT FEEL THE LOVE FROM YOUR ACTING!!
Stage Director
...I'M NO GOOD AT THIS.
プイ HMPH
Oh!
Class 1-5 Romeo
OH NO! RENJI-KUN IS LOSING MOTIVATION!!
MR. WARDROBE! COME HERE, PLEASE!
LEAVE YOU WARDROBE CONCERNS TO ME, HONEY!
HAHAHA!
WHAT A HANDSOME YOUNG MAN YOU ARE. ♡
WE'LL HELP TOO!
ぴとっ SNUGGLE
YOU'LL FEEL MORE LIKE ROMEO ONCE YOU LOOK THE PART! ♡
FEEL MORE LIKE ROMEO?

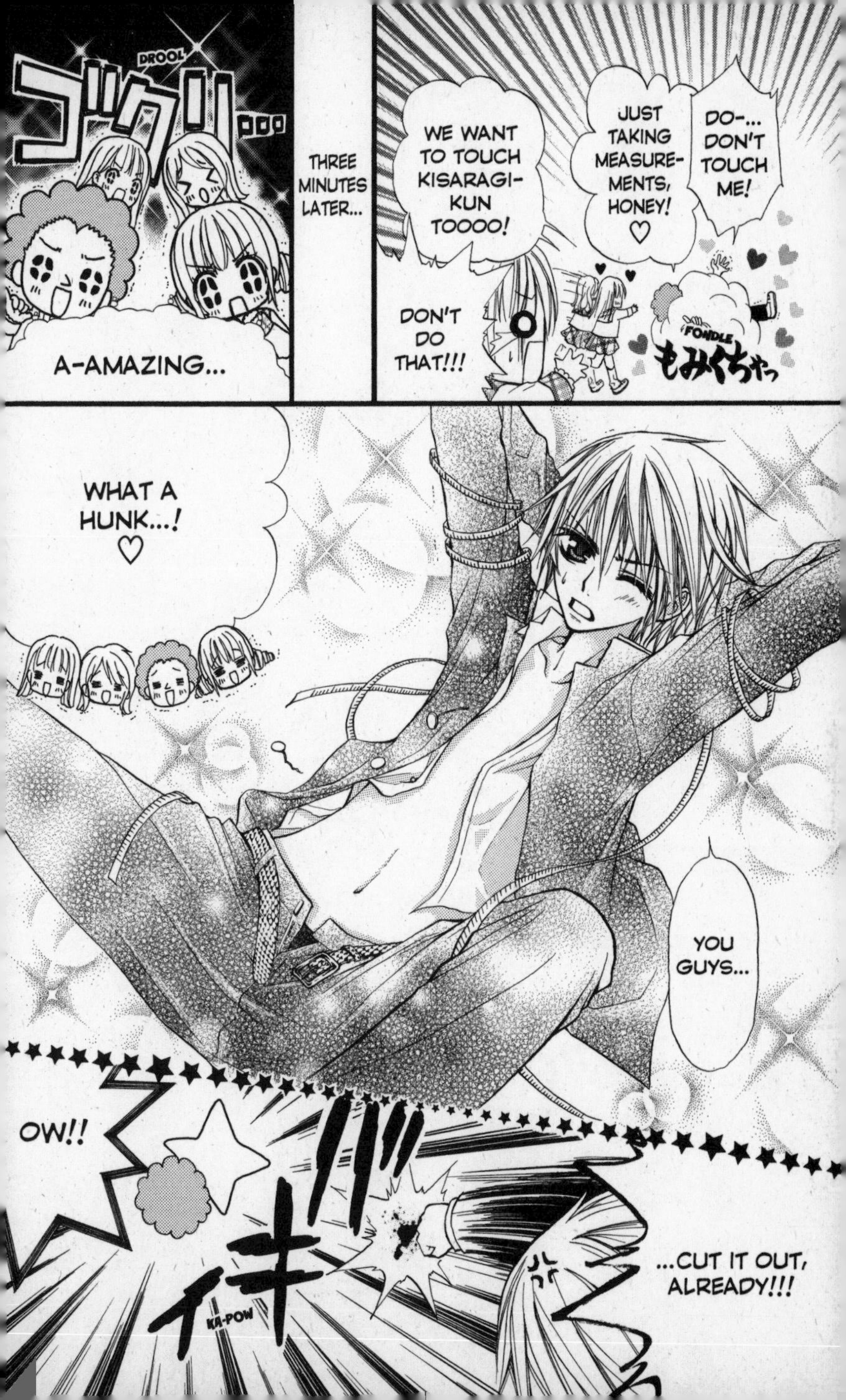
DO-... DON'T TOUCH ME!
JUST TAKING MEASUREMENTS, HONEY! ♡
WE WANT TO TOUCH KISARAGI-KUN TOOOO!
FONDLE
もみくちゃっ
DON'T DO THAT!!!
THREE MINUTES LATER...
DROOL
ゴクリ
A-AMAZING...
YOU GUYS...
WHAT A HUNK...! ♡
...CUT IT OUT, ALREADY!!!
KA-POW
OW!!

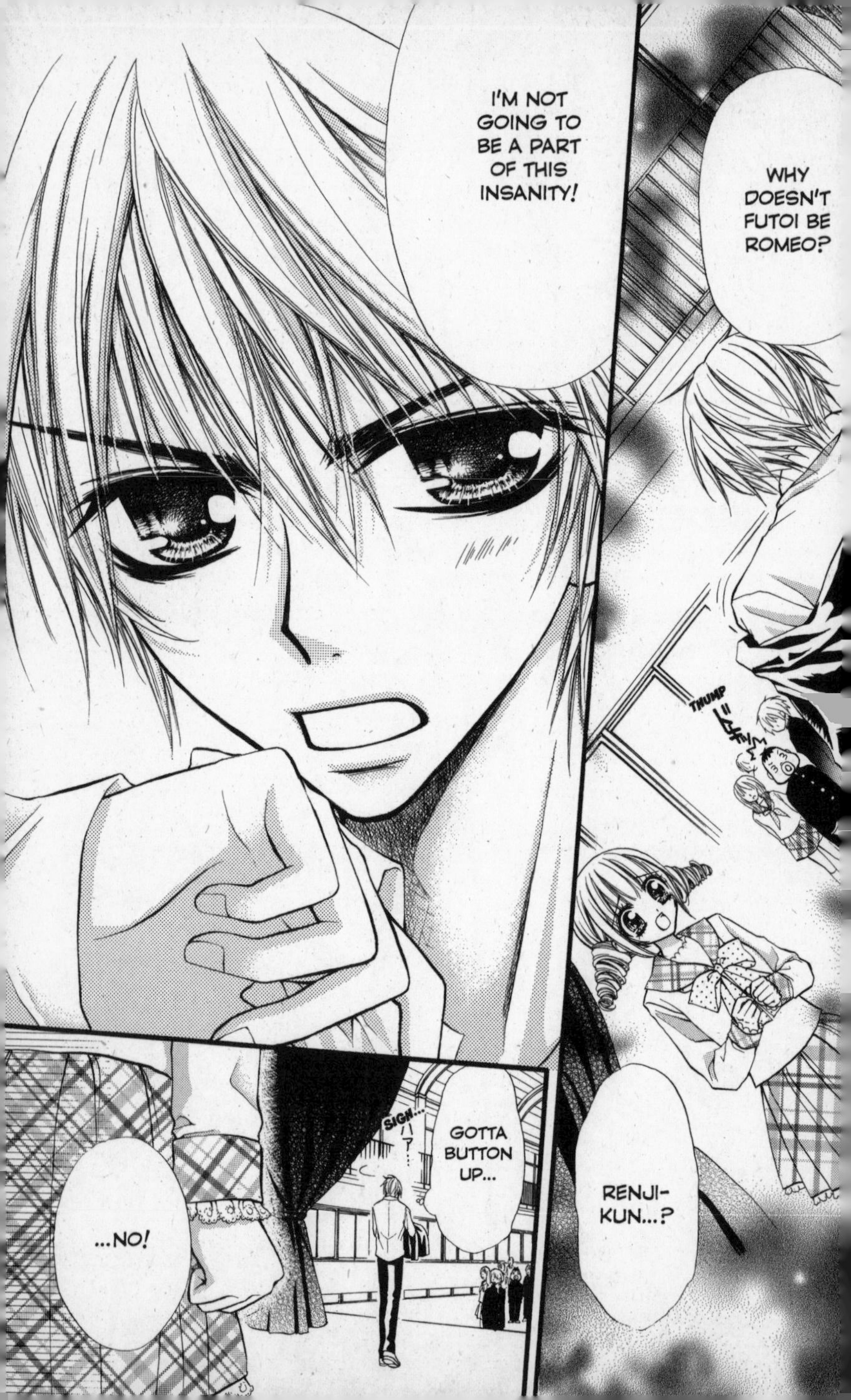
WHY DOESN'T FUTOI BE ROMEO?
THUMP
RENJI-KUN...?
I'M NOT GOING TO BE A PART OF THIS INSANITY!
SIGH...
GOTTA BUTTON UP...
...NO!

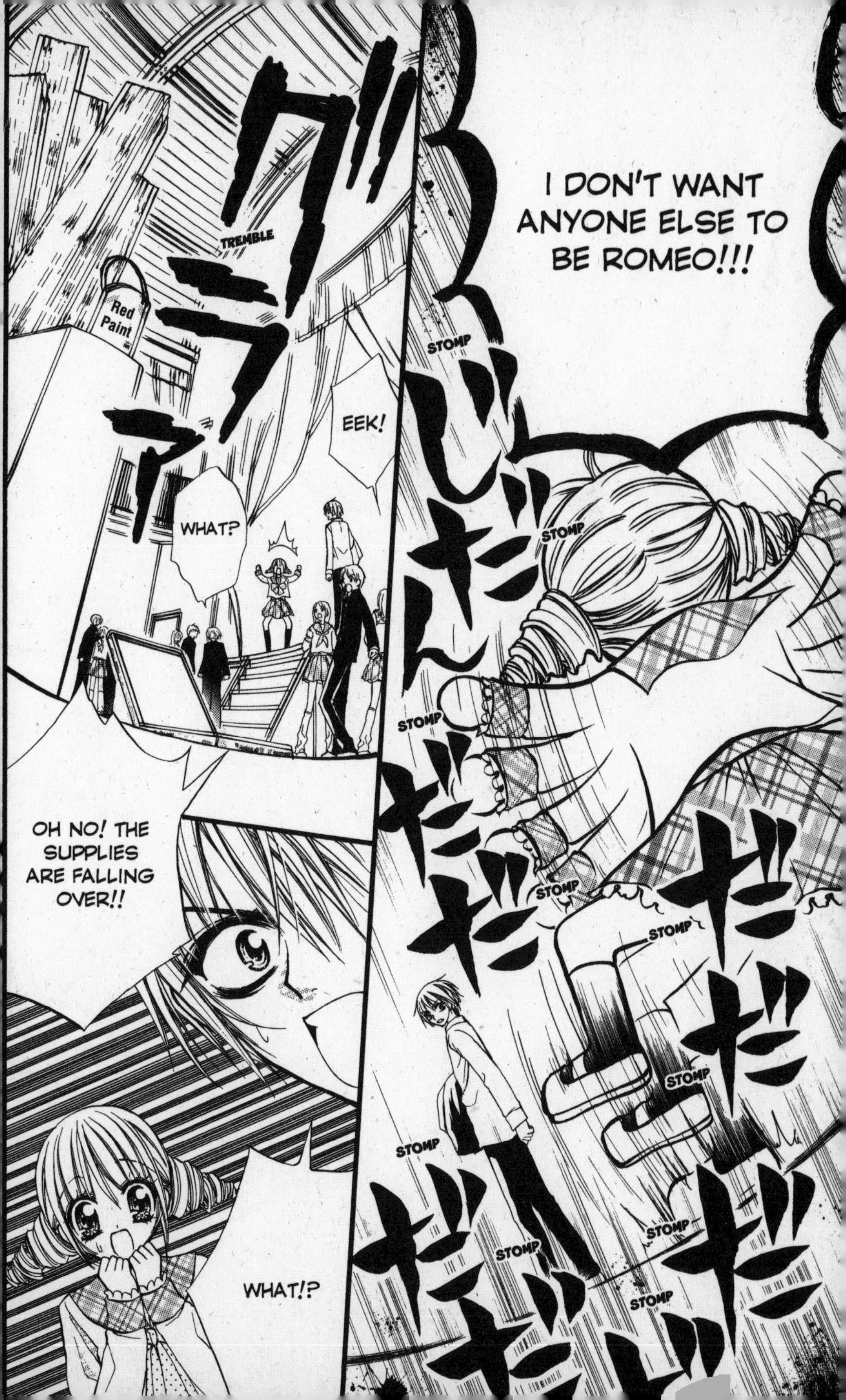
I DON'T WANT ANYONE ELSE TO BE ROMEO!!!
STOMP
STOMP
STOMP
STOMP
STOMP
STOMP
STOMP
STOMP
STOMP
STOMP
TREMBLE
Red Paint
EEK!
WHAT?
OH NO! THE SUPPLIES ARE FALLING OVER!!
WHAT!?

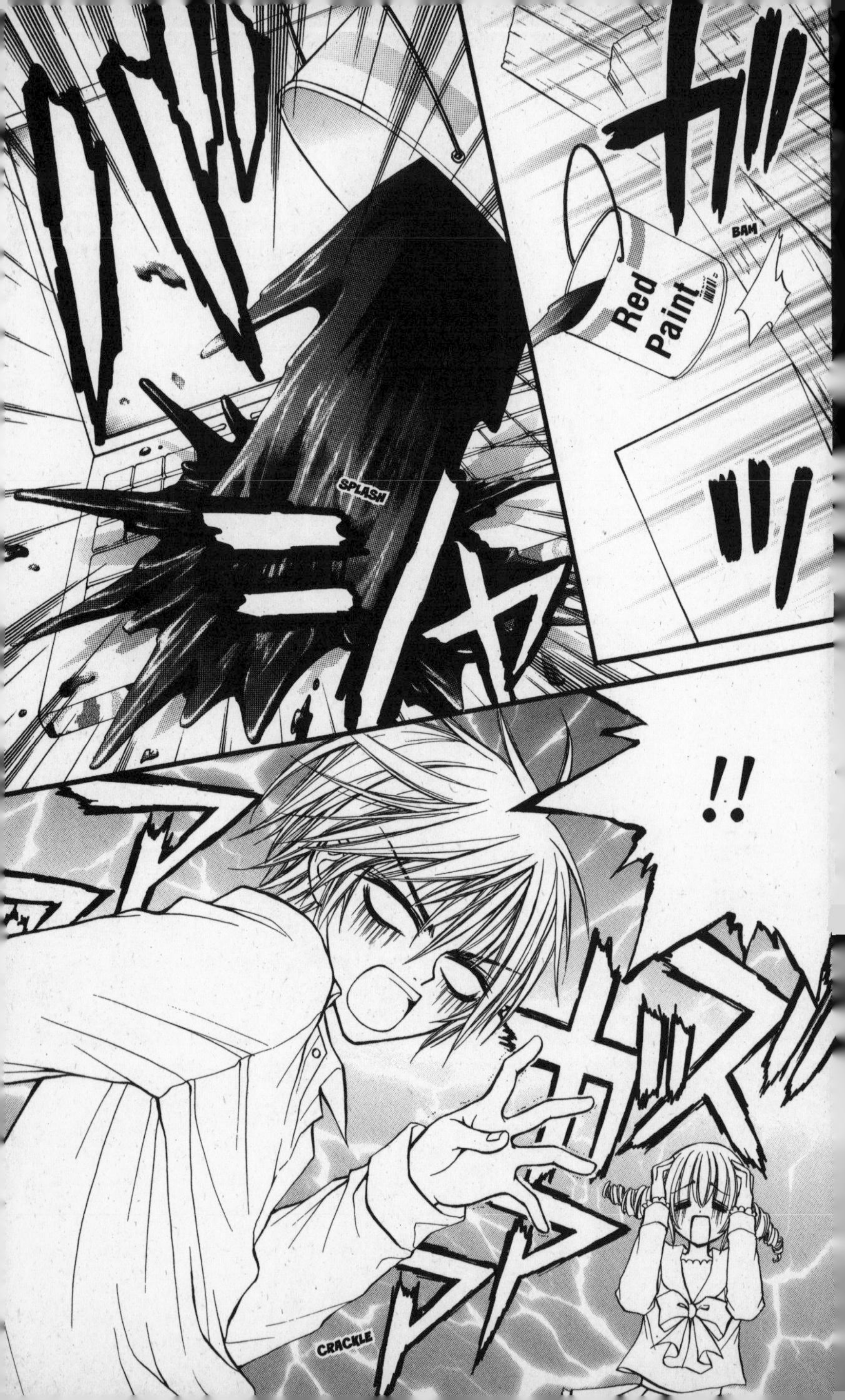
BAM
Red Paint
SPLASH
!!
CRACKLE

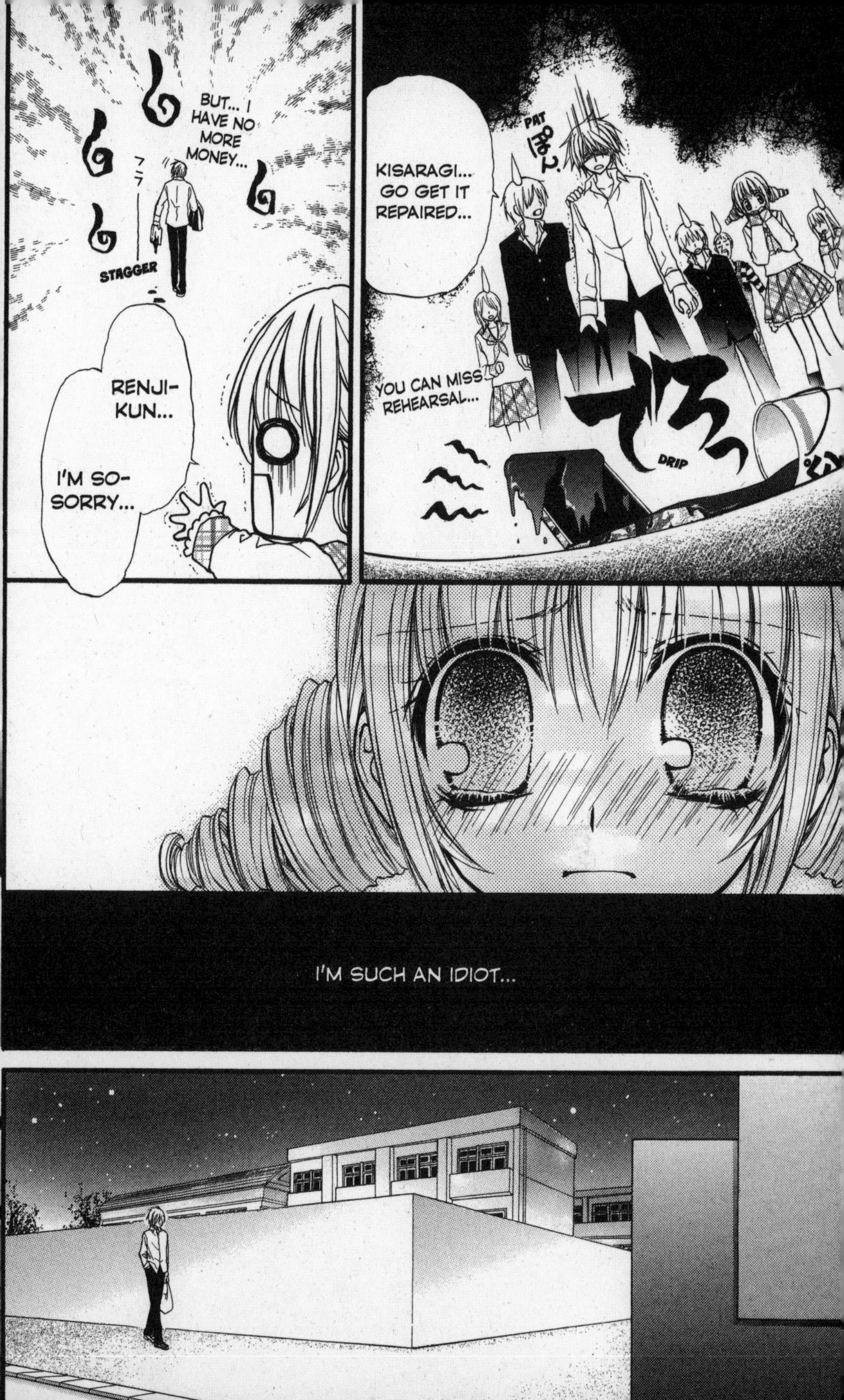
PAT
ぽん
KISARAGI... GO GET IT REPAIRED...
YOU CAN MISS REHEARSAL...
DRIP
BUT... I HAVE NO MORE MONEY...
STAGGER
RENJI-KUN...
I'M SO-SORRY...
I'M SUCH AN IDIOT...

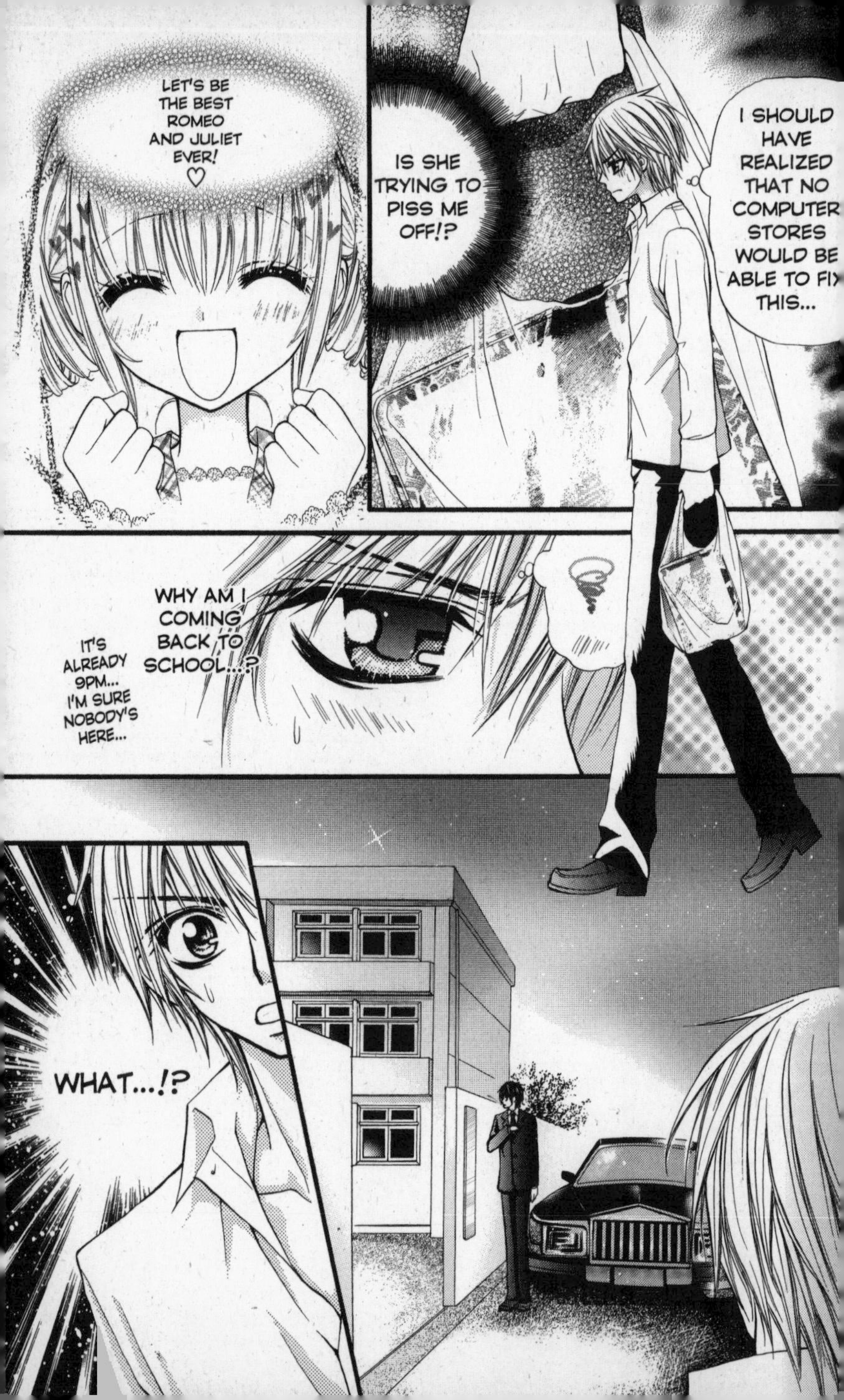
I SHOULD HAVE REALIZED THAT NO COMPUTER STORES WOULD BE ABLE TO FIX THIS...
IS SHE TRYING TO PISS ME OFF!?
LET'S BE THE BEST ROMEO AND JULIET EVER! ♡
WHY AM I COMING BACK TO SCHOOL...?
IT'S ALREADY 9PM... I'M SURE NOBODY'S HERE...
WHAT...!?

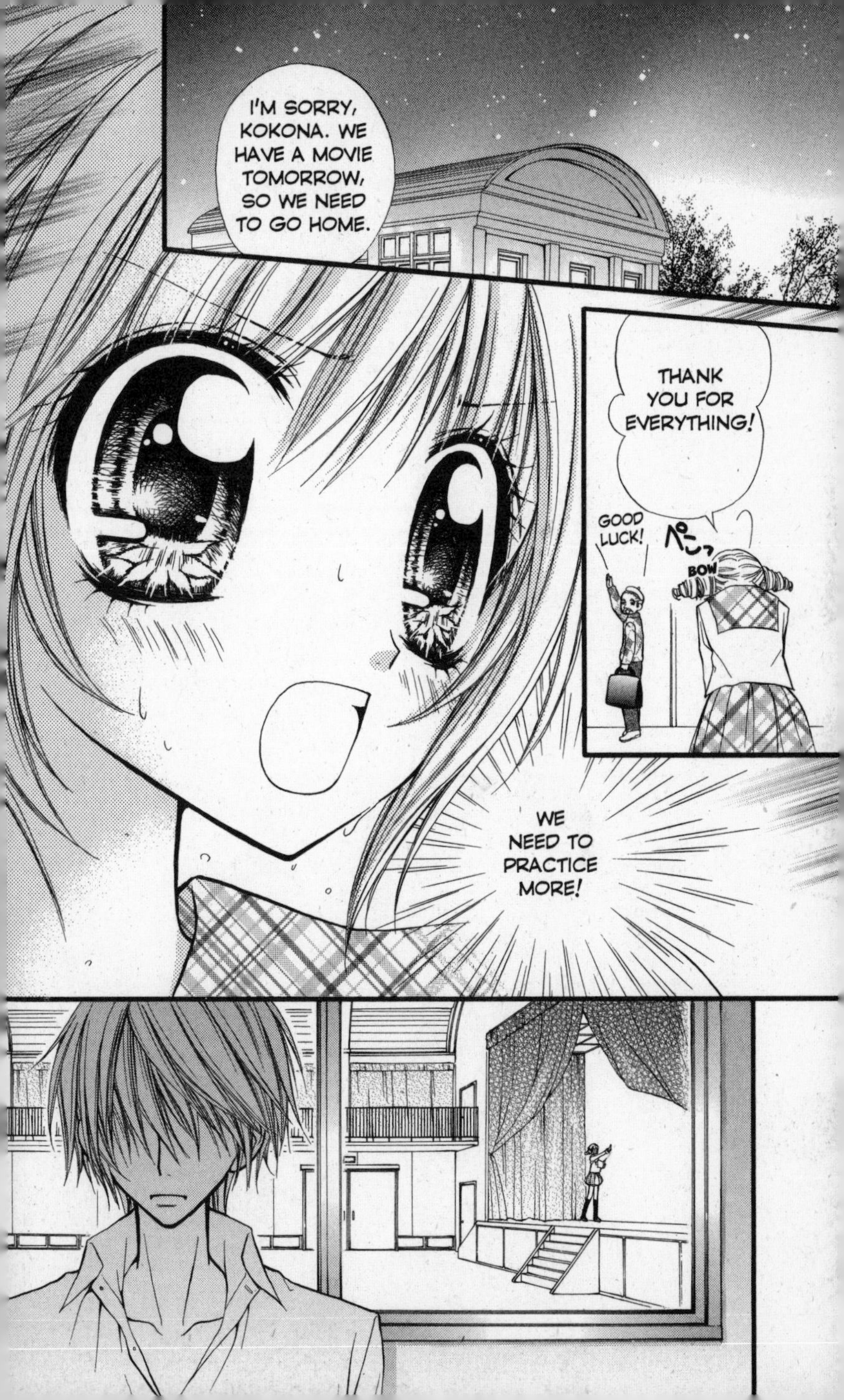
I'M SORRY, KOKONA. WE HAVE A MOVIE TOMORROW, SO WE NEED TO GO HOME.
THANK YOU FOR EVERYTHING!
ぺこっ
BOW
GOOD LUCK!
WE NEED TO PRACTICE MORE!

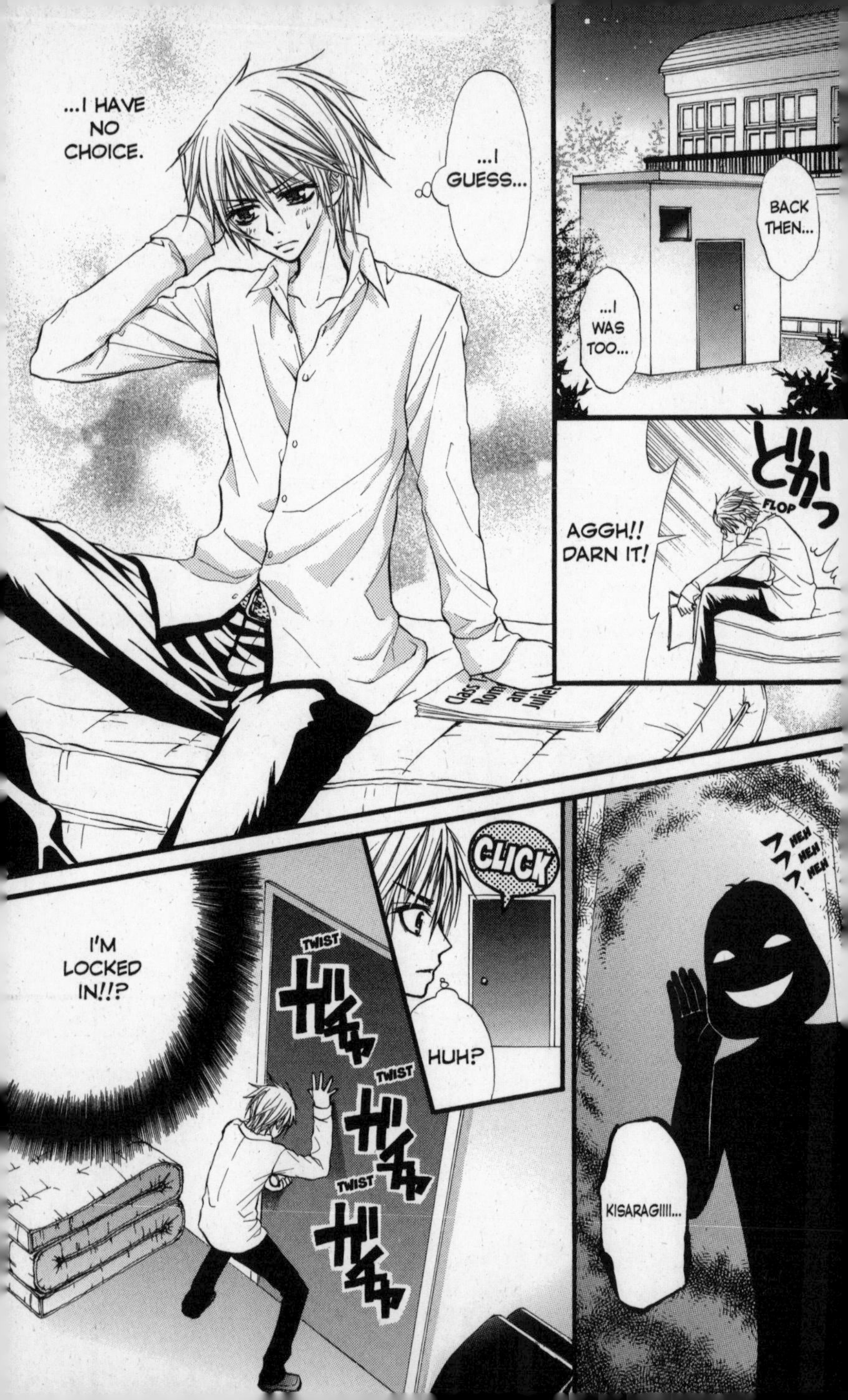
BACK THEN...
...I WAS TOO...
AGGH!! DARN IT!
とかっ
FLOP
...I GUESS...
...I HAVE NO CHOICE.
フフフ...
HEH HEH HEH
KISARAGIIII...
CLICK
HUH?
I'M LOCKED IN!!?
TWIST
ガチャ
TWIST
ガチャ
TWIST
ガチャ

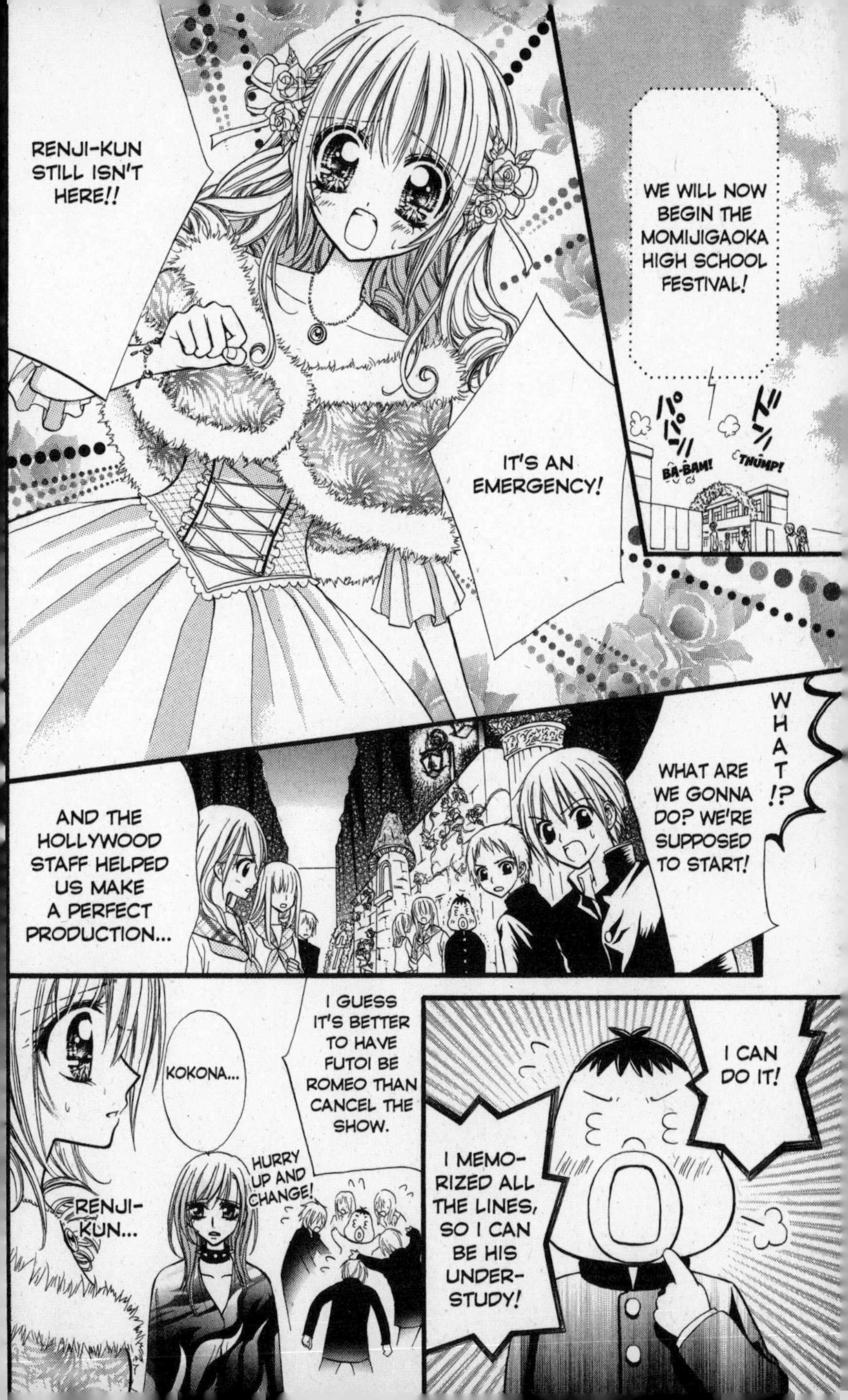
WE WILL NOW BEGIN THE MOMIJIGAOKA HIGH SCHOOL FESTIVAL!
THUMP!
BA-BAM!
RENJI-KUN STILL ISN'T HERE!!
IT'S AN EMERGENCY!
WHAT!?
WHAT ARE WE GONNA DO? WE'RE SUPPOSED TO START!
AND THE HOLLYWOOD STAFF HELPED US MAKE A PERFECT PRODUCTION...
I CAN DO IT!
I MEMO-RIZED ALL THE LINES, SO I CAN BE HIS UNDER-STUDY!
I GUESS IT'S BETTER TO HAVE FUTOI BE ROMEO THAN CANCEL THE SHOW.
HURRY UP AND CHANGE!
KOKONA...
RENJI-KUN...

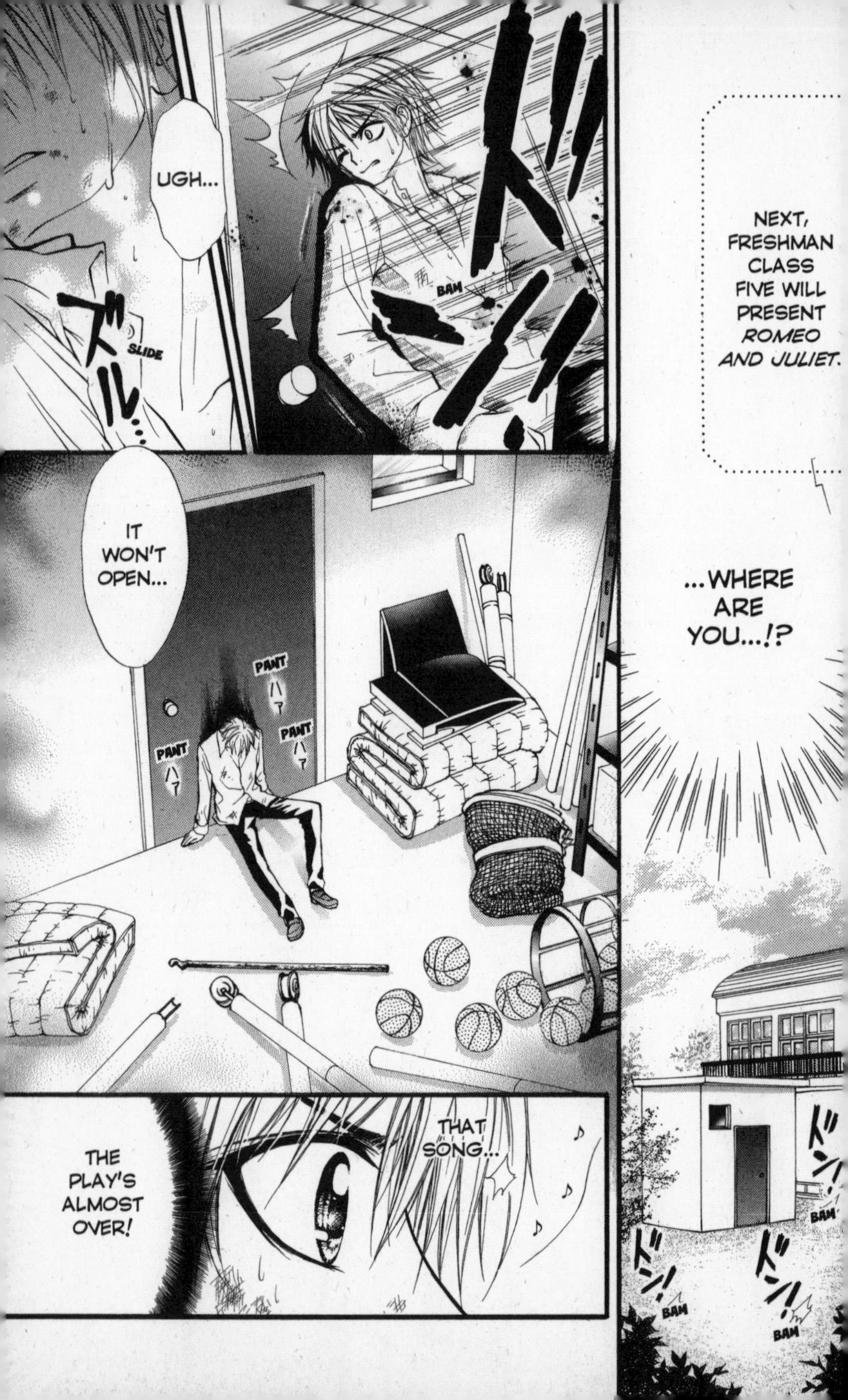

NEXT, FRESHMAN CLASS FIVE WILL PRESENT *ROMEO AND JULIET.*
...WHERE ARE YOU...!?
ドン!
BAM
ドン!
BAM
ドン!
BAM
ドン!
BAM
BAM
UGH...
ズル...
SLIDE
IT WON'T OPEN...
PANT
ハァ
PANT
ハァ
PANT
ハァ
THAT SONG...
THE PLAY'S ALMOST OVER!

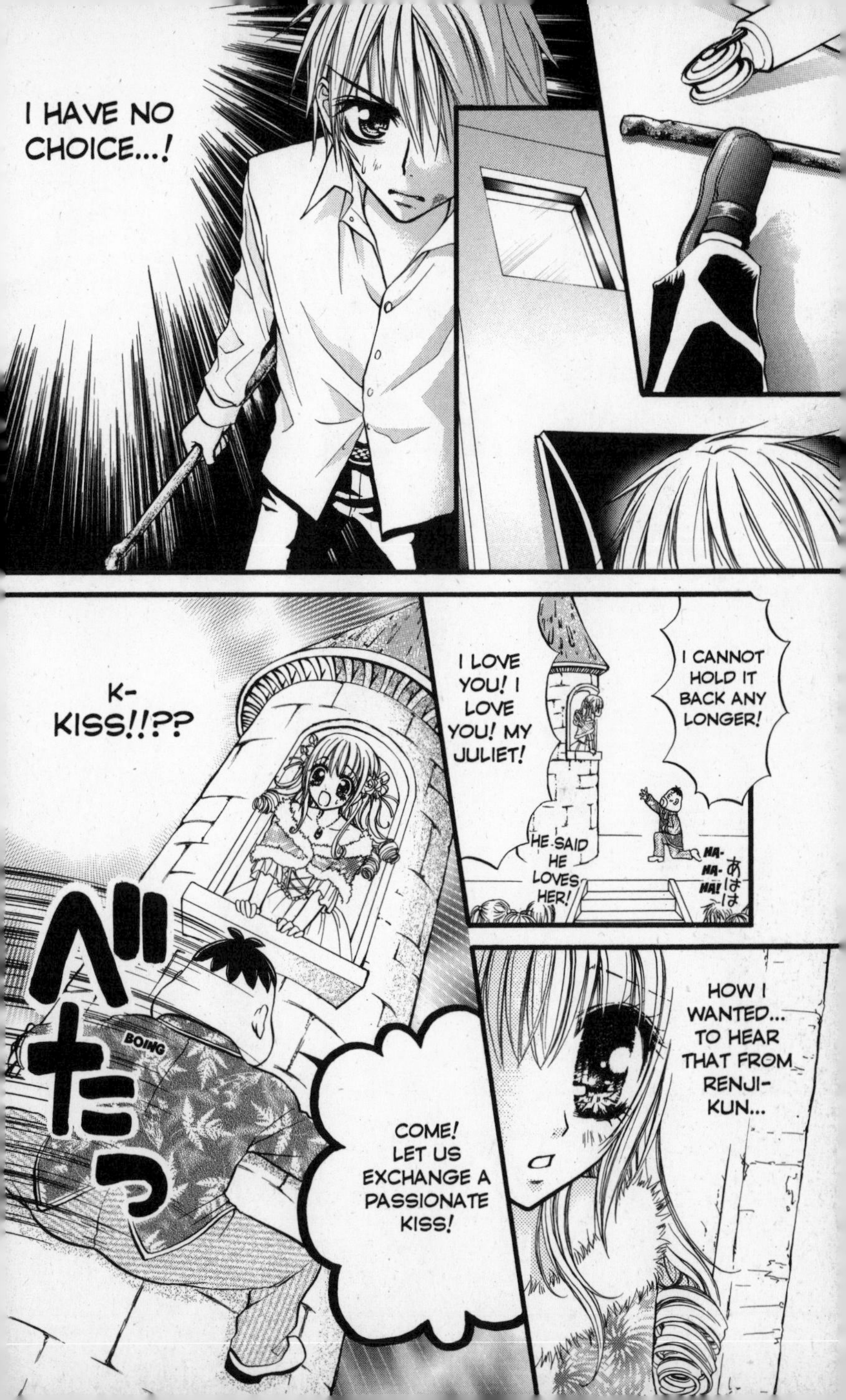
I HAVE NO CHOICE...!
I CANNOT HOLD IT BACK ANY LONGER!
I LOVE YOU! I LOVE YOU! MY JULIET!
HA-HA-HA!
あはは
HE SAID HE LOVES HER!
HOW I WANTED... TO HEAR THAT FROM RENJI-KUN...
K-KISS!!??
BOING
COME! LET US EXCHANGE A PASSIONATE KISS!
べたっ

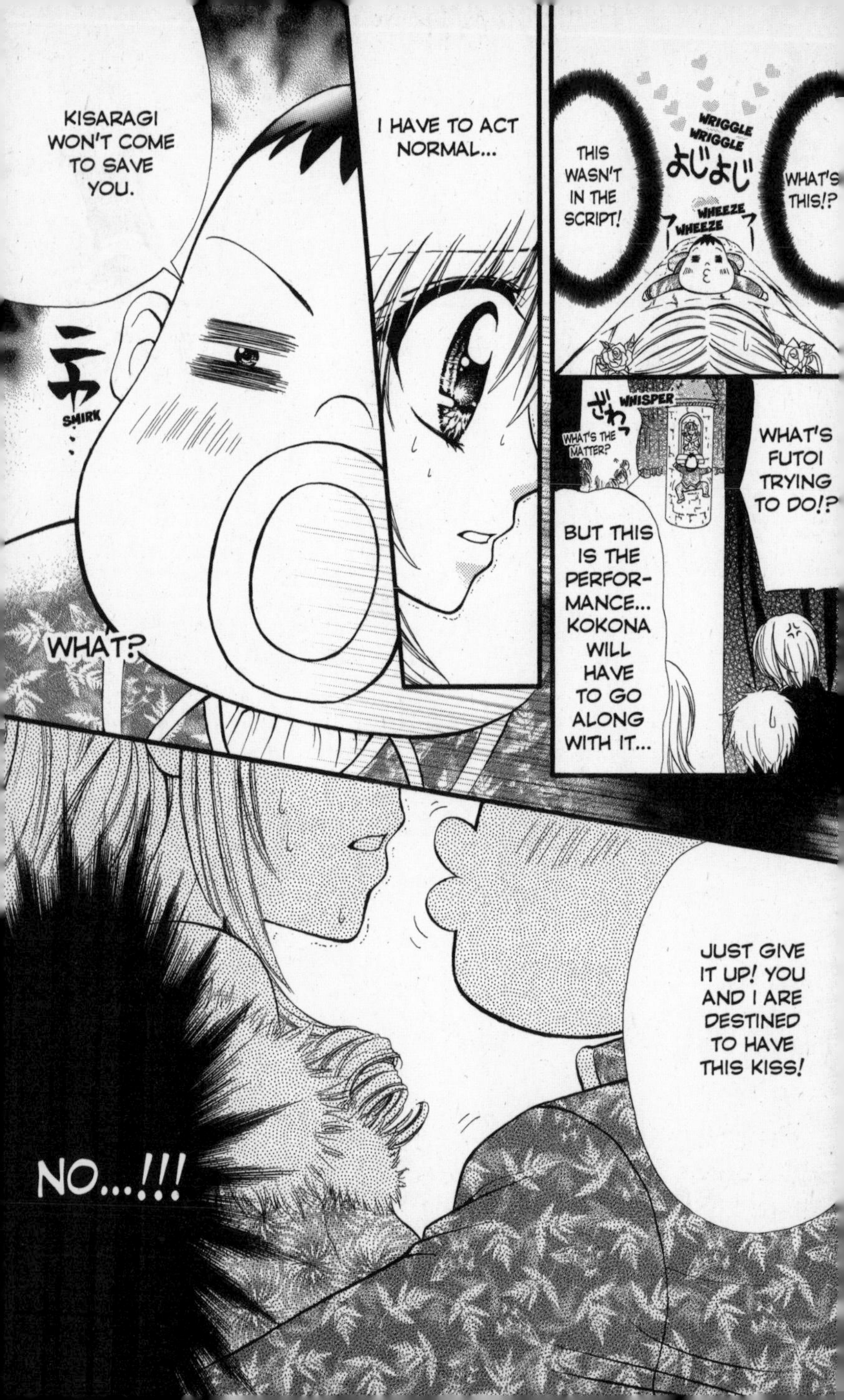
WHAT'S THIS!?
WRIGGLE WRIGGLE
よじよじ
WHEEZE WHEEZE
THIS WASN'T IN THE SCRIPT!
WHAT'S FUTOI TRYING TO DO!?
ざわっ
WHISPER
WHAT'S THE MATTER?
BUT THIS IS THE PERFORMANCE... KOKONA WILL HAVE TO GO ALONG WITH IT...
I HAVE TO ACT NORMAL...
KISARAGI WON'T COME TO SAVE YOU.
ニヤ…
SMIRK
WHAT?
JUST GIVE IT UP! YOU AND I ARE DESTINED TO HAVE THIS KISS!
NO...!!!

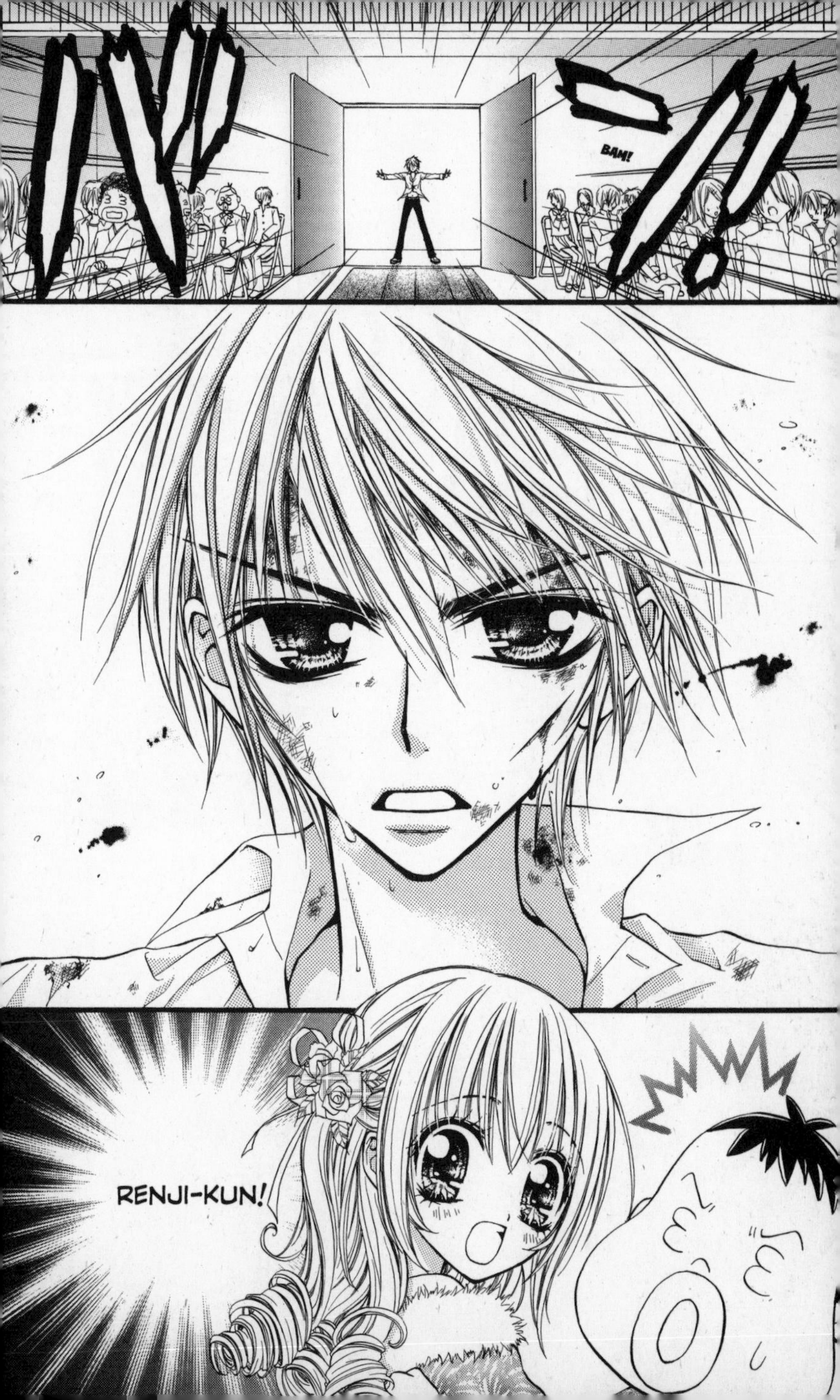
BAM!
RENJI-KUN!

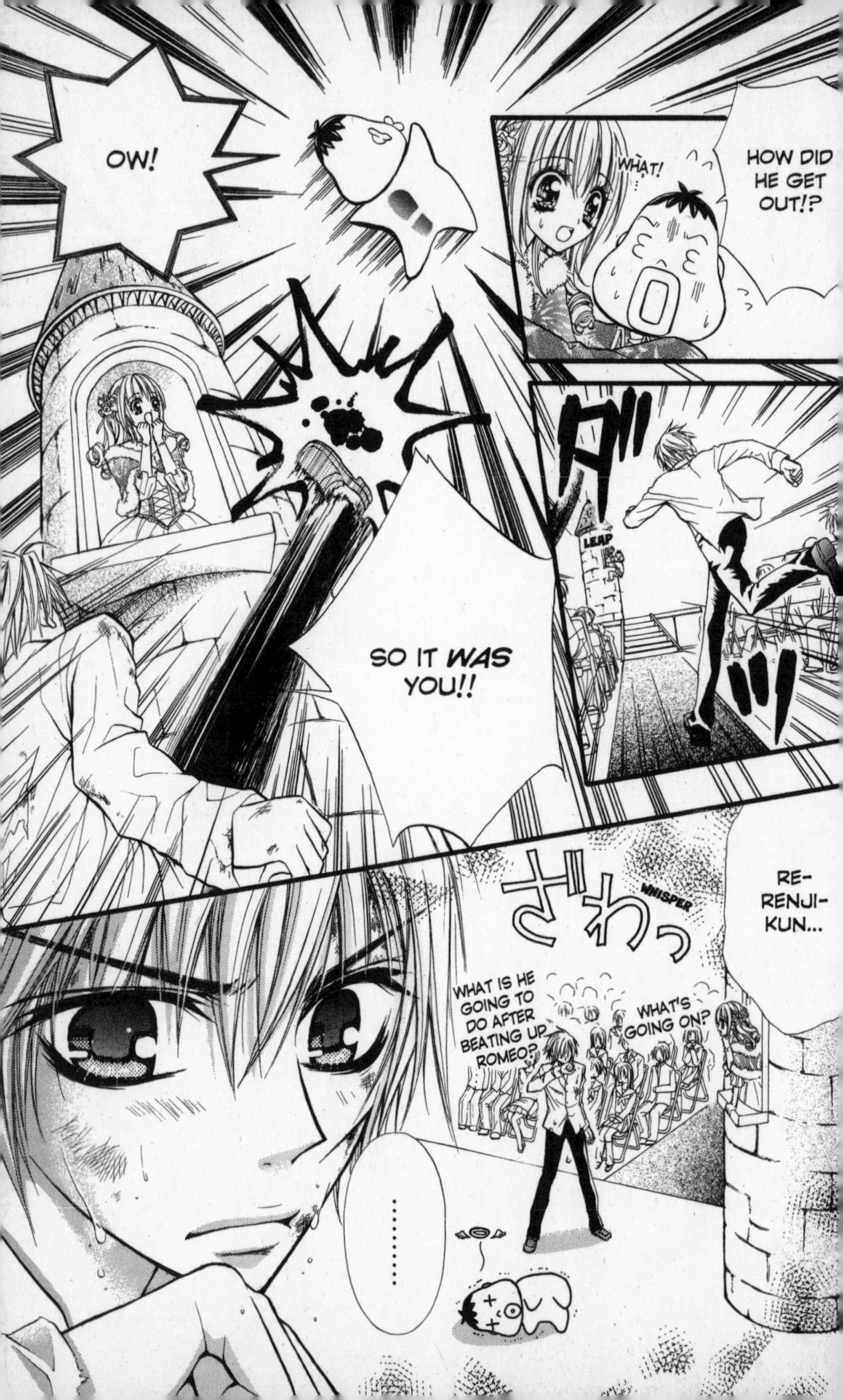
WHAT!
HOW DID HE GET OUT!?
ダッ
LEAP
OW!
SO IT WAS YOU!!
RE-RENJI-KUN...
ざわっ
WHISPER
WHAT'S GOING ON?
WHAT IS HE GOING TO DO AFTER BEATING UP ROMEO?
......

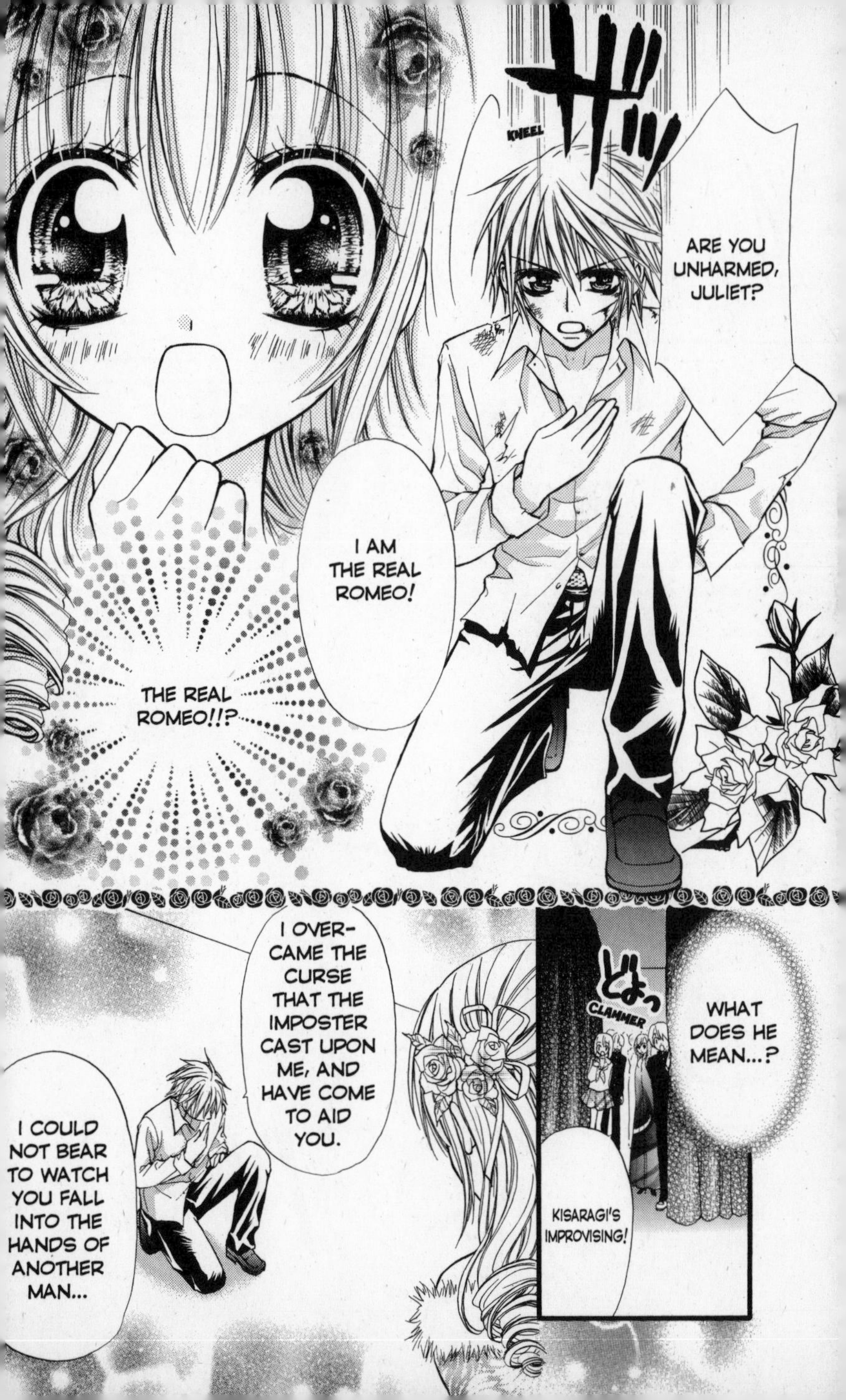
ザッ
KNEEL
ARE YOU UNHARMED, JULIET?
I AM THE REAL ROMEO!
THE REAL ROMEO!!?
どよっ
CLAMMER
WHAT DOES HE MEAN...?
KISARAGI'S IMPROVISING!
I OVER-CAME THE CURSE THAT THE IMPOSTER CAST UPON ME, AND HAVE COME TO AID YOU.
I COULD NOT BEAR TO WATCH YOU FALL INTO THE HANDS OF ANOTHER MAN...

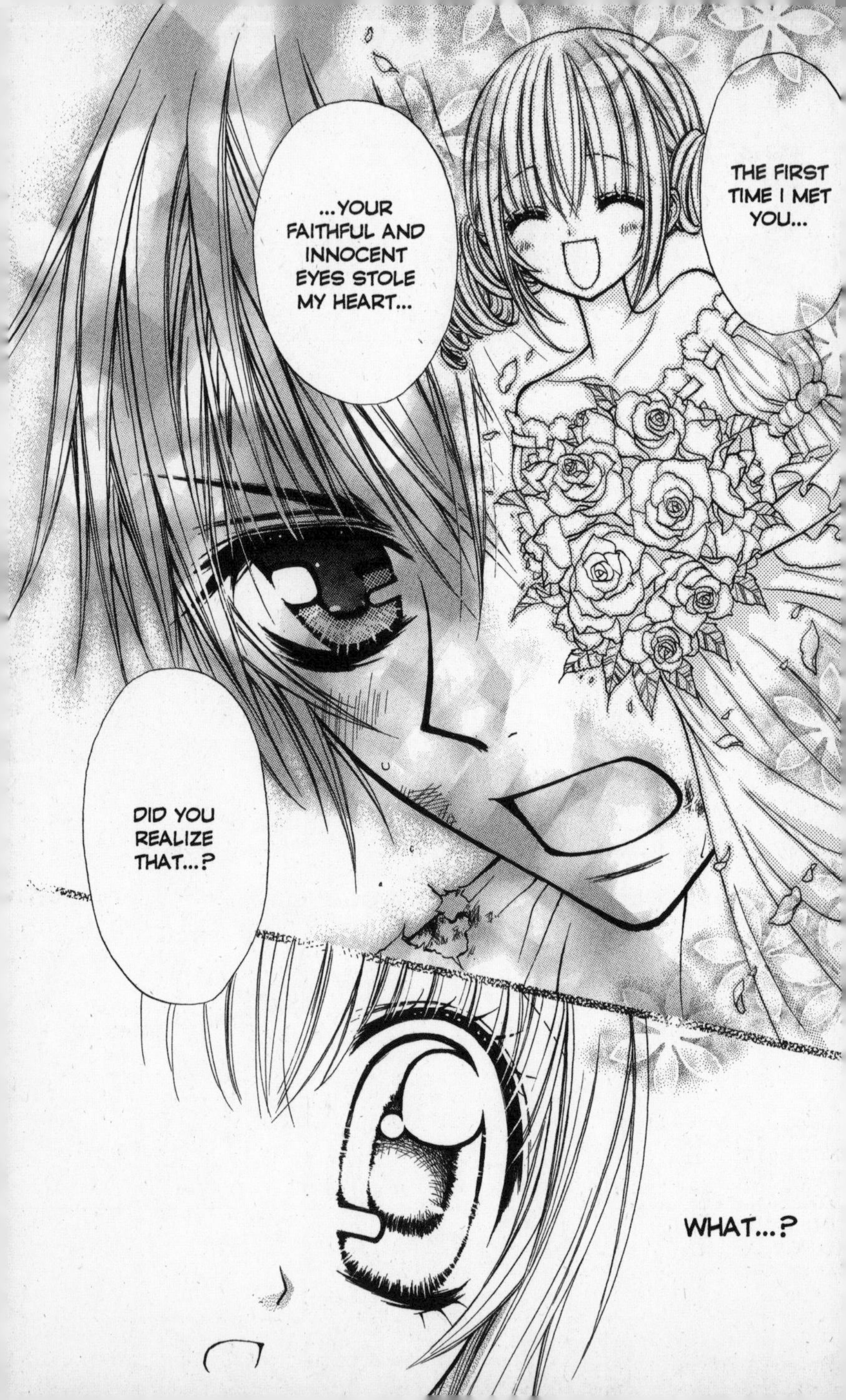
THE FIRST TIME I MET YOU...
...YOUR FAITHFUL AND INNOCENT EYES STOLE MY HEART...
DID YOU REALIZE THAT...?
WHAT...?

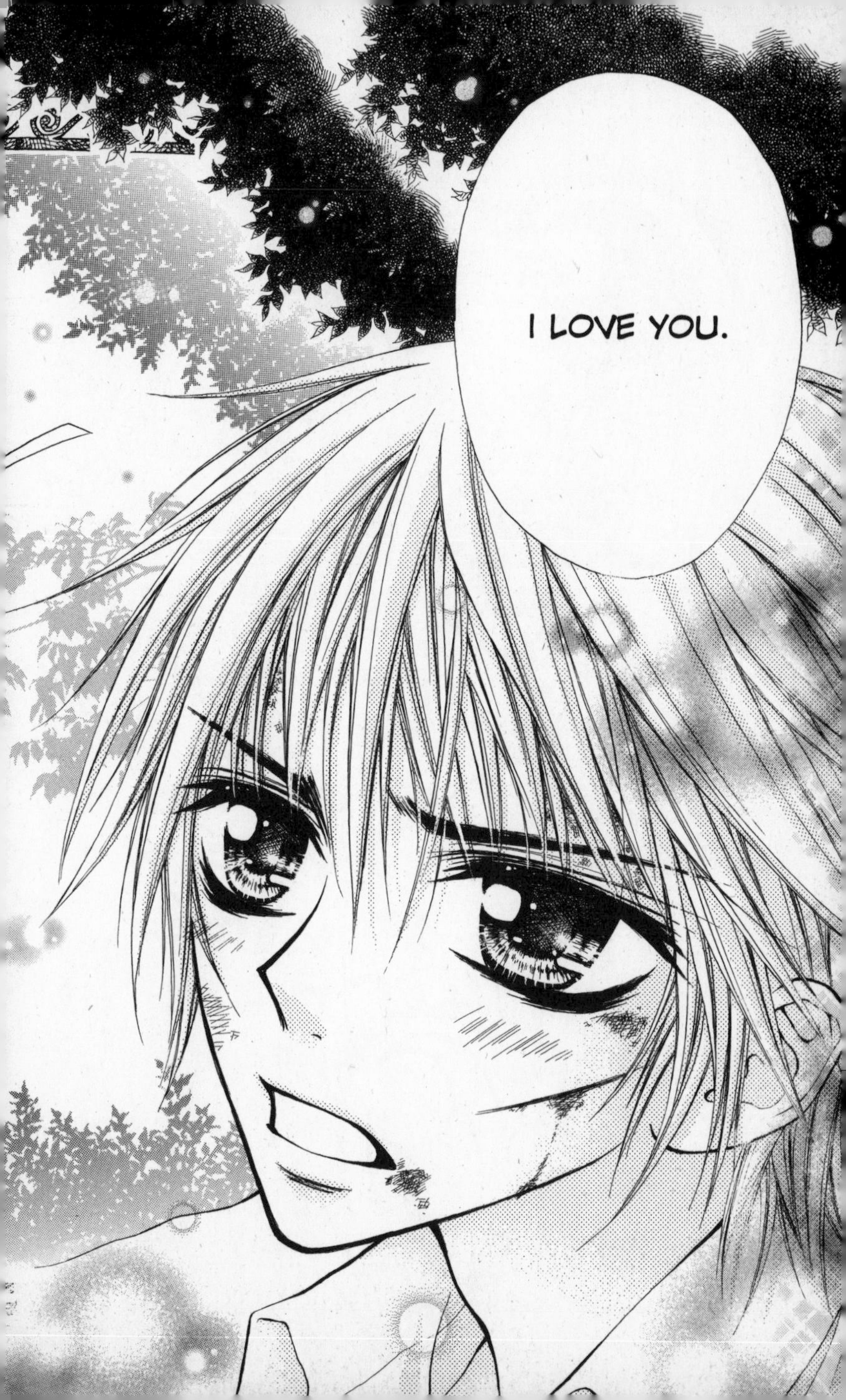
I LOVE YOU.

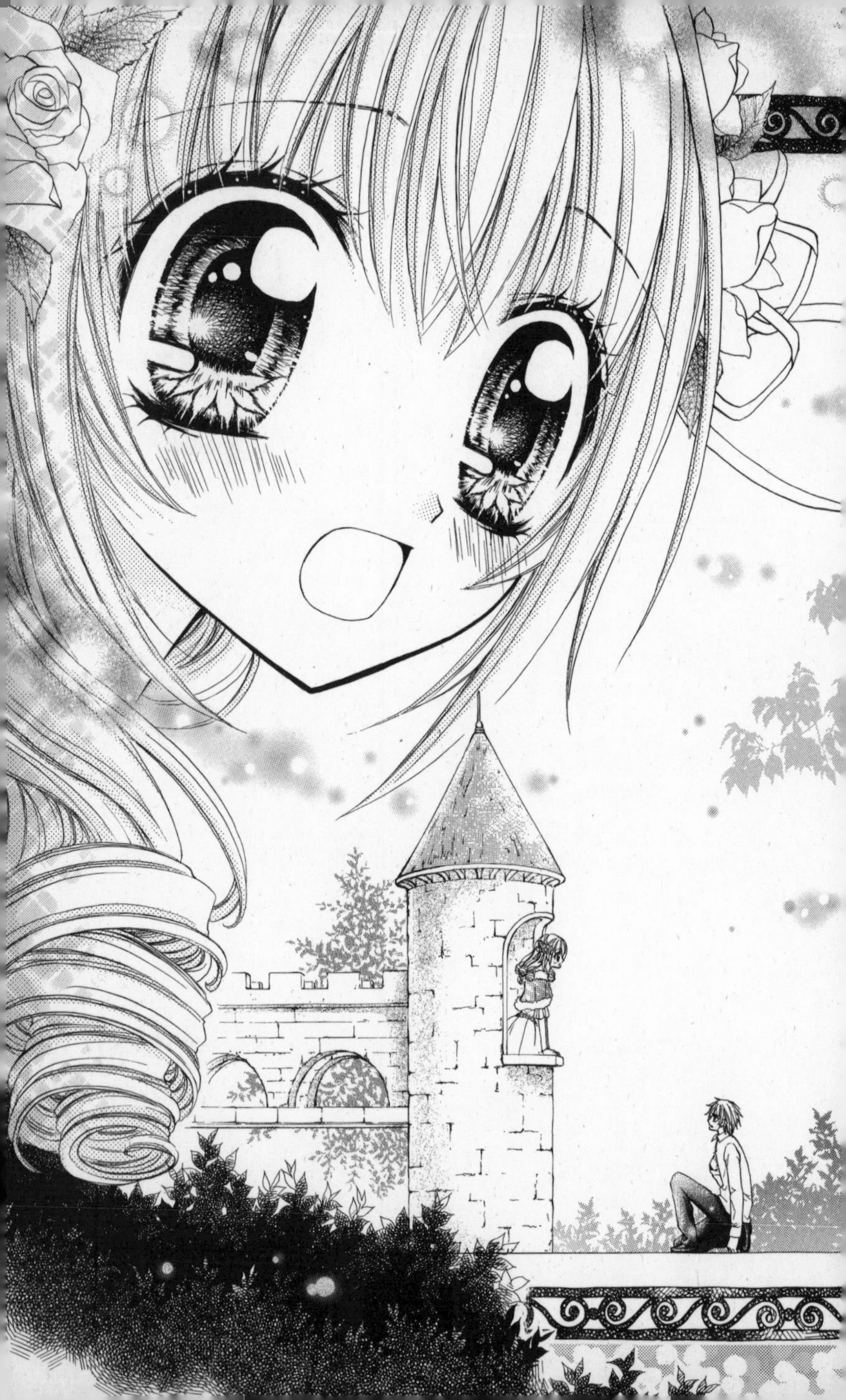

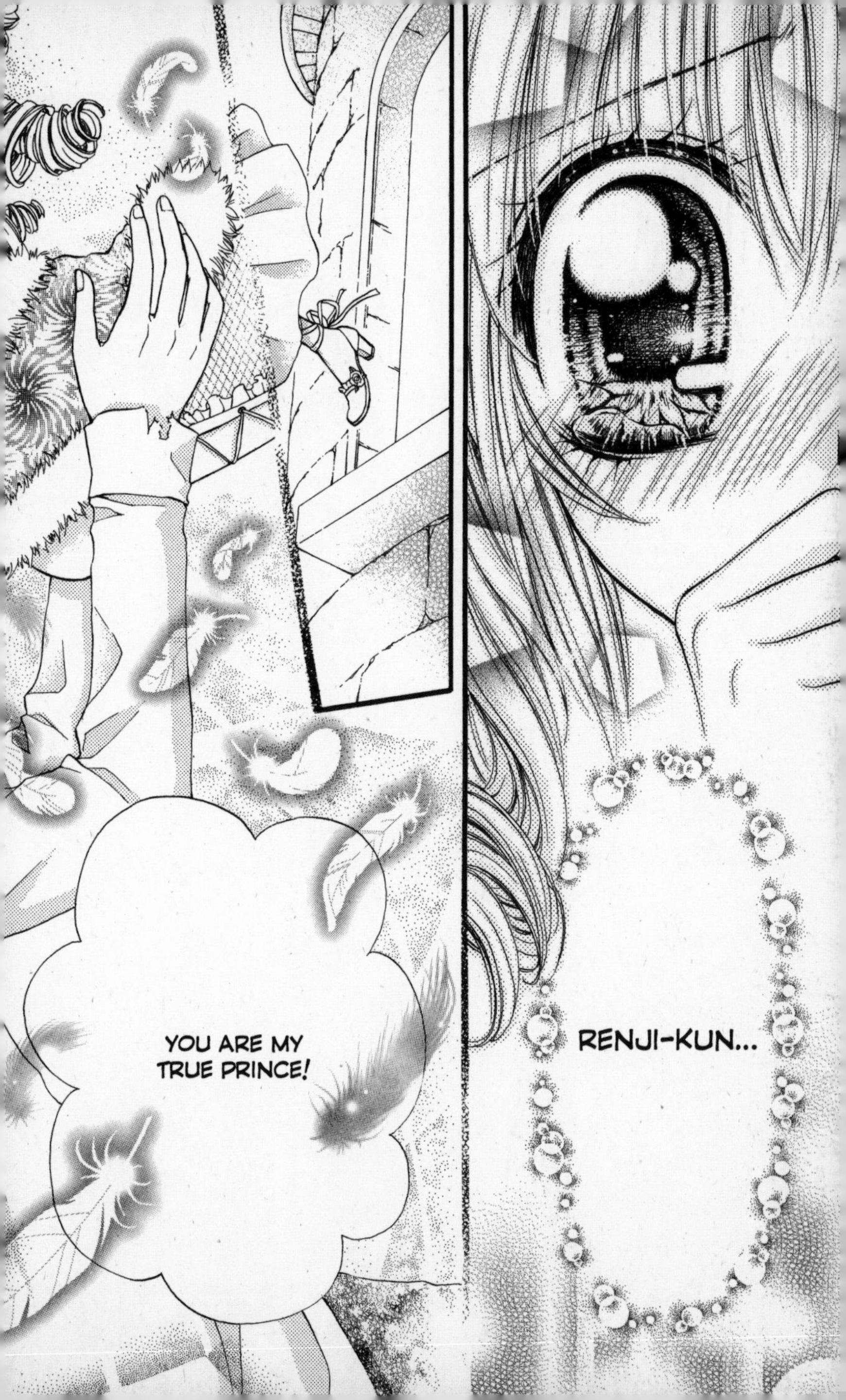
RENJI-KUN...
YOU ARE MY TRUE PRINCE!

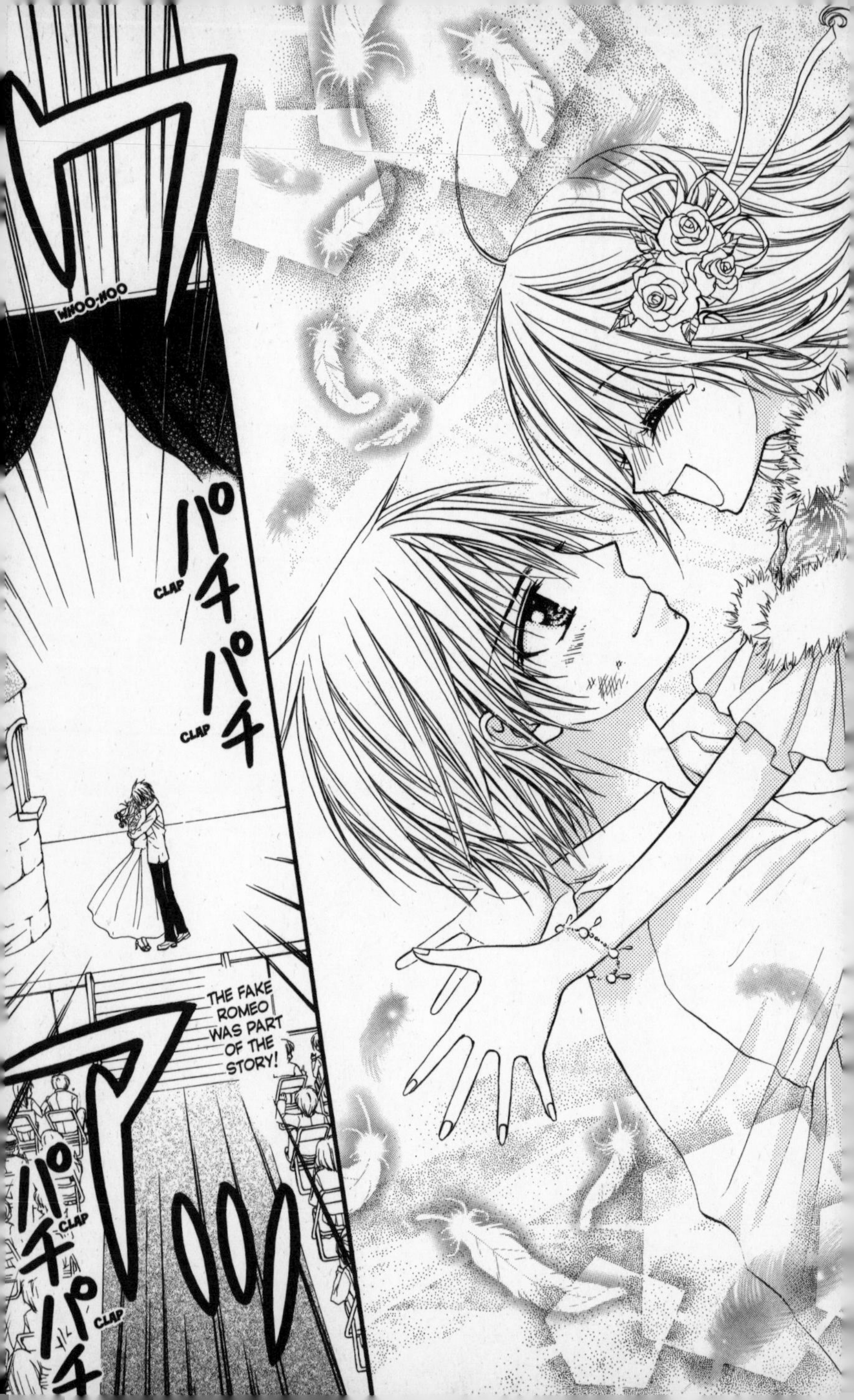
WHOO-HOO
パチパチ
CLAP
CLAP
THE FAKE ROMEO WAS PART OF THE STORY!
パチパチ
CLAP
CLAP

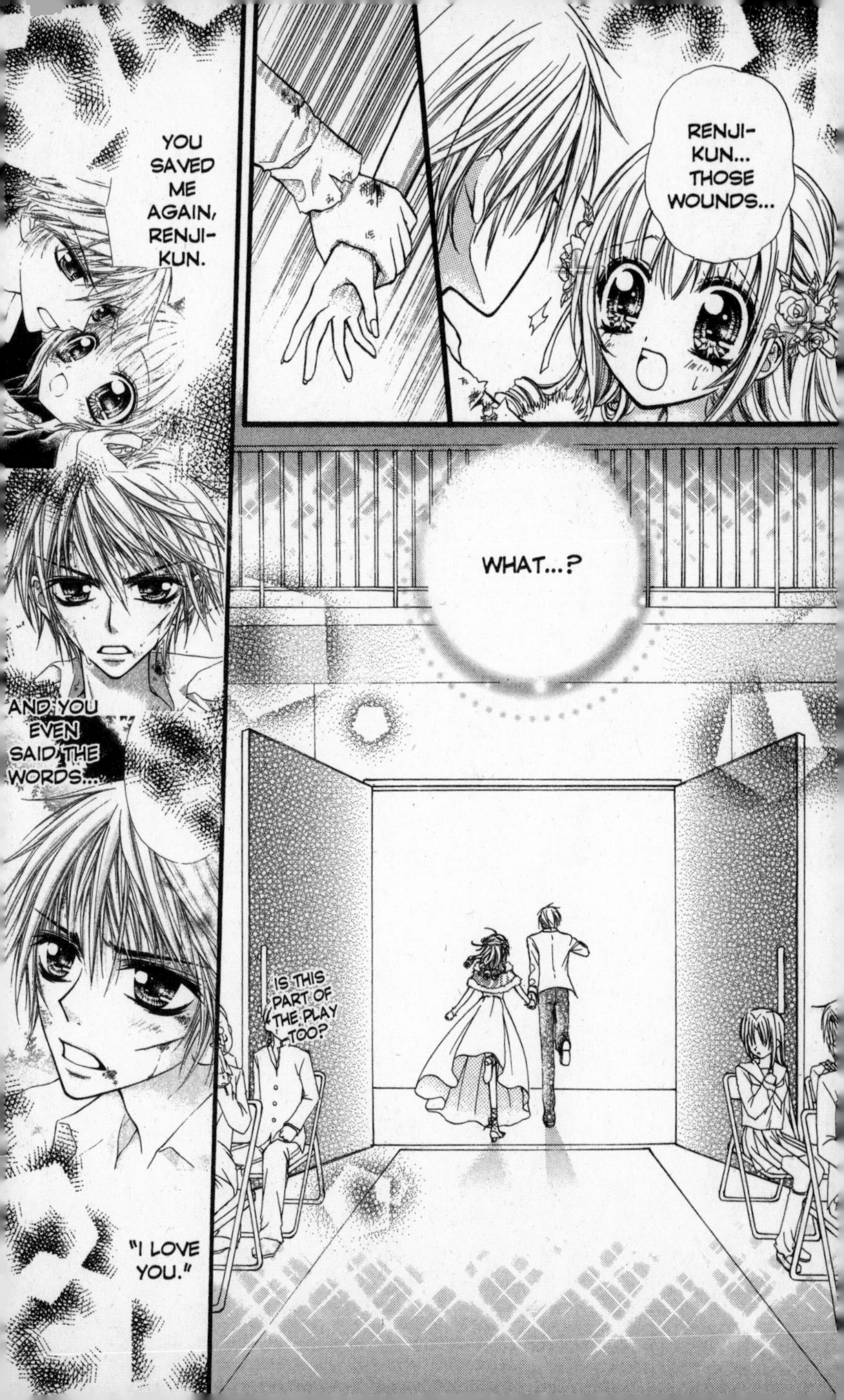
RENJI-KUN... THOSE WOUNDS...
WHAT...?
IS THIS PART OF THE PLAY TOO?
YOU SAVED ME AGAIN, RENJI-KUN.
AND YOU EVEN SAID THE WORDS...
"I LOVE YOU."

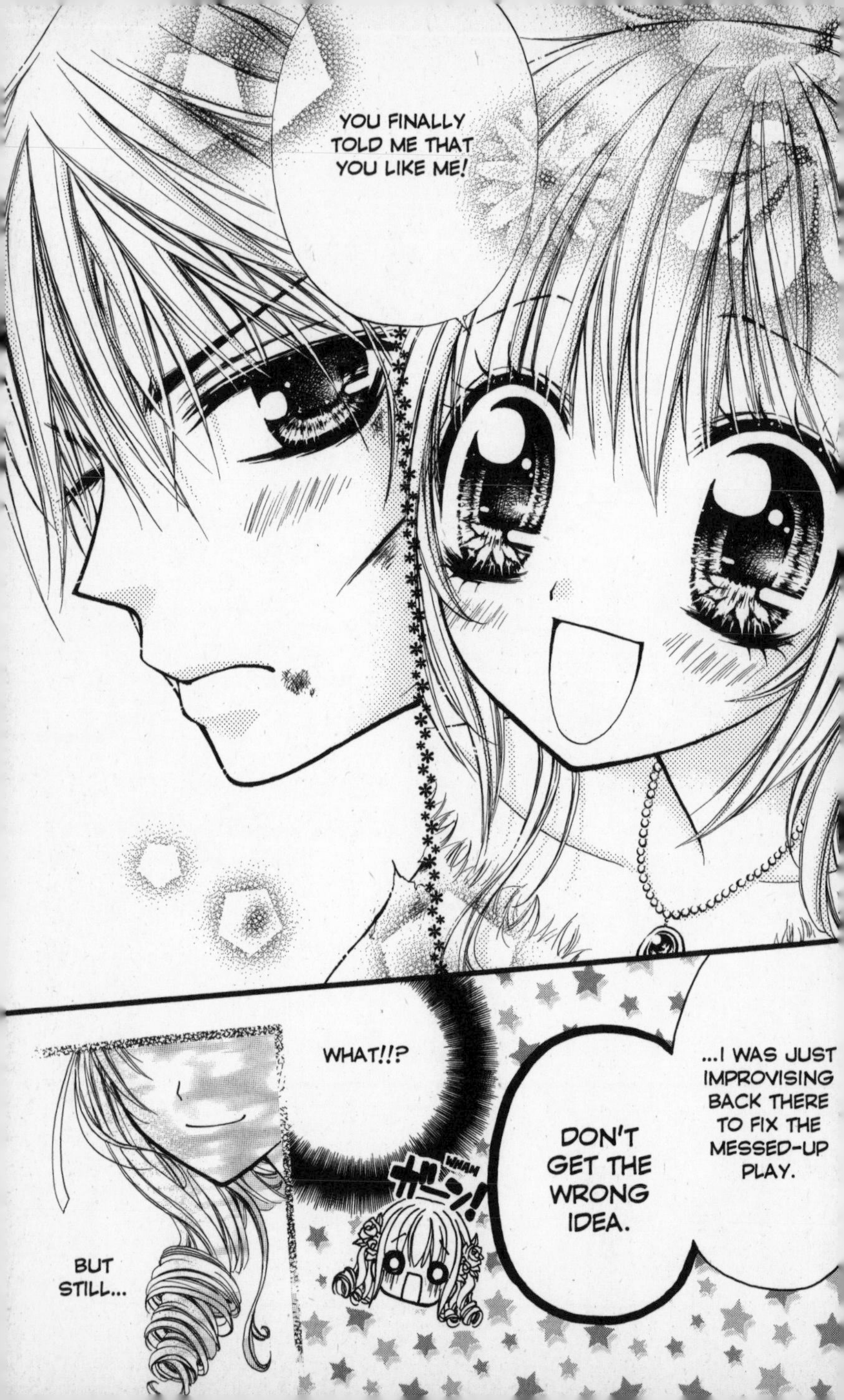
YOU FINALLY TOLD ME THAT YOU LIKE ME!
...I WAS JUST IMPROVISING BACK THERE TO FIX THE MESSED-UP PLAY.
DON'T GET THE WRONG IDEA.
WHAM
WHAT!!?
BUT STILL...

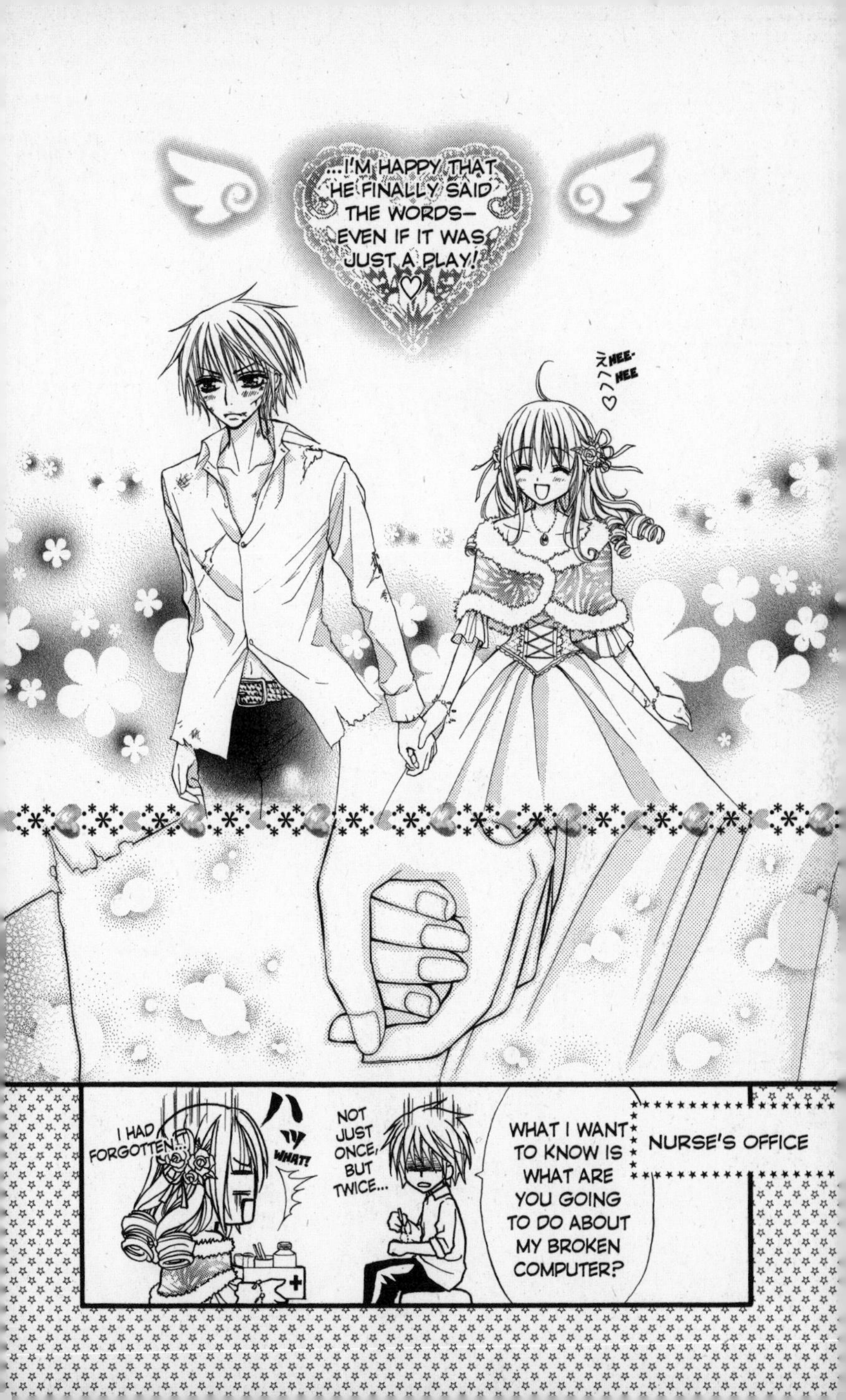
...I'M HAPPY THAT HE FINALLY SAID THE WORDS— EVEN IF IT WAS JUST A PLAY! ♡
HEE-HEE ♡
NURSE'S OFFICE
WHAT I WANT TO KNOW IS WHAT ARE YOU GOING TO DO ABOUT MY BROKEN COMPUTER?
NOT JUST ONCE, BUT TWICE...
WHAT!
I HAD FORGOTTEN...

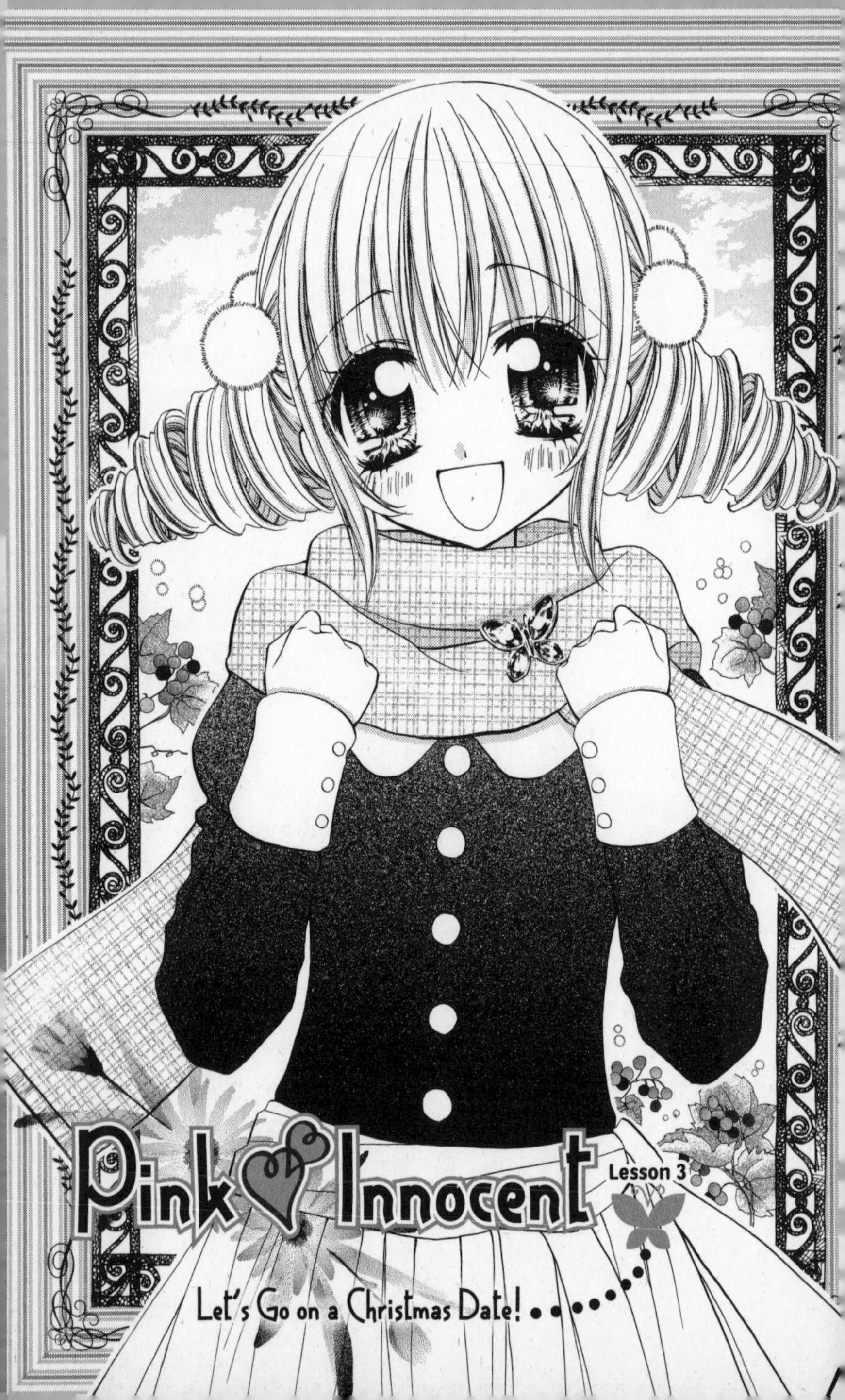
Pink Innocent
Lesson 3
Let's Go on a Christmas Date!

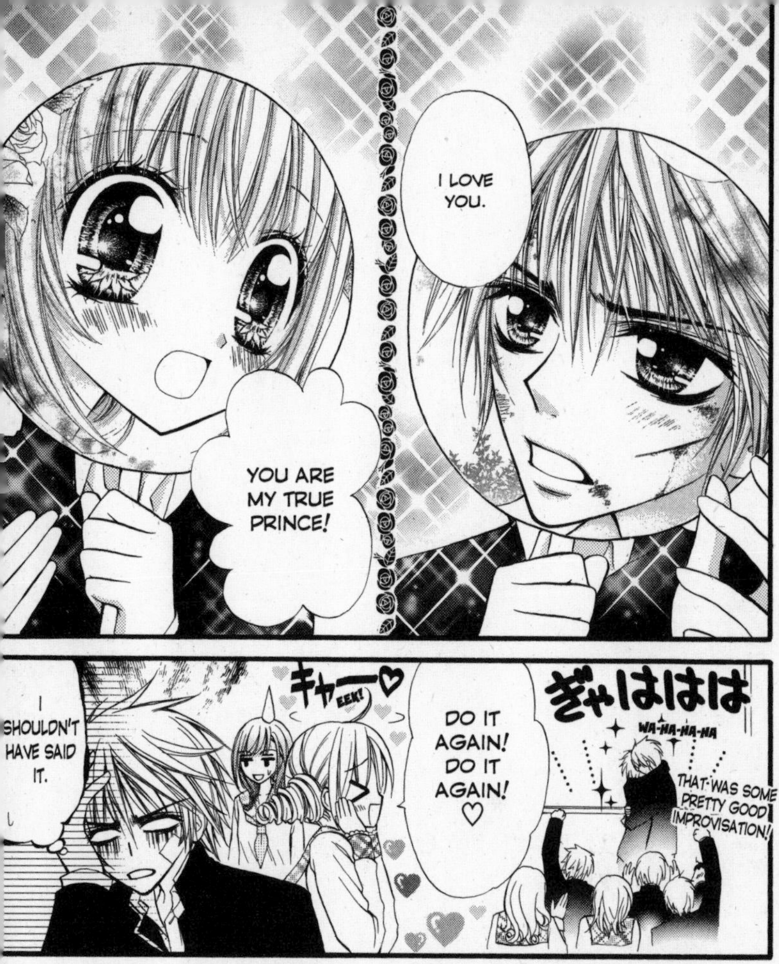
I LOVE YOU.
YOU ARE MY TRUE PRINCE!
ぎゃははは
WA-HA-HA-HA
THAT WAS SOME PRETTY GOOD IMPROVISATION!
DO IT AGAIN! DO IT AGAIN! ♡
キャー♡
EEK!
I SHOULDN'T HAVE SAID IT.

KOKONA'S LOVE BLOG

Hello, Kokona here. Computer-obsessed Renji-kun saved me instead of his computer, and I felt his true love for me!♡ But I still wanted to hear him say the words! I tried to get him to say it during our *Romeo and Juliet* play for the school festival, but everything went wrong.... Right before the play Renji-kun disappeared, and an understudy Romeo tried to kiss me during the play! But then Renji-kun came and saved me, and told me that he loves me!!

Comment

Aery: Kisaragi may say that it was only part of the play, but most people wouldn't go that far for no reason. Be happy, Kokona! ☆

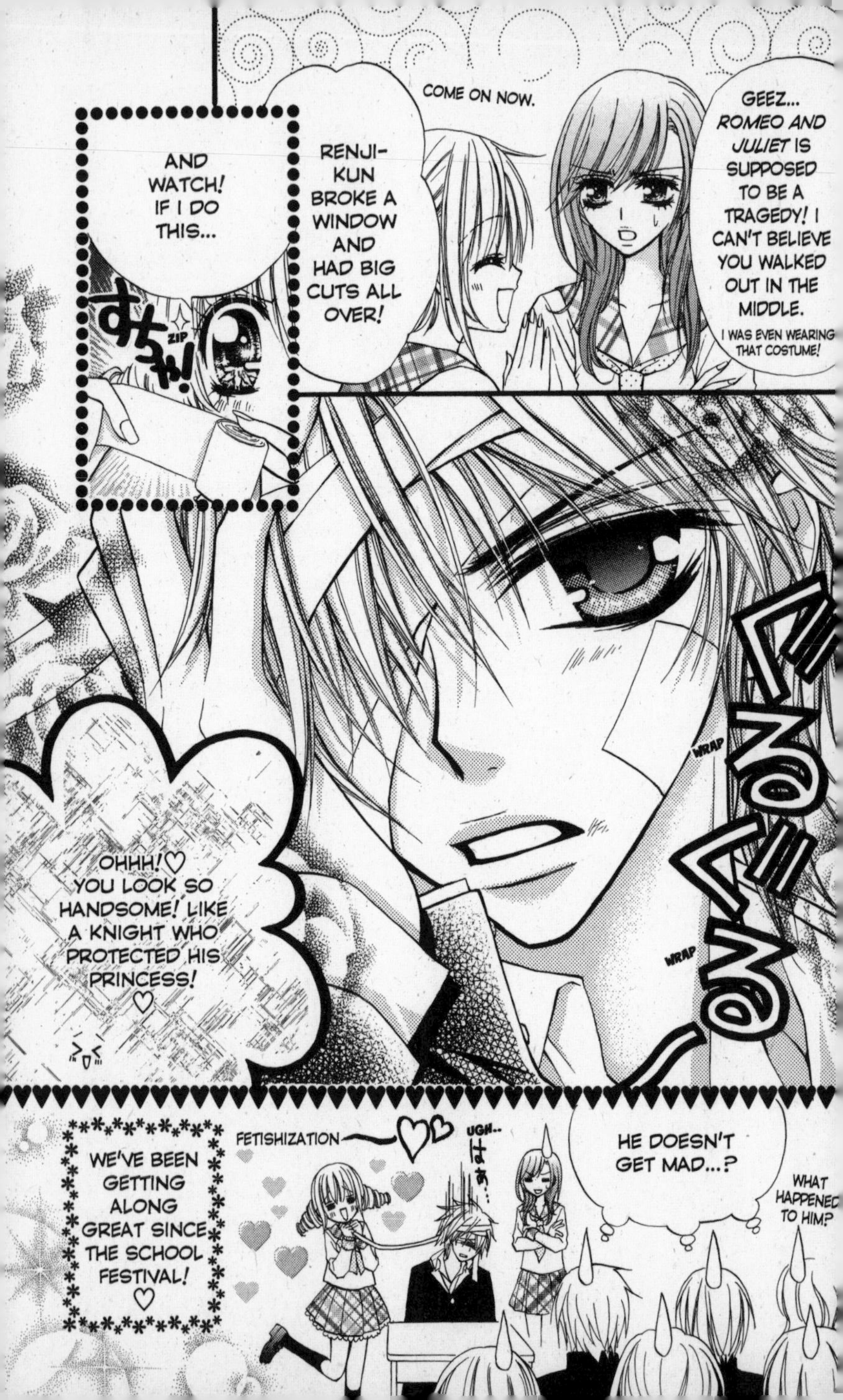
GEEZ... ROMEO AND JULIET IS SUPPOSED TO BE A TRAGEDY! I CAN'T BELIEVE YOU WALKED OUT IN THE MIDDLE.
I WAS EVEN WEARING THAT COSTUME!
COME ON NOW.
RENJI-KUN BROKE A WINDOW AND HAD BIG CUTS ALL OVER!
AND WATCH! IF I DO THIS...
すちゃ!
ZIP
WRAP
WRAP
OHHH!♡ YOU LOOK SO HANDSOME! LIKE A KNIGHT WHO PROTECTED HIS PRINCESS! ♡
WHAT HAPPENED TO HIM?
HE DOESN'T GET MAD...?
UGH..
はぁ...
FETISHIZATION~♡♡
WE'VE BEEN GETTING ALONG GREAT SINCE THE SCHOOL FESTIVAL! ♡

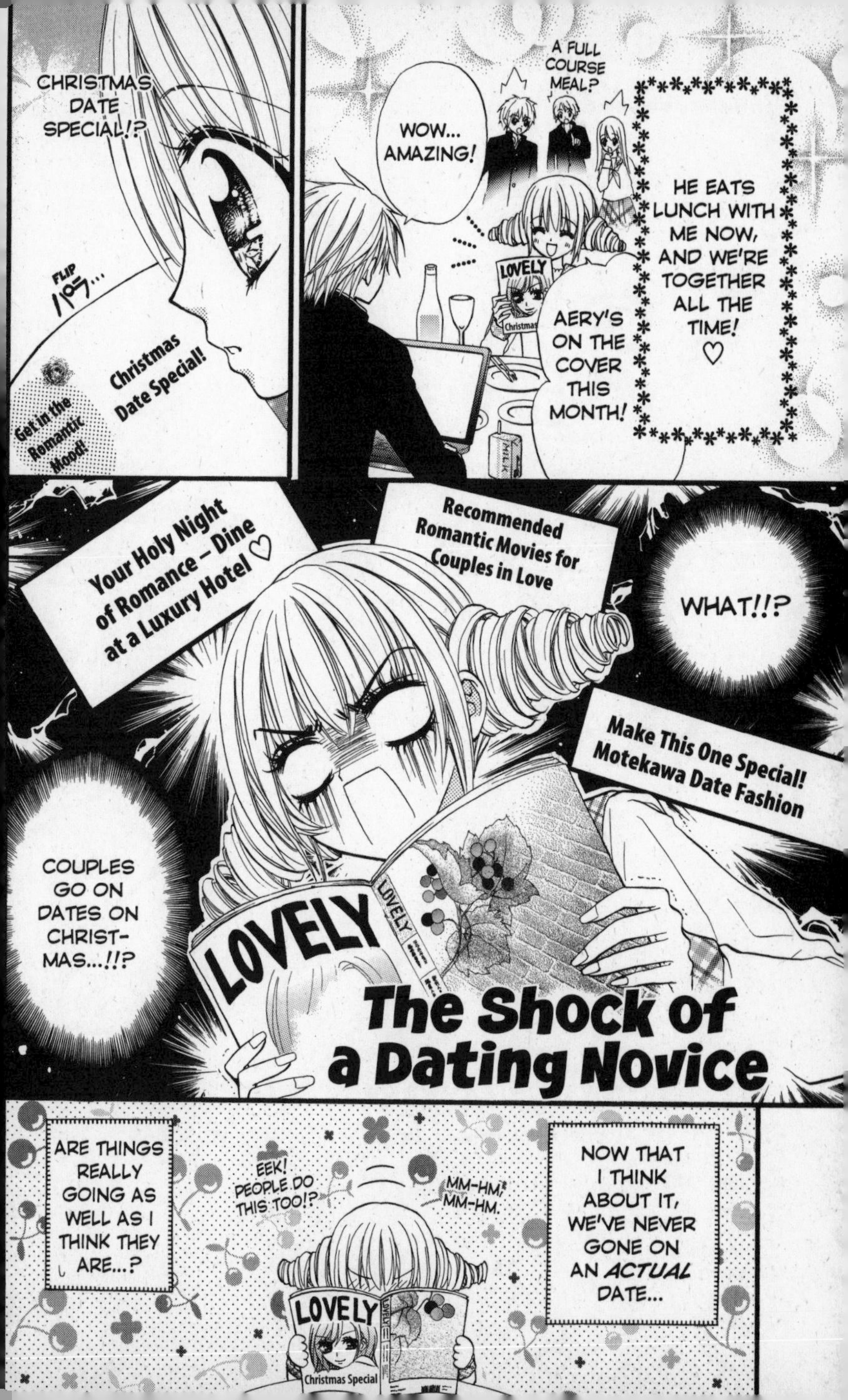

A FULL COURSE MEAL?
HE EATS LUNCH WITH ME NOW, AND WE'RE TOGETHER ALL THE TIME! ♡
WOW... AMAZING!
.....
AERY'S ON THE COVER THIS MONTH!
LOVELY
Christmas
MILK
CHRISTMAS DATE SPECIAL!?
FLIP...
Christmas Date Special!
Get in the Romantic Mood!
Recommended Romantic Movies for Couples in Love
WHAT!!?
Your Holy Night of Romance – Dine at a Luxury Hotel ♡
Make This One Special! Motekawa Date Fashion
COUPLES GO ON DATES ON CHRIST-MAS...!!?
LOVELY
The Shock of a Dating Novice
NOW THAT I THINK ABOUT IT, WE'VE NEVER GONE ON AN *ACTUAL* DATE...
MM-HM, MM-HM.
EEK! PEOPLE DO THIS TOO!?
ARE THINGS REALLY GOING AS WELL AS I THINK THEY ARE...?
LOVELY
Christmas Special

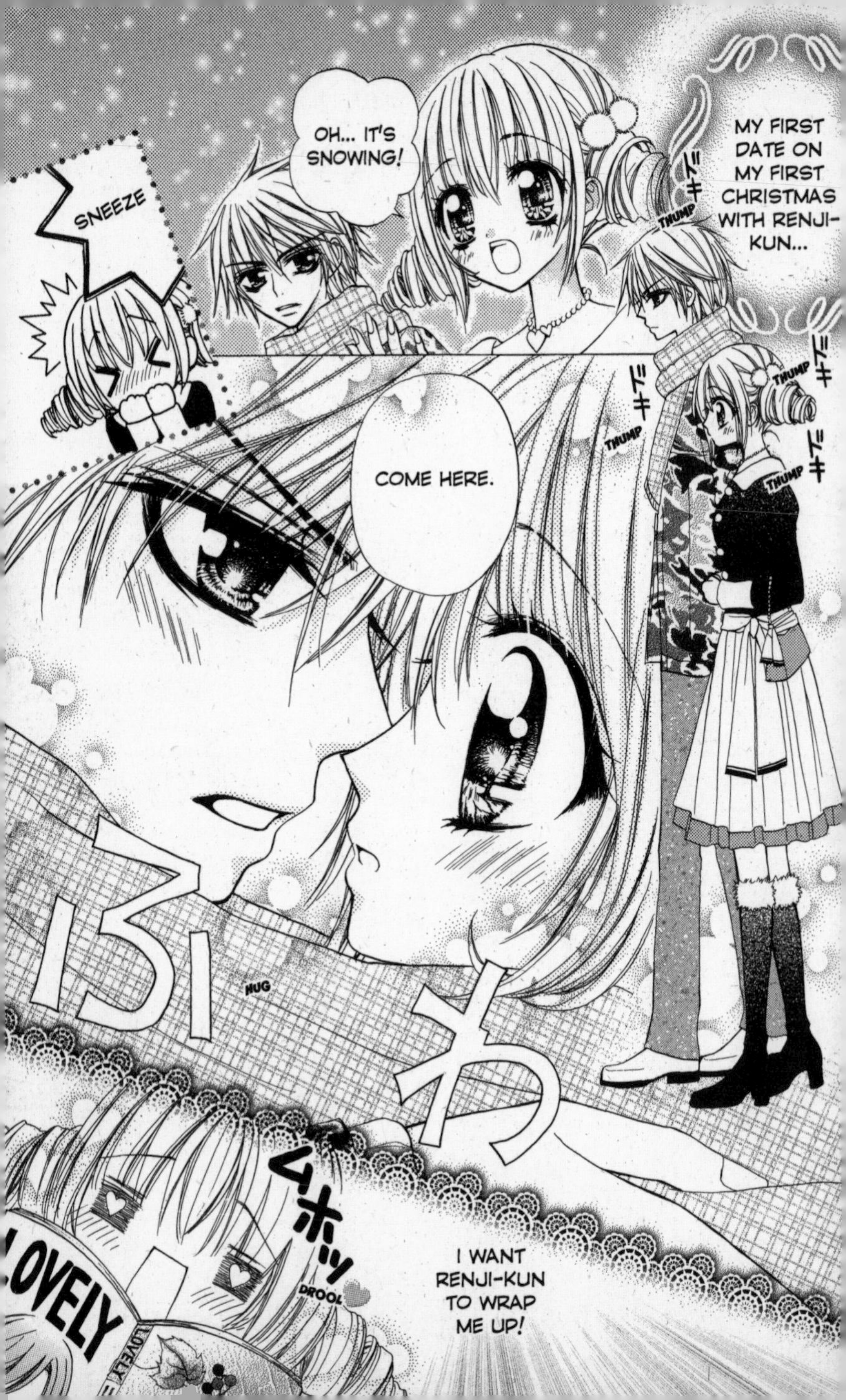
MY FIRST DATE ON MY FIRST CHRISTMAS WITH RENJI-KUN...
ドキ
THUMP
OH... IT'S SNOWING!
SNEEZE
ドキ
THUMP
ドキ
THUMP
ドキ
THUMP
COME HERE.
ふわ
HUG
I WANT RENJI-KUN TO WRAP ME UP!
ホッ
DROOL
LOVELY
LOVELY

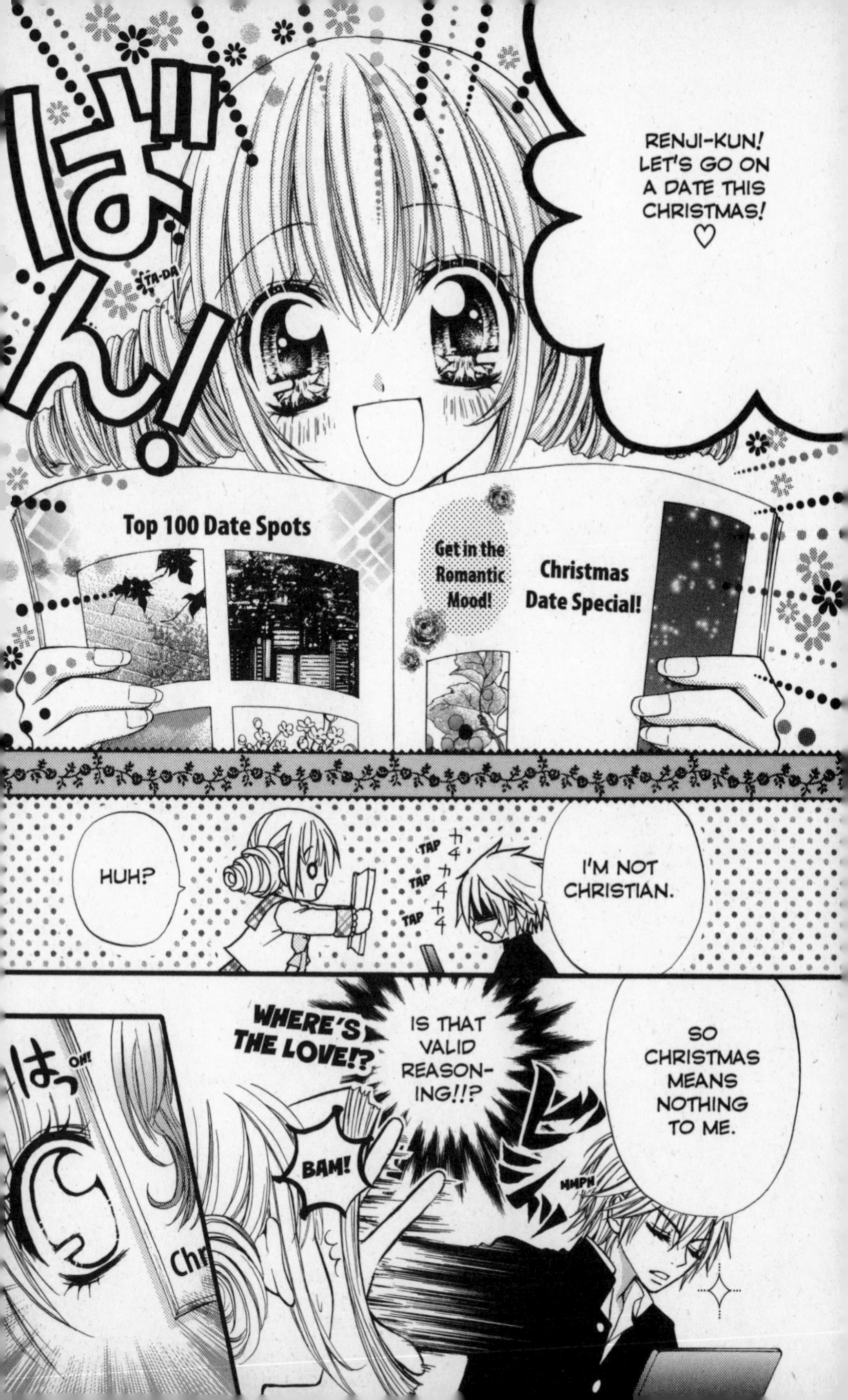
RENJI-KUN! LET'S GO ON A DATE THIS CHRISTMAS! ♡
Christmas Date Special!
Get in the Romantic Mood!
Top 100 Date Spots
ぱん!
TA-DA
I'M NOT CHRISTIAN.
TAP
TAP
TAP
HUH?
SO CHRISTMAS MEANS NOTHING TO ME.
HMPN
IS THAT VALID REASON-ING!!?
WHERE'S THE LOVE!?
BAM!
はっ
OH!
Chr

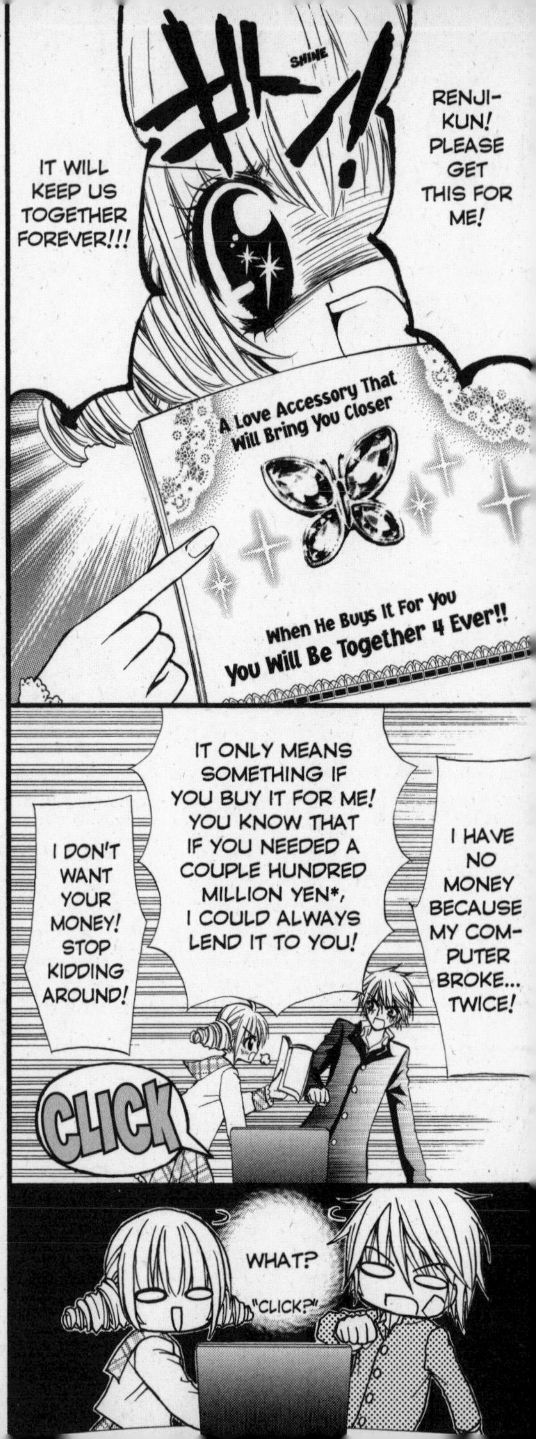
SHINE
RENJI-KUN! PLEASE GET THIS FOR ME!
IT WILL KEEP US TOGETHER FOREVER!!!
A Love Accessory That Will Bring You Closer
When He Buys It For You
You Will Be Together 4 Ever!!
I HAVE NO MONEY BECAUSE MY COMPUTER BROKE... TWICE!
IT ONLY MEANS SOMETHING IF YOU BUY IT FOR ME! YOU KNOW THAT IF YOU NEEDED A COUPLE HUNDRED MILLION YEN*, I COULD ALWAYS LEND IT TO YOU!
I DON'T WANT YOUR MONEY! STOP KIDDING AROUND!
CLICK
WHAT?
"CLICK?"

*A COUPLE MILLION DOLLARS.

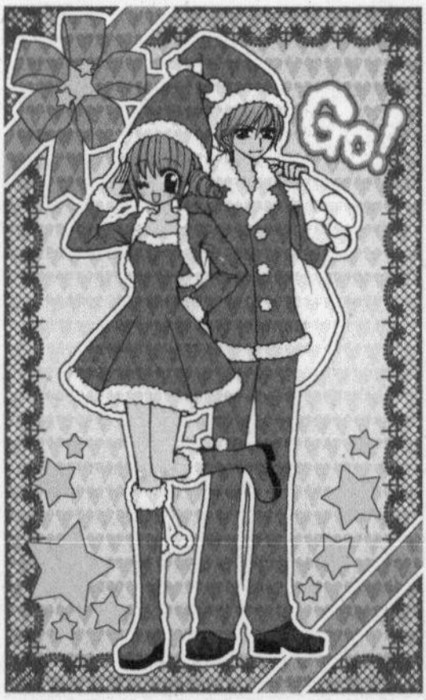
Go!

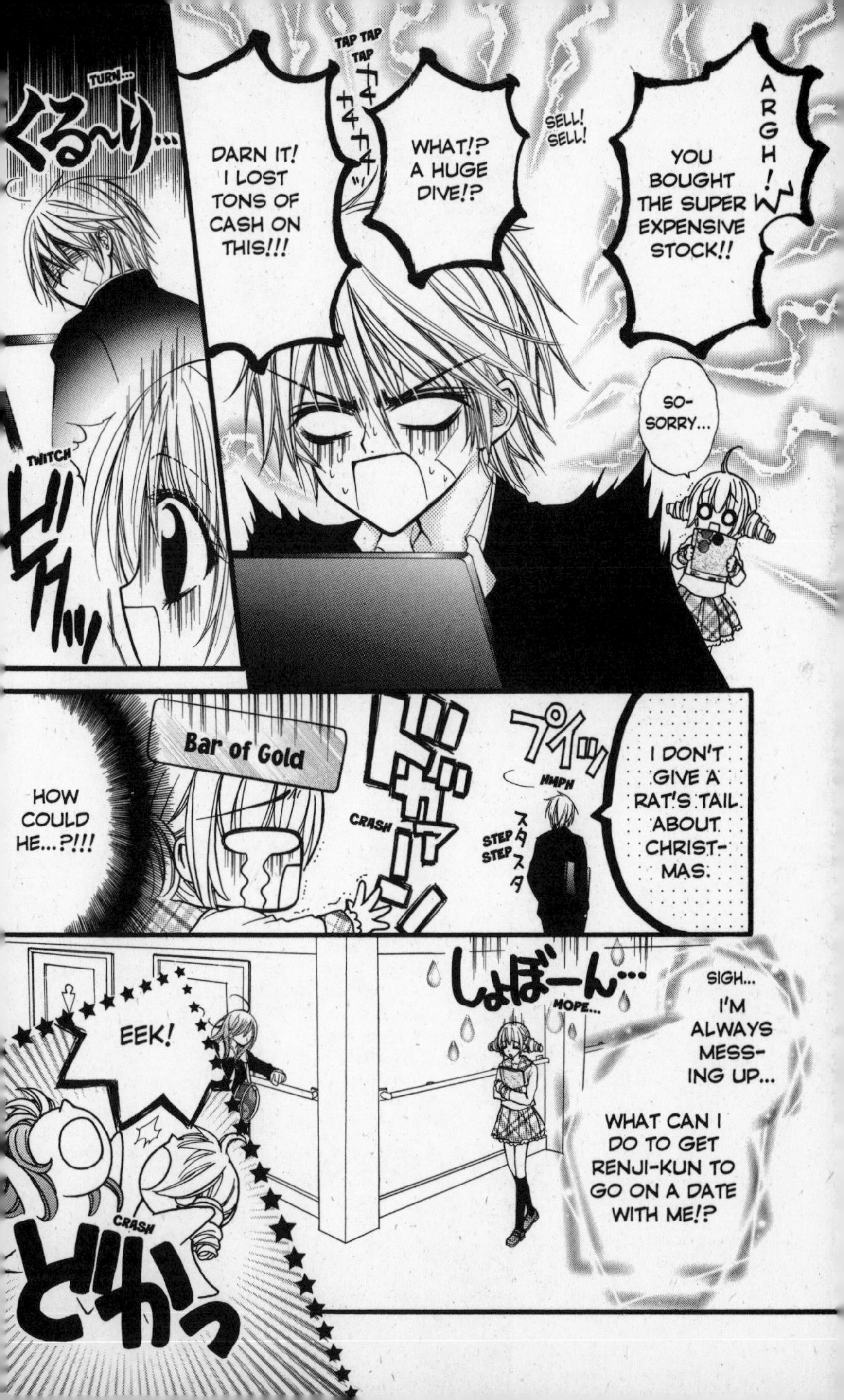
ARGH!
YOU BOUGHT THE SUPER EXPENSIVE STOCK!!
SELL! SELL!
WHAT!? A HUGE DIVE!?
TAP TAP TAP
DARN IT! I LOST TONS OF CASH ON THIS!!!
SO-SORRY...
くる〜り…
TURN...
TWITCH
I DON'T GIVE A RAT'S TAIL ABOUT CHRISTMAS.
プイッ
HMPH
スタスタ
STEP STEP
CRASH
Bar of Gold
HOW COULD HE...?!!!
SIGH...
I'M ALWAYS MESSING UP...
WHAT CAN I DO TO GET RENJI-KUN TO GO ON A DATE WITH ME!?
しょぼーん…
MOPE...
EEK!
CRASH
どわっ

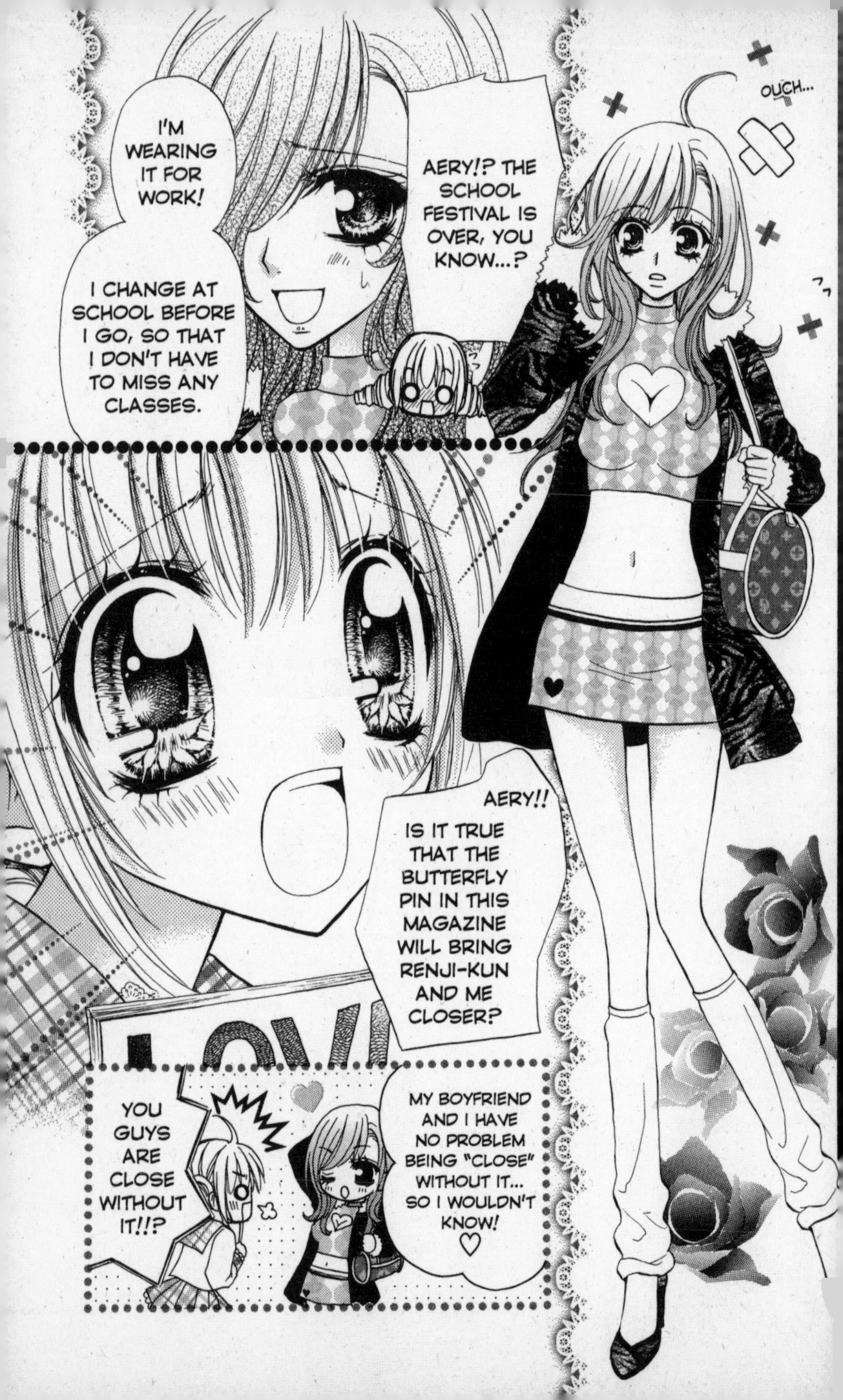
OUCH...
AERY!? THE SCHOOL FESTIVAL IS OVER, YOU KNOW...?
I'M WEARING IT FOR WORK!
I CHANGE AT SCHOOL BEFORE I GO, SO THAT I DON'T HAVE TO MISS ANY CLASSES.
AERY!!
IS IT TRUE THAT THE BUTTERFLY PIN IN THIS MAGAZINE WILL BRING RENJI-KUN AND ME CLOSER?
LOVE
MY BOYFRIEND AND I HAVE NO PROBLEM BEING "CLOSE" WITHOUT IT... SO I WOULDN'T KNOW! ♡
YOU GUYS ARE CLOSE WITHOUT IT!!?

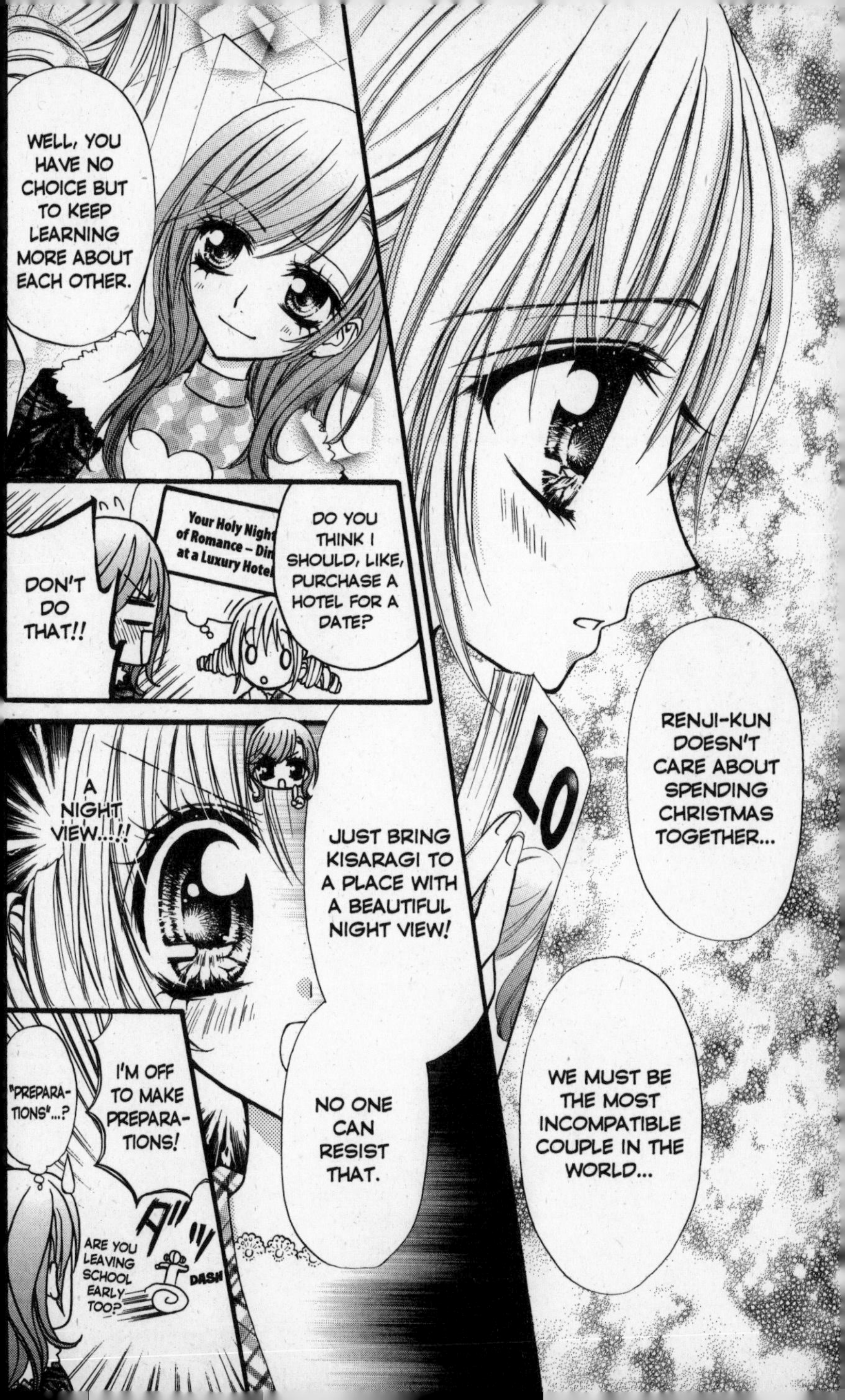
RENJI-KUN DOESN'T CARE ABOUT SPENDING CHRISTMAS TOGETHER...
WE MUST BE THE MOST INCOMPATIBLE COUPLE IN THE WORLD...
WELL, YOU HAVE NO CHOICE BUT TO KEEP LEARNING MORE ABOUT EACH OTHER.
DO YOU THINK I SHOULD, LIKE, PURCHASE A HOTEL FOR A DATE?
Your Holy Night of Romance – Din at a Luxury Hotel
DON'T DO THAT!!
JUST BRING KISARAGI TO A PLACE WITH A BEAUTIFUL NIGHT VIEW!
A NIGHT VIEW...!!
NO ONE CAN RESIST THAT.
I'M OFF TO MAKE PREPARA-TIONS!
"PREPARA-TIONS"...?
DASH
ARE YOU LEAVING SCHOOL EARLY TOO?

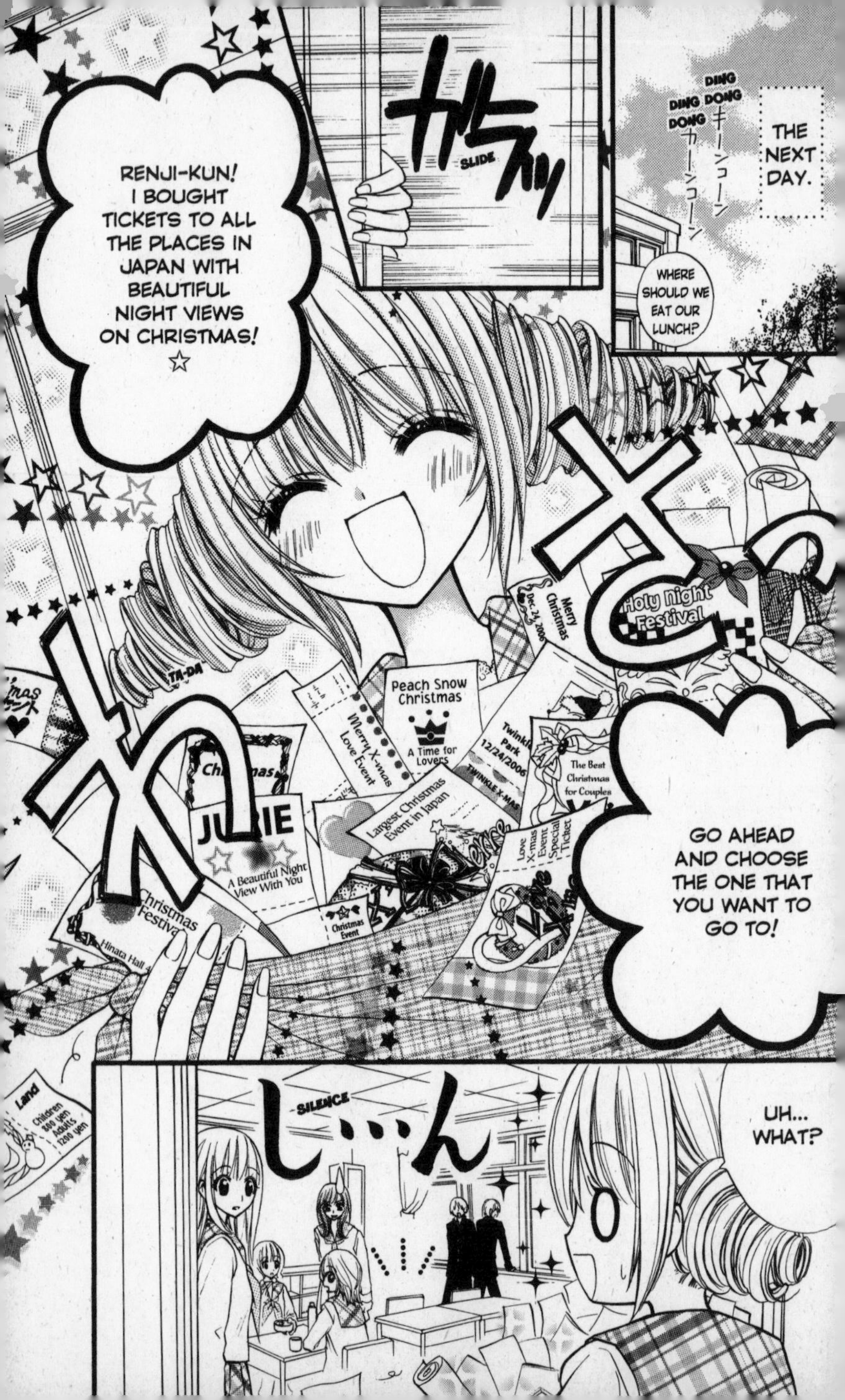
THE NEXT DAY.
DING DONG DING DONG
キーンコーン カーンコーン
WHERE SHOULD WE EAT OUR LUNCH?
SLIDE
ガラッ
RENJI-KUN! I BOUGHT TICKETS TO ALL THE PLACES IN JAPAN WITH BEAUTIFUL NIGHT VIEWS ON CHRISTMAS! ☆
GO AHEAD AND CHOOSE THE ONE THAT YOU WANT TO GO TO!
TA-DA
Merry Christmas Dec. 24, 2006
Holy night Festival
Peach Snow Christmas
A Time for Lovers
Merry X-mas Love Event
Twinkle Park 12/24/2006
TWINKLE X-MAS
The Best Christmas for Couples
Largest Christmas Event in Japan
Love X-mas Event Special Ticket
A Beautiful Night View With You
Christmas Event
Christmas Festival
Hinata Hall
Children 800 yen Adults 1200 yen
UH... WHAT?
SILENCE
し…ん

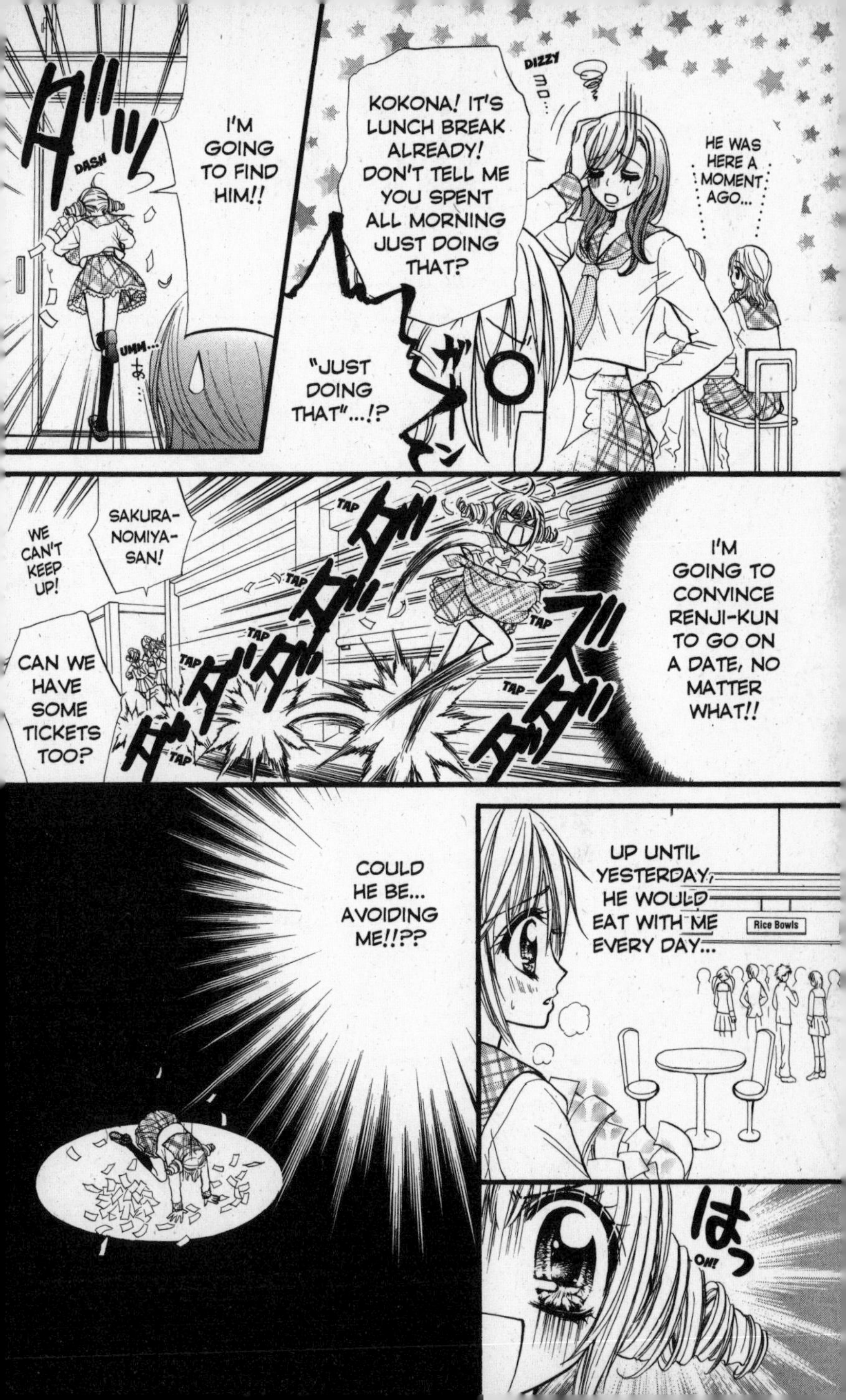

DIZZY
ヨロ…
KOKONA! IT'S LUNCH BREAK ALREADY! DON'T TELL ME YOU SPENT ALL MORNING JUST DOING THAT?
HE WAS HERE A MOMENT AGO...
"JUST DOING THAT"...!?
DASH
I'M GOING TO FIND HIM!!
UMM...
あ…
I'M GOING TO CONVINCE RENJI-KUN TO GO ON A DATE, NO MATTER WHAT!!
TAP
TAP
TAP
TAP
TAP
TAP
SAKURA-NOMIYA-SAN!
WE CAN'T KEEP UP!
CAN WE HAVE SOME TICKETS TOO?
UP UNTIL YESTERDAY, HE WOULD EAT WITH ME EVERY DAY...
Rice Bowls
はっ
OH!
COULD HE BE... AVOIDING ME!!??

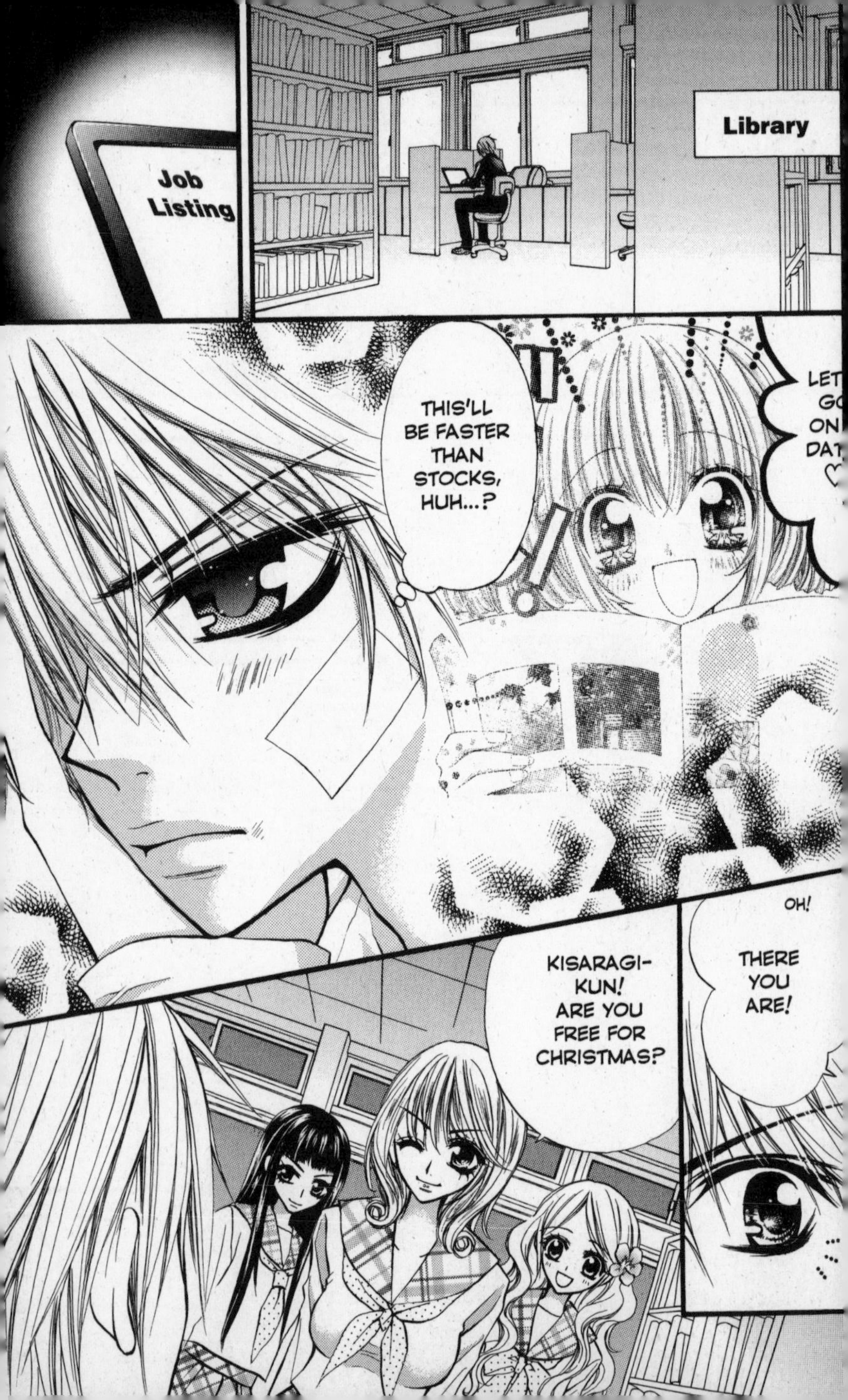

Library
Job Listing
LET GO ON DAT ♡
THIS'LL BE FASTER THAN STOCKS, HUH...?
OH!
THERE YOU ARE!
...
KISARAGI-KUN! ARE YOU FREE FOR CHRISTMAS?

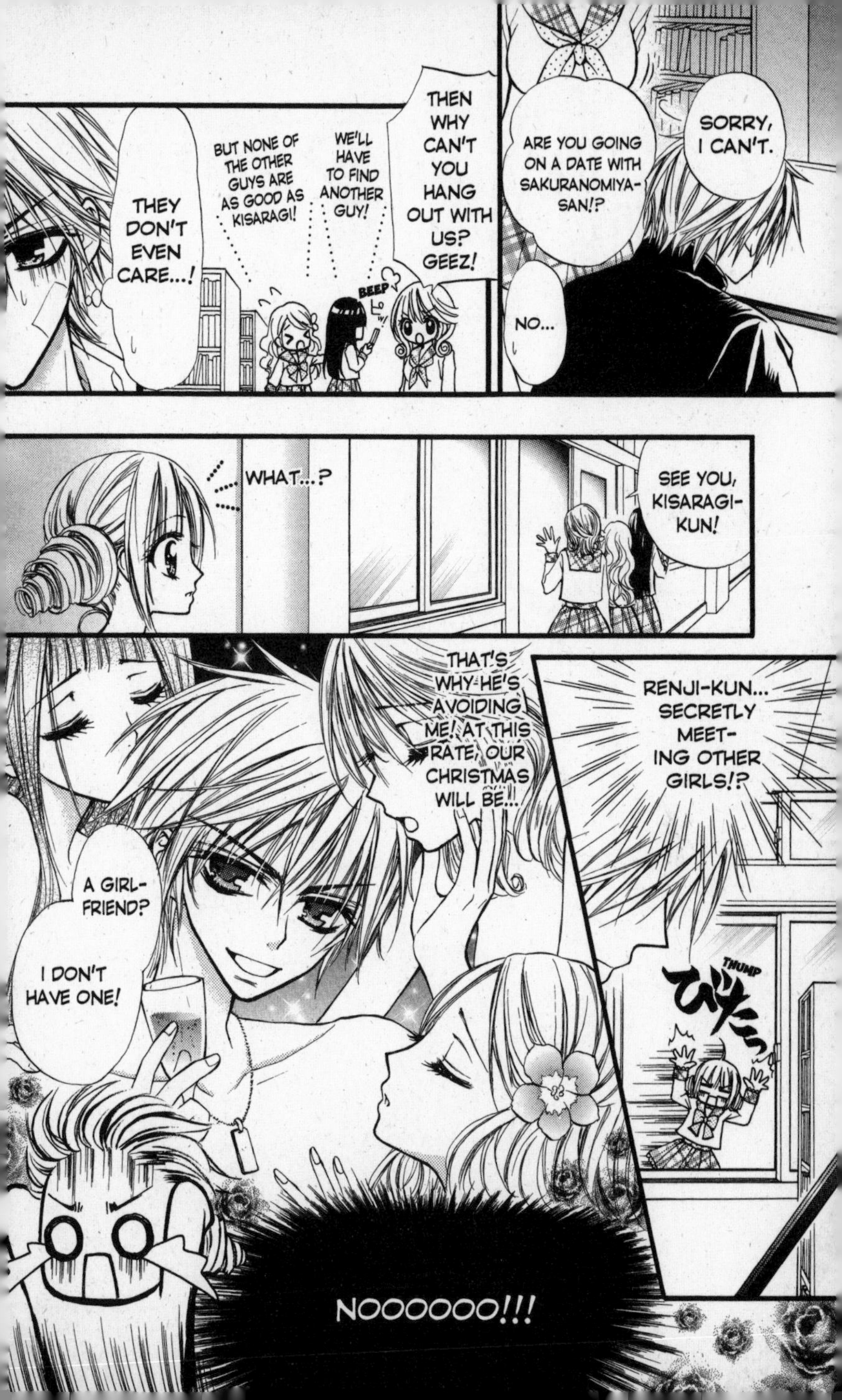
SORRY, I CAN'T.
ARE YOU GOING ON A DATE WITH SAKURANOMIYA-SAN!?
NO...
THEN WHY CAN'T YOU HANG OUT WITH US? GEEZ!
WE'LL HAVE TO FIND ANOTHER GUY!
BUT NONE OF THE OTHER GUYS ARE AS GOOD AS KISARAGI!
BEEP
THEY DON'T EVEN CARE...!
SEE YOU, KISARAGI-KUN!
WHAT...?
RENJI-KUN... SECRETLY MEET-ING OTHER GIRLS!?
THUMP
THAT'S WHY HE'S AVOIDING ME! AT THIS RATE, OUR CHRISTMAS WILL BE...
A GIRL-FRIEND?
I DON'T HAVE ONE!
NOOOOOO!!!

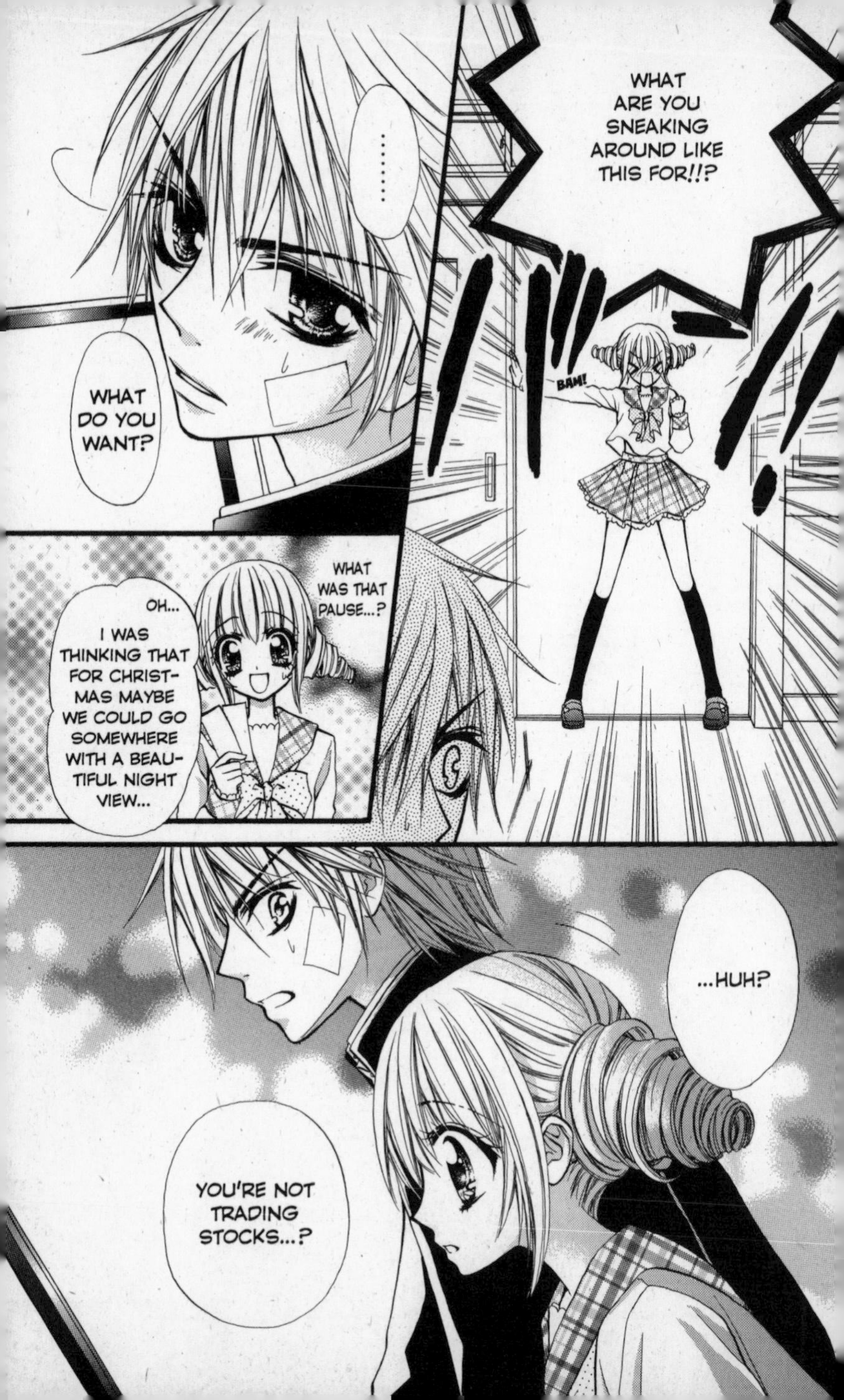
WHAT ARE YOU SNEAKING AROUND LIKE THIS FOR!!?
BAM!
......
WHAT DO YOU WANT?
WHAT WAS THAT PAUSE...?
OH... I WAS THINKING THAT FOR CHRIST-MAS MAYBE WE COULD GO SOMEWHERE WITH A BEAU-TIFUL NIGHT VIEW...
...HUH?
YOU'RE NOT TRADING STOCKS...?

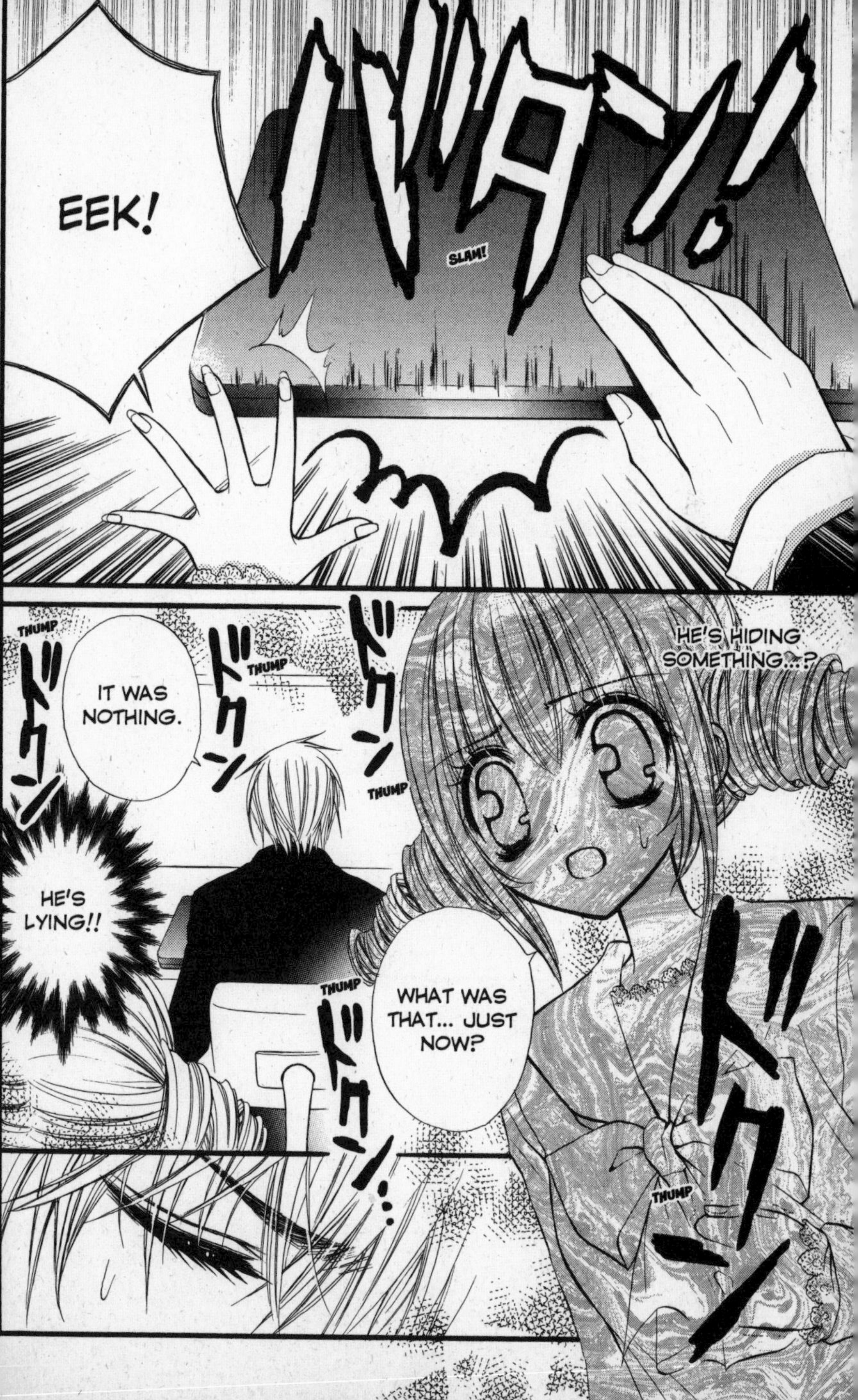
EEK!
SLAM!
HE'S HIDING SOMETHING...?
THUMP
WHAT WAS THAT... JUST NOW?
THUMP
THUMP
IT WAS NOTHING.
THUMP
THUMP
HE'S LYING!!

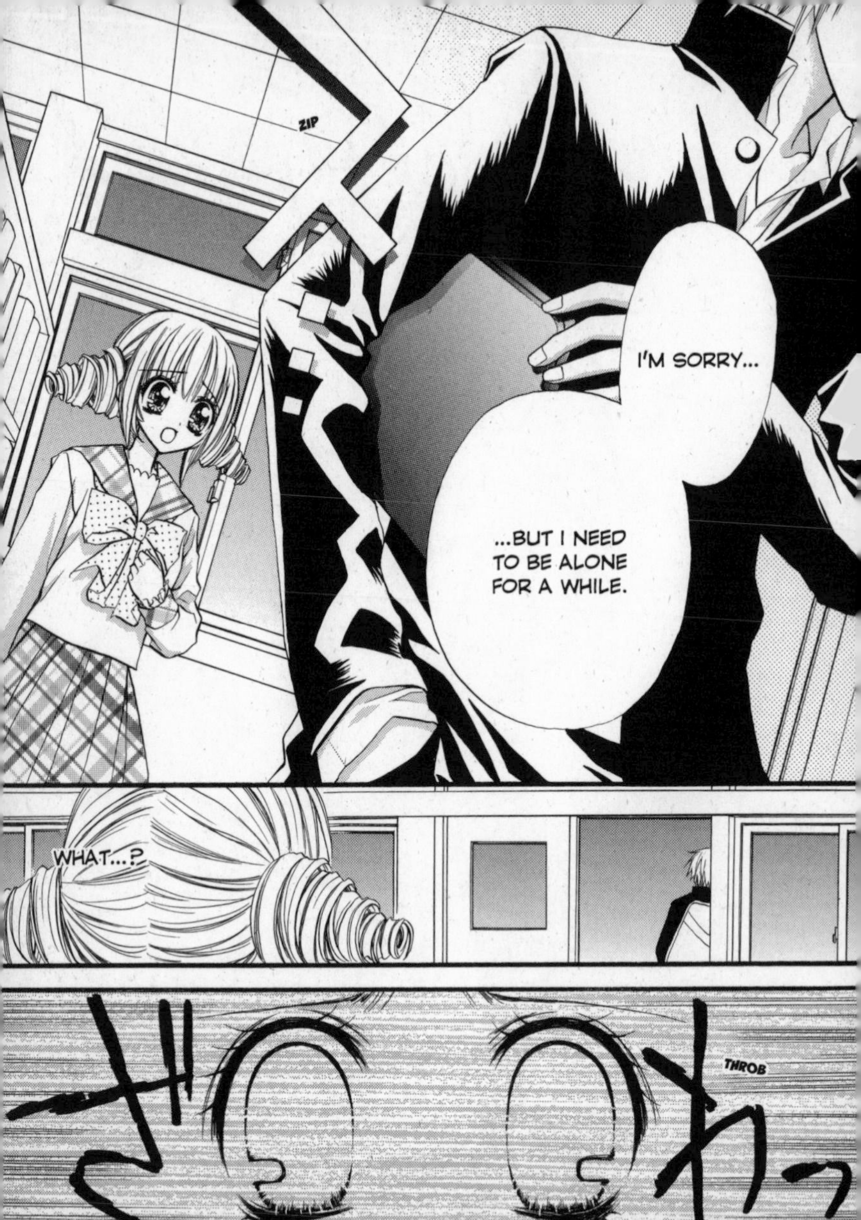
I'M SORRY...
...BUT I NEED TO BE ALONE FOR A WHILE.
ZIP
WHAT...?
THROB
ざわっ

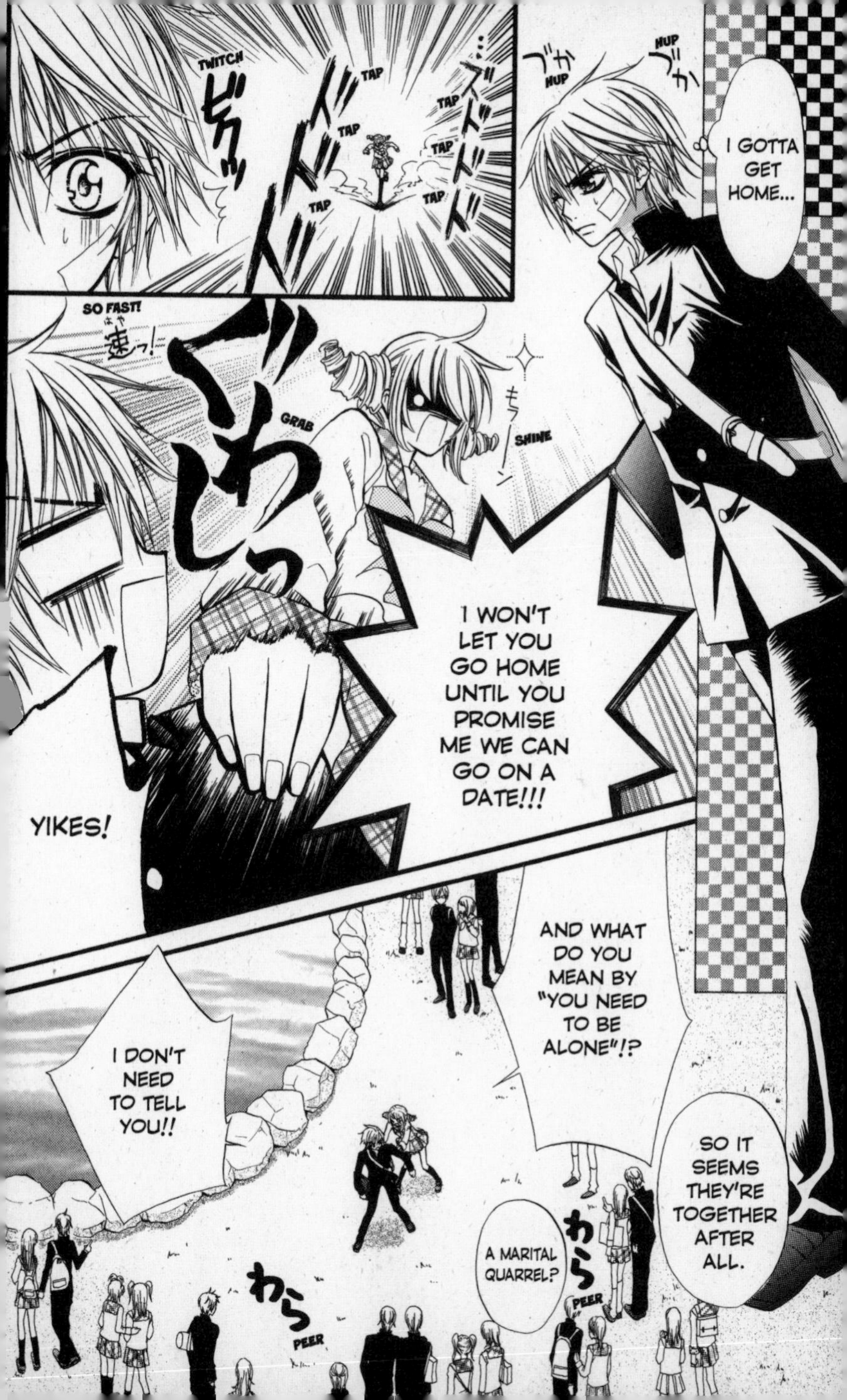
HUP
HUP
I GOTTA GET HOME...
TWITCH
TAP
TAP
TAP
TAP
TAP
TAP
SO FAST!
速っ!
GRAB
SHINE
I WON'T LET YOU GO HOME UNTIL YOU PROMISE ME WE CAN GO ON A DATE!!!
YIKES!
AND WHAT DO YOU MEAN BY "YOU NEED TO BE ALONE"!?
I DON'T NEED TO TELL YOU!!
SO IT SEEMS THEY'RE TOGETHER AFTER ALL.
わら
PEER
A MARITAL QUARREL?
わら
PEER

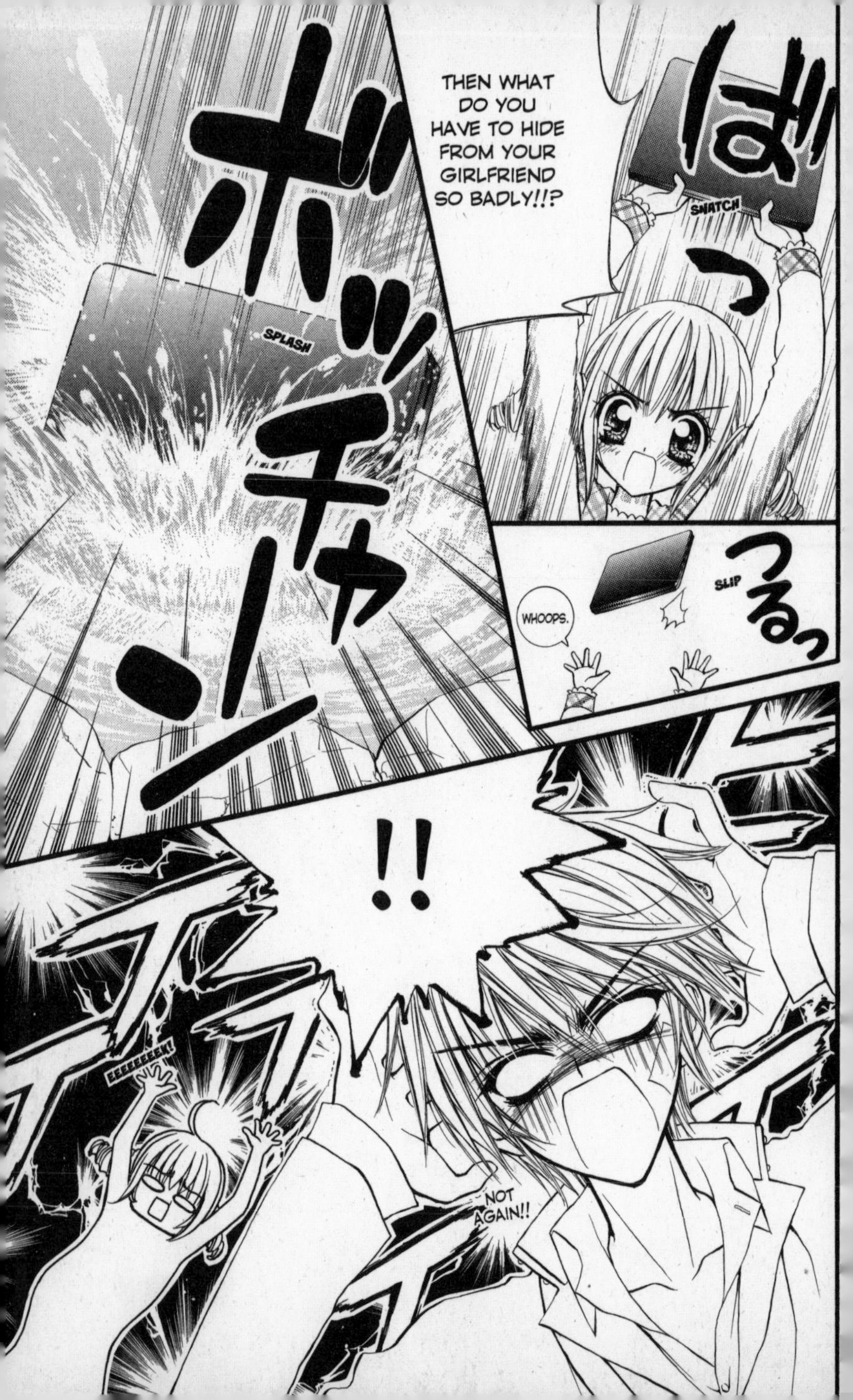

ばっ
SNATCH
THEN WHAT DO YOU HAVE TO HIDE FROM YOUR GIRLFRIEND SO BADLY!!?
つるっ
SLIP
WHOOPS.
ボッチャーン
SPLASH
!!
NOT AGAIN!!
EEEEEEEEK!

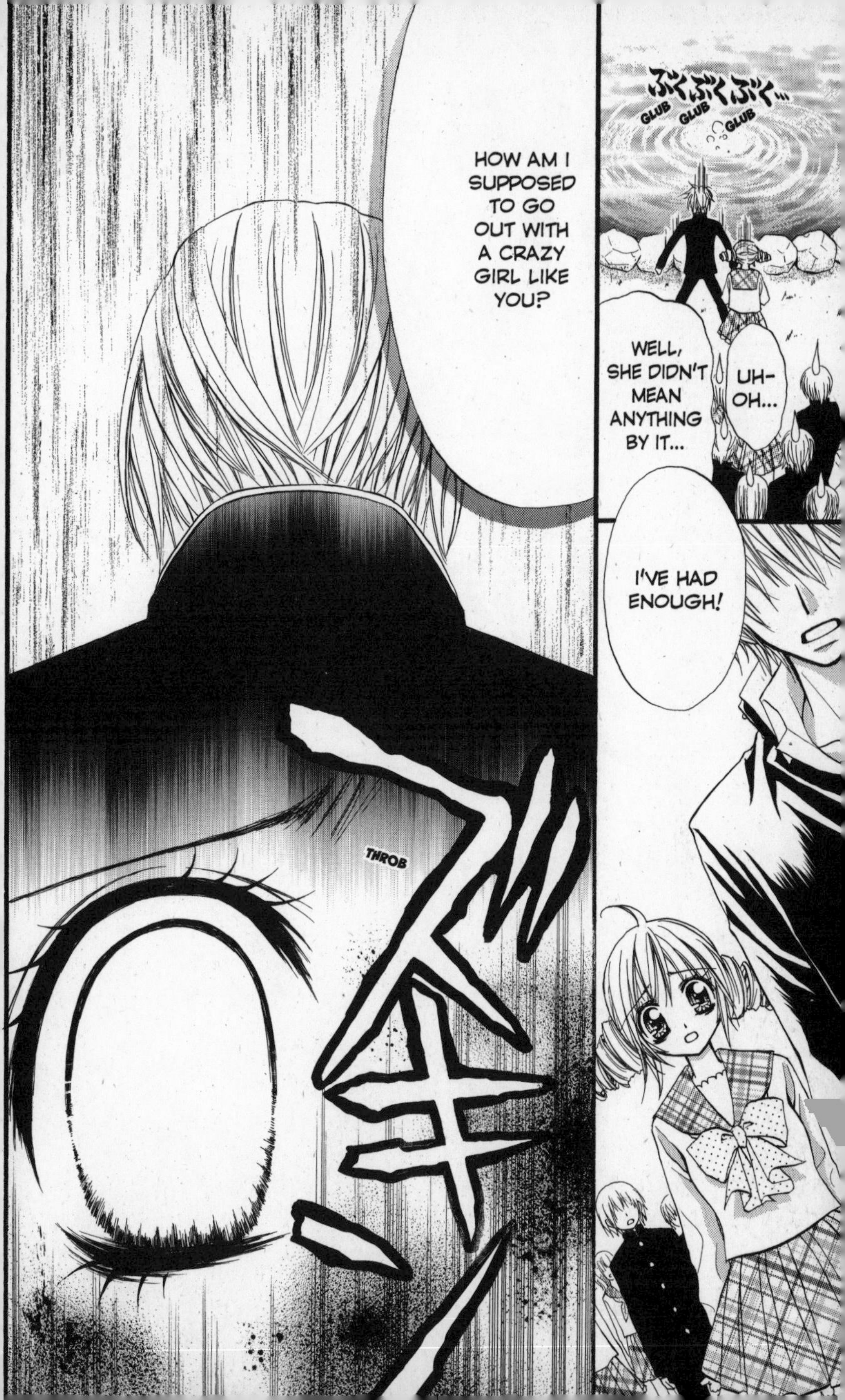
ぶくぶくぶく…
GLUB GLUB GLUB
UH-OH...
WELL, SHE DIDN'T MEAN ANYTHING BY IT...
I'VE HAD ENOUGH!
HOW AM I SUPPOSED TO GO OUT WITH A CRAZY GIRL LIKE YOU?
ズキッ
THROB

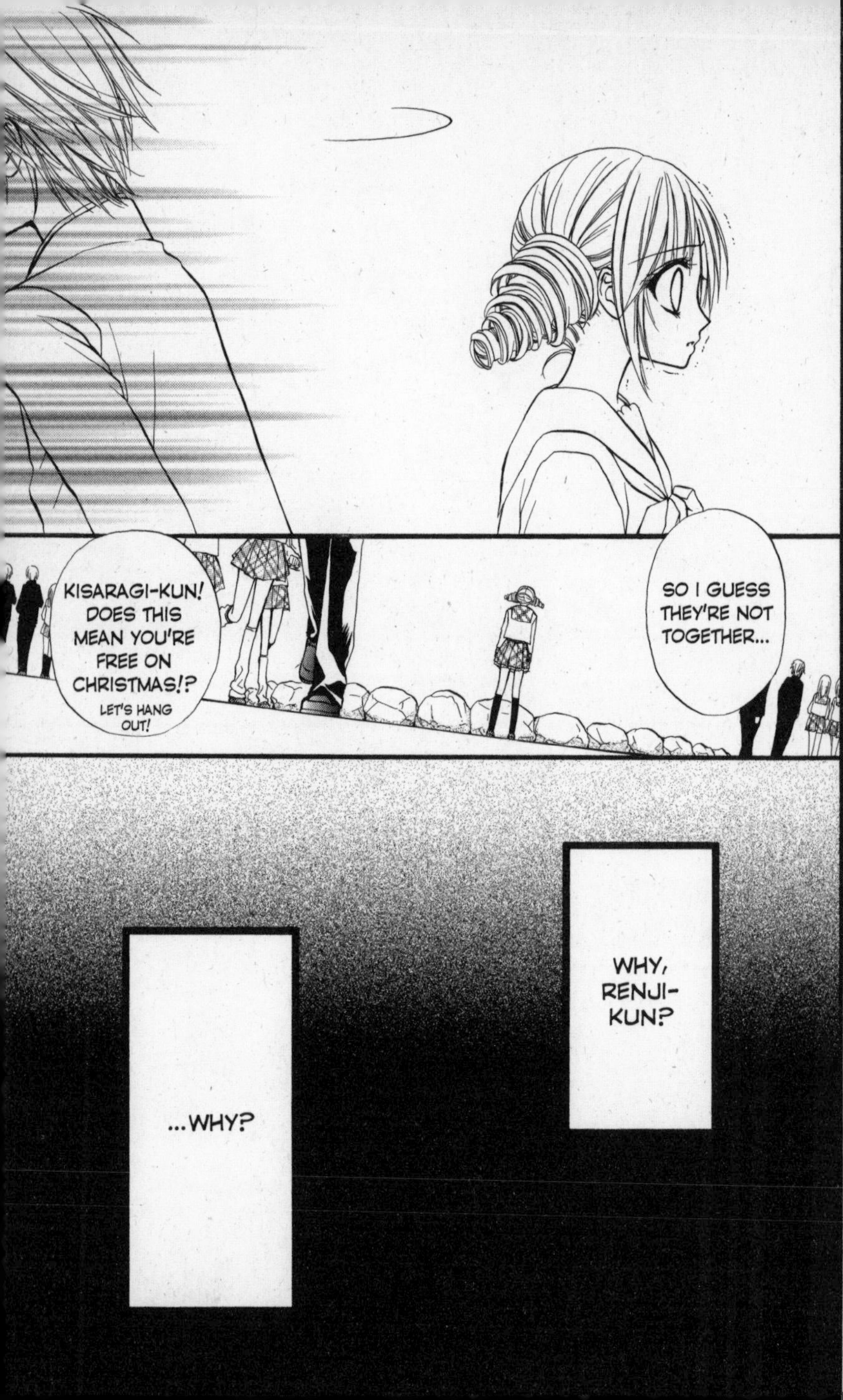
SO I GUESS THEY'RE NOT TOGETHER...
KISARAGI-KUN! DOES THIS MEAN YOU'RE FREE ON CHRISTMAS!?
LET'S HANG OUT!
WHY, RENJI-KUN?
...WHY?

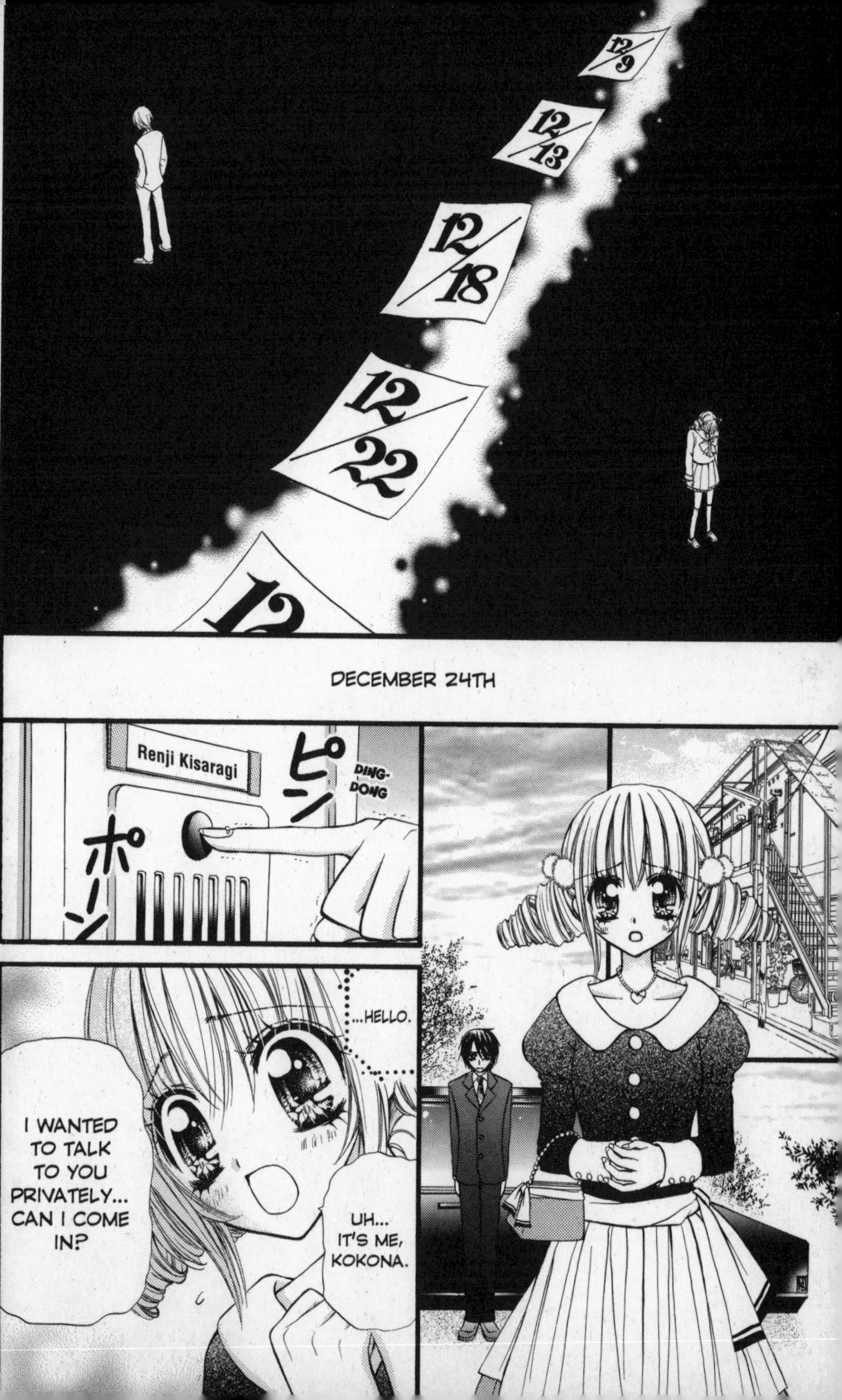
12/9
12/13
12/18
12/22
12
DECEMBER 24TH
Renji Kisaragi
ピンポーン
DING-DONG
...HELLO.
UH... IT'S ME, KOKONA.
I WANTED TO TALK TO YOU PRIVATELY... CAN I COME IN?

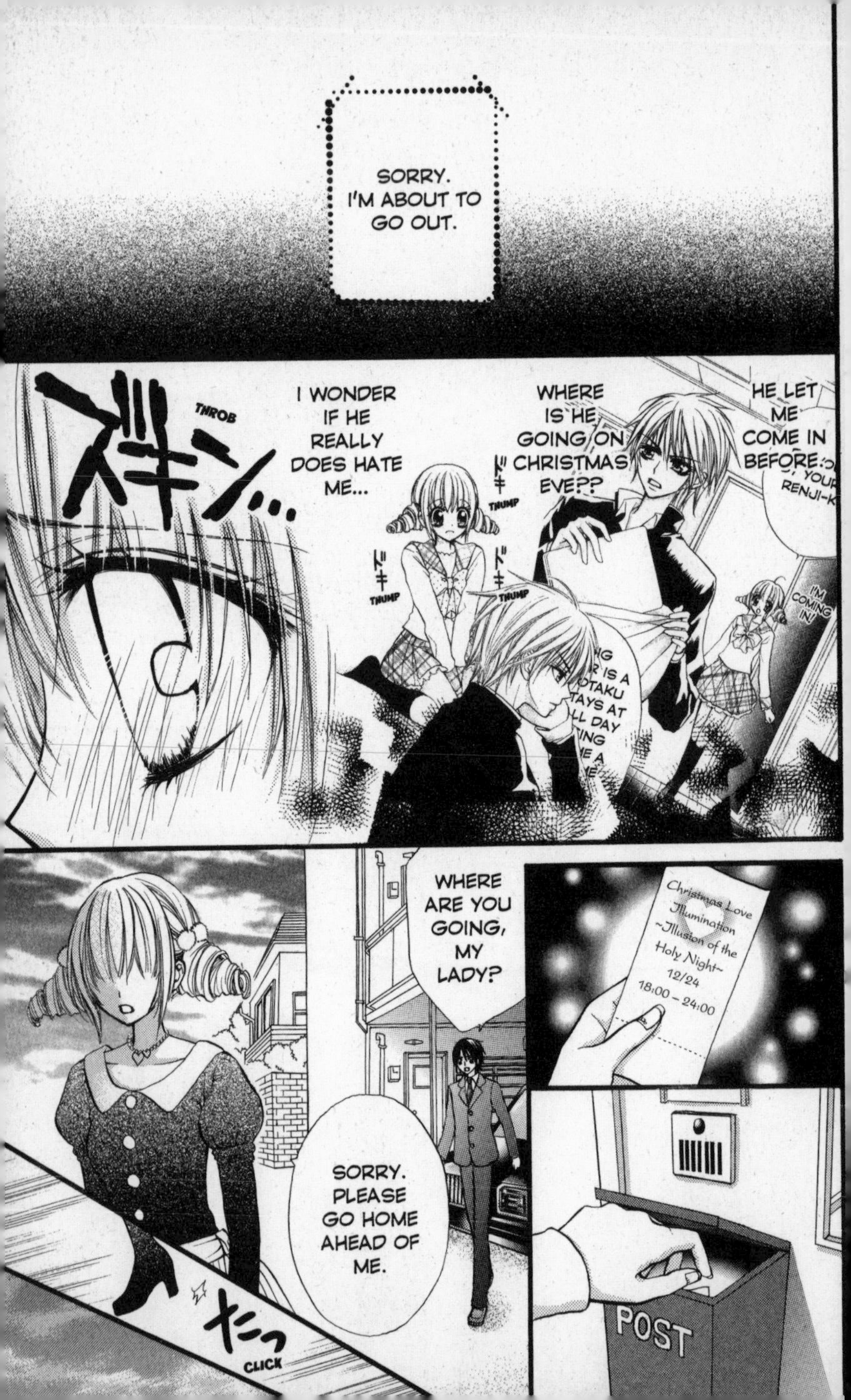
SORRY. I'M ABOUT TO GO OUT.
HE LET ME COME IN BEFORE.
I'M COMING IN!
WHERE IS HE GOING ON CHRISTMAS EVE??
THUMP
THUMP
THUMP
I WONDER IF HE REALLY DOES HATE ME...
THROB
Christmas Love Illumination ~Illusion of the Holy Night~ 12/24 18:00 – 24:00
POST
WHERE ARE YOU GOING, MY LADY?
SORRY. PLEASE GO HOME AHEAD OF ME.
CLICK

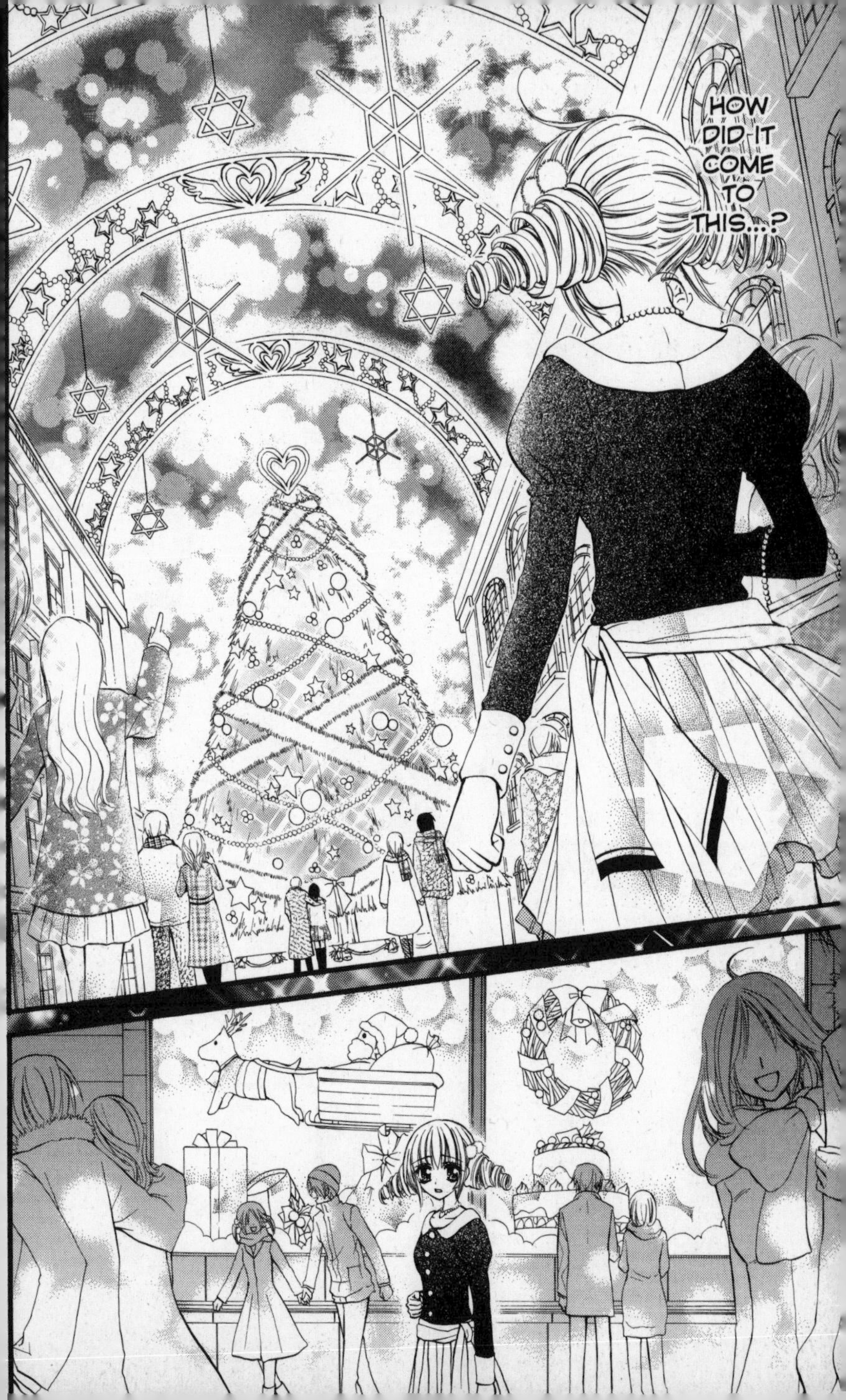
HOW DID IT COME TO THIS...?

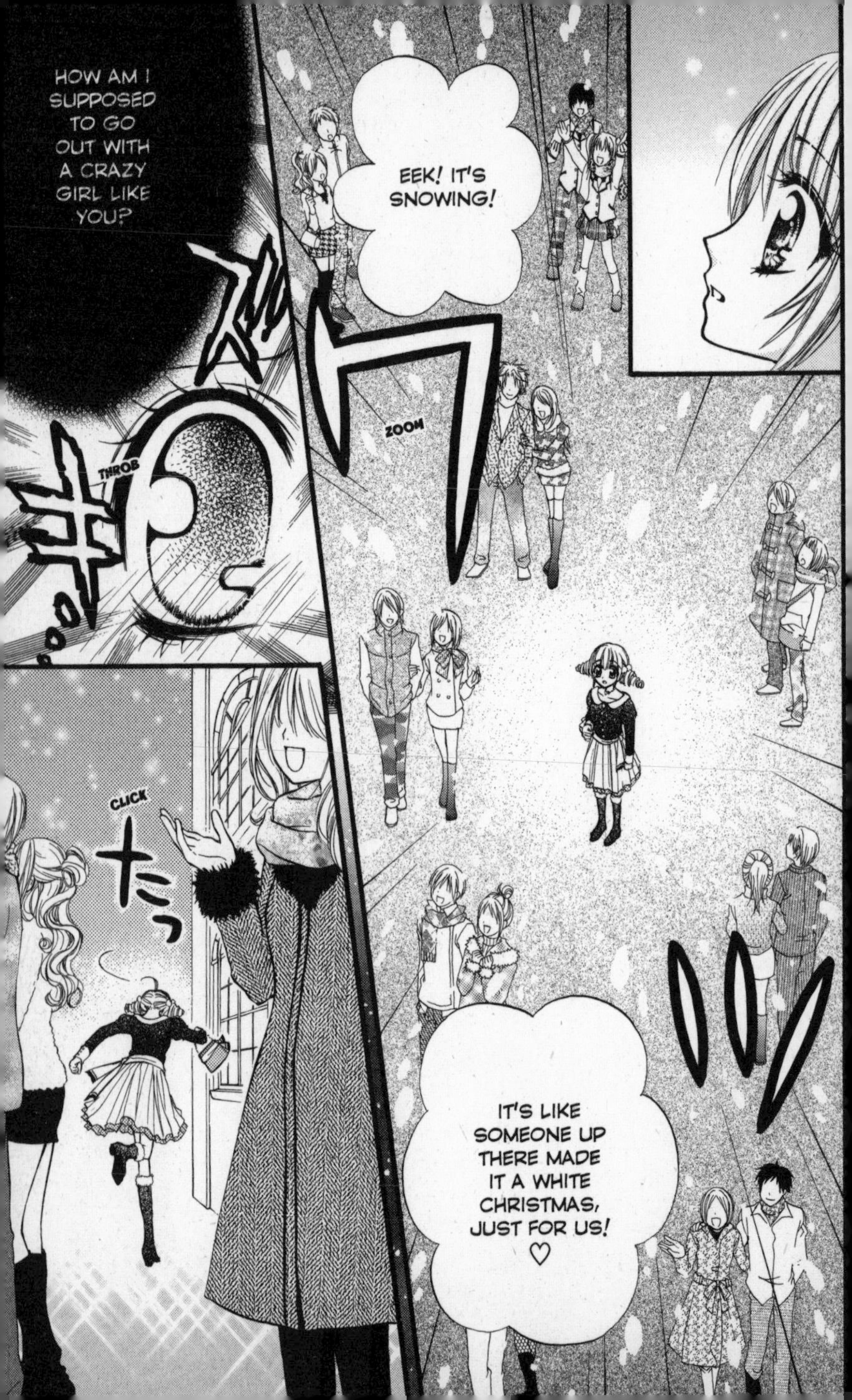
EEK! IT'S SNOWING!
ZOOM
IT'S LIKE SOMEONE UP THERE MADE IT A WHITE CHRISTMAS, JUST FOR US! ♡
HOW AM I SUPPOSED TO GO OUT WITH A CRAZY GIRL LIKE YOU?
THROB
CLICK

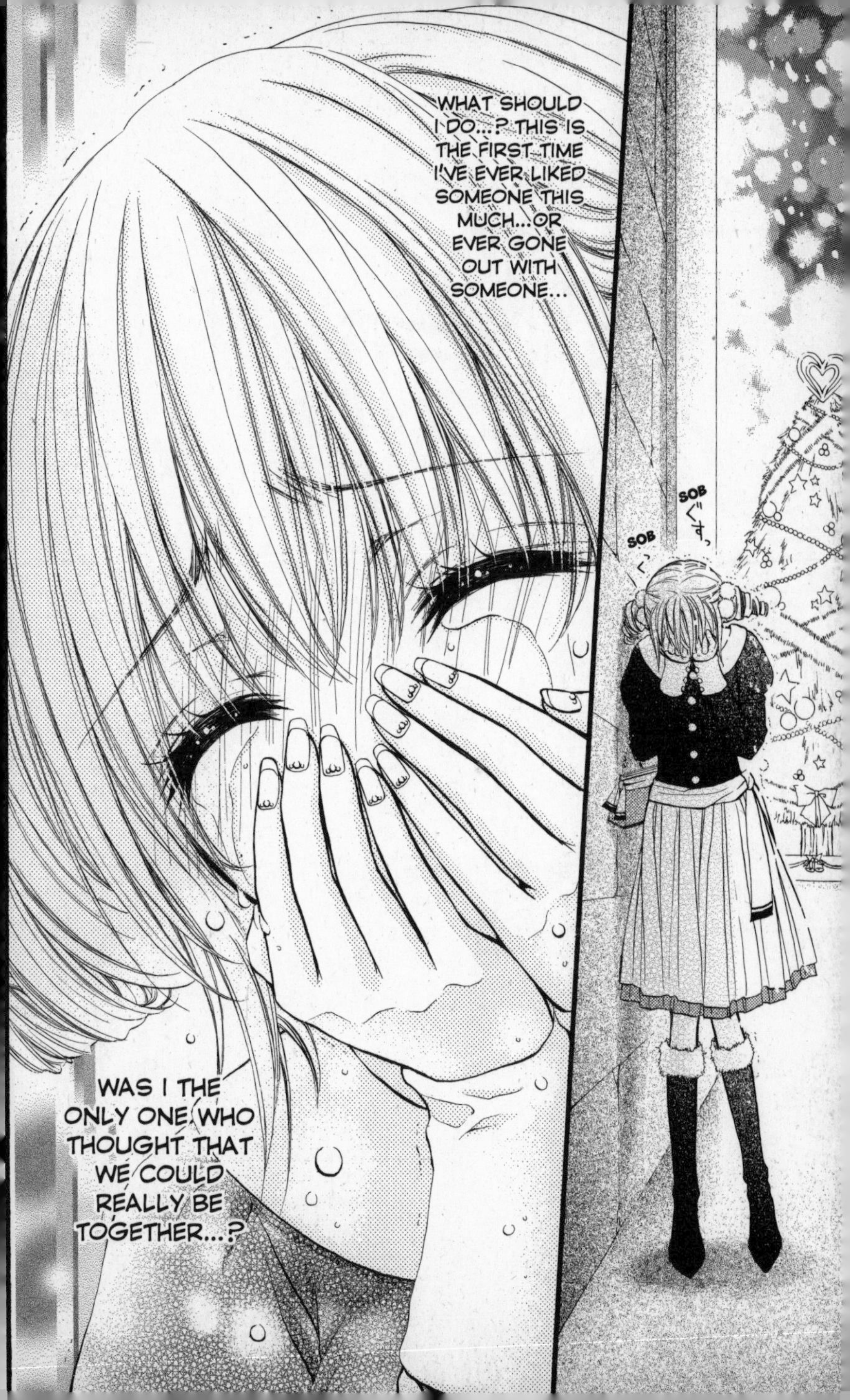
SOB
ぐすっ
SOB
ぐ
WHAT SHOULD I DO...? THIS IS THE FIRST TIME I'VE EVER LIKED SOMEONE THIS MUCH...OR EVER GONE OUT WITH SOMEONE...
WAS I THE ONLY ONE WHO THOUGHT THAT WE COULD REALLY BE TOGETHER...?

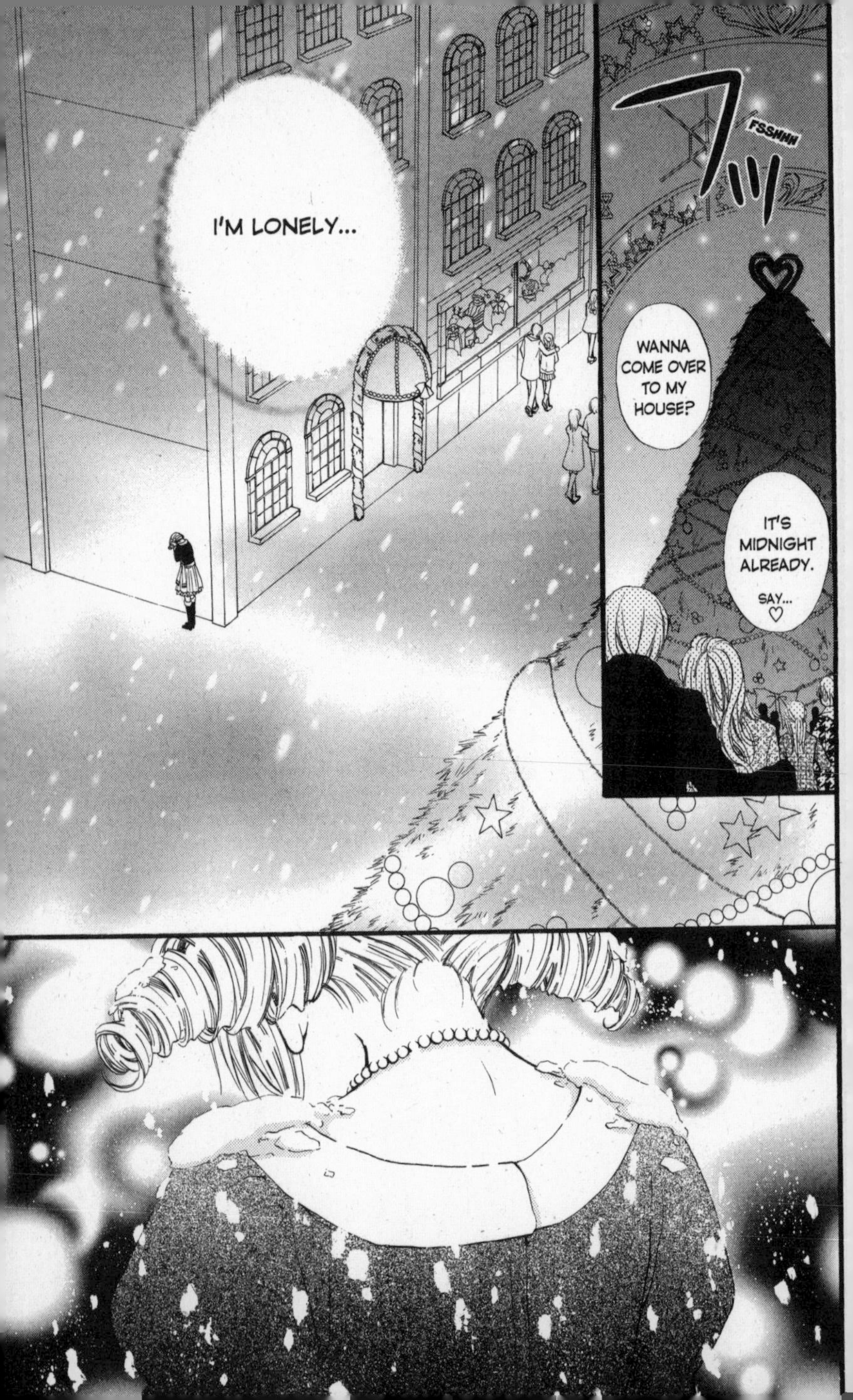
フッ
FSSHHH
WANNA COME OVER TO MY HOUSE?
IT'S MIDNIGHT ALREADY.
SAY... ♡
I'M LONELY...

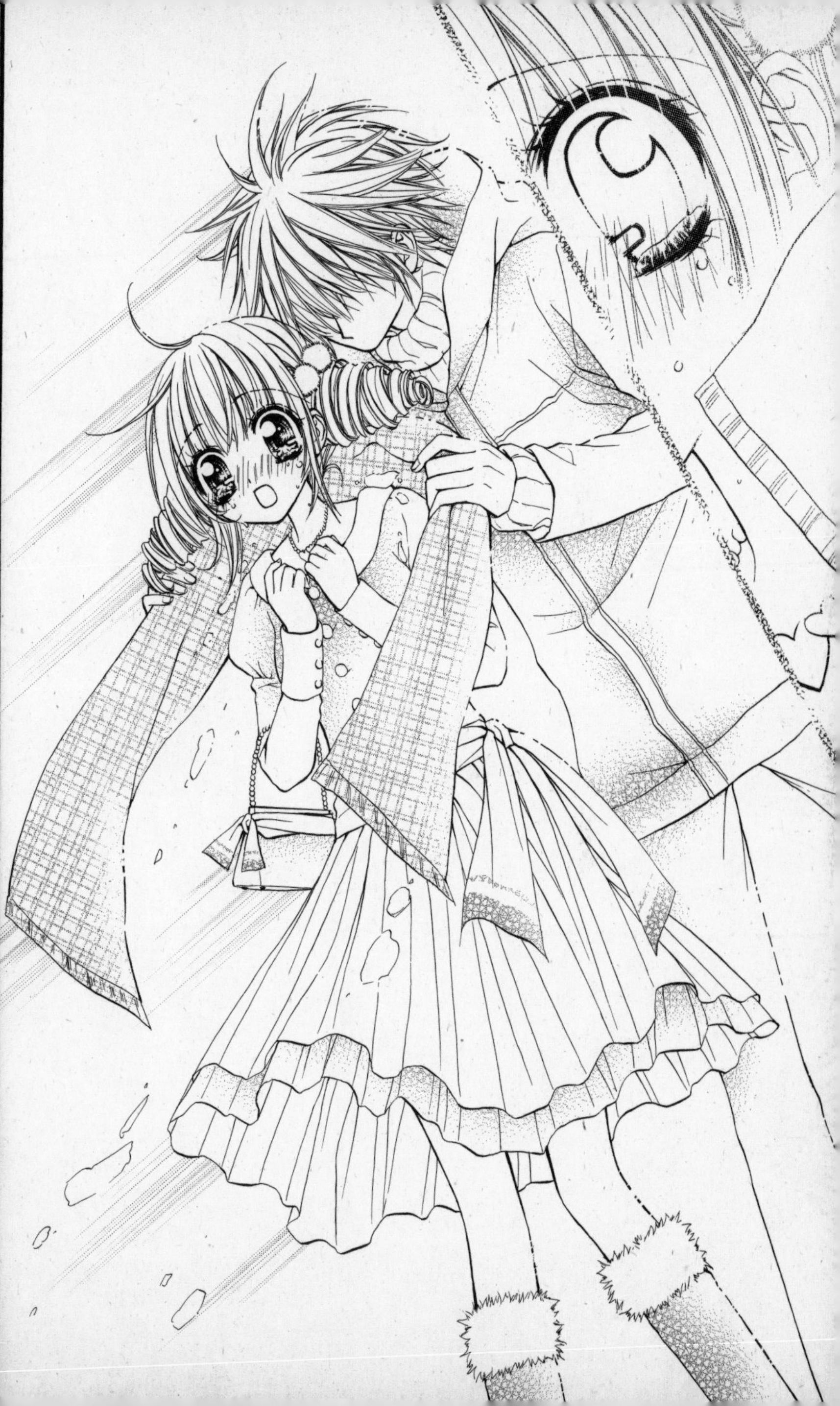

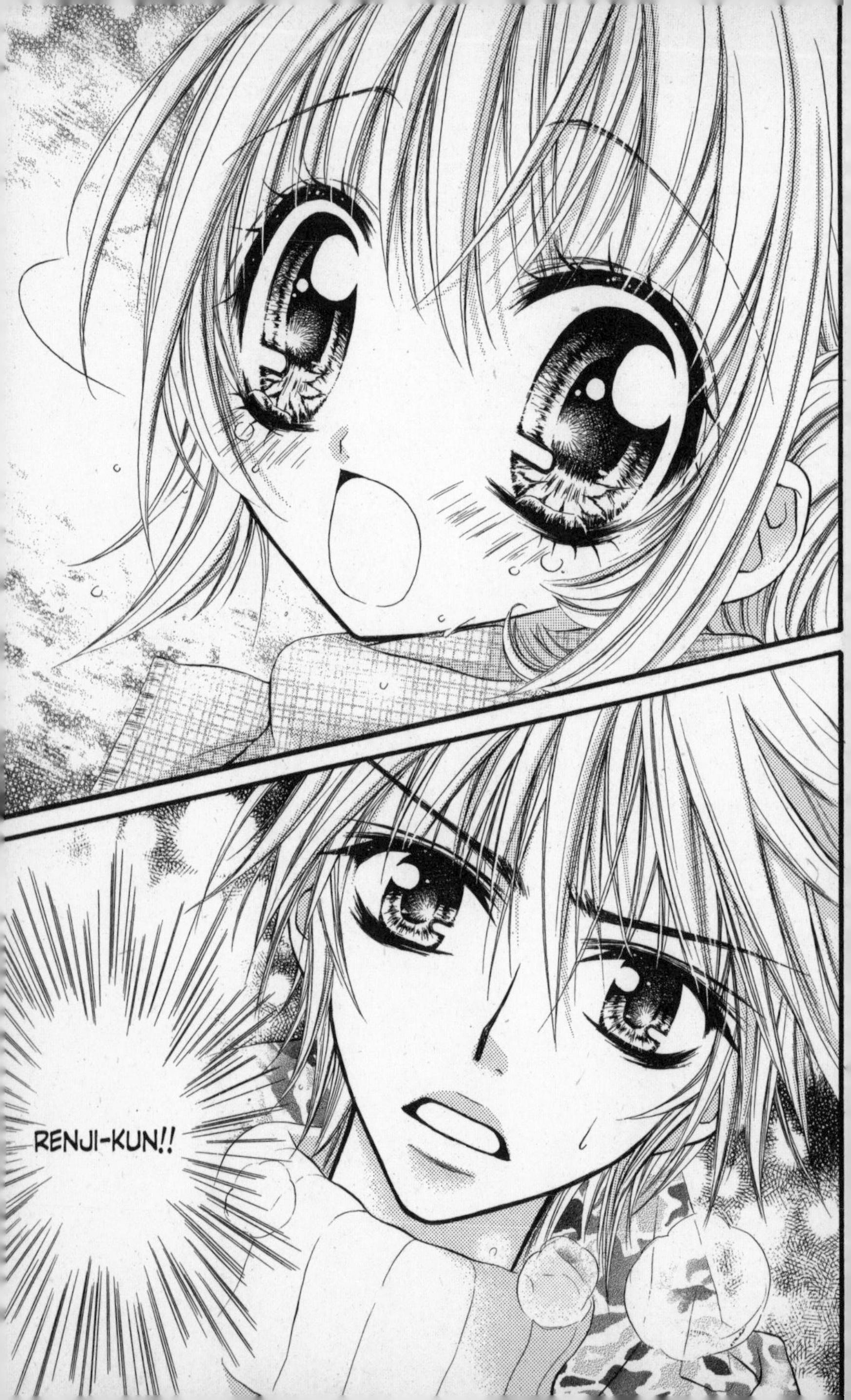
RENJI-KUN!!

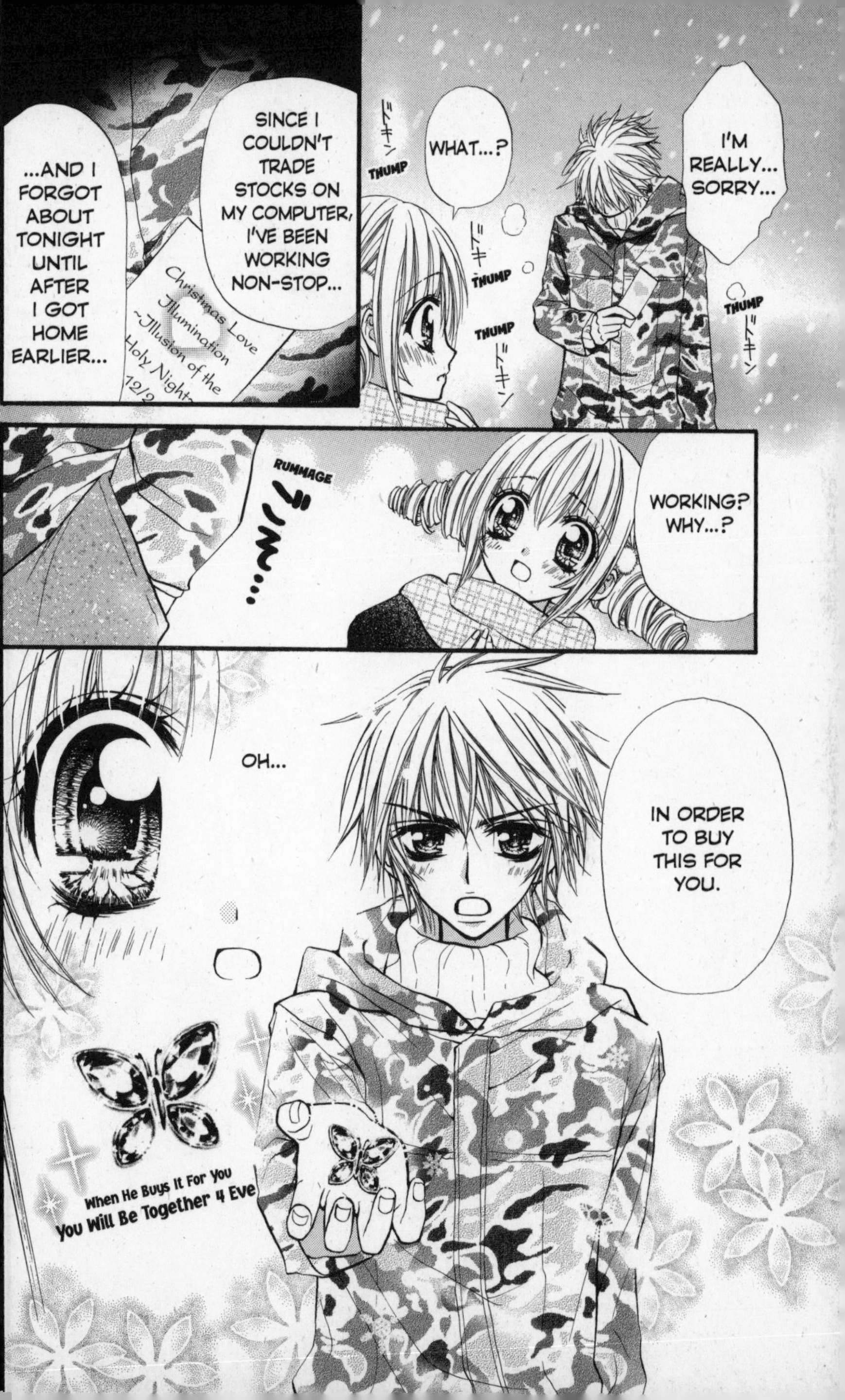
I'M REALLY... SORRY...
THUMP
WHAT...?
THUMP
THUMP
THUMP
SINCE I COULDN'T TRADE STOCKS ON MY COMPUTER, I'VE BEEN WORKING NON-STOP...
...AND I FORGOT ABOUT TONIGHT UNTIL AFTER I GOT HOME EARLIER...
Christmas Love Illumination ~Illusion of the Holy Night
12/2
WORKING? WHY...?
RUMMAGE
IN ORDER TO BUY THIS FOR YOU.
OH...
When He Buys It For You
You Will Be Together 4 Eve

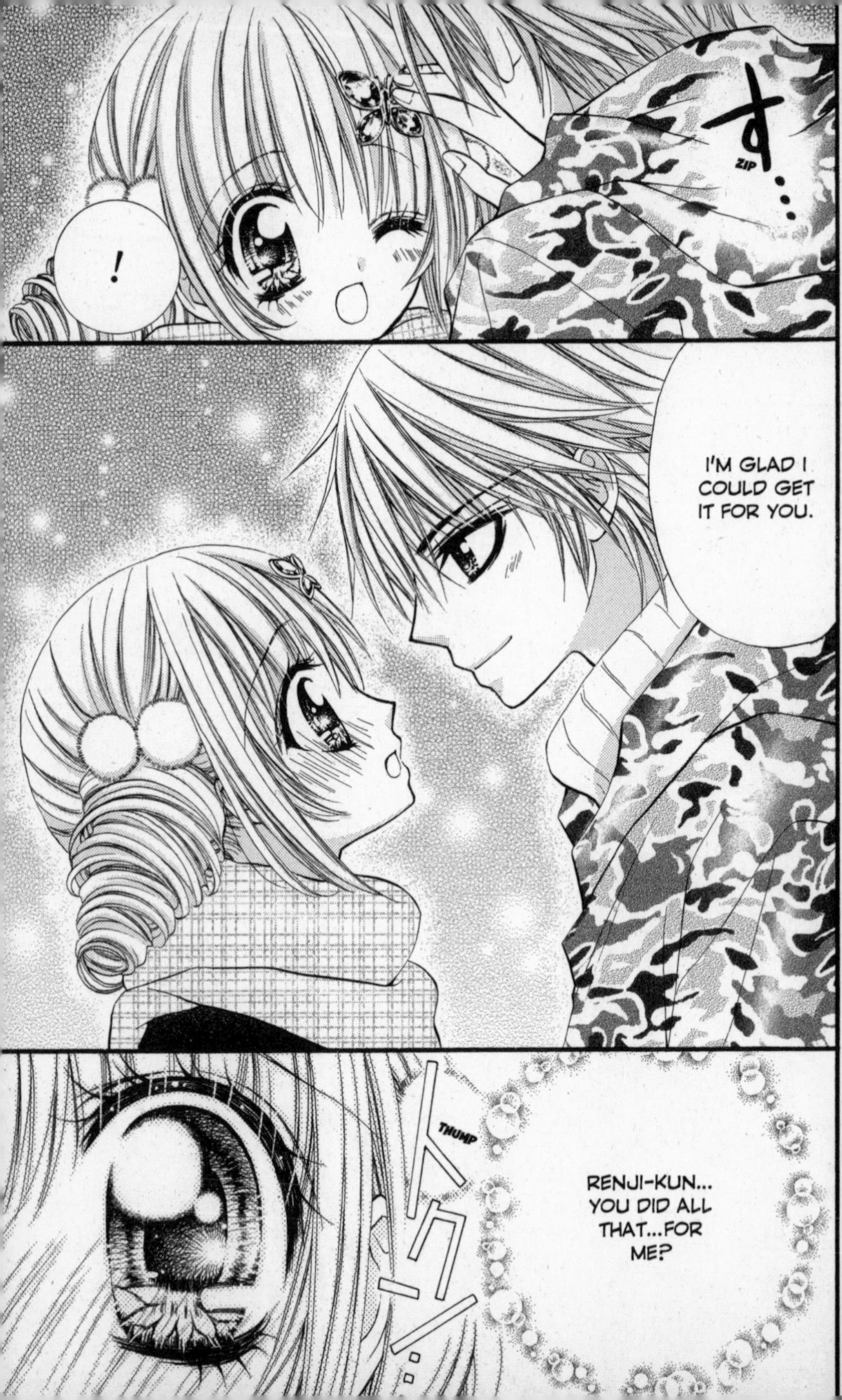

す
ZIP
...
!
I'M GLAD I COULD GET IT FOR YOU.
RENJI-KUN... YOU DID ALL THAT...FOR ME?
THUMP

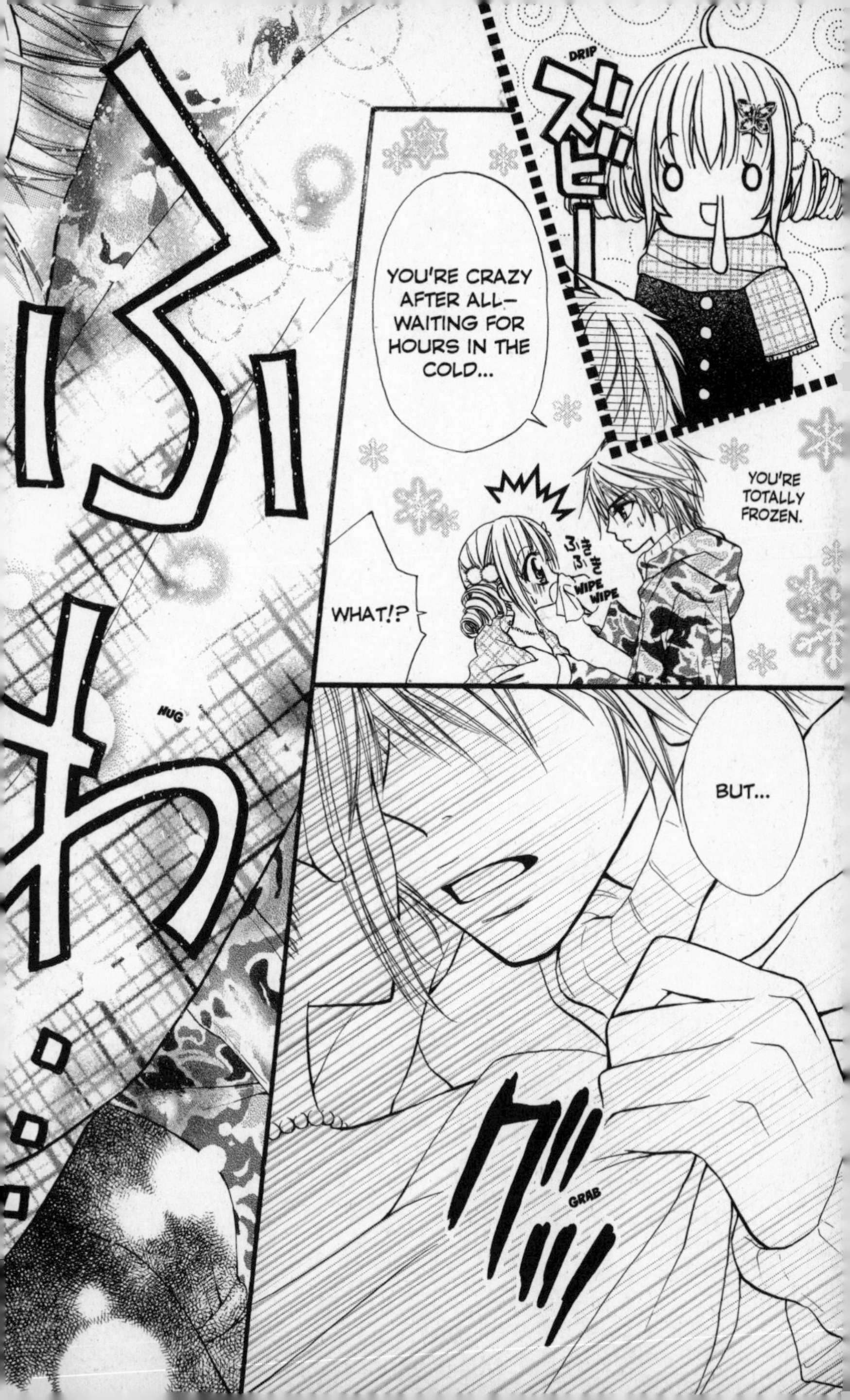

ズビ
DRIP
YOU'RE TOTALLY FROZEN.
ふきふき
WIPE WIPE
WHAT!?
YOU'RE CRAZY AFTER ALL— WAITING FOR HOURS IN THE COLD...
BUT...
GRAB
HUG
ふわ...

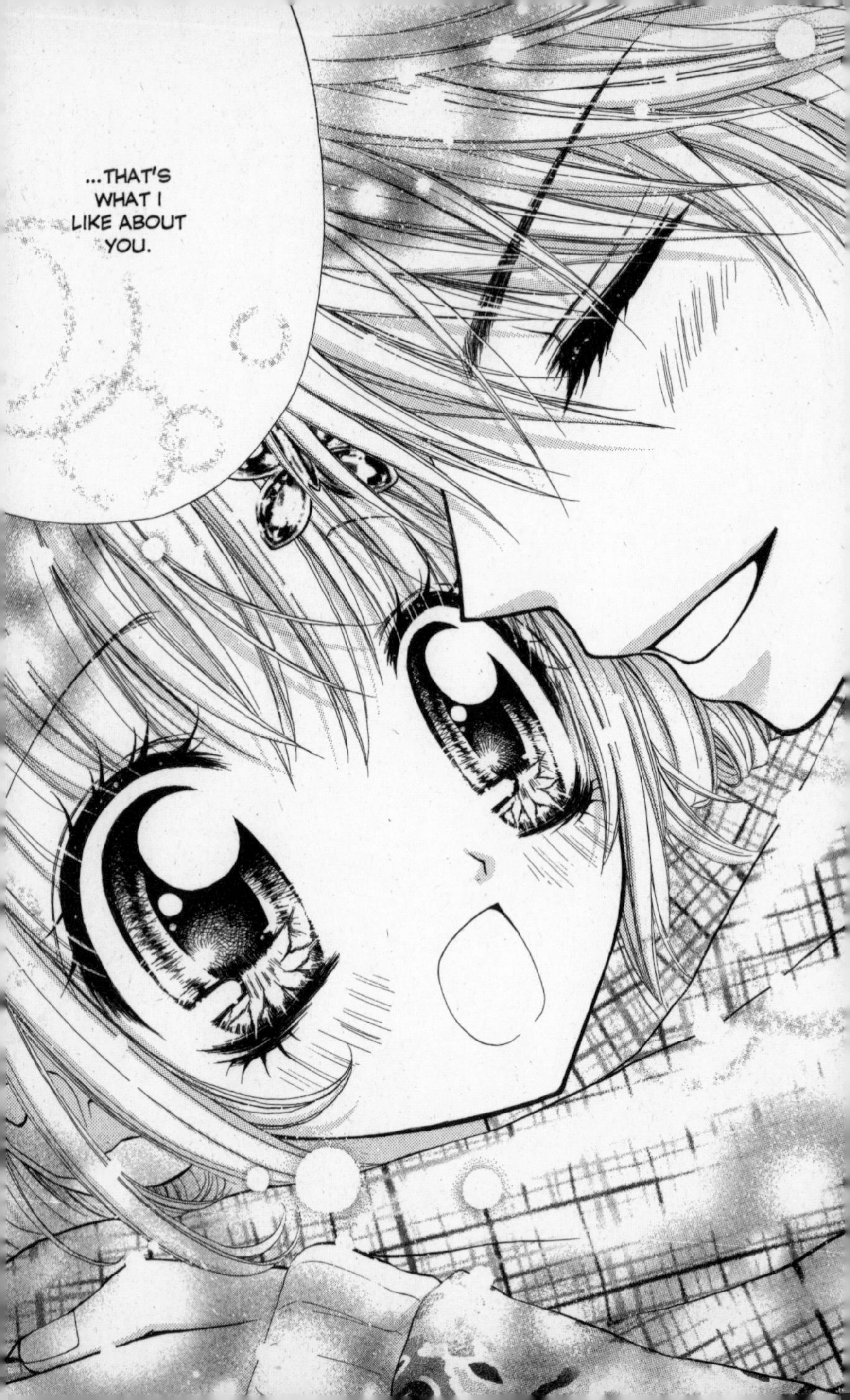
...THAT'S WHAT I LIKE ABOUT YOU.

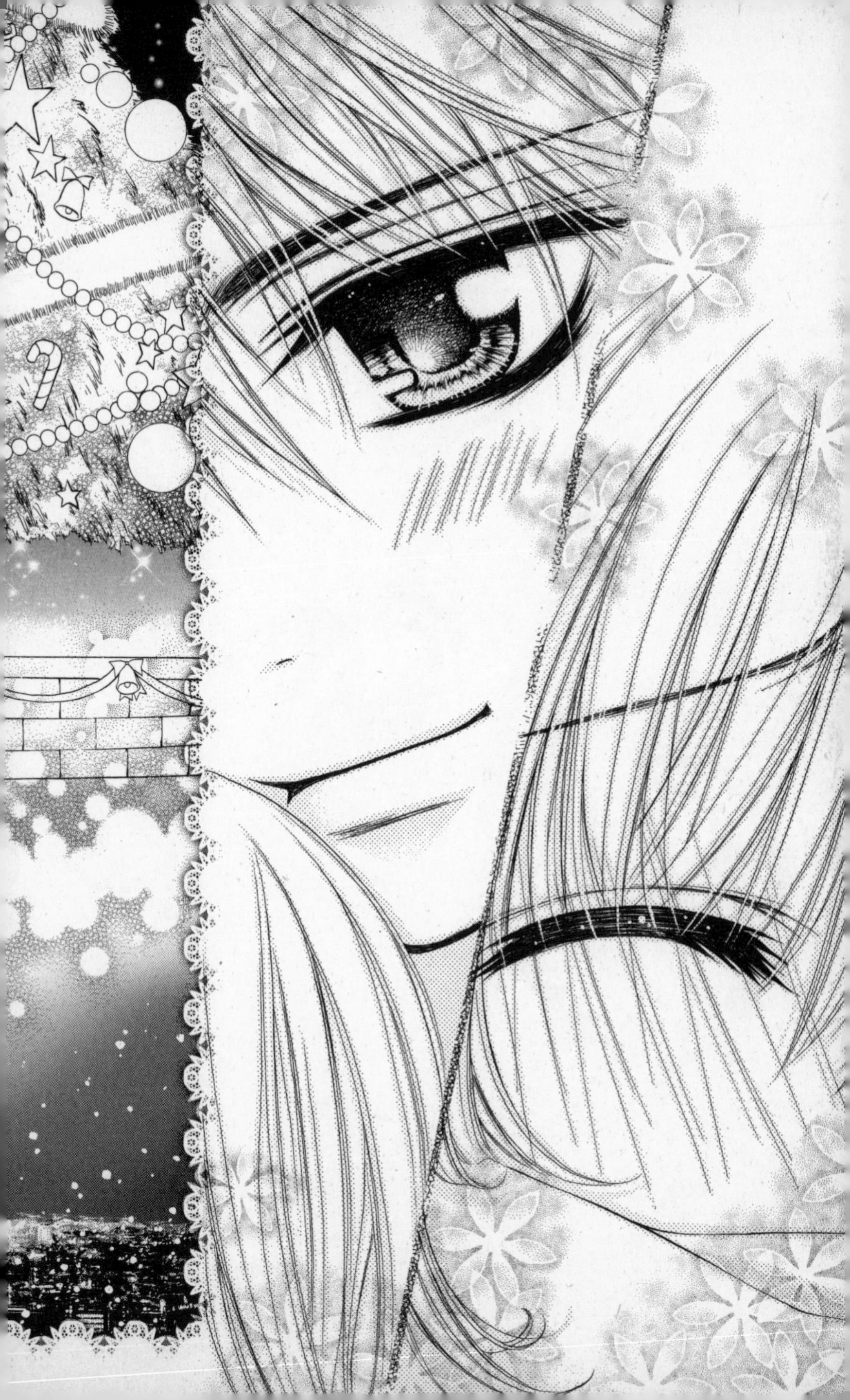

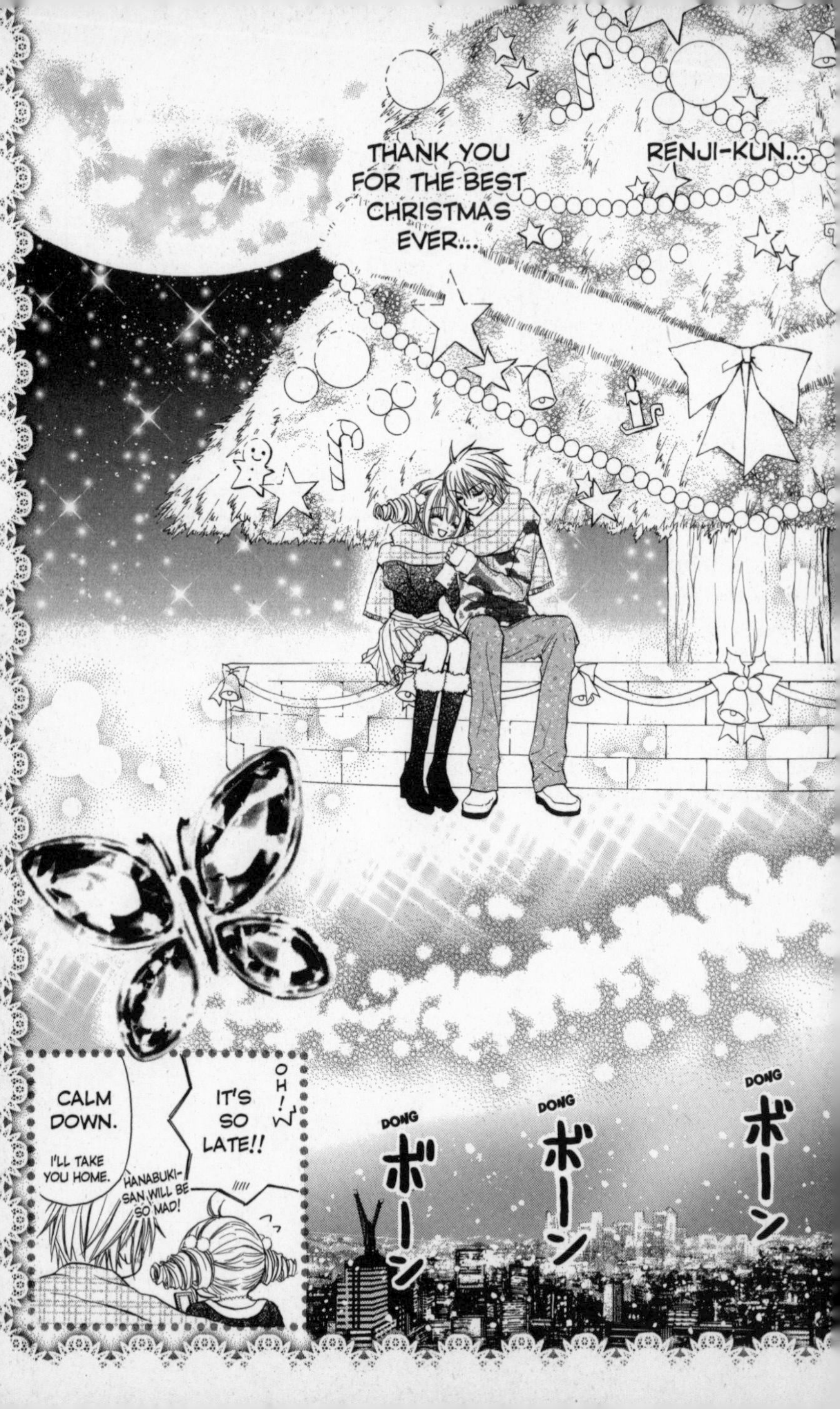
RENJI-KUN...
THANK YOU FOR THE BEST CHRISTMAS EVER...
DONG
ボーン
DONG
ボーン
DONG
ボーン
OH!!
IT'S SO LATE!!
HANABUKI-SAN WILL BE SO MAD!
CALM DOWN.
I'LL TAKE YOU HOME.

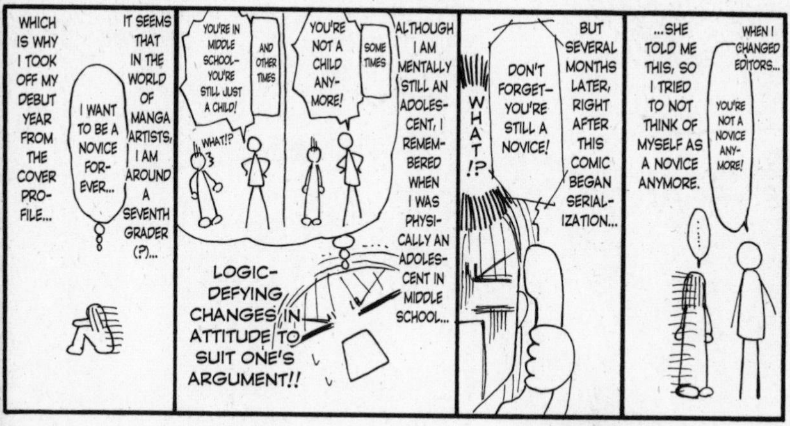
WHEN I CHANGED EDITORS...
YOU'RE NOT A NOVICE ANY-MORE!
...SHE TOLD ME THIS, SO I TRIED TO NOT THINK OF MYSELF AS A NOVICE ANYMORE.
...
BUT SEVERAL MONTHS LATER, RIGHT AFTER THIS COMIC BEGAN SERIALIZATION...
DON'T FORGET— YOU'RE STILL A NOVICE!
WHAT!?
ALTHOUGH I AM MENTALLY STILL AN ADOLESCENT, I REMEMBERED WHEN I WAS PHYSICALLY AN ADOLESCENT IN MIDDLE SCHOOL...
SOMETIMES
YOU'RE NOT A CHILD ANYMORE!
AND OTHER TIMES
YOU'RE IN MIDDLE SCHOOL— YOU'RE STILL JUST A CHILD!
WHAT!?
LOGIC-DEFYING CHANGES IN ATTITUDE TO SUIT ONE'S ARGUMENT!!
IT SEEMS THAT IN THE WORLD OF MANGA ARTISTS, I AM AROUND A SEVENTH GRADER (?)...
I WANT TO BE A NOVICE FOREVER...
WHICH IS WHY I TOOK OFF MY DEBUT YEAR FROM THE COVER PROFILE...

After I changed editors, the company sent me tickets again to go to Universal Studios Japan! I went with four of the publishing staff who always help with my drafts, and I was rather shocked when I discovered that the editor was the third youngest in the group...!
I was...the oldest... The ages of the other four lined up perfectly—each was one year older than the next! Ha!

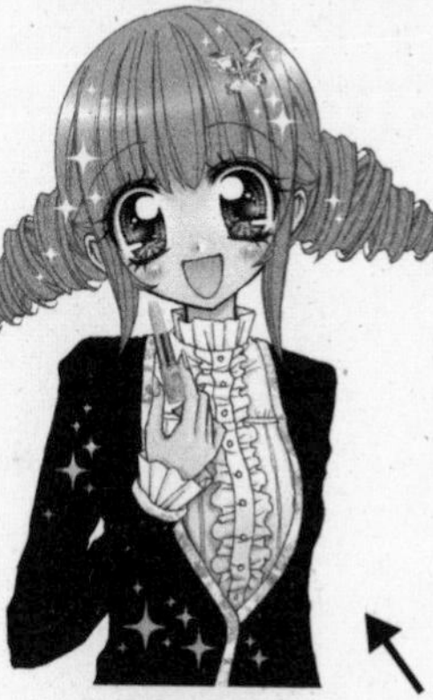

I was happy when my editor liked this drawing. It was great to be able to do the clothes in just black and white.

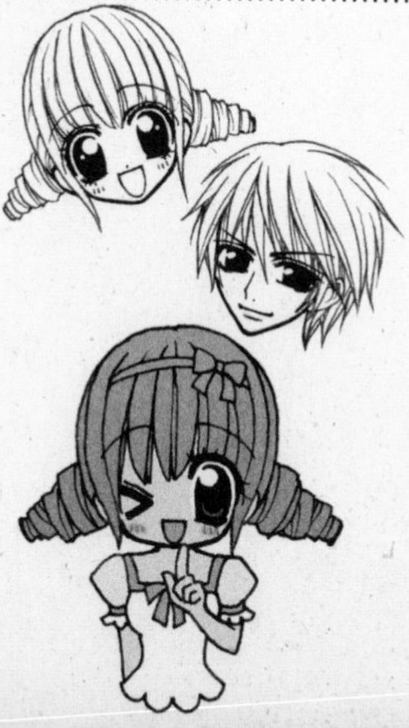

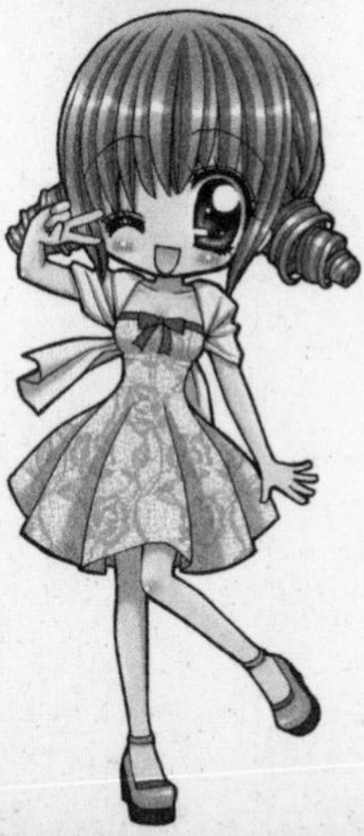

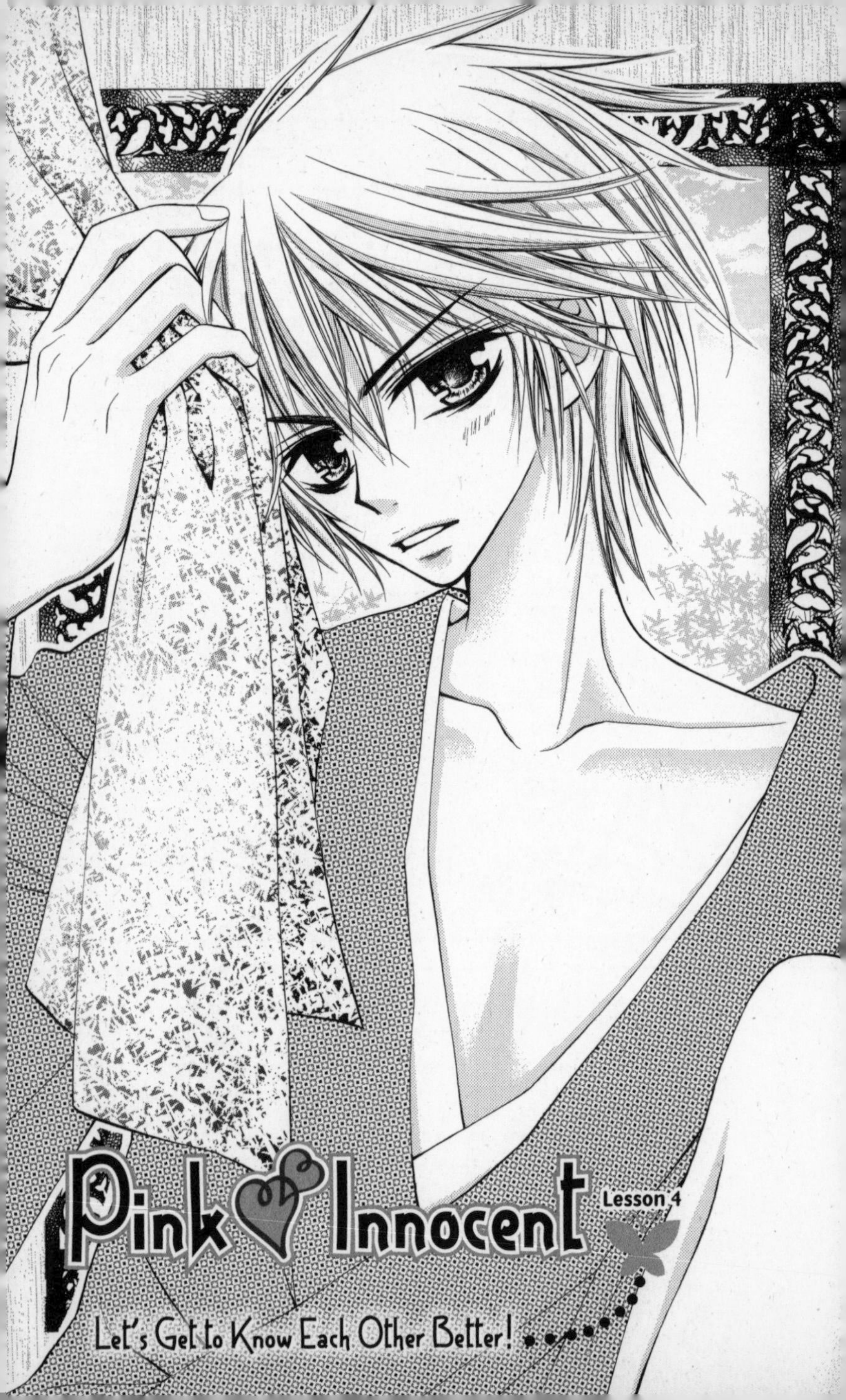
Pink Innocent
Lesson 4
Let's Get to Know Each Other Better!

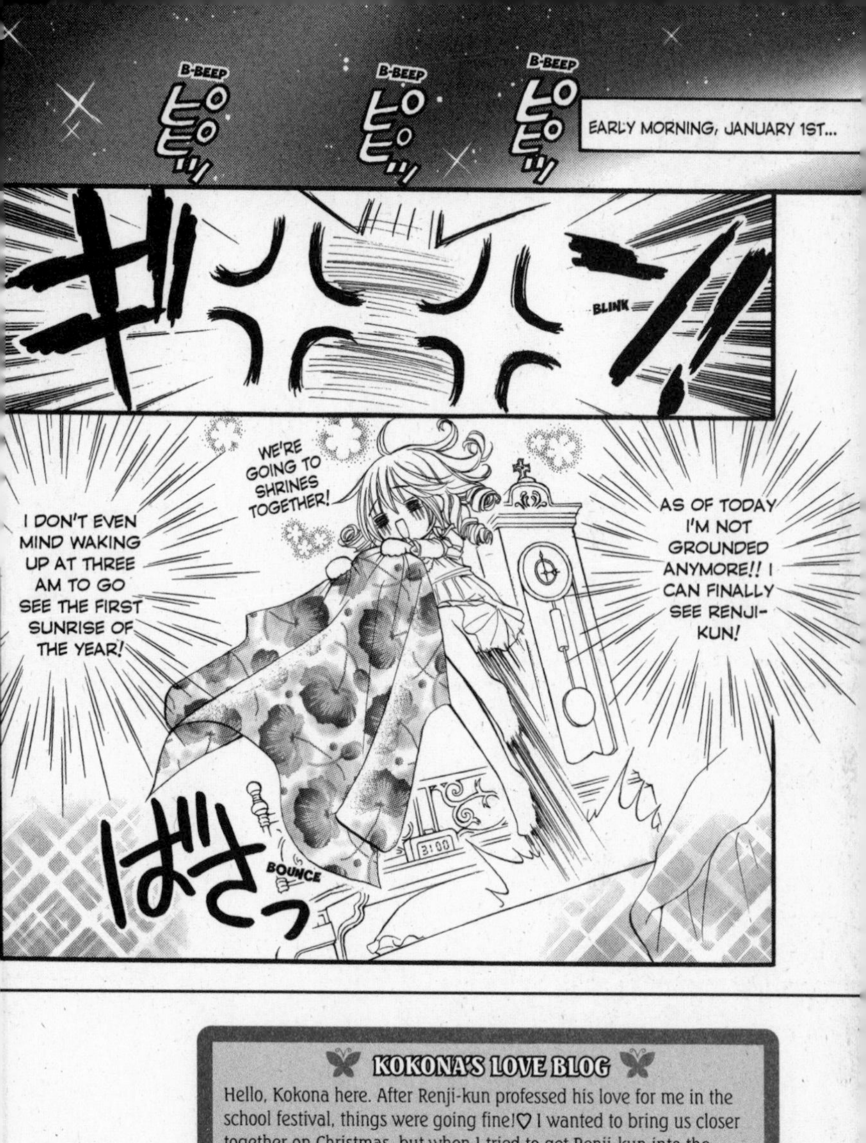
EARLY MORNING, JANUARY 1ST...
B-BEEP
B-BEEP
B-BEEP
BLINK
AS OF TODAY I'M NOT GROUNDED ANYMORE!! I CAN FINALLY SEE RENJI-KUN!
WE'RE GOING TO SHRINES TOGETHER!
I DON'T EVEN MIND WAKING UP AT THREE AM TO GO SEE THE FIRST SUNRISE OF THE YEAR!
3:00
BOUNCE

KOKONA'S LOVE BLOG

Hello, Kokona here. After Renji-kun professed his love for me in the school festival, things were going fine!♡ I wanted to bring us closer together on Christmas, but when I tried to get Renji-kun into the mood, I ended up making him mad. It was Christmas Eve and we still hadn't made up, so I went to see the illumination by myself. I was wallowing in my sadness, but then Renji-kun came!! He had been working in secret to buy my a present!! I was really touched.♡

Comment

Aery: The butterfly pin he gave you is cute! ☆ It's really cool that he worked to buy a present, just for you!

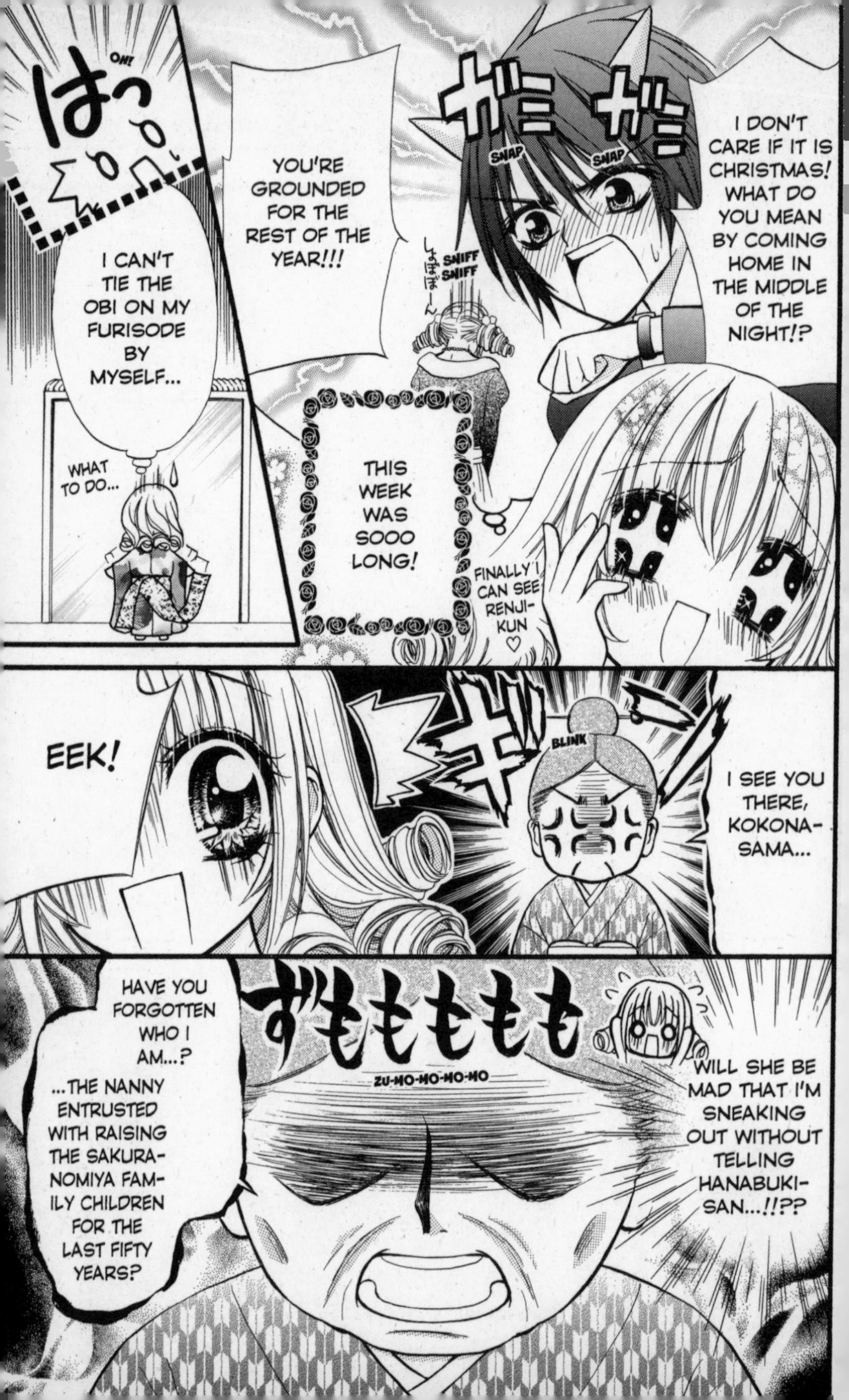

ガミ ガミ
SNAP SNAP
I DON'T CARE IF IT IS CHRISTMAS! WHAT DO YOU MEAN BY COMING HOME IN THE MIDDLE OF THE NIGHT!?
YOU'RE GROUNDED FOR THE REST OF THE YEAR!!!
しょぼぼーん
SNIFF SNIFF
THIS WEEK WAS SOOO LONG!
FINALLY I CAN SEE RENJI-KUN ♡
はっ
OH!
I CAN'T TIE THE OBI ON MY FURISODE BY MYSELF...
WHAT TO DO...
I SEE YOU THERE, KOKONA-SAMA...
BLINK
ギッ
EEK!
WILL SHE BE MAD THAT I'M SNEAKING OUT WITHOUT TELLING HANABUKI-SAN...!!??
ずもももも
ZU-MO-MO-MO-MO
HAVE YOU FORGOTTEN WHO I AM...? ...THE NANNY ENTRUSTED WITH RAISING THE SAKURA-NOMIYA FAMILY CHILDREN FOR THE LAST FIFTY YEARS?

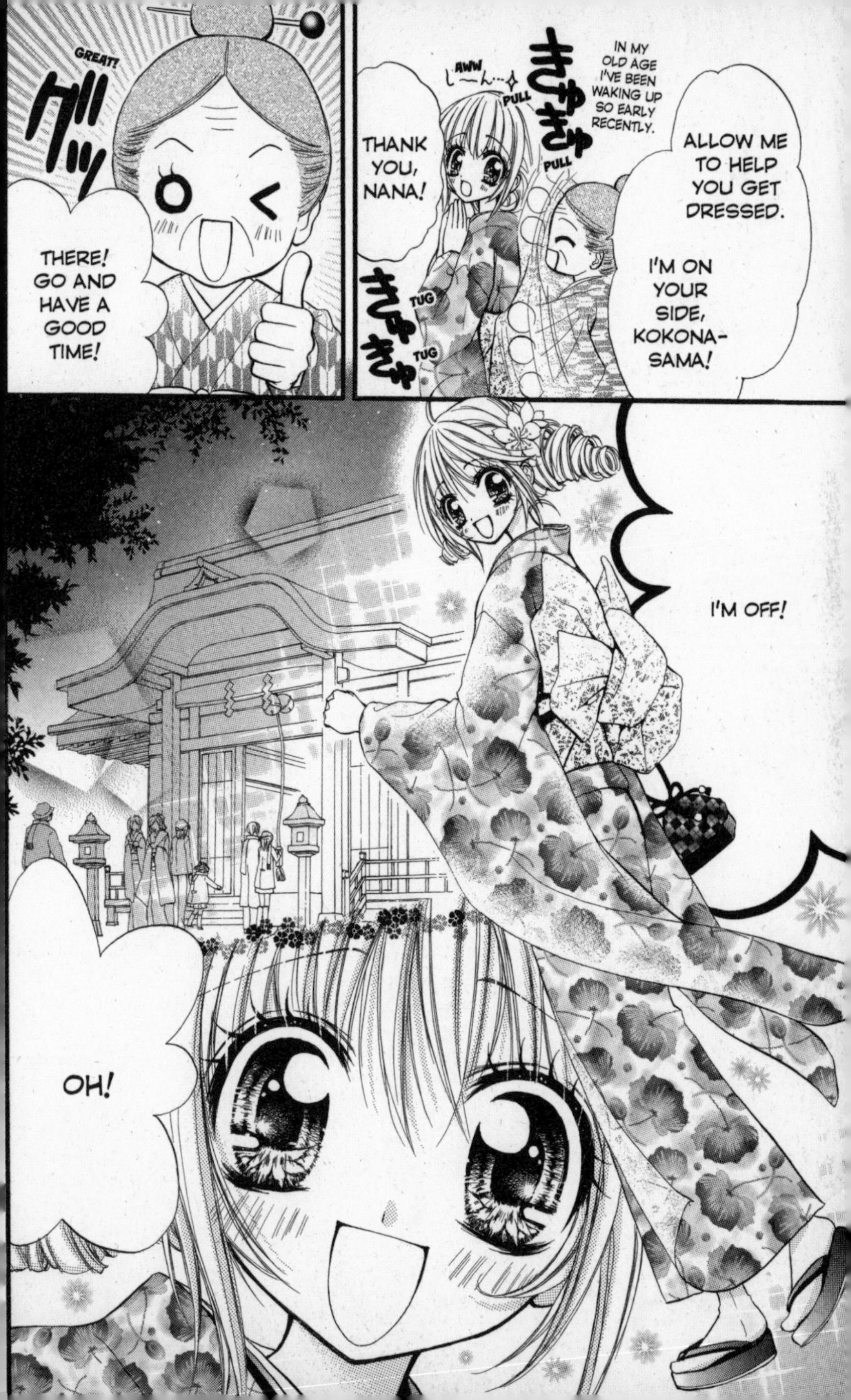
ALLOW ME TO HELP YOU GET DRESSED.
IN MY OLD AGE I'VE BEEN WAKING UP SO EARLY RECENTLY.
きゅきゅ
PULL
PULL
AWW
じ〜ん…
THANK YOU, NANA!
I'M ON YOUR SIDE, KOKONA-SAMA!
きゅきゅ
TUG
TUG
GREAT!
グッ
THERE! GO AND HAVE A GOOD TIME!
I'M OFF!
OH!

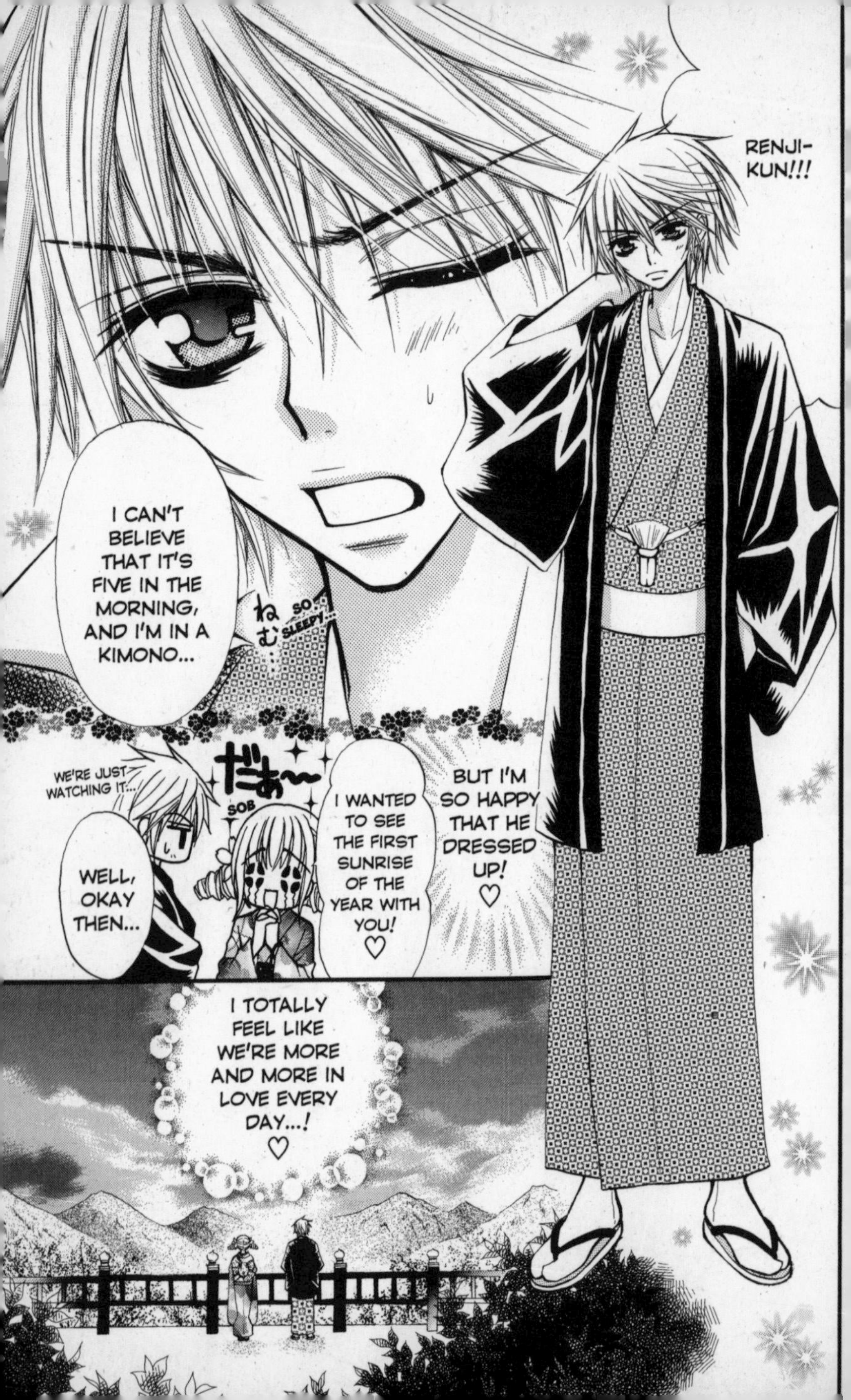
RENJI-KUN!!!
I CAN'T BELIEVE THAT IT'S FIVE IN THE MORNING, AND I'M IN A KIMONO...
ねむ
SO SLEEPY...
BUT I'M SO HAPPY THAT HE DRESSED UP! ♡
I WANTED TO SEE THE FIRST SUNRISE OF THE YEAR WITH YOU! ♡
だぁ～
SOB
WE'RE JUST WATCHING IT...
WELL, OKAY THEN...
I TOTALLY FEEL LIKE WE'RE MORE AND MORE IN LOVE EVERY DAY...! ♡

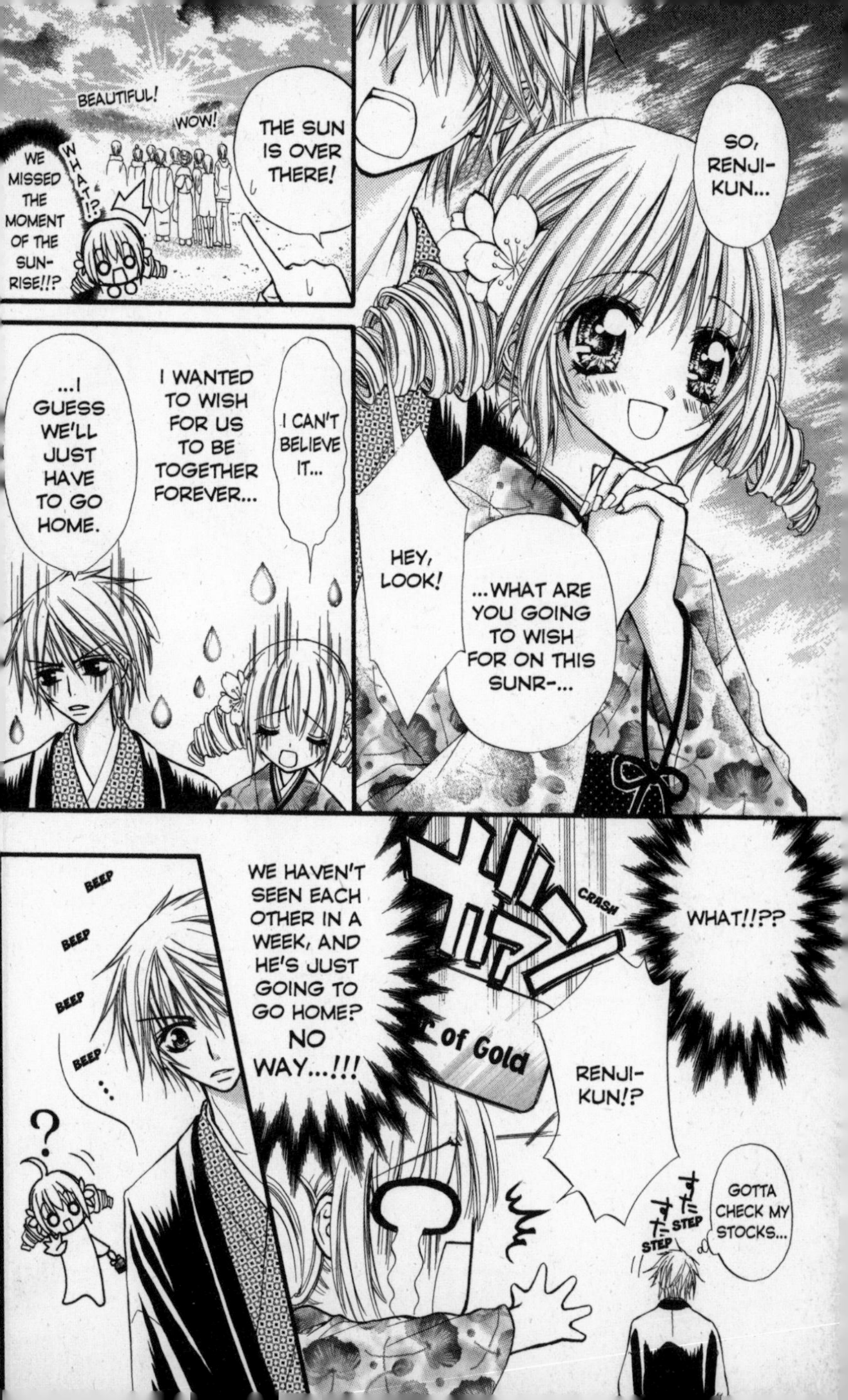
SO, RENJI-KUN...
...WHAT ARE YOU GOING TO WISH FOR ON THIS SUNR-...
HEY, LOOK!
THE SUN IS OVER THERE!
WOW!
BEAUTIFUL!
WHAT!?
WE MISSED THE MOMENT OF THE SUN-RISE!!?
I CAN'T BELIEVE IT...
I WANTED TO WISH FOR US TO BE TOGETHER FOREVER...
...I GUESS WE'LL JUST HAVE TO GO HOME.
WHAT!!??
CRASH
of Gold
RENJI-KUN!?
GOTTA CHECK MY STOCKS...
STEP
STEP
WE HAVEN'T SEEN EACH OTHER IN A WEEK, AND HE'S JUST GOING TO GO HOME? NO WAY...!!!
BEEP
BEEP
BEEP
BEEP
...
?

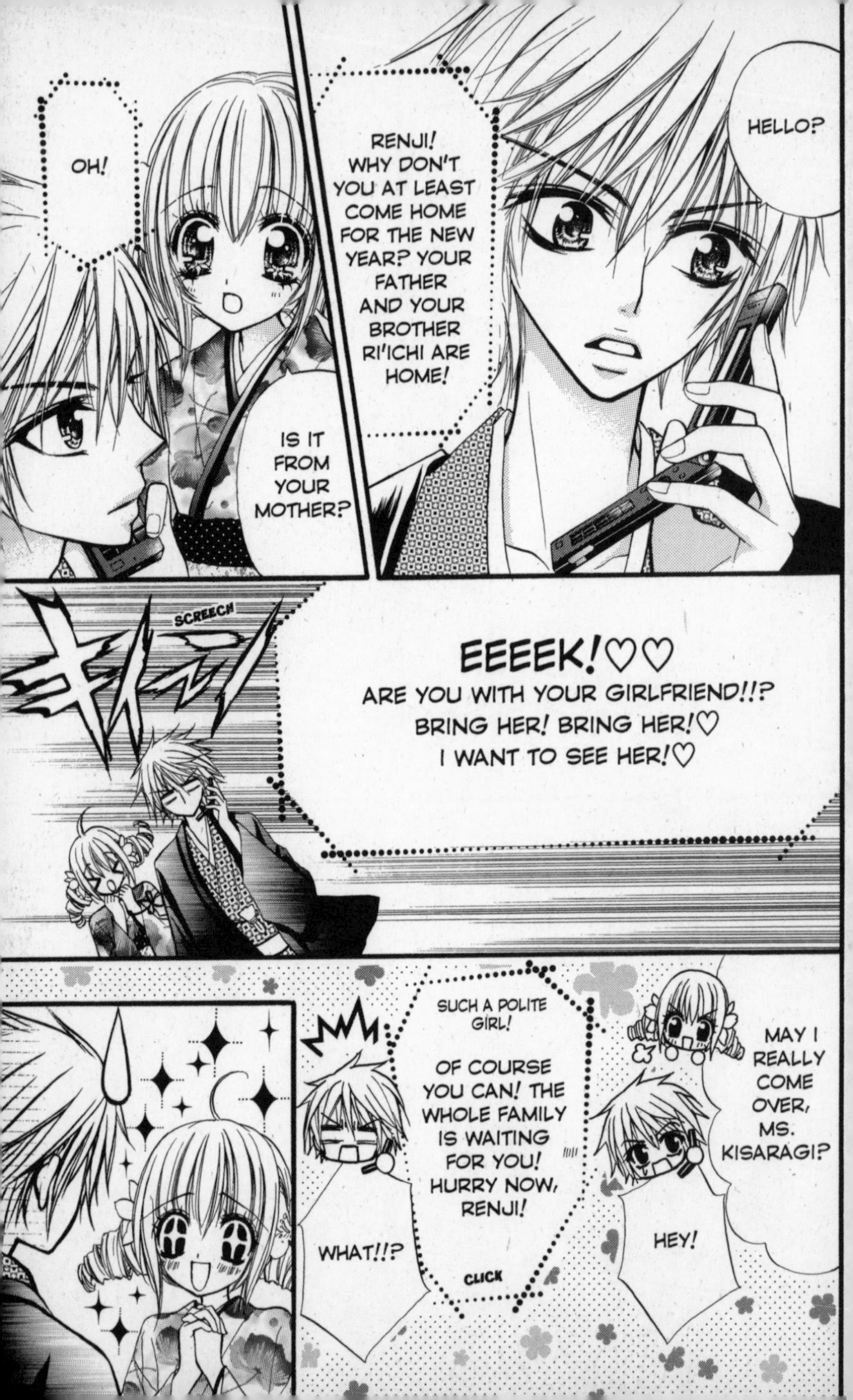
HELLO?
RENJI! WHY DON'T YOU AT LEAST COME HOME FOR THE NEW YEAR? YOUR FATHER AND YOUR BROTHER RI'ICHI ARE HOME!
OH!
IS IT FROM YOUR MOTHER?
SCREECH
EEEEK!♡♡
ARE YOU WITH YOUR GIRLFRIEND!!? BRING HER! BRING HER!♡ I WANT TO SEE HER!♡
MAY I REALLY COME OVER, MS. KISARAGI?
HEY!
SUCH A POLITE GIRL!
OF COURSE YOU CAN! THE WHOLE FAMILY IS WAITING FOR YOU! HURRY NOW, RENJI!
CLICK
WHAT!!?

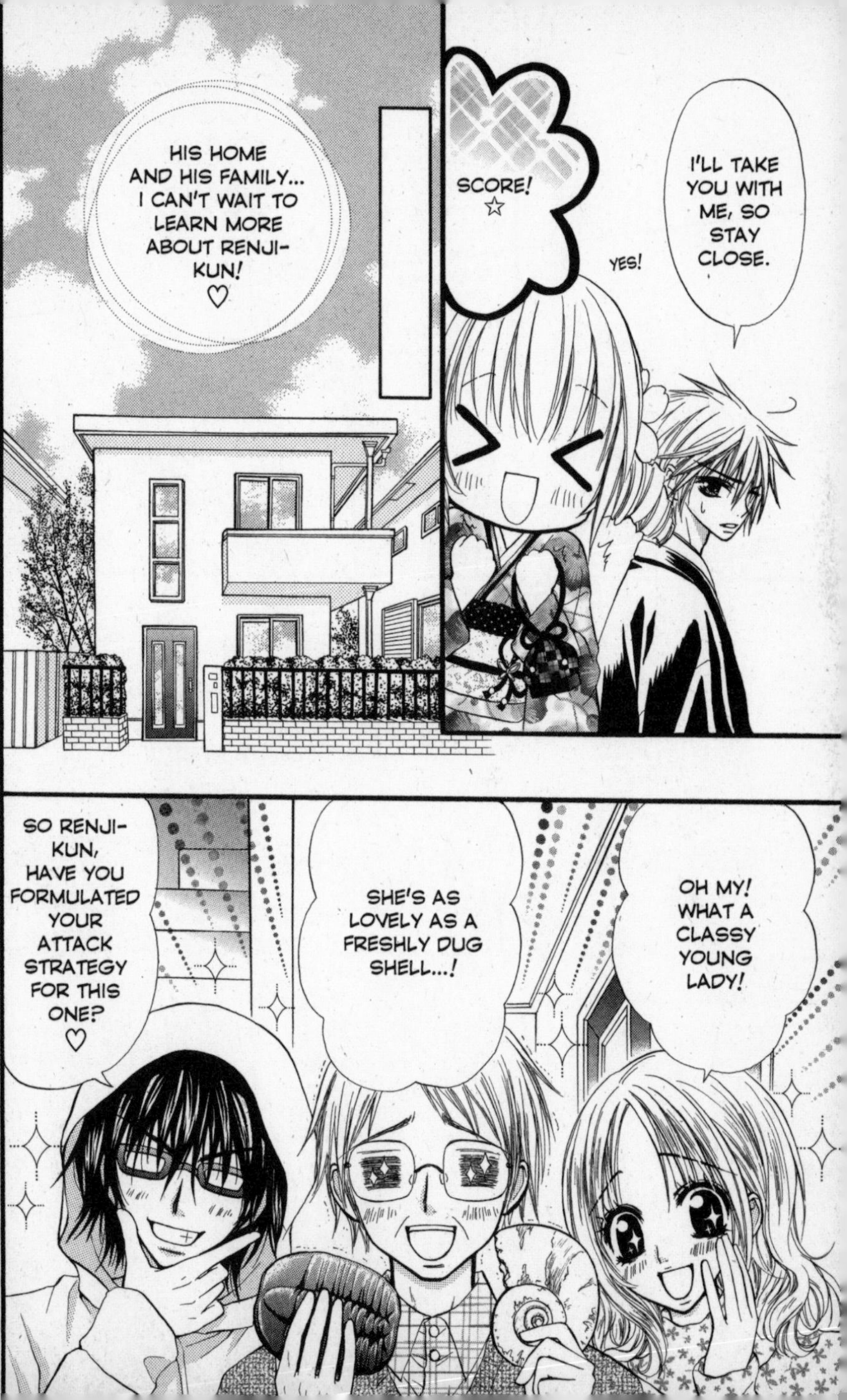
I'LL TAKE YOU WITH ME, SO STAY CLOSE.
YES!
SCORE! ☆
HIS HOME AND HIS FAMILY... I CAN'T WAIT TO LEARN MORE ABOUT RENJI-KUN! ♡
OH MY! WHAT A CLASSY YOUNG LADY!
SHE'S AS LOVELY AS A FRESHLY DUG SHELL...!
SO RENJI-KUN, HAVE YOU FORMULATED YOUR ATTACK STRATEGY FOR THIS ONE? ♡

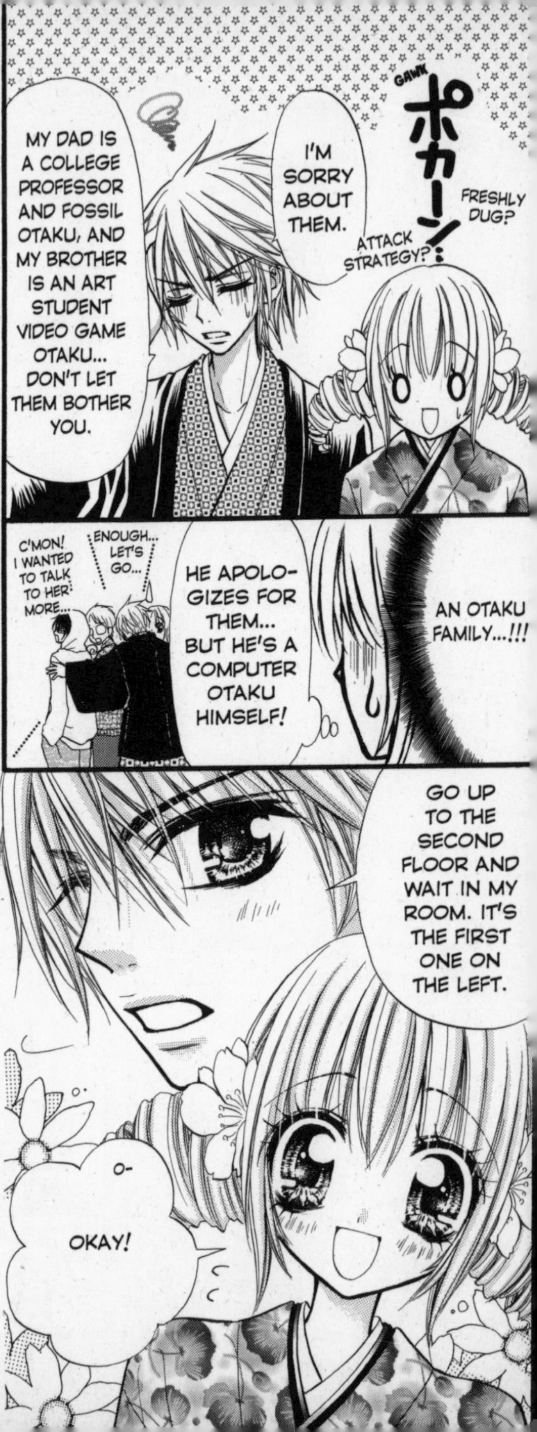
GAWK
ポカーン!
FRESHLY DUG?
ATTACK STRATEGY?
I'M SORRY ABOUT THEM.
MY DAD IS A COLLEGE PROFESSOR AND FOSSIL OTAKU, AND MY BROTHER IS AN ART STUDENT VIDEO GAME OTAKU... DON'T LET THEM BOTHER YOU.
AN OTAKU FAMILY...!!!
HE APOLOGIZES FOR THEM... BUT HE'S A COMPUTER OTAKU HIMSELF!
ENOUGH... LET'S GO...
C'MON! I WANTED TO TALK TO HER MORE...
GO UP TO THE SECOND FLOOR AND WAIT IN MY ROOM. IT'S THE FIRST ONE ON THE LEFT.
O- OKAY!

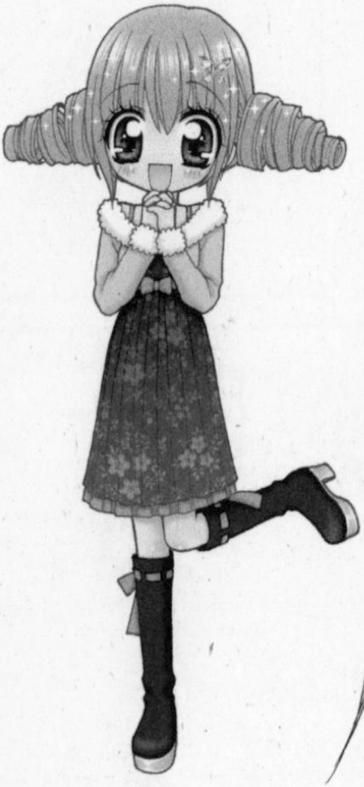

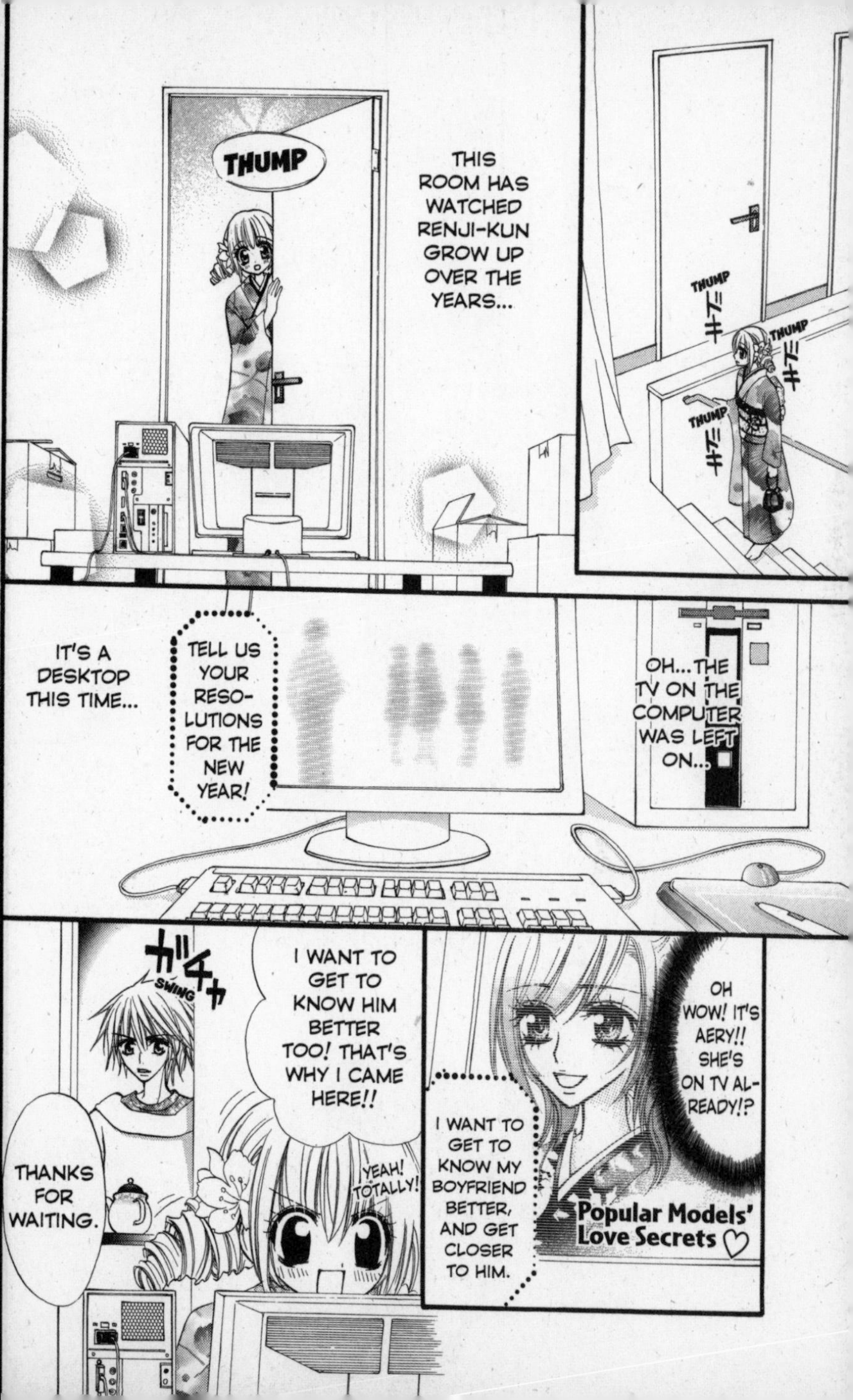
THUMP
THUMP
THUMP
THIS ROOM HAS WATCHED RENJI-KUN GROW UP OVER THE YEARS...
THUMP
OH... THE TV ON THE COMPUTER WAS LEFT ON...
TELL US YOUR RESO-LUTIONS FOR THE NEW YEAR!
IT'S A DESKTOP THIS TIME...
OH WOW! IT'S AERY!! SHE'S ON TV AL-READY!?
I WANT TO GET TO KNOW MY BOYFRIEND BETTER, AND GET CLOSER TO HIM.
Popular Models' Love Secrets ♡
I WANT TO GET TO KNOW HIM BETTER TOO! THAT'S WHY I CAME HERE!!
SWING
YEAH! TOTALLY!
THANKS FOR WAITING.

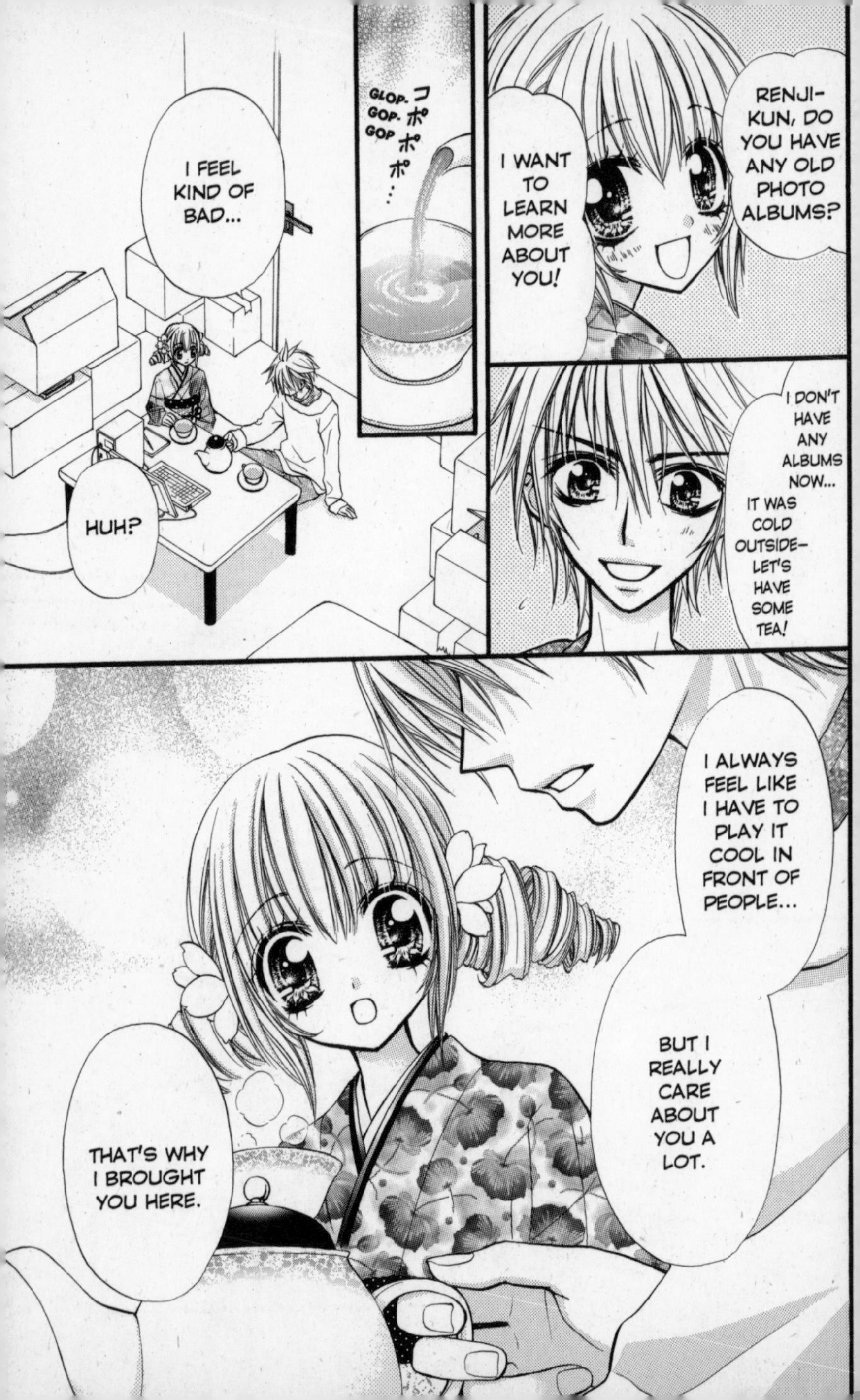
RENJI-KUN, DO YOU HAVE ANY OLD PHOTO ALBUMS?
I WANT TO LEARN MORE ABOUT YOU!
I DON'T HAVE ANY ALBUMS NOW...
IT WAS COLD OUTSIDE—LET'S HAVE SOME TEA!
GLOP. GOP. GOP
コポポポ…
I FEEL KIND OF BAD...
HUH?
I ALWAYS FEEL LIKE I HAVE TO PLAY IT COOL IN FRONT OF PEOPLE...
BUT I REALLY CARE ABOUT YOU A LOT.
THAT'S WHY I BROUGHT YOU HERE.

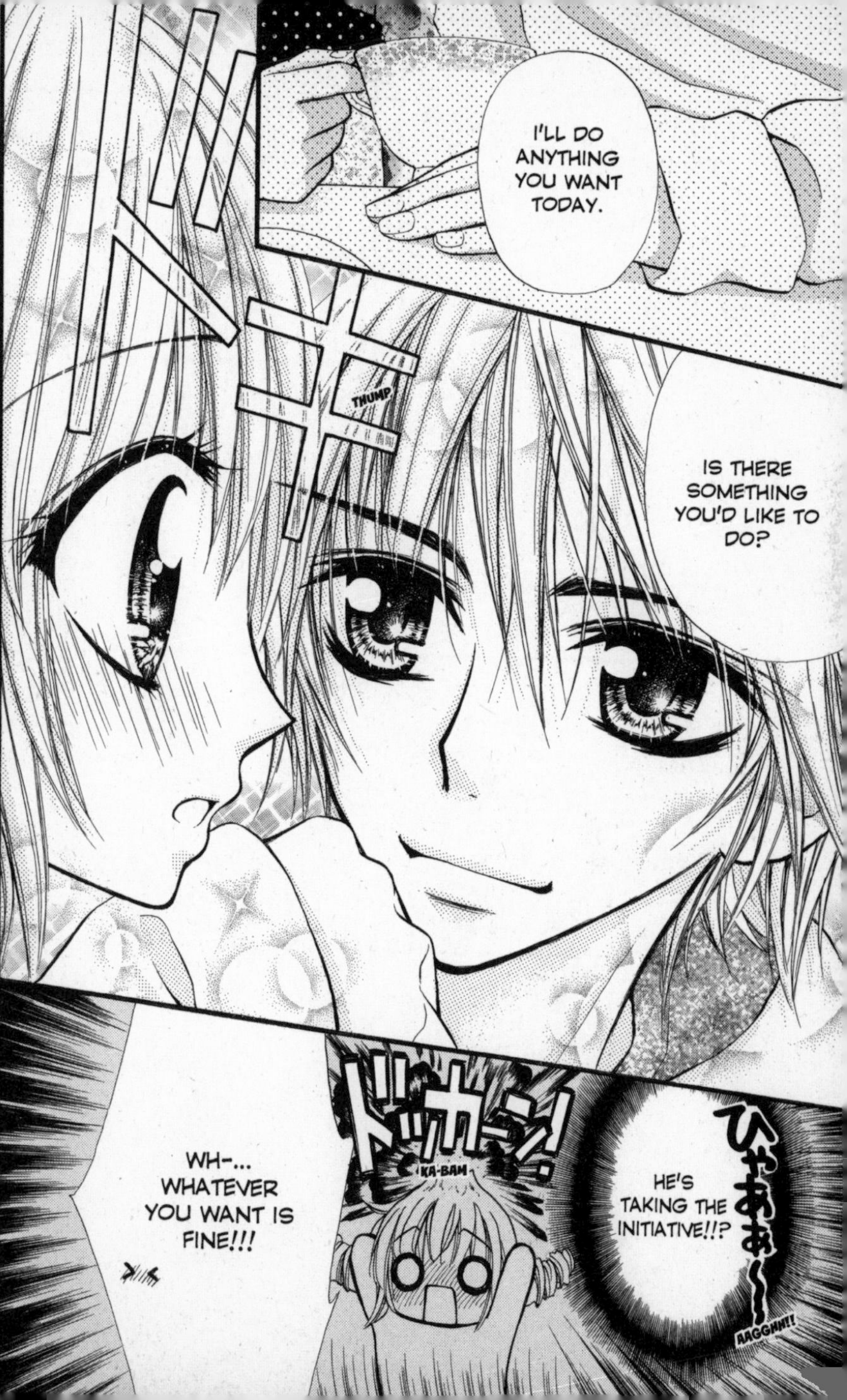
I'LL DO ANYTHING YOU WANT TODAY.
IS THERE SOMETHING YOU'D LIKE TO DO?
THUMP
ひゃあぁ~
AAGGHH!!
HE'S TAKING THE INITIATIVE!!?
ドッカーン!
KA-BAM
WH-... WHATEVER YOU WANT IS FINE!!!

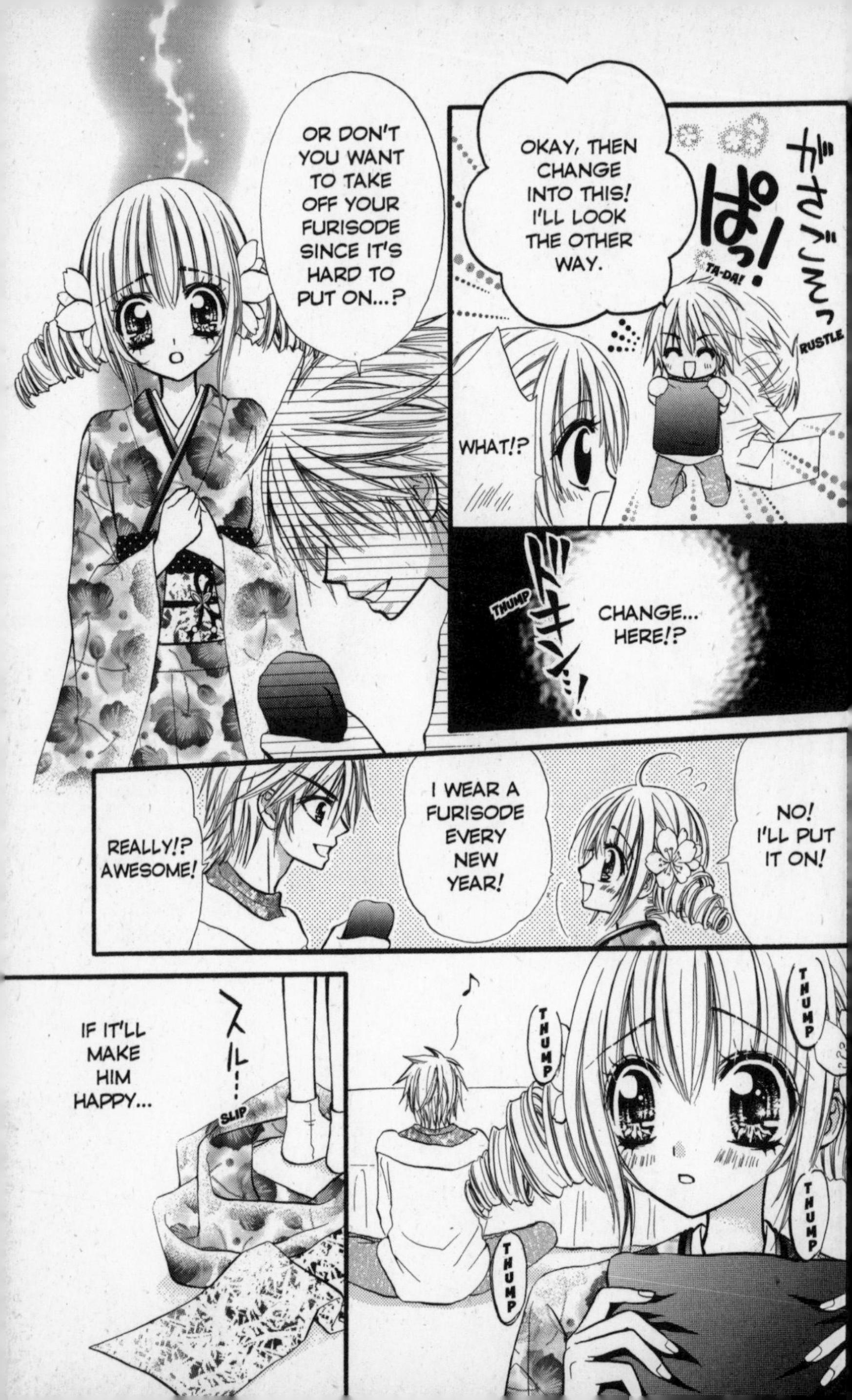
OKAY, THEN CHANGE INTO THIS! I'LL LOOK THE OTHER WAY.
がさごそっ
RUSTLE
ぱっ!
TA-DA!
WHAT!?
ドキン…!
THUMP
CHANGE... HERE!?
OR DON'T YOU WANT TO TAKE OFF YOUR FURISODE SINCE IT'S HARD TO PUT ON...?
NO! I'LL PUT IT ON!
I WEAR A FURISODE EVERY NEW YEAR!
REALLY!? AWESOME!
THUMP
THUMP
THUMP
THUMP
♪
スル…
SLIP
IF IT'LL MAKE HIM HAPPY...

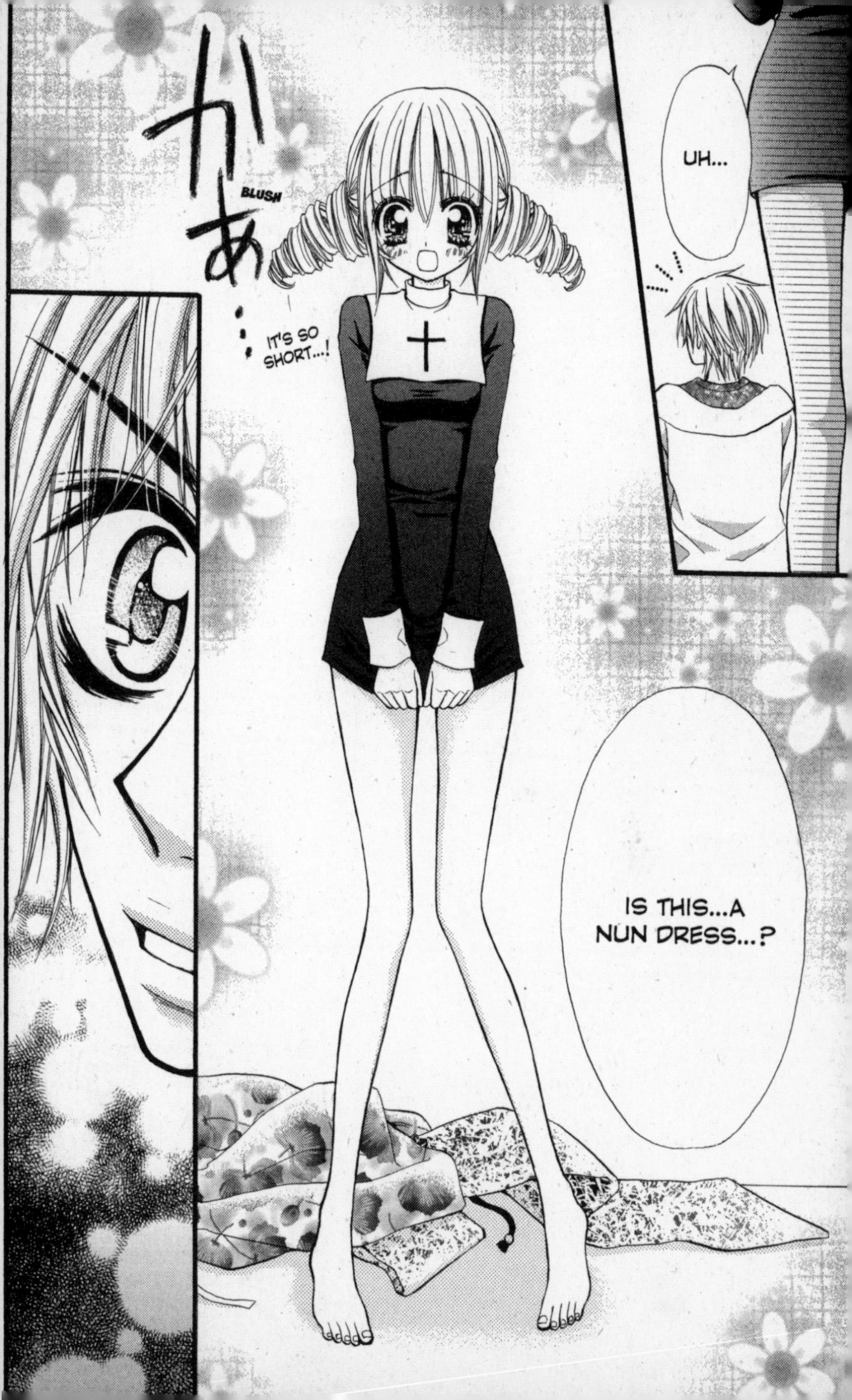
UH...
...!!
かあ
BLUSH
IT'S SO SHORT...!
IS THIS...A NUN DRESS...?

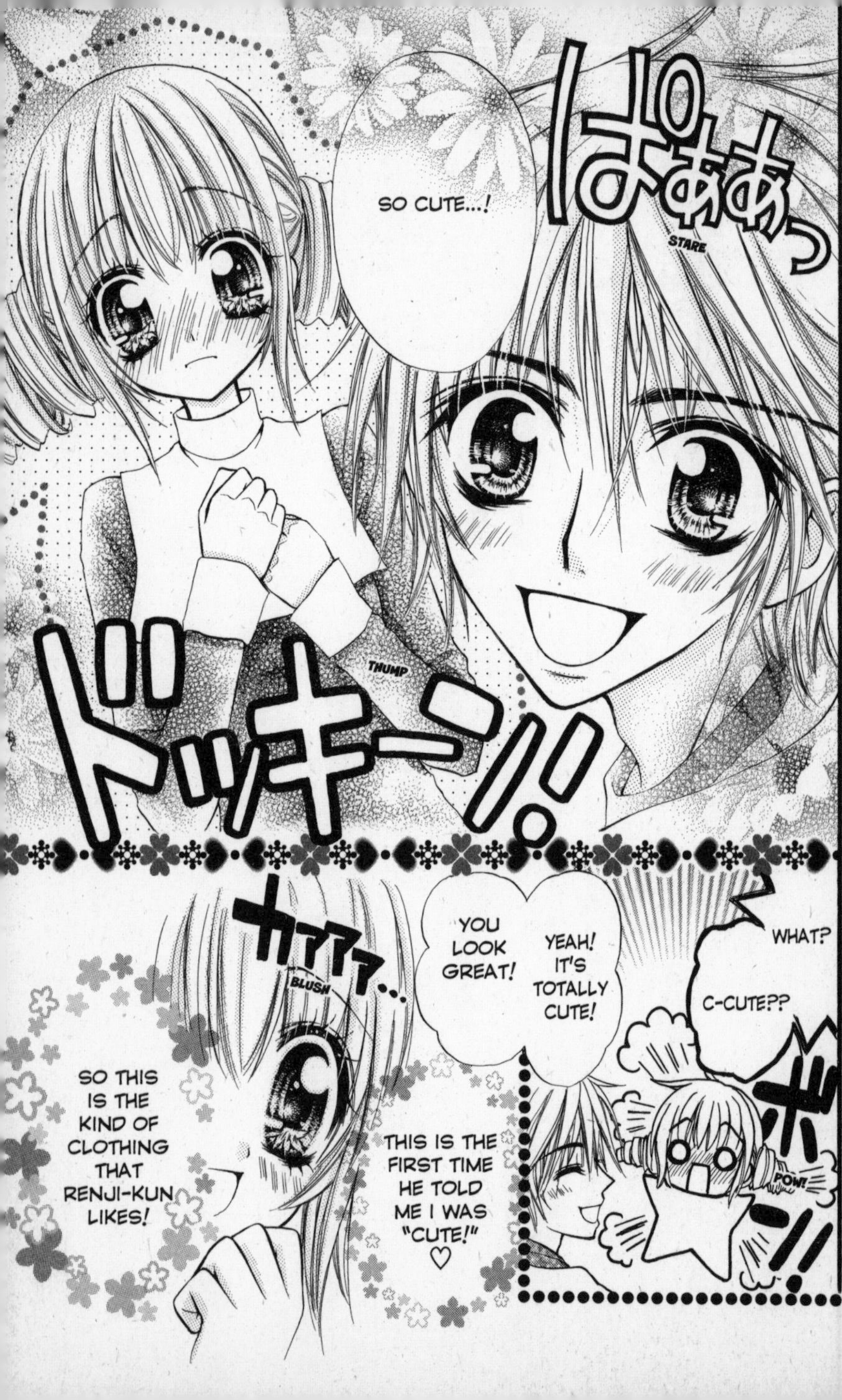
ぱあああっ
STARE
SO CUTE...!
ドッキーン!!
THUMP
WHAT?
C-CUTE??
ボン!!
POW!
YOU LOOK GREAT!
YEAH! IT'S TOTALLY CUTE!
カァァァ...
BLUSH
THIS IS THE FIRST TIME HE TOLD ME I WAS "CUTE!" ♡
SO THIS IS THE KIND OF CLOTHING THAT RENJI-KUN LIKES!

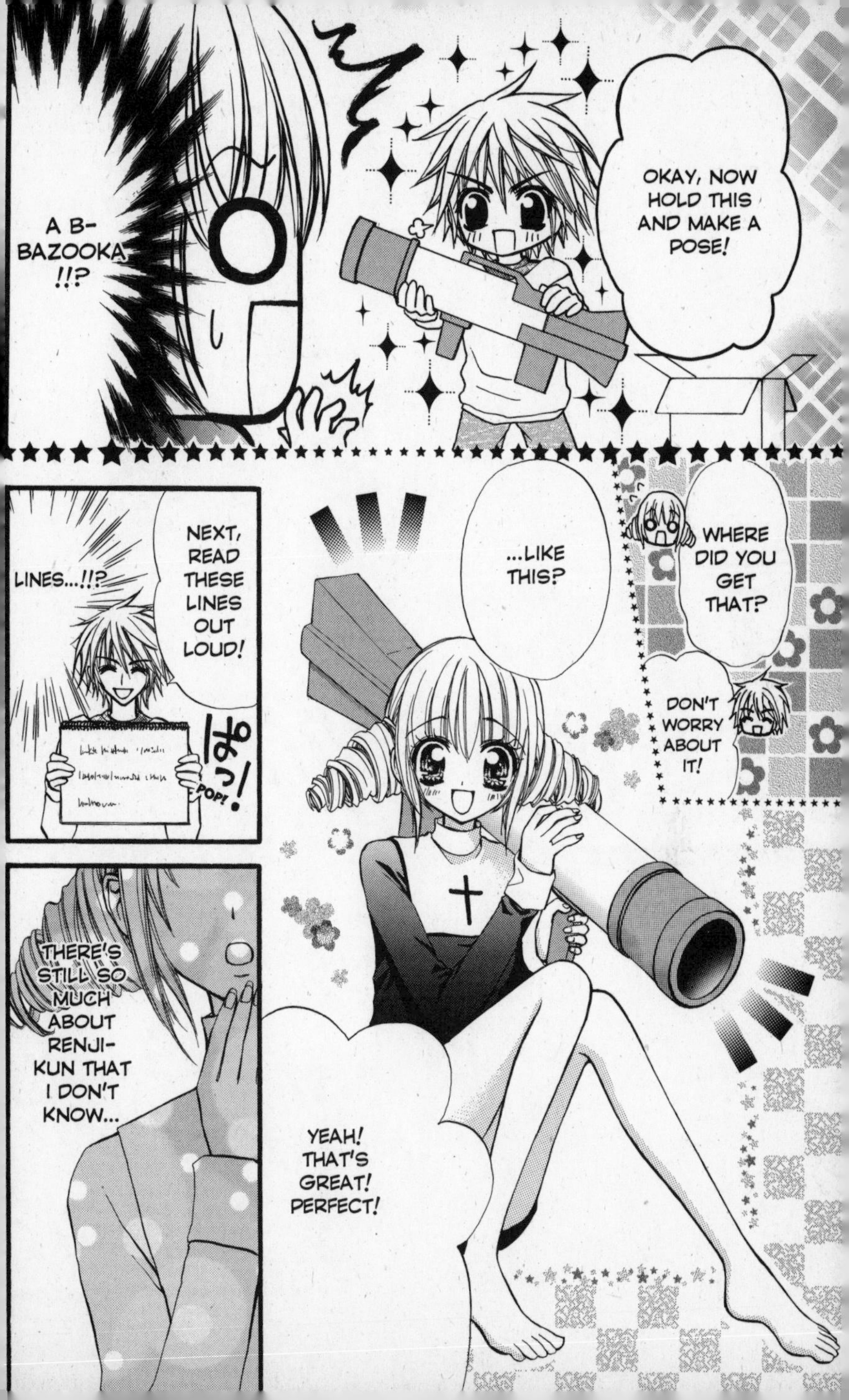
OKAY, NOW HOLD THIS AND MAKE A POSE!
A B-BAZOOKA!!?
WHERE DID YOU GET THAT?
DON'T WORRY ABOUT IT!
...LIKE THIS?
YEAH! THAT'S GREAT! PERFECT!
NEXT, READ THESE LINES OUT LOUD!
LINES...!!?
ぽっ
POP!
THERE'S STILL SO MUCH ABOUT RENJI-KUN THAT I DON'T KNOW...

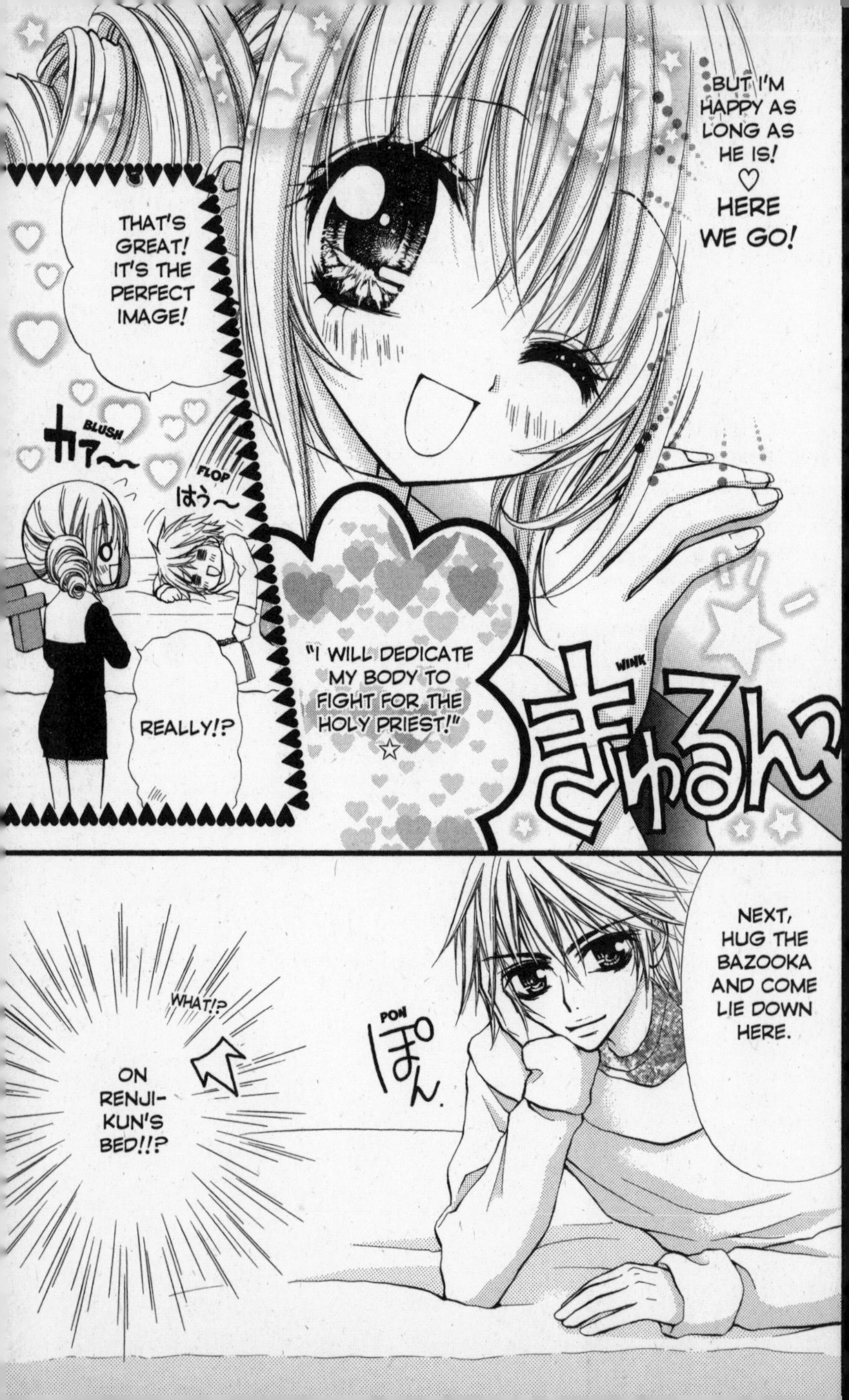
BUT I'M HAPPY AS LONG AS HE IS! ♡ HERE WE GO!
"I WILL DEDICATE MY BODY TO FIGHT FOR THE HOLY PRIEST!" ☆
きゅるんっ
WINK
THAT'S GREAT! IT'S THE PERFECT IMAGE!
カァ〜〜
BLUSH
はぅ〜
FLOP
REALLY!?
NEXT, HUG THE BAZOOKA AND COME LIE DOWN HERE.
ぽん.
PON
WHAT!?
ON RENJI-KUN'S BED!!?

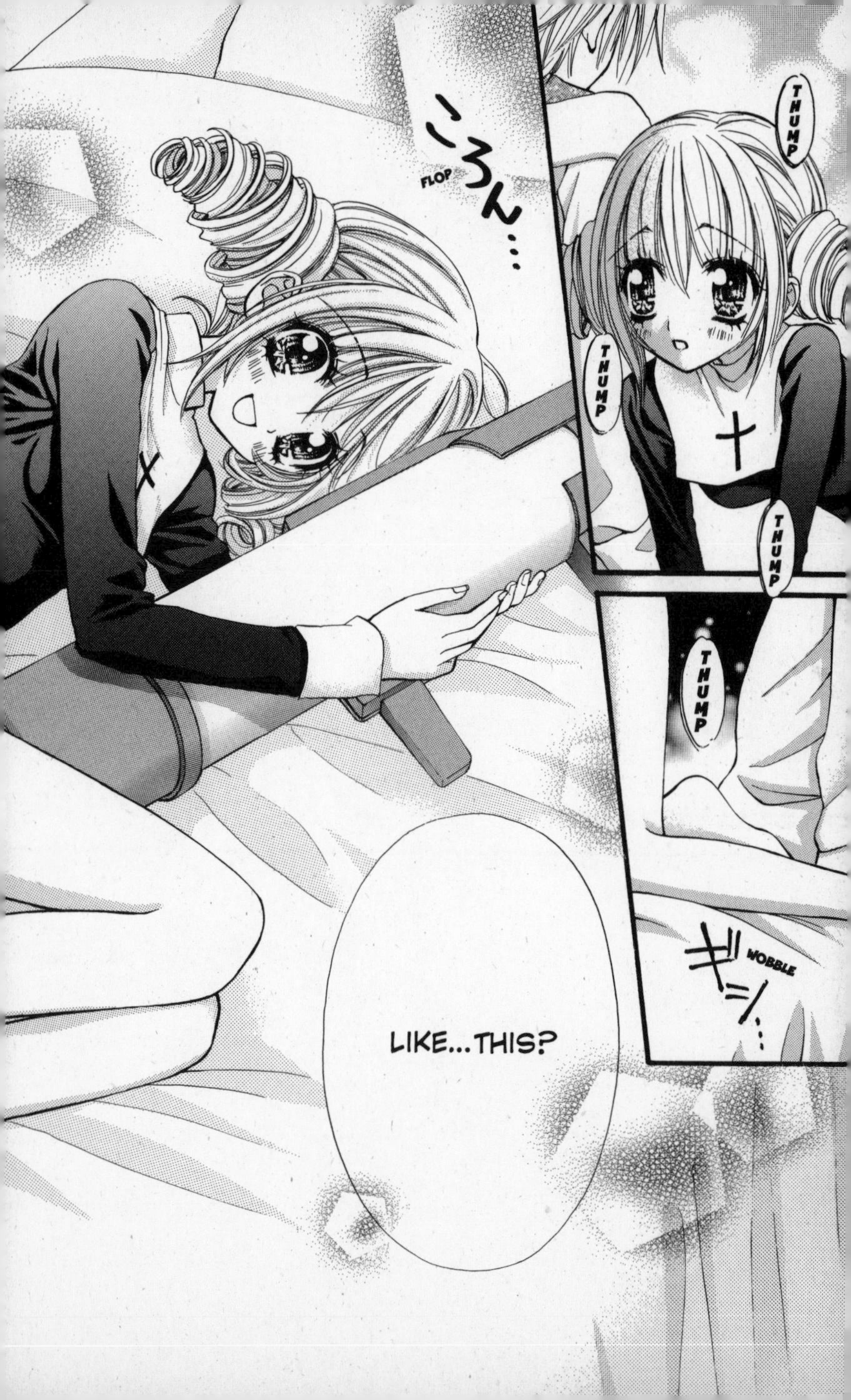
THUMP
THUMP
THUMP
THUMP
WOBBLE
ころん…
FLOP
LIKE...THIS?

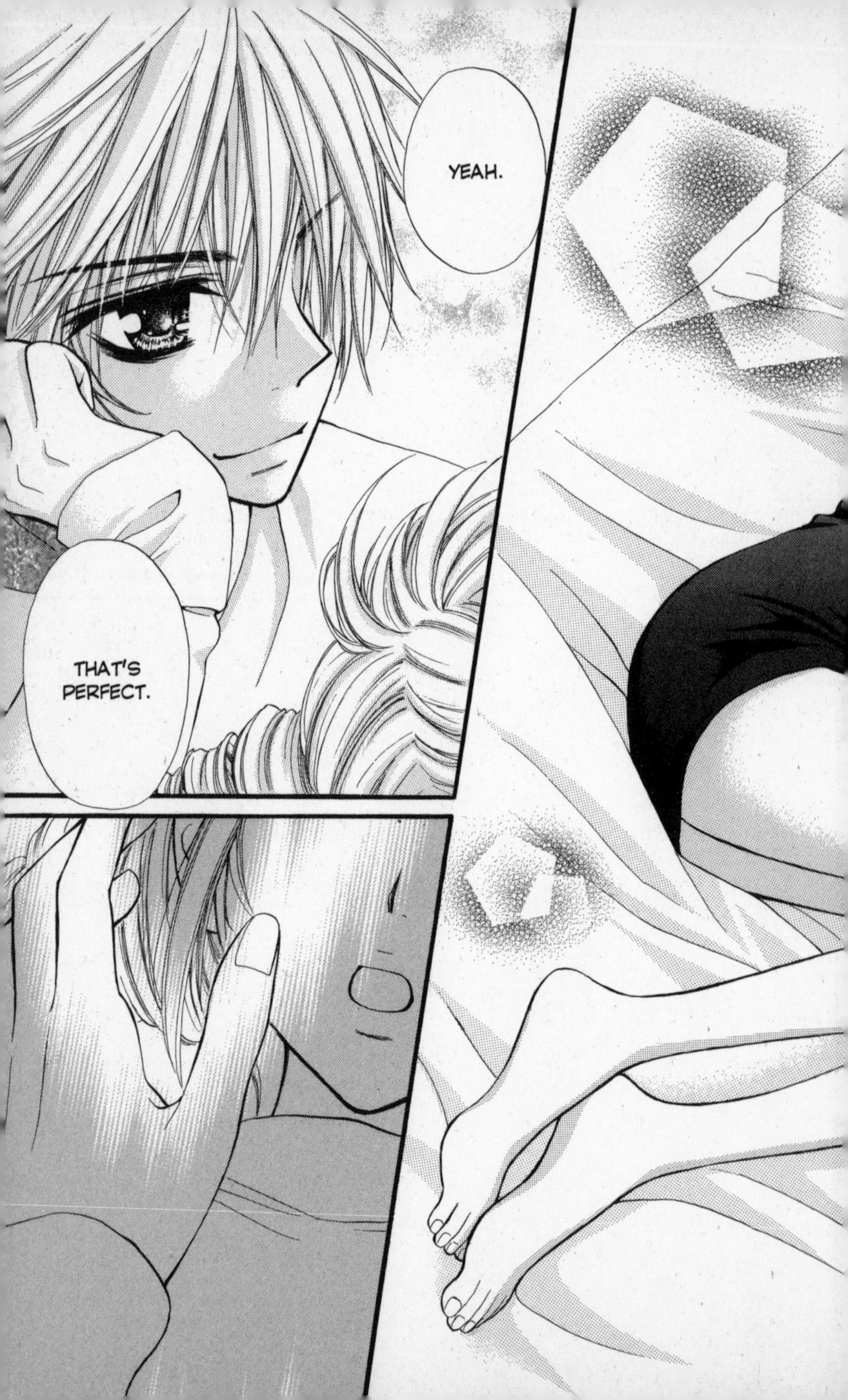
YEAH.
THAT'S PERFECT.

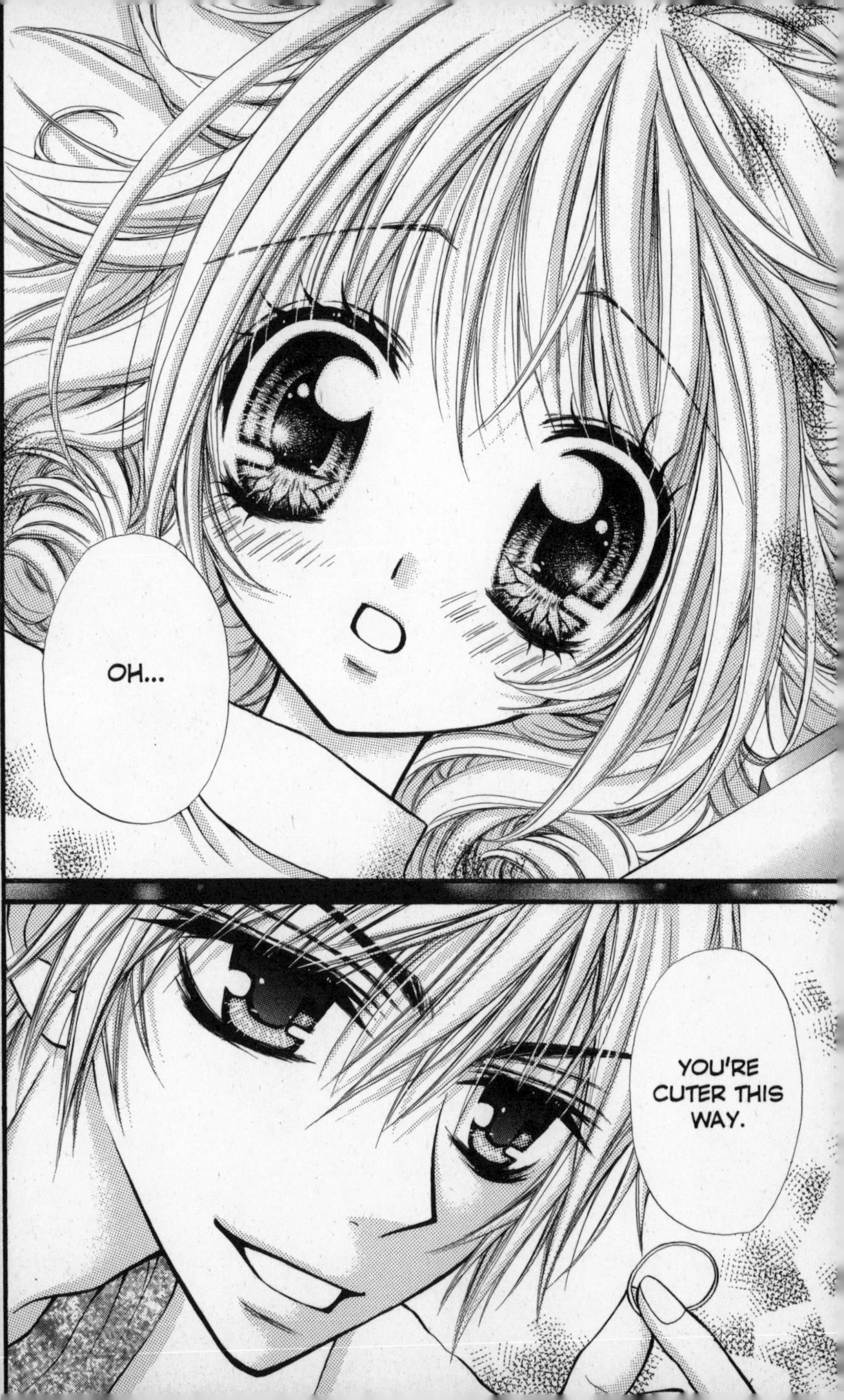
OH...
YOU'RE CUTER THIS WAY.

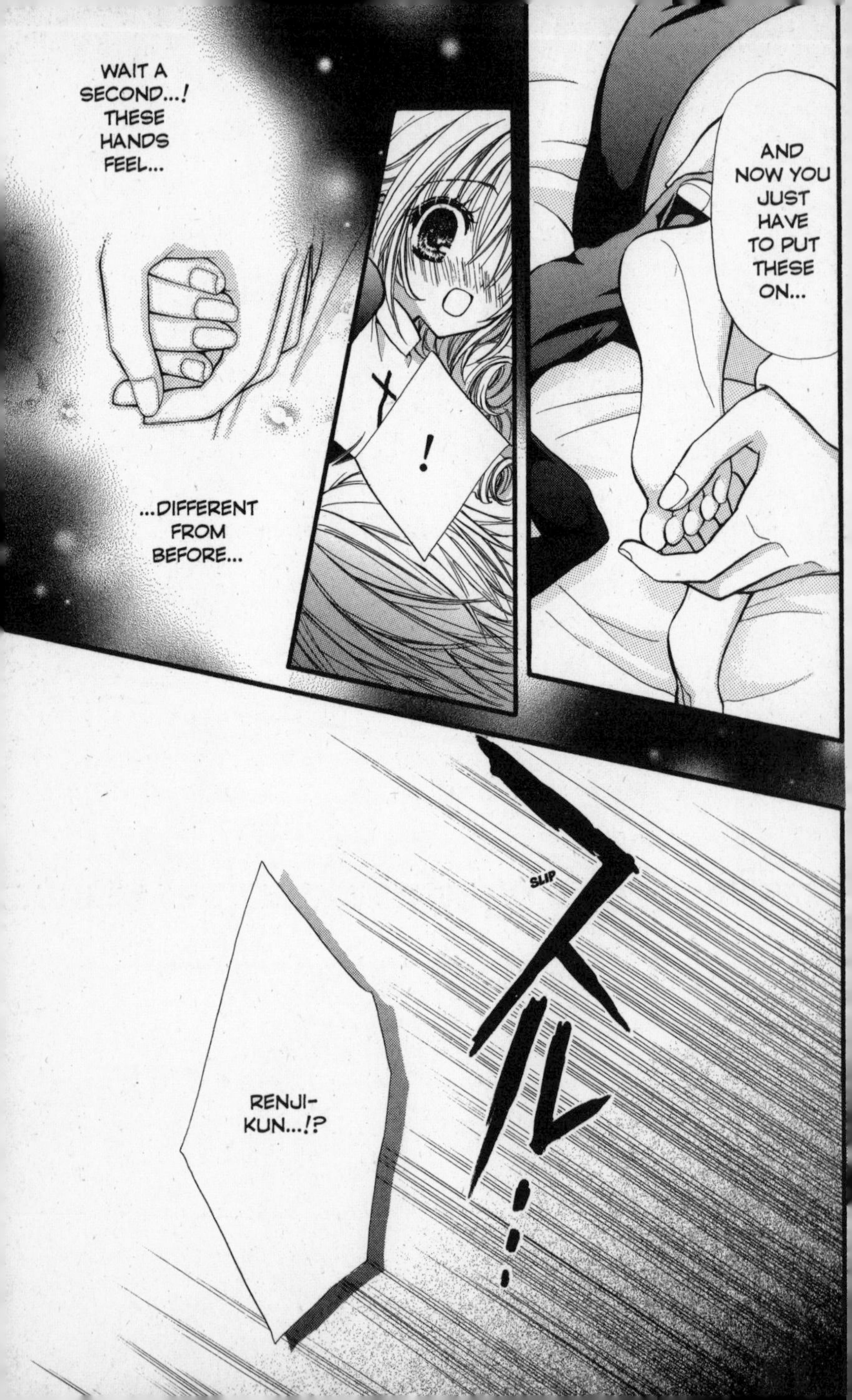
AND NOW YOU JUST HAVE TO PUT THESE ON...
!
WAIT A SECOND...! THESE HANDS FEEL...
...DIFFERENT FROM BEFORE...
SLIP
RENJI-KUN...!?

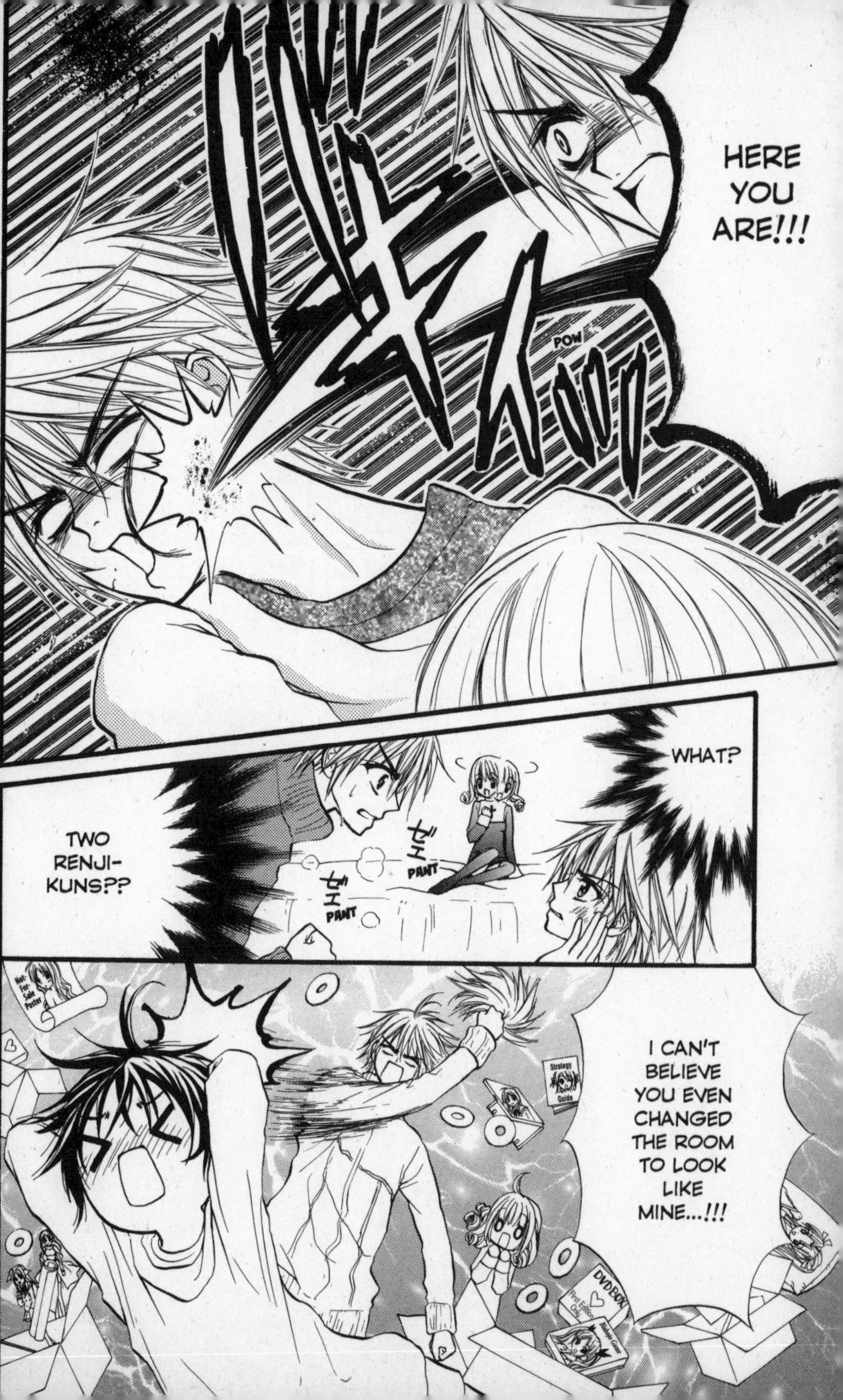
HERE YOU ARE!!!
POW
WHAT?
ゼェ PANT
ゼェ PANT
TWO RENJI-KUNS??
I CAN'T BELIEVE YOU EVEN CHANGED THE ROOM TO LOOK LIKE MINE...!!!
DVD BOX
First Edition Only
Strategy Guide
Not-For-Sale Poster

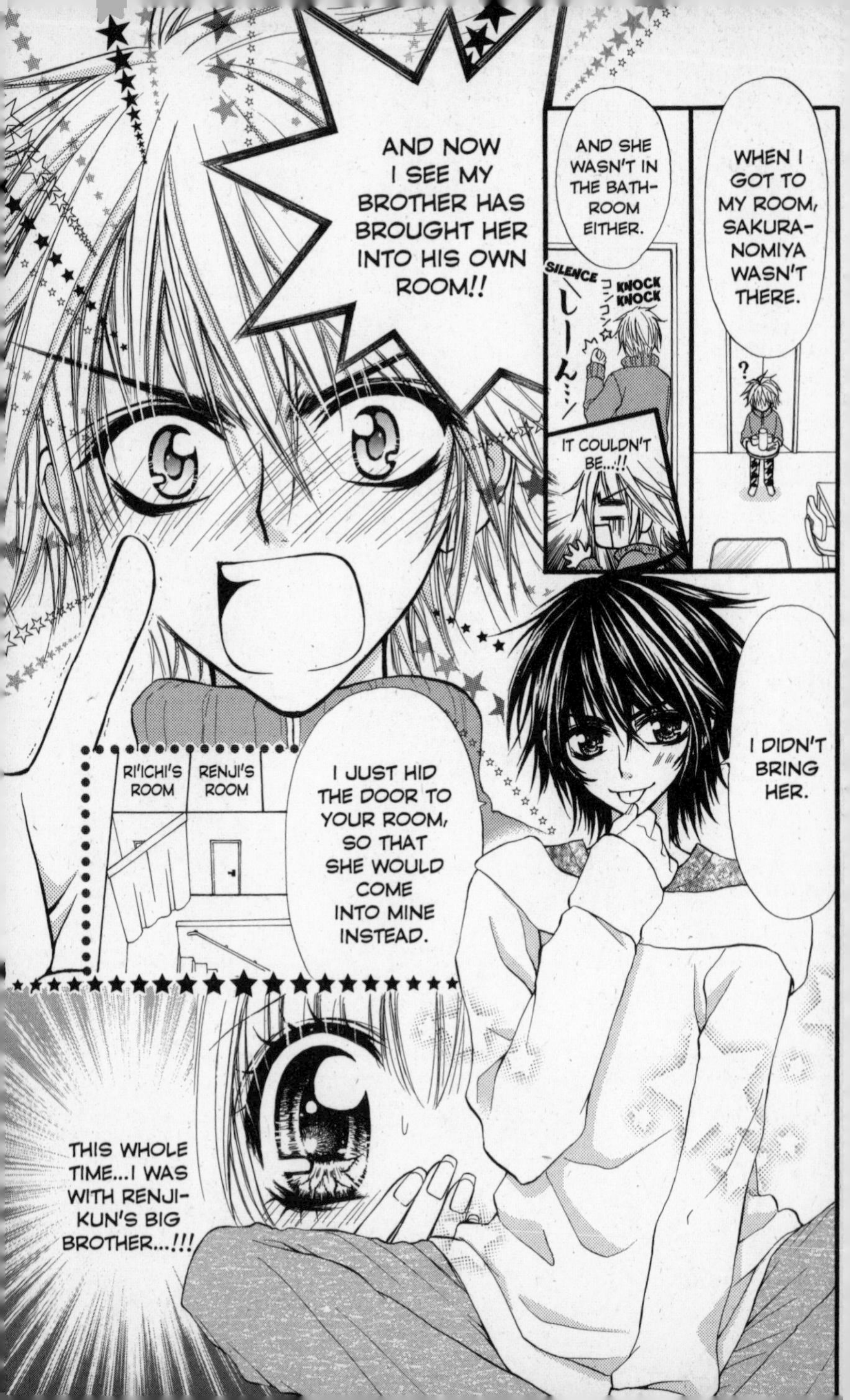
WHEN I GOT TO MY ROOM, SAKURA-NOMIYA WASN'T THERE.
AND SHE WASN'T IN THE BATH-ROOM EITHER.
KNOCK KNOCK
コンコン
SILENCE
しーん…
IT COULDN'T BE...!!
AND NOW I SEE MY BROTHER HAS BROUGHT HER INTO HIS OWN ROOM!!
I DIDN'T BRING HER.
I JUST HID THE DOOR TO YOUR ROOM, SO THAT SHE WOULD COME INTO MINE INSTEAD.
RENJI'S ROOM
RI'ICHI'S ROOM
THIS WHOLE TIME...I WAS WITH RENJI-KUN'S BIG BROTHER...!!!

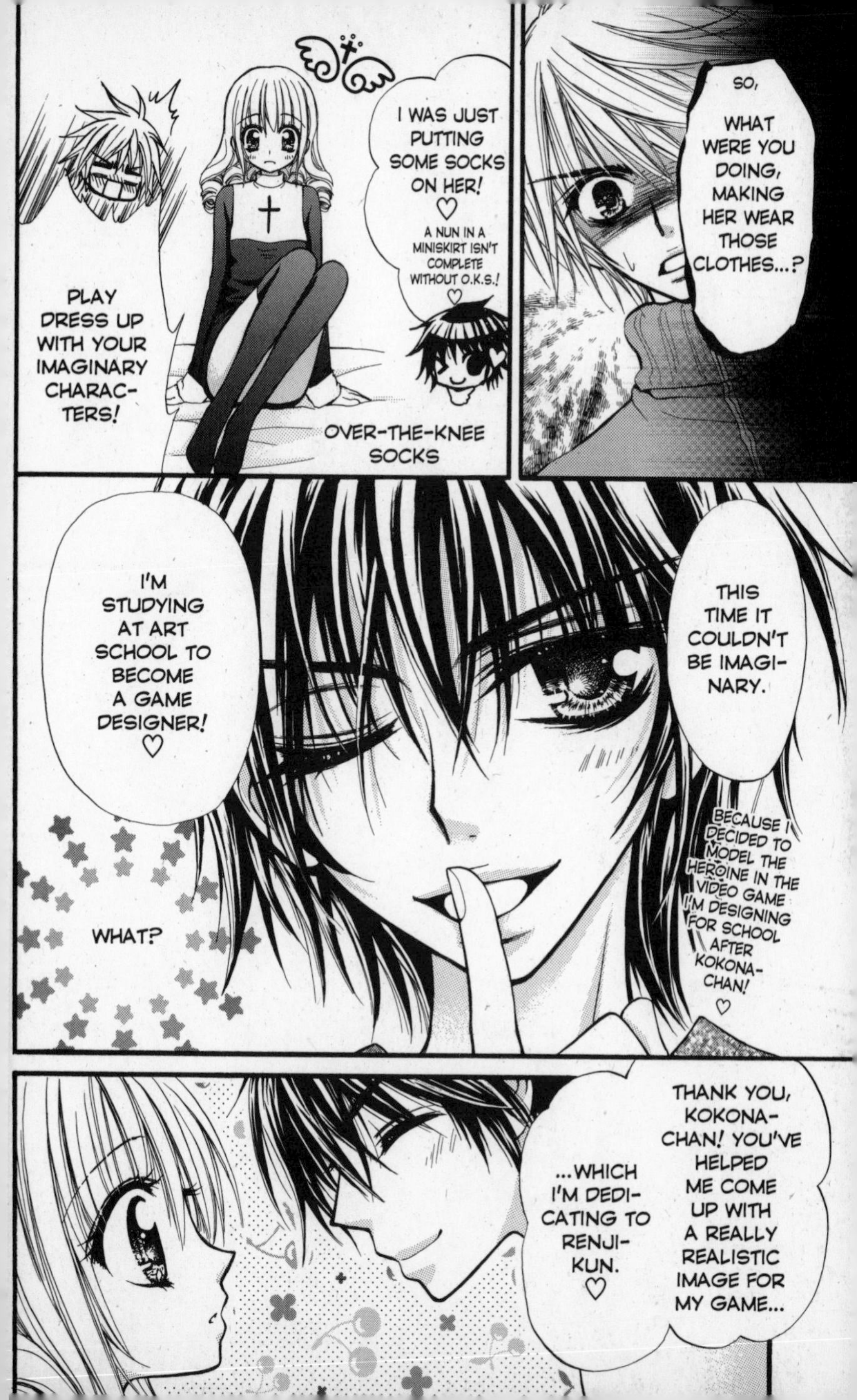
SO, WHAT WERE YOU DOING, MAKING HER WEAR THOSE CLOTHES...?
I WAS JUST PUTTING SOME SOCKS ON HER! ♡
A NUN IN A MINISKIRT ISN'T COMPLETE WITHOUT O.K.S.! ♡
OVER-THE-KNEE SOCKS
PLAY DRESS UP WITH YOUR IMAGINARY CHARACTERS!
THIS TIME IT COULDN'T BE IMAGINARY.
I'M STUDYING AT ART SCHOOL TO BECOME A GAME DESIGNER! ♡
BECAUSE I DECIDED TO MODEL THE HEROINE IN THE VIDEO GAME I'M DESIGNING FOR SCHOOL AFTER KOKONA-CHAN! ♡
WHAT?
THANK YOU, KOKONA-CHAN! YOU'VE HELPED ME COME UP WITH A REALLY REALISTIC IMAGE FOR MY GAME...
...WHICH I'M DEDICATING TO RENJI-KUN. ♡

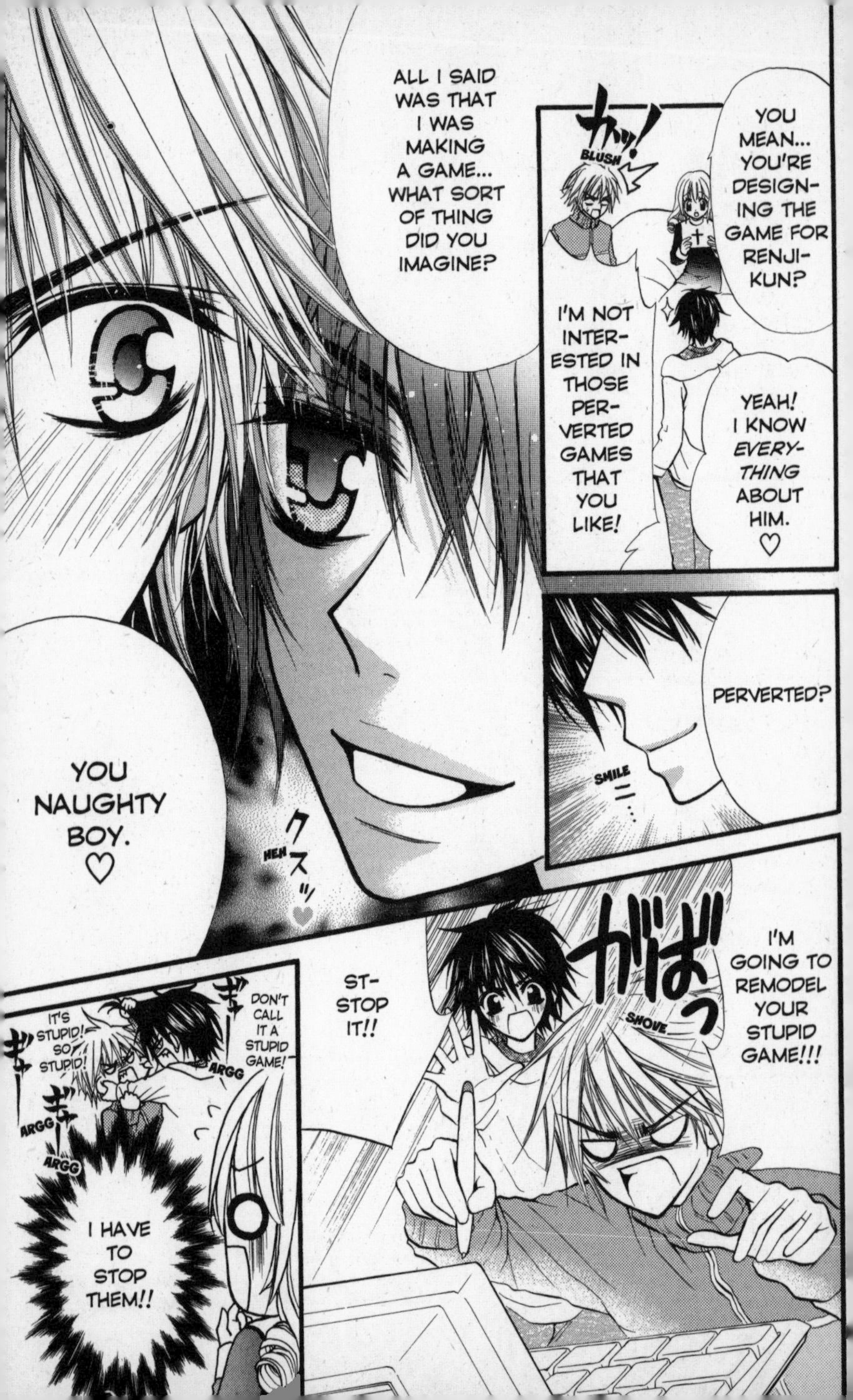

YOU MEAN... YOU'RE DESIGNING THE GAME FOR RENJI-KUN?
カッ! BLUSH
YEAH! I KNOW *EVERYTHING* ABOUT HIM. ♡
I'M NOT INTERESTED IN THOSE PERVERTED GAMES THAT YOU LIKE!
PERVERTED?
SMILE
ALL I SAID WAS THAT I WAS MAKING A GAME... WHAT SORT OF THING DID YOU IMAGINE?
クスッ HEH
YOU NAUGHTY BOY. ♡
I'M GOING TO REMODEL YOUR STUPID GAME!!!
がばっ SHOVE
ST-STOP IT!!
DON'T CALL IT A STUPID GAME!
ARGG
IT'S STUPID! SO STUPID!
ARGG
ARGG
I HAVE TO STOP THEM!!

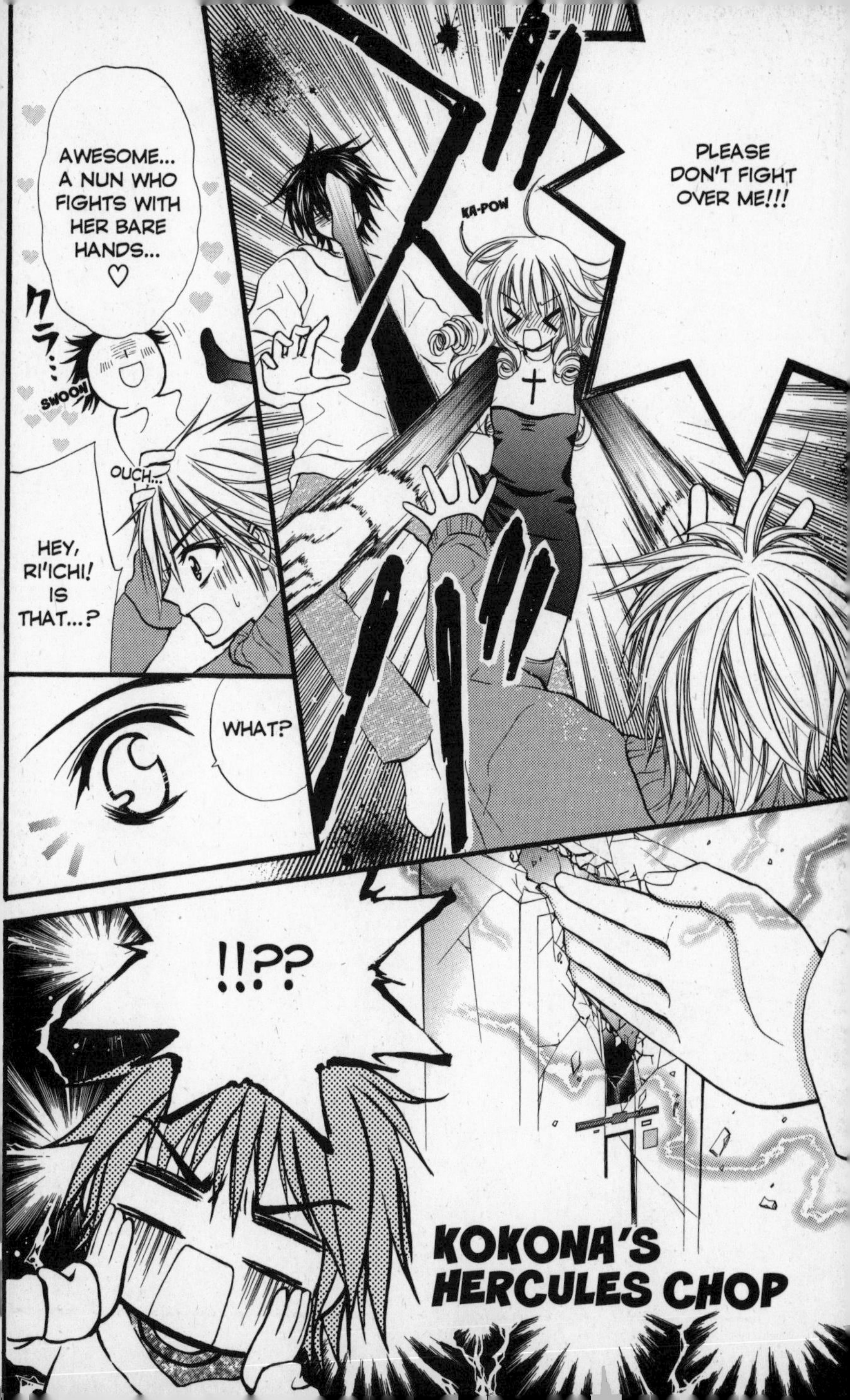
PLEASE DON'T FIGHT OVER ME!!!
KA-POW
AWESOME... A NUN WHO FIGHTS WITH HER BARE HANDS... ♡
クラ…
SWOON
OUCH...
HEY, RI'ICHI! IS THAT...?
WHAT?
!!??
KOKONA'S HERCULES CHOP

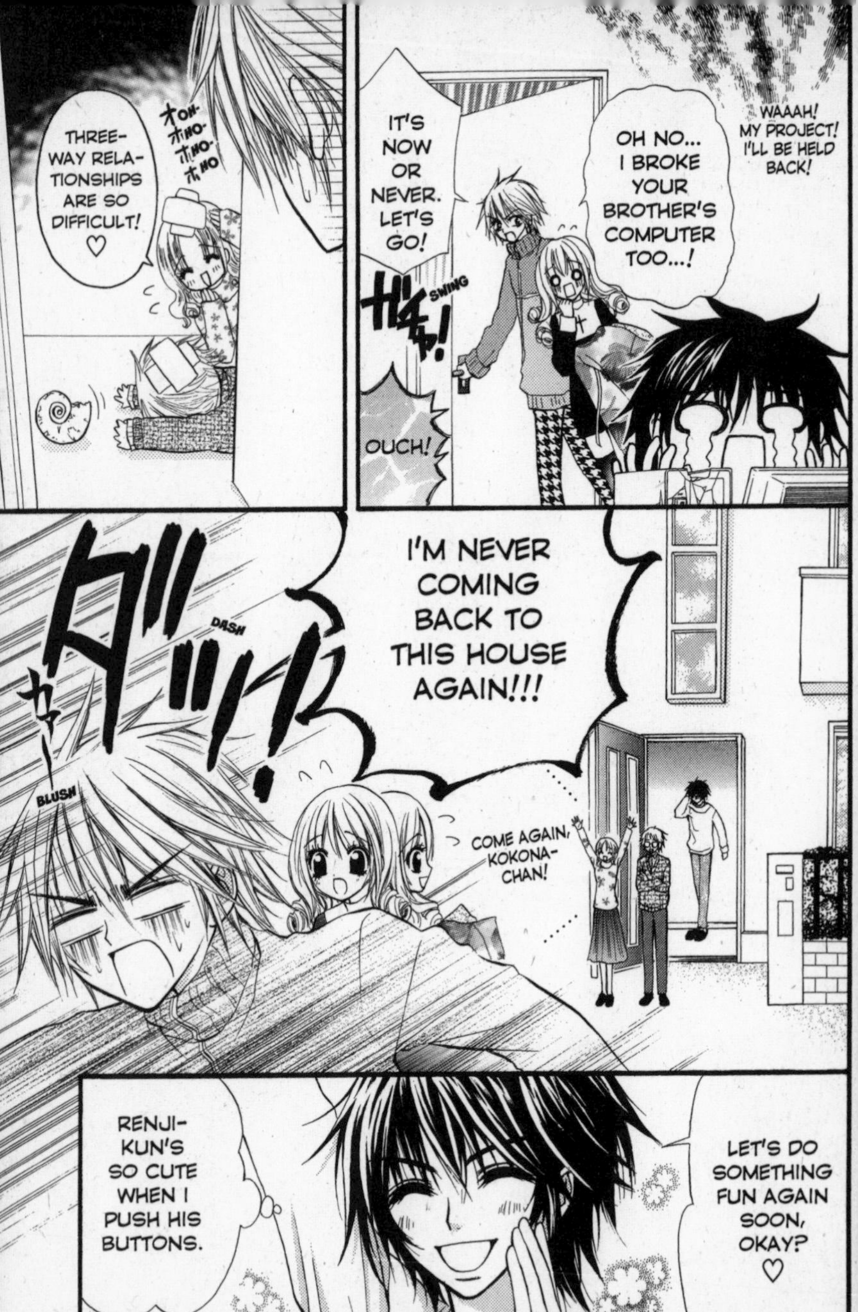
WAAAH! MY PROJECT! I'LL BE HELD BACK!
OH NO... I BROKE YOUR BROTHER'S COMPUTER TOO...!
IT'S NOW OR NEVER. LET'S GO!
SWING
OUCH!
OH-HO-HO-HO
THREE-WAY RELATIONSHIPS ARE SO DIFFICULT! ♡
I'M NEVER COMING BACK TO THIS HOUSE AGAIN!!!
COME AGAIN, KOKONA-CHAN!
DASH
BLUSH
LET'S DO SOMETHING FUN AGAIN SOON, OKAY? ♡
RENJI-KUN'S SO CUTE WHEN I PUSH HIS BUTTONS.

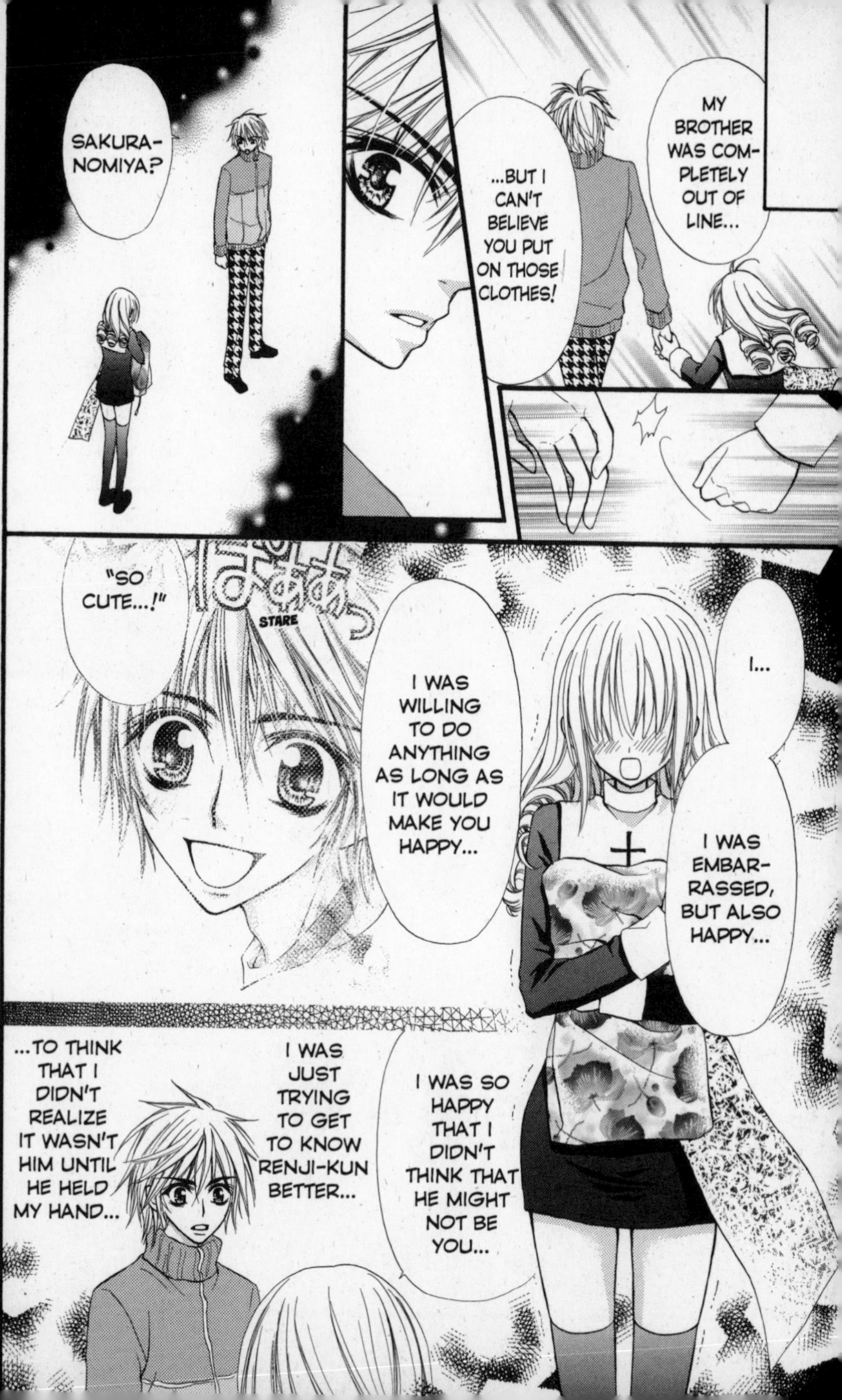
MY BROTHER WAS COMPLETELY OUT OF LINE...
...BUT I CAN'T BELIEVE YOU PUT ON THOSE CLOTHES!
SAKURANOMIYA?
I...
I WAS EMBARRASSED, BUT ALSO HAPPY...
I WAS WILLING TO DO ANYTHING AS LONG AS IT WOULD MAKE YOU HAPPY...
"SO CUTE...!"
STARE
I WAS SO HAPPY THAT I DIDN'T THINK THAT HE MIGHT NOT BE YOU...
I WAS JUST TRYING TO GET TO KNOW RENJI-KUN BETTER...
...TO THINK THAT I DIDN'T REALIZE IT WASN'T HIM UNTIL HE HELD MY HAND...

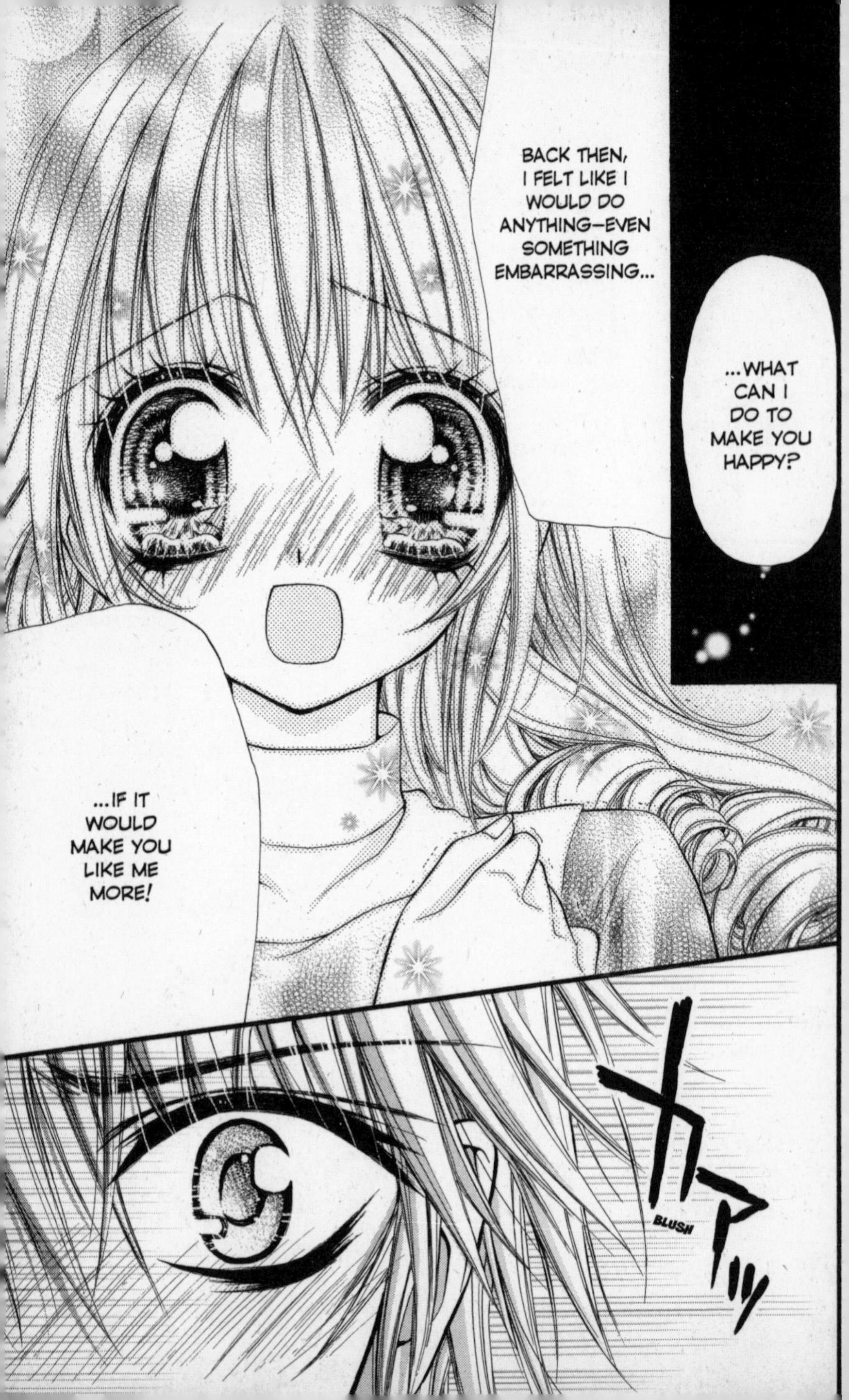
...WHAT CAN I DO TO MAKE YOU HAPPY?
BACK THEN, I FELT LIKE I WOULD DO ANYTHING—EVEN SOMETHING EMBARRASSING...
...IF IT WOULD MAKE YOU LIKE ME MORE!
BLUSH

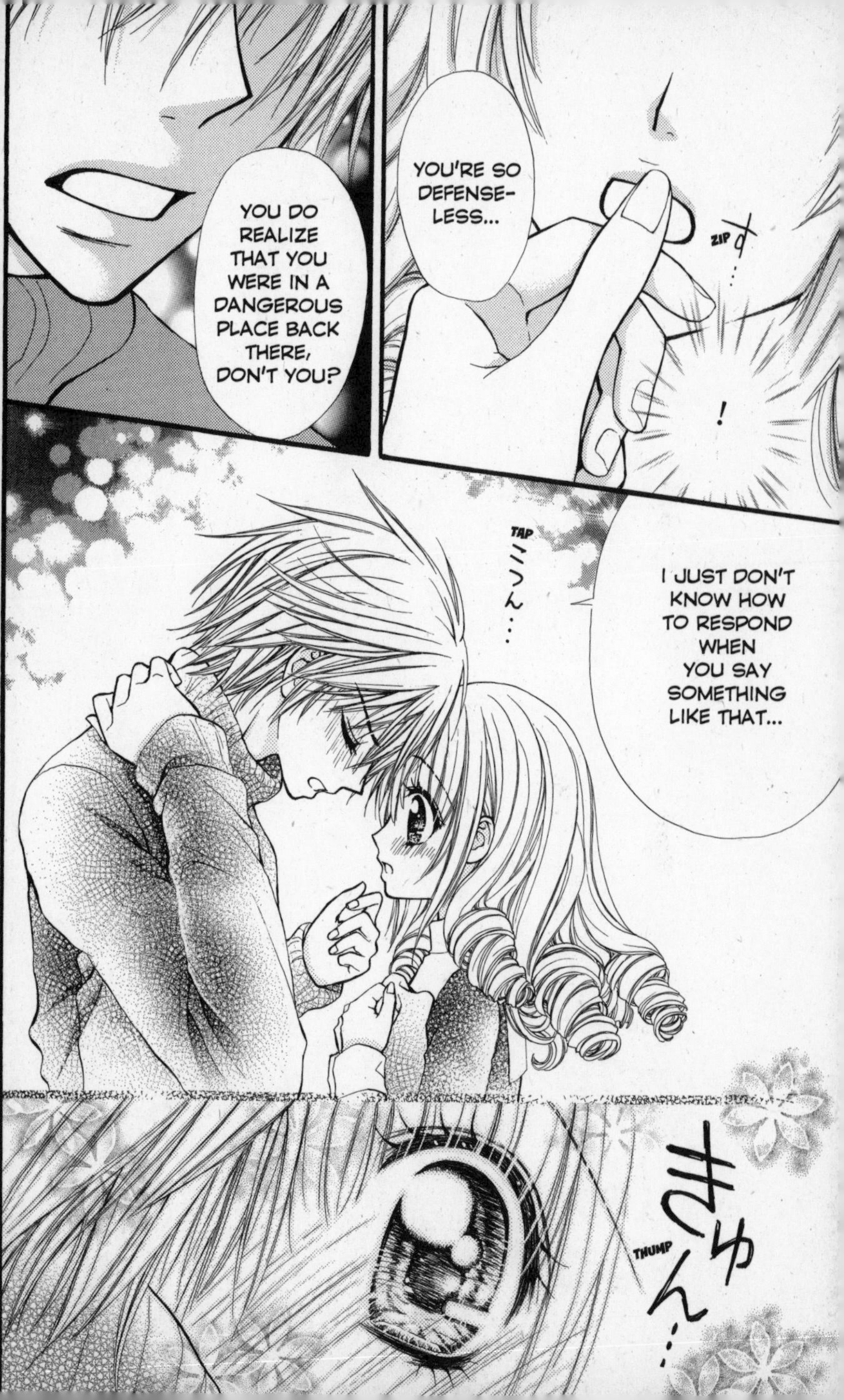
YOU'RE SO DEFENSE-LESS...
ZIP す…
!
YOU DO REALIZE THAT YOU WERE IN A DANGEROUS PLACE BACK THERE, DON'T YOU?
I JUST DON'T KNOW HOW TO RESPOND WHEN YOU SAY SOMETHING LIKE THAT...
TAP こつん…
THUMP きゅん…

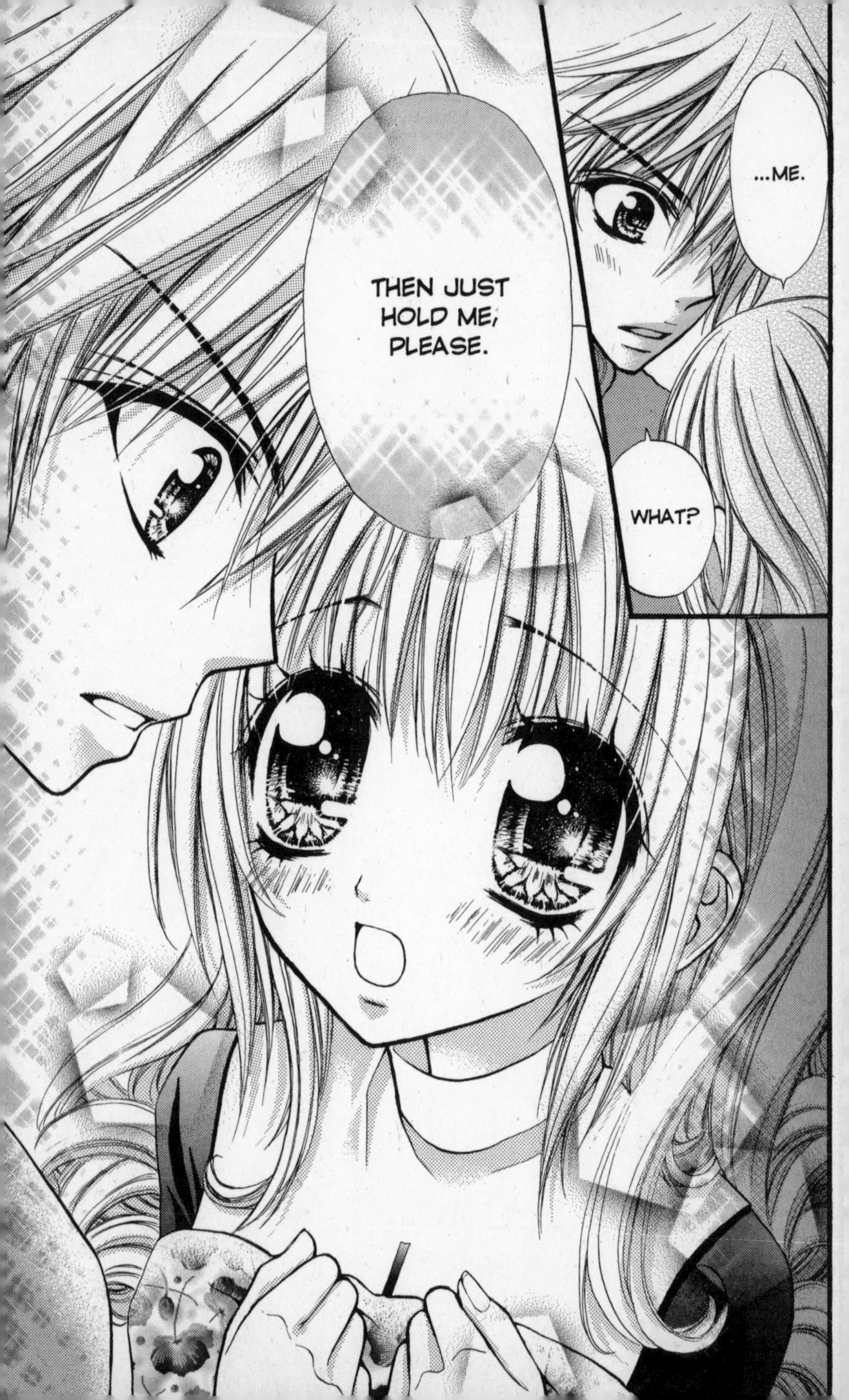
...ME.
WHAT?
THEN JUST HOLD ME, PLEASE.

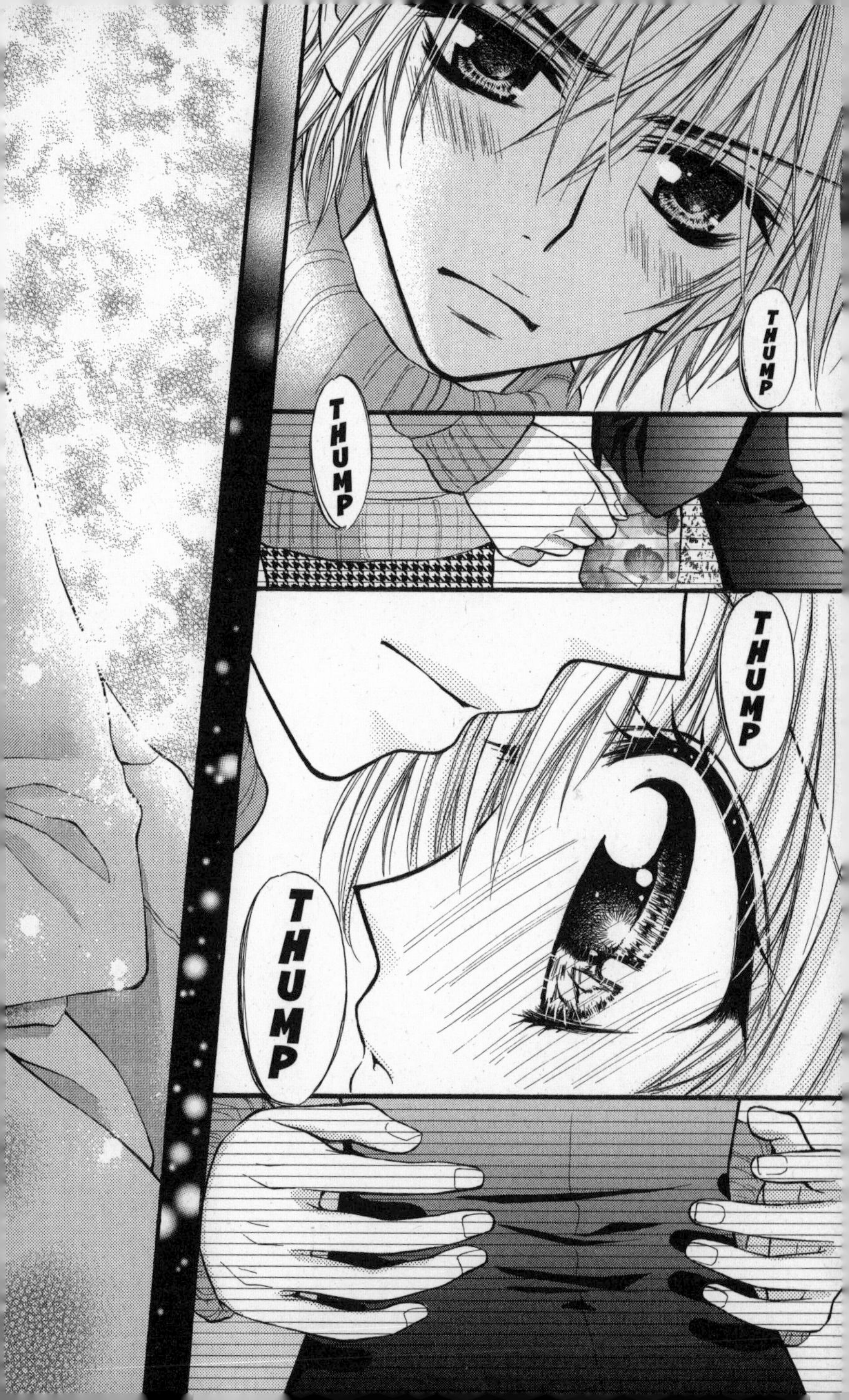
THUMP
THUMP
THUMP
THUMP

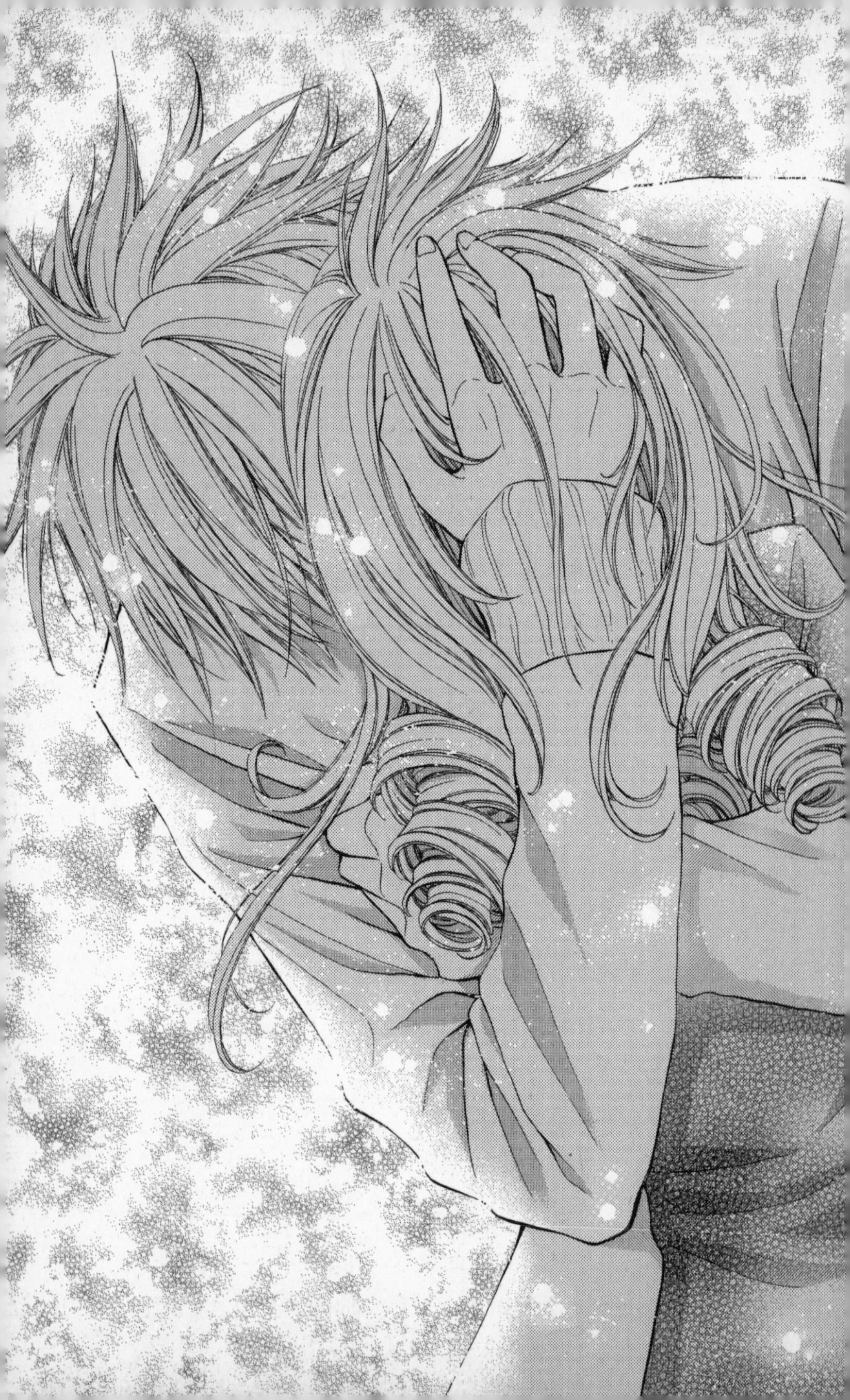

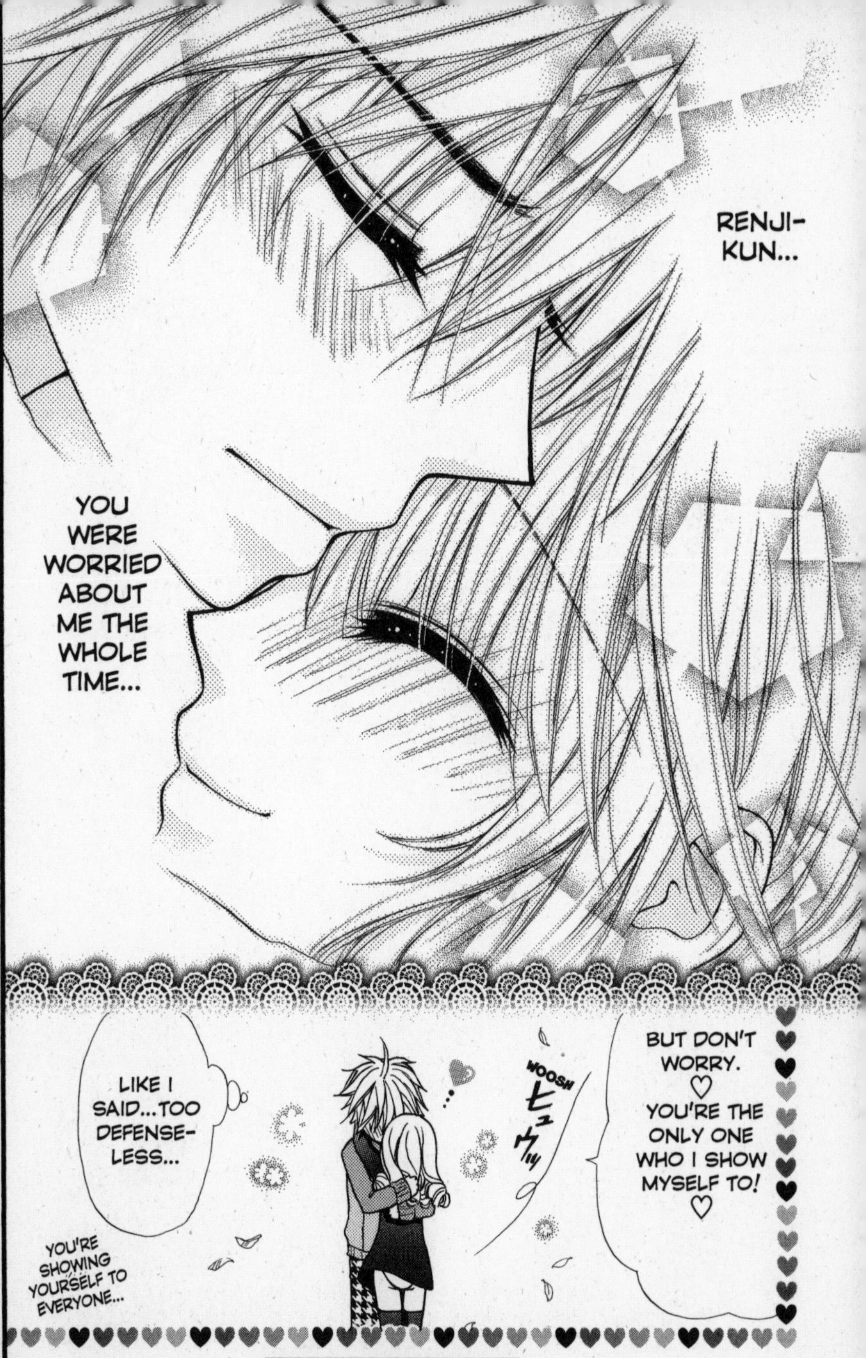
RENJI-KUN...
YOU WERE WORRIED ABOUT ME THE WHOLE TIME...
BUT DON'T WORRY. ♡ YOU'RE THE ONLY ONE WHO I SHOW MYSELF TO! ♡
WOOSH
ヒュウッ
LIKE I SAID...TOO DEFENSE-LESS...
YOU'RE SHOWING YOURSELF TO EVERYONE...

To Be Continued in Volume 2

Preview images from the original serialization!

This one was printed really large! (Ha-ha)

↓

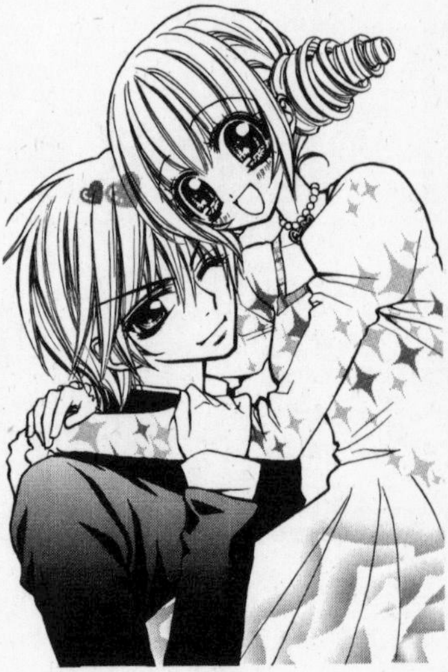

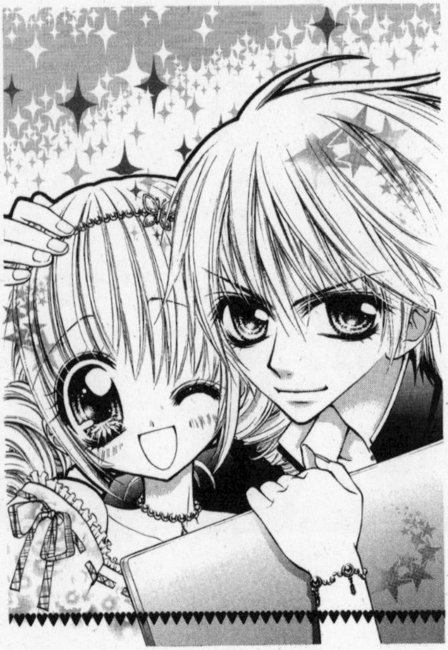

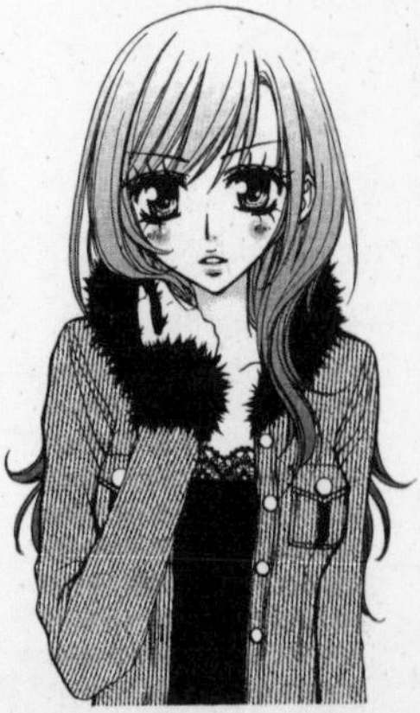

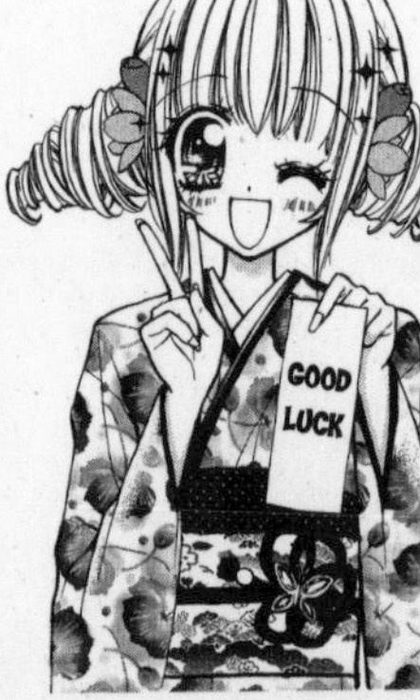
GOOD LUCK

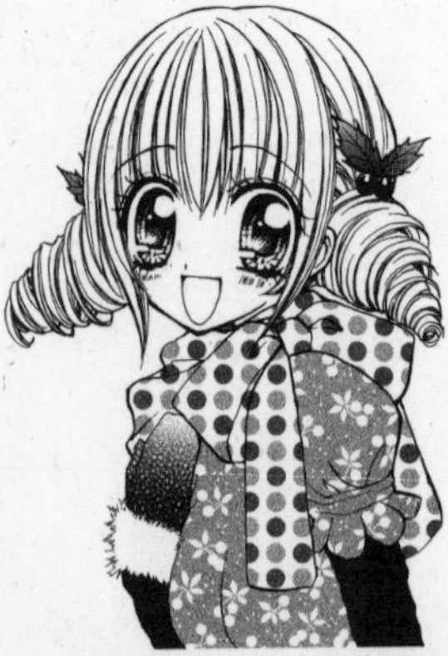

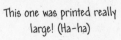

	Kokona Sakuranomiya
Height	152 cm
Weight	38 kg
Star Sign	Aries
Blood Type	Type B
Favorite Subject	Gym
Least Favorite Subject	None
Class	1-5 (Momojigaoka High School)
Favorite Colors	Pink and White
Favorite Food	Full Course Meals
Most Wanted Item	Memories with Renji-kun
Hobbies	Fantasizing about Love
Character Flaw	Victim Complex
Favorite Word	Enthusiasm
Special Talent	Sky Diving

Kokona's profile was uploaded to the Nakayoshi website "Diginaka!"
To prepare for this, I had to think of a profile!⚬ I researched astrology and tried to pick a birthday that suited the character's personality, but different astrologers say different things, so I wasn't sure which one to believe!⚬
I am actually quite surprised that a lot of people have written that *Pink Innocent* is a "wild-type" love story. Unlike Kokona, I never do anything to initiate romance...because I'm never confident that people will like me....
(Hmm...)

I often wonder how people would classify my style. A while after my debut, I think my old editor told me once to "become more stupid!"⚬ Until then, I had drawn very serious manga about career problems and the protection of overhunted animals....All of my friends from my student days who saw my first comics as Momoyuki were totally shocked!
After training with blood and tears (?), I wonder if I have finally become an idiot....

A Happy New Year! 2007

Kotori

Thanks to everyone for your warm letters of support! It's very encouraging to know that there are people who enjoy my work!

I'd love to hear everyone's thoughts on this new series too!♡

Kotori Momoyuki
Nakayoshi Editorial Department
Post Office Box 91,
Akasaka Post Office, Tokyo
107-8652

←I drew this picture for an autographed New Year's greeting card gift campaign.

Thank you for reading the whole book!
I will try my best to keep challenging myself to make manga that everyone can enjoy, and that will stay in everyone's heart, so thank you for your continued support!
I hope to meet you again in the second volume!

. . . .

Special Thanks
Chika Sezaki-sama   Kino Fujiwara-sama   Kanae Seiya-sama   Saki-sama
Soara Fujita-sama   Kanako Asai-sama   Tomoyuki Kawashima-sama
Kawai-sama   Haribara-sama   Madoka Aotsuki-sama   NOSE-sama
Tanbo Mino-sama   Editor: Aya Oriuchi

I would like to thank all of the people who worked on the production of this book, and all the people who have added it to their collection.

12/30/2006 Kotori Momoyuki

KC Series by
Kotori Momoyuki:
Rabu Rabo (Love Lab)
Total 1 Volume
Ōji-sama no Tsukurikata
(*How to Make a Prince*)
Total 2 Volumes
Pink Innocent 1

Profile:
Born June 30th,
Cancer, Blood Type A.
Originally from Osaka.
Hobbies: Piano,
Desktop Music.

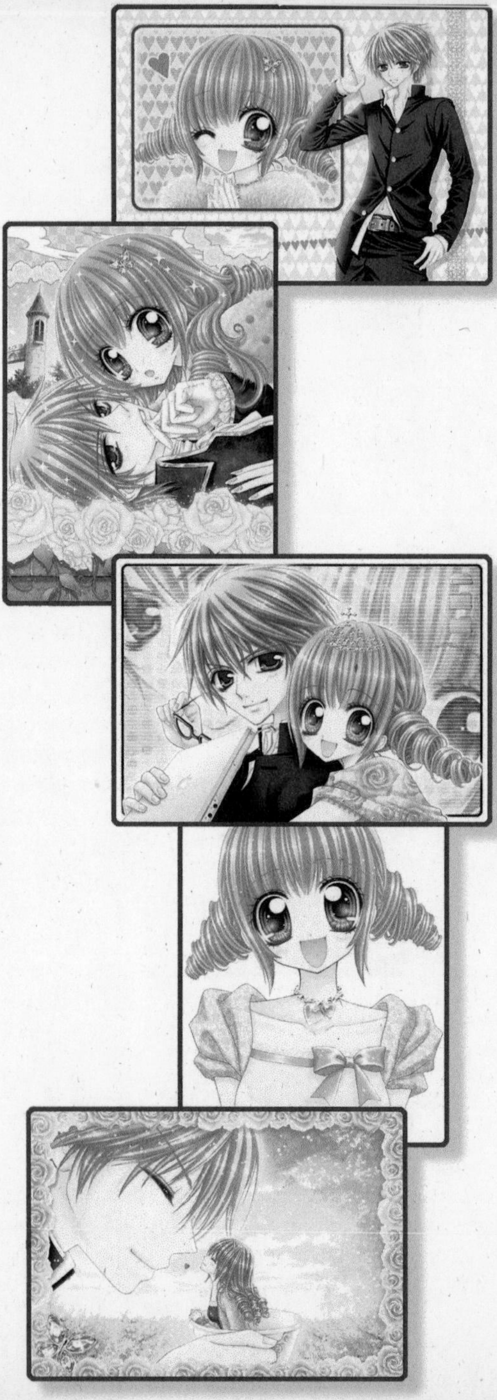

TRANSLATION NOTES

Japanese is a tricky language for most Westerners, and translation is often more art than science. For your edification and reading pleasure, here are notes on some of the places where we could have gone in a different direction with our translation of the work, or where a Japanese cultural reference is used.

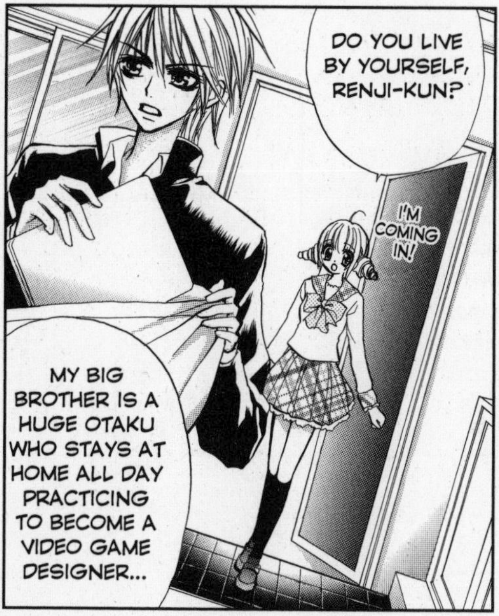
DO YOU LIVE BY YOURSELF, RENJI-KUN?
I'M COMING IN!
MY BIG BROTHER IS A HUGE OTAKU WHO STAYS AT HOME ALL DAY PRACTICING TO BECOME A VIDEO GAME DESIGNER...

Otaku, page 26
Otaku is the Japanese word for someone obsessed with any one particular subject area. It is often translated as "nerd," although it can mean obsession in any area from computers (as in the case of Renji), video games (as in the case of Ri'ichi), or even fossils (as in the case of Renji's father).

Part-time model, page 61
Dokusha moderu, literally "reader models," is a phenomenon where fashion magazines recruit regular girls from its readership to pose and work as models in the magazine. Like reality shows in the U.S., this cultural phenomenon allows viewers and readers to relate to their idols, who respectively attain mini-celebrity status. We can witness the rise of Aery's fame through this and the next volume!

Christmas dates, page 92

As Renji points out, Japan is not a Christian country, and Christmas has very little religious or cultural significance. Instead, the appearance of the holiday (lights, wreaths, and of course presents) is more prominent, and it has become the biggest day for couples after Valentine's Day. As we see later in the book, New Year's in Japan is what many associate with Christmas in the West—a quieter time to spend with family, and participate in religious activities (shrine visits, etc.).

Obi/Furisode, page 127

Obi is the wrap-around sash for traditional Japanese dress. *Obi*s for women's kimonos are very elaborate, often costing more than the actual kimono, and require another person to fasten. A *furisode* (literally "swinging sleeves") is the most formal style of kimono worn by unmarried women, and is characterized by its long, flowing sleeves.

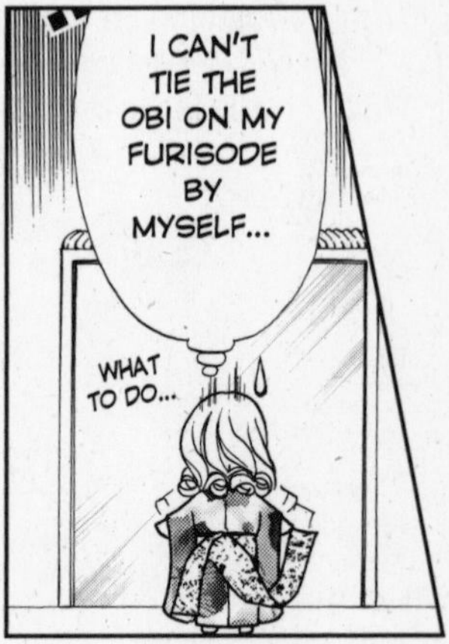
I CAN'T TIE THE OBI ON MY FURISODE BY MYSELF...
WHAT TO DO...

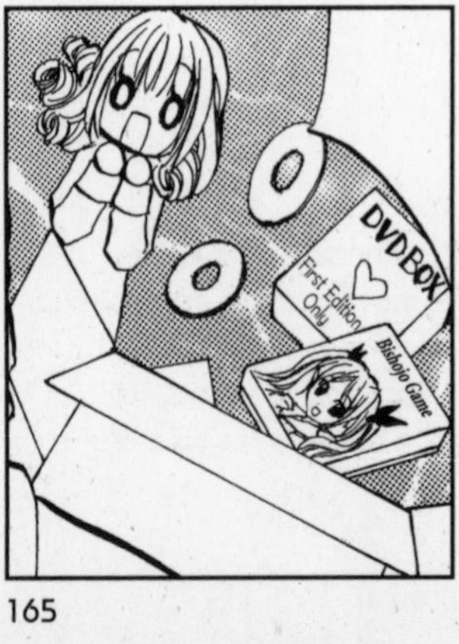
DVD BOX
First Edition Only
Bishojo Game

***Bishojo* game, page 146**

Bishojo (literally "beautiful girl") games are video games (popular among *otaku*) based on a dating scenario where the main character must win the heart of one of the many beautiful girls in the game. These games range from innocuous to more mature.

Preview of *Pink Innocent* Volume 2

We're pleased to present you a preview from *Pink Innocent* volume 2.
Please check our website (www.delreymanga.com) to see when
this volume will be available in English. For now you'll have to make
do with Japanese!

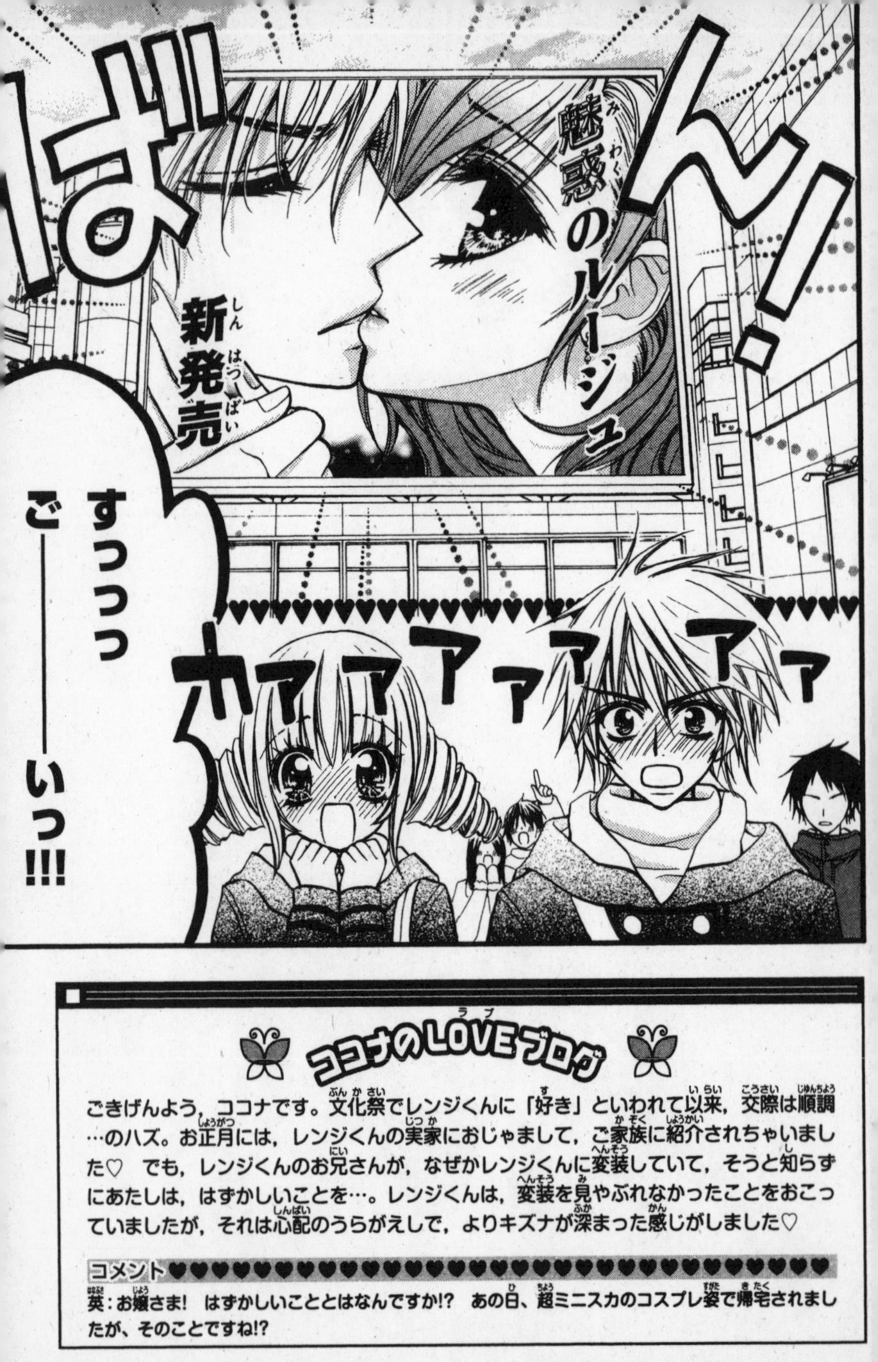
ばん!!
魅惑のルージュ
新発売
ホアアアアアア
すっっっご———いっ!!!

ココナのLOVEブログ

ごきげんよう，ココナです。文化祭でレンジくんに「好き」といわれて以来，交際は順調…のハズ。お正月には，レンジくんの実家におじゃまして，ご家族に紹介されちゃいました♡　でも，レンジくんのお兄さんが，なぜかレンジくんに変装していて，そうと知らずにあたしは，はずかしいことを…。レンジくんは，変装を見やぶれなかったことをおこっていましたが，それは心配のうらがえしで，よりキズナが深まった感じがしました♡

コメント♥♥♥♥♥♥♥♥♥♥♥♥♥♥♥♥♥♥♥♥♥♥♥♥♥♥♥♥♥♥♥♥

英：お嬢さま!　はずかしいこととはなんですか!?　あの日、超ミニスカのコスプレ姿で帰宅されましたが、そのことですね!?

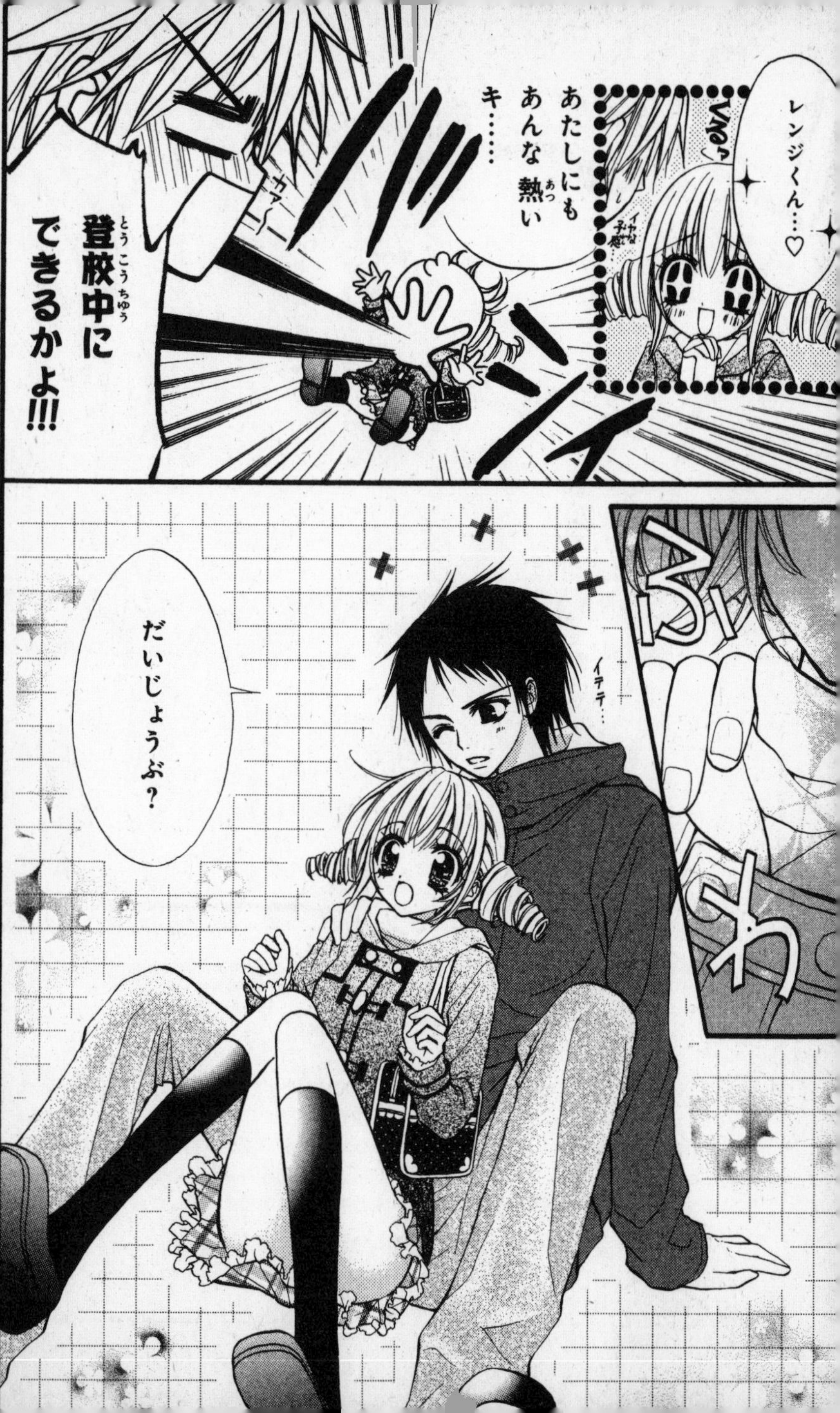
レンジくん…♡
ぐるっ
イヤな予感
あたしにもあんな熱いキ……
カァ〜
登校中にできるかよ!!!
ふわ
イテテ…
だいじょうぶ？

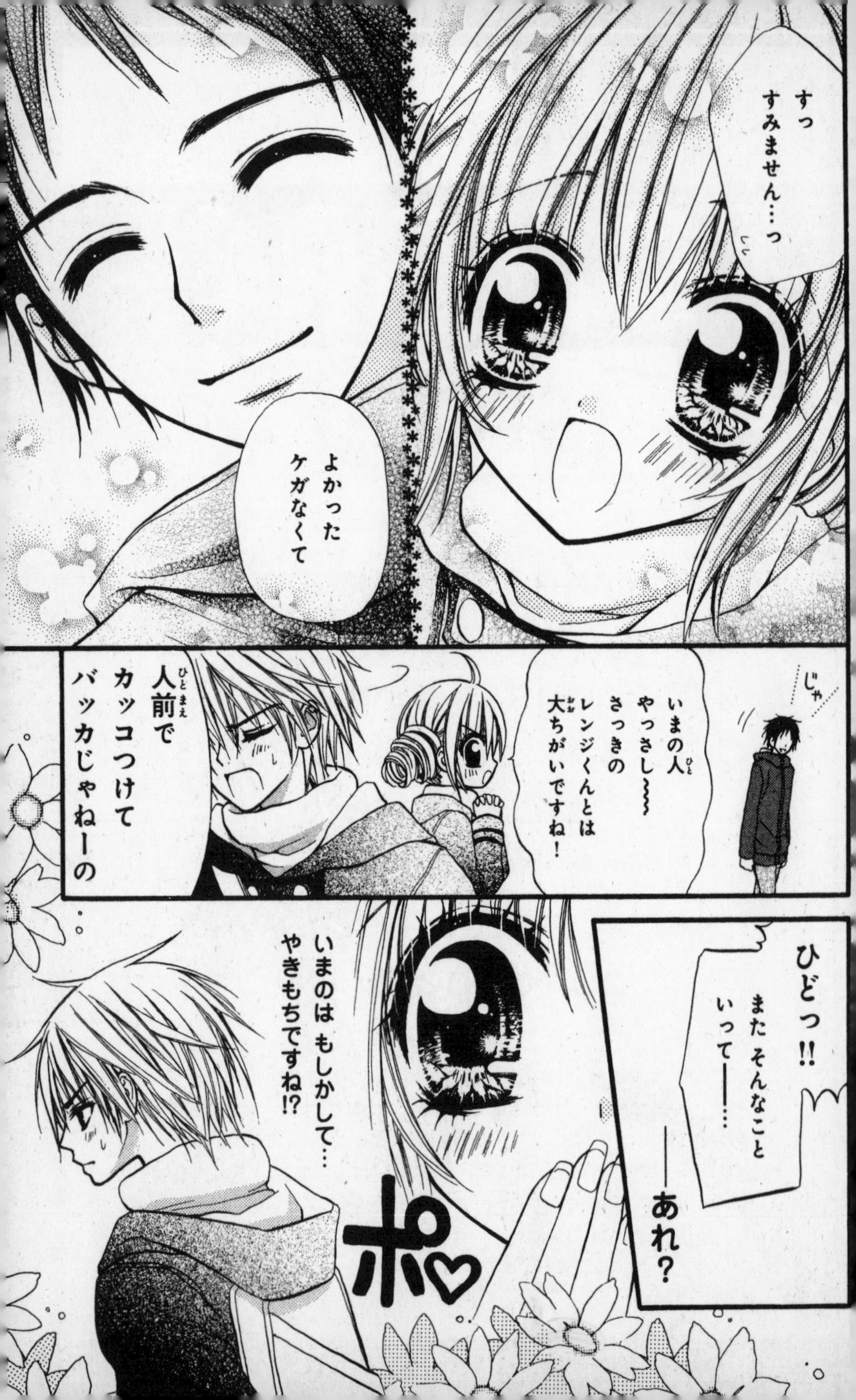
すっ すみません…っ
よかった ケガなくて
じゃ
いまの人 やっさし〜〜〜 さっきの レンジくんとは 大ちがいですね!
人前で カッコつけて バッカじゃねーの
ひどっ!!
また そんなこと いって——…
——あれ?
いまのは もしかして… やきもちですね!?
ポ♡

TOMARE!

[STOP!]

You're going the wrong way!

Manga is a completely different type of reading experience.

To start at the *beginning*, go to the *end*!

That's right! Authentic manga is read the traditional Japanese way—from right to left. Exactly the *opposite* of how American books are read. It's easy to follow: Just go to the other end of the book, and read each page—and each panel—from right side to left side, starting at the top right. Now you're experiencing manga as it was meant to be!